Betty Ahnson

MACMILLAN S[...]

The books in this series prese[...]
and in a sophisticated manner with more conceptual underpinning
than has previously been provided.

The series is intended primarily for undergraduate and postgraduate
students taking small business and related courses at universities and
polytechnics. Books in the series will also be suitable for those
working for professional examinations and for well-informed managers of small and growing businesses.

PUBLISHED

Paul Burns and Jim Dewhurst (eds): *Small Business and Entrepreneurship*
Paul Burns and Jim Dewhurst (eds): *Small Business in Europe*
Jim Dewhurst and Paul Burns: *Small Business: Planning, Finance and Control*
Terry Hill: *Small Business: Production/Operations Management*
Derek Waterworth: *Small Business: Marketing for the Small Business*

Series Standing Order

If you would like to receive future titles in this series as they are
published, you can make use of our standing order facility. To place a
standing order please contact your bookseller or, in case of difficulty,
write to us at the address below with your name and address and the
name of the series. Please state with which title you wish to begin your
standing order. (If you live outside the United Kingdom we may not
have the rights for your area, in which case we will forward your order
to the publisher concerned.)

Customer Services Department, Macmillan Distribution Ltd
Houndmills, Basingstoke, Hampshire, RG21 2XS, England.

SMALL BUSINESS

Planning, Finance and Control

SECOND EDITION

Jim Dewhurst and Paul Burns

MACMILLAN EDUCATION

© Jim Dewhurst and Paul Burns 1983, 1989

All rights reserved. No reproduction, copy or transmission of this publication may be made without written permission.

No paragraph of this publication may be reproduced, copied or transmitted save with written permission or in accordance with the provisions of the Copyright Act 1956 (as amended), or under the terms of any licence permitting limited copying issued by the Copyright Licensing Agency, 33–4 Alfred Place, London WC1E 7DP.

Any person who does any unauthorised act in relation to this publication may be liable to criminal prosecution and civil claims for damages.

First edition 1983
Reprinted 1985, 1986
Second edition 1989

Published by

British Library Cataloguing in Publication Data
Dewhurst, Jim
Small business.—2nd ed.
1. Great Britain. Small firms. Financial management
I. Title   II. Burns, Paul, *1949–*
658.1'592'0941
ISBN 0-333-46718-3 (hardcover)
ISBN 0-333-46719-1 (paperback)

Contents

	Preface to the Second Edition	vi
1	Ave	1
2	The Genesis of a Business	9
3	Setting Up a Business	28
4	Strategy and Planning	43
5	The Business Plan	60
6	Bank Finance	101
7	Bank Services for Small Business	116
8	Risk Capital	132
9	Taxation and Allowances	156
10	An Introduction to Accounting and the Companies Acts	190
11	Costs and Profit	206
12	Controlling Costs	228
13	Financial Planning and Budgeting	236
14	Control and Delegation Through Budgets	253
15	Accounting Systems	269
16	Understanding Financial Information	293
17	Alternative Choice Decisions	315
18	Capital Investment Appraisal	337
19	The Management of Working Capital: Inventory and Cash	365
20	Credit Control	377
21	Vale	389
	Select Bibliography	406

Preface to the Second Edition

Since the book was first published (1983) a number of measures – many initiated by the government – relating to the supply of funds to small businesses have come into effect. The position now is that the UK businessman is no longer disadvantaged *vis-à-vis* his counterpart in the common market in terms of the provision of finance. It is probably true to say that a good business idea, properly planned and presented, need never be short of risk capital.

The problem indeed is more one of proper planning and presentation. More and more the small business manager must be able to plan ahead, preferably with the use of a micro-computer and a suitable spreadsheet. Our first edition has been completely updated; in this new edition the emphasis is on the steps that need to be taken for effective overall planning.

We have had a great deal of help from colleagues and friends in the preparation of this book. We would like, especially, to mention Sue Burns, and her work on Chapter 9. For all practical purposes this represents a complete rewrite of the Chapter 6 on taxation in our earlier edition. National Westminster, Midland, Barclays and Lloyds Bank plc have all supplied us with useful information: Lloyds Bank has allowed us to reproduce their structure chart.

We would also like to thank Carolyn Jane Claridge and Susan Anne Claridge for giving us permission to use their business plan. We wish them every success with their restaurant.

We may, at times, use sexist words and phrases, though only, we hope, where predominant usage sanctions it (an example would be 'businessman' rather than 'businessperson'). Throughout we ask readers to accept that 'he' or 'him' subsumes 'she' or 'her'. Otherwise, to put it bluntly, this book would be inordinately long!

January 1988　　　　　　　　　　　　　　　　　　　　Jim Dewhurst
　　　　　　　　　　　　　　　　　　　　　　　　　　　Paul Burns

CHAPTER 1

Ave

INTRODUCTION	1
SIZE	3
THE NUMBERS OF SMALL BUSINESSES	5
THE BOOK	8

Introduction

In all the short history of modern business there is nothing so strange as this. On the one hand we have the traditional belief in the rightness and power of size. Rationalisation, standardisation and concentration are the watchwords. Economies of scale rule the industrial world. In the United Kingdom we say we must be big to stand up against the ruthless cost-effective multinational corporations based in the USA and Japan. And indeed in the United Kingdom we have gone further along this road of concentration than any other country in the world. Yet this predilection for economic orthodoxy has not brought us economic success. And even some economic theory is now emphasising the diseconomies of scale.

There is another viewpoint which has a growing number of adherents. Perhaps, these people argue, economic success is not the sole criterion by which we should judge all things. Perhaps people matter. Perhaps a society should be concerned to some extent with the quality of life, job satisfaction and good human relationships. Much evidence is now produced that some primitive races are more relaxed, more caring and (unbelievably!) apparently happier than we are. Some evidence has been produced recently that people working in small business units in a civilised society are more committed than those working in large, amorphous, corporations.

One extreme conclusion we might draw from this is that we should reject our modern way of life and try a return to some primitive pre-industrial society. This is absurd. Man (but please see the sexual disclaimer earlier in the preface!) has competitive, striving, basic urges in his make-up. Put another way the average man in the United Kingdom – in so far as he exists – does not want to see us 'deteriorate' back into some third-rate primitive society.

What are the alternatives? One solution, ably put by Fritz Schumacher, was that an *intermediate technology* should be developed. To use his own words, this would be a technology that is 'simpler, very much cheaper, very much easier to maintain than the highly sophisticated technology of the modern West'. But the question to which he gave this answer was: 'What would be the appropriate technology for Rural India or Rural Latin America or maybe the City slums?' Now it may well be that for a comparatively rural, primitive society, intermediate technology (rather than a sudden forced transformation to high technology) may be the answer. But we are neither a primitive society nor all city slums.

The situation in the United Kingdom is indeed almost the complete reverse. The Industrial Revolution started here and we have already gone further along the road of industrial success and then apparent rigidity and relative decline than any other country. What can we do? How can we combine our present state of industrial homeostasis with an enlightened approach? The clue must surely lie in our difficulty in seeing that size and technological/managerial efficiency are not the same, or at any rate are not hopelessly interlocked. The arguments against an undue concern with size (except in certain parts of the economy) are strong. The arguments in favour of applying modern technological and managerial control techniques are equally strong. What this book is concerned to show is that in a free-thinking, democratic society it is possible to use sophisticated, sometimes highly quantitative, techniques in the control of small businesses without impairing those special characteristics of a small business which we (and particularly those who work with it) admire so much.

This book therefore develops the theme that small business is beneficial, that it is flexible, that it can adapt to new situations more easily than large corporations, that it is innovative, that it already probably makes a larger contribution *pro rata* than large business, and that with efficient control and management techniques the benefit it gives can be much greater.

We do not use the words 'small' or 'smaller' here or throughout in any tight restrictive sense. We are not trying to keep businesses small. We are seeking to make small businesses more effective and efficient in the very broadest senses (at one extreme this does include human aspects such as job satisfaction). In many cases increase in efficiency may mean growth. There is nothing wrong with this. All we are arguing here is that size does not necessarily lead to efficiency.

More precisely efficiency comes as the result of making good decisions and implementing them properly.

Size

In 1969 a Committee of Inquiry on Small Firms (the 'Bolton' Committee) was set up. It reported in November 1971 (Cmnd 4811). The Committee, sensibly realised that its first job was to define a small business. It made heavy weather of it. Recognising that one single definition would not cover industries as divergent as manufacturing and service, the Committee used eight definitions for varying industry groups. These ranged from under 200 employees for manufacturing, to under £50,000 turnover for retailing, and up to 5 vehicles or less for road transport. But any definition which was based on turnover, or indeed any other measure of size expressed in financial terms (such as capital employed or net assets) suffered from terrible inherent disadvantages in times of inflation. A firm which is selling the same number of units from one year to the next, and so, in real terms, is staying exactly still, may, because of inflation, move up from being a small firm to being classed as a large firm.

The 'Wilson' Committee on the Financing of Small Firms, March 1979 (Cmnd 7503), updated the Bolton turnover requirements for small firms by an index based on the general index of retail prices. This brought the definitions temporarily in line but it in no way solved this particular problem. In the EEC small firms are usually categorised by employees, but there is no general agreement on the number that is covered by the term 'small'. Probably the most common definitions are that those firms with less than 100 employees are small and those with 100 to 500 are medium. But many countries (e.g. West Germany) regard 10 employees as the top limit for small firms, and France and Sweden agree with the Bolton (manufacturing) 200 employees limit! In any case, Bolton was certainly right in arguing that one definition will not work easily right across the board. As it says, 'in retail distribution a firm employing 200 people would typically have at least 10 shops with a total turnover of several million pounds and would be a very large organisation in terms of the distributive trades'.

However, the advantages from having a definition which somehow covers all industries are obviously very great. The 1981 Companies Act laid down, for the first time in British history, formats for the balance-sheets and profit-and-loss accounts, and, though not of importance here, these proscriptive formats apply to all companies, but only for the copies of their accounts filed with the Registrar of Companies. There were certain size exemptions. These were repeated in the 1985 Companies Act. Businesses were split into medium-sized and small (though in practical terms both would normally be regarded as small). These definitions are:

1. MEDIUM

A company may be classified as medium-sized if, for the financial year and the one immediately preceding it, two (at least) out of the following three conditions apply:
(a) turnover did not exceed £5.75m
(b) balance-sheet total did not exceed £2.8m
(c) average weekly number of employees did not exceed 250

2. SMALL

A company may be classified as small if, for the financial year and the one immediately preceding it, two (at least) of the following three conditions apply:
(a) turnover did not exceed £1.4m
(b) balance-sheet total did not exceed £0.7m
(c) average weekly number of employees did not exceed 50

For both categories the 'balance-sheet total' means the total of all its assets (as specified in the prescribed formats) without deduction of any liabilities.

Although comparisons are obviously difficult, these definitions cover firms appreciably larger than those that the Wilson Committee gave. They tie up better, however, with EEC definitions and they do allow a little extra to cover inflationary growth and also to give some flexibility.

The Bolton report was rightly very conscious of the necessity but also the inadequacy of quantitative definitions, such as the one we have discussed. It contrasted the 'statistical' definition (such as its own of one for each of the eight industrial sectors!) with what it called the 'economic' definition.

This economic definition makes a great deal of sense. It has three parts:

1. MARKET SHARE
2. INDEPENDENCE
3. PERSONALISED MANAGEMENT

The characteristic of a small firm's share of the market is that it is not large enough to enable it to influence the prices or national quantities of goods sold to any significant extent.

Independence means that the owner has control of the business himself. It therefore rules out those small subsidiaries which, though in many ways fairly autonomous, nevertheless have to refer major decisions (e.g. on capital investment) to a higher level of authority.

Personalised management is the most characteristic factor of all. It implies that the owner actively participates in all aspects of the management of the business, and in all major decision-making processes. There is little devolution or delegation of authority. One person is involved when anything material is concerned.

But if one owner/manager has to manage everything, what a wide range of skills he must need! Unlike the chief executive of a large corporation who can employ a secretary, a financial director, a treasurer, a solicitor and an accountant, all well informed in their own professional fields, and all willing and able to advise him, the small business proprietor has to be himself, a 'man for all seasons'.

It is obvious that this has been the case for many years. What is different now is that there are a battery of sophisticated, quantitative techniques which, for the first time, partly through the use of computers, are becoming available to small-business managers.

It is not the thesis of this book that the computer solves everything. Far from it, put the wrong figures into it, subject it to the wrong analysis, and the print-out will be a recipe for disaster. What is necessary is a good understanding of the more advanced methods now available: when they can be used, how to use them, and what are their limitations. It is a function of this book to provide some insight into these decision-making techniques.

The numbers of small businesses

We can now look at the small business in the larger context of the UK industrial environment and, in particular, at the number of small businesses. The degree to which many industries in this country had been concentrated into a few large corporations is now widely known. The Bolton Committee said that 'to our surprise the process of concentration has gone further here than elsewhere: *no* country was found where small firms had a lower share in manufacturing than in the UK' (*our italics*). The Committee also noted that there had been no official study of the likely consequences of the entry of the

Table 1.1 Manufacturing industry: index of trend in shares of small and medium-sized businesses (rate of change of share, % per annum)

Number of firms	Establishments/Enterprises Small	Medium	Large
1973–81 Belgium	0.2	−2.1	1.0
1971–81 Denmark			
1977–81 France			
1977–82 West Germany	0.3	−1.0	−0.8
1969–78 Greece	−0.1	3.2	0.0
1973–82 Republic of Ireland	0.5	−1.8	−4.8
1971–81 Italy	0.0	−1.6	−1.8
1974–78 Luxembourg[a]	2.0	−2.0	−3.2
1978–83 Netherlands	0.4	−1.2	−3.1
1975–80 UK – establishments	{ 0.6	−2.9	−3.2
– enterprises	{ 0.2	−3.5	−2.9

[a] Smallest category 20–49

Employment			
1973–81 Belgium	0.6	−0.7	0.3
1971–81 Denmark[a]	1.0	← −0.3 →	
1977–81 France	4.9	−0.5	−4.8
1977–82 West Germany	−0.3	−0.1	0.1
1969–78 Greece	−1.3	2.1	1.0
1973–82 Republic of Ireland	1.8	0.1	−2.7
1971–81 Italy	1.2	−0.9	−1.3
1974–78 Luxembourg[b]	4.6	1.6	−2.0
1971–79 Netherlands	0.6	← 0.2 →	
1975–80 UK – establishments	{ 2.4	0.3	−0.8
– enterprises	{ 2.2	0.1	−0.6

[a] Smallest category 6–49
[b] Smallest category 20–49

Sources: National sources and Economist Intelligence Unit estimates.

(then) separate United Kingdom into the EEC. However, it went on to forecast the likely effects. It argued that the decline of the small firm in the UK could be attributed, at any rate in part, to advances in transport and communication. Any large businesses could easily serve the whole country; the day of the small firm serving exclusively a small local area was practically over. Looked at this way, the creation of the EEC was just an inevitable extension of the geographical area which served as a practical unit for selling and distribution. In fact, even at the time of the Bolton report, there was already evidence that 'in the Netherlands the formation [of the EEC] was followed by a

Table 1.2 Services: index of trend in shares of small and medium-sized businesses (rate of change of share, % per annum)

Numbers	Establishments/Enterprises Small	Medium	Large
1973–81 Belgium	0.1	−2.4	0.0
1971–81 Denmark			
France			
West Germany			
1969–78 Greece	−0.0	← 3.0	→
1971–77 Republic of Ireland	−0.0	← 3.0	→
1971–81 Italy	−0.1	9.5	5.2
1975–78 Luxembourg[a]	0.0	← 1.6	→
1978–83 Netherlands	−0.1	1.4	4.5

Employment			
1973–81 Belgium	0.2	−0.8	0.7
1971–81 Denmark			
1977–81 France	1.3	−0.2	−7.7
West Germany			
1969–78 Greece	−0.8	← 3.3	→
1971–77 Republic of Ireland	0.15	← −0.5	→
1971–81 Italy	−1.3	5.2	−1.4
1975–78 Luxembourg	0.4	← 1.5	→
1975–78 Netherlands	−0.2	← 0.1	→

Sources: National sources and Economist Intelligence Unit estimates.

tendency to larger scale production and an increase in the number of mergers and takeovers'.

There is some evidence that, even before the government's initiatives in the early to mid-1980s, the trend in the decline in the numbers of small firms in the United Kingdom had been reversed. The Economist Intelligence Unit, in their 10-country Survey of Small Businesses, gave two tables. We have condensed these. Our first (Table 1.1) shows for manufacturing industry the rates of change in the proportionate share of various sizes of establishments or enterprises as a percentage of the whole for the 10 constituent member countries of the report. UK figures are available both for establishments and enterprises. The second table (1.2) deals with service industries and is included mainly for interest as there are no figures given for the UK.

The reports of Bolton *et al.* however did show clearly that the decline in the number of small businesses (though it may have been halted recently) has been dramatic. But is this a serious matter? Do small firms really contribute all that much to the economy? Perhaps the day of the small business has finally gone and that is a good thing!

In the last chapter of this book, after we have discussed a number of financial, and some non-financial, measures of the performance of businesses, we shall be in a better position to compare relative contributions.

The book

In the main body of this text, however, we concentrate on the small business in the United Kingdom, and with the provision of information, and with the planning, which we think are essential for proper decision-making. Throughout we address an academic audience. This book is primarily intended for use on small business courses in business schools, universities, polytechnics and colleges. It does, however, include substantial sections on practical matters of use both to students and to serious small business managers.

CHAPTER 2

The Genesis of a Business

THE BUSINESS IDEA	9
IS IT WORTH WHILE?	10
Sales estimates	11
Costs and profitability	16
Capital requirements	19
HOW WILL IT BE FINANCED?	22
How much borrowing?	23
What type of borrowing?	24
Summary	25
Appendix 1 *Sources of market information*	26

The business idea

Setting up a business needs a business idea. The idea does not have to be original but it does have to meet the needs of a clearly identified group of customers. It also has to be sufficiently different from products or services offered by competitors to have some chance of survival in the market place. It is that uniqueness that will make people buy your product or service. That uniqueness may be confined to the fact that you are the only off-licence in the area, but it has to be sufficient to make you stand out.

Most people base their business upon skills, experience or qualifications they have, perhaps gained in a previous job, or through a hobby. Others spot 'gaps in the market', opportunities that are not being taken by existing businesses. These might come from identifying new fast-growing markets, or identifying where customer needs are being badly served by existing businesses. Of course, the entrepreneur must ask himself whether he will like the work and whether he is willing to put in the time needed to make the business successful.

There is also the question of how the venture will be financed, and whether the entrepreneur can afford to launch the business.

The entrepreneur is the key to the successful launch of any business. He is the person who perceives the market opportunity and then has the motivation, drive and ability to mobilise resources to meet it. However, it is difficult to create a picture of him. Colin Barrow[1] tries to catalogue certain typical characteristics:

- Self-confident all-rounder . . . the person who can 'make the product, market it and count the money, but above all they have the confidence that lets them move comfortably through unchartered waters'.
- The ability to bounce back . . . the person who can cope with making mistakes and still has the confidence to try again.
- Innovative skills . . . not an 'inventor' in the traditional sense but one who is able to carve out a new niche in the market place, often invisible to others.
- Results orientated . . . to make the business successful requires the drive that only comes from setting goals and targets and getting pleasure from achieving them.
- Professional risk taker . . . to succeed means taking measured risks. Often the successful entrepreneur exhibits an incremental approach to risk taking, at each stage exposing himself to only a limited, measured amount of personal risk and moving from one stage to another as each decisions is proved.
- Total commitment . . . hard work, energy and single-mindedness are essential elements in the entrepreneurial profile.

Anybody wishing to set up a new business must ask himself whether he has the qualities needed to make the business a success.

Is it worth while?

Many people set up small businesses simply because they prefer to be their own boss and work at their own pace. They go into the business with little more than blind optimism about the marketability of one, single product. Unfortunately, their chances of success on this basis are slim.

This chapter is about the initial considerations necessary before setting up a small business. It asks three basic questions?

---

[1] Colin Barrow, *Routes to Success*, Kogan Page, 1986.

- Is it worth while?
- How will it be financed?
- What are the legal considerations?

Sales estimates

All business operations are geared to sales, and the first step in estimating whether a business will be profitable and what capital it will need is to estimate the sales potential for its products or services. It is no good producing if you cannot sell all your produce – though sometimes constraints, such as limited production capacity, may mean that you could sell more than you produce.

Estimating sales for an established business can be relatively straightforward; you can rely on market information you and the sales force have gained, you may have established regular customers and know their requirements, you may be able to apply one of the many mathematical techniques to estimate sales in the future. For a completely new business, it is far more difficult; you have no market information coming from a sales force, you have no regular customers, you have no history on which to base projections. The new small business launches itself on to the market with a lot of faith – but it should temper that faith with good judgement.

The most important person to any business is the customer, and sales will depend on his buying behaviour. Generally we can say that there are two categories of product or service, each with very different customers. First, there are consumer goods: either fast-moving products such as ice-cream, or durable products, such as washing-machines; sales of the latter depend on getting the product tried, while sales of the former are dependent upon repeat purchases. Second, there are industrial goods: either materials (such as timber), parts (screws) and services (advertising), or capital items (such as fork-lift trucks); again, sales of the latter depend on getting the product tried, often by one particular person, whereas sales of the former are dependent upon repeat purchases. Every business needs to understand the customer and his buying habits.

The first step in forecasting the sales for a small business is to look at the overall market. Market demand for a product is not a single number, it is a function dependent upon the industry marketing effort. The forecast demand within a market will thus depend upon forecast industry marketing effort.

A useful analytical tool in looking at the problems facing market estimation for small businesses is the product/market matrix shown

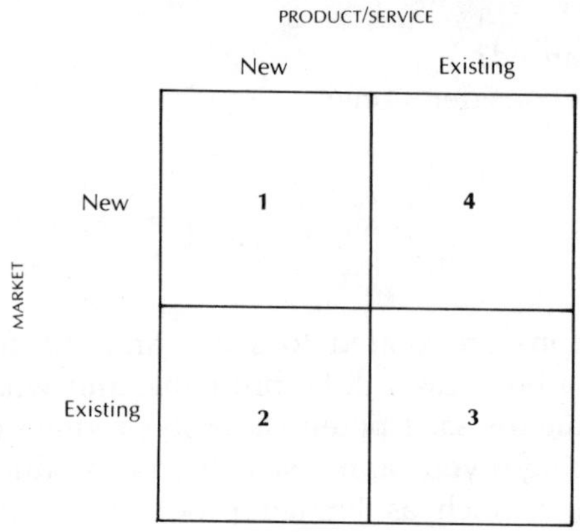

                          PRODUCT/SERVICE

	New	Existing
New	1	4
Existing	2	3

MARKET

Figure 2.1 The product/market matrix

in Figure 2.1. It allows one to focus on the divergent problems facing new small businesses introducing different types of products or services into different types of market. The matrix classifies four types of product or service launch:

1. NEW PRODUCT OR SERVICE/NEW MARKET. This small business has the most difficult and risky product launch of all – introducing a completely new product on to a completely new market. An example of this is the tremendously successful personal microcomputer industry, which initially had many small businesses entering the field.
2. EXISTING MARKET/NEW PRODUCT OR SERVICE. This small business introduces a new product or service which displaces or competes against old products in an existing market. Recently a company called Straw Box Systems Ltd was formed to produce and sell tough boxes made from straw, competing against traditional softwood boxes in the packaging of fresh fruit and vegetables.
3. EXISTING MARKET/EXISTING PRODUCT OR SERVICE. This small business introduces an old product or service into an old or existing market: for example, a new off-licence in a town centre with five shops already selling beers, wine and spirits. Such a business will have limited growth potential and sales will be made, probably, at the expense of competitors.
4. EXISTING PRODUCT OR SERVICE/NEW MARKET. This small business introduces an old product or service into a new market: for example, if our off-licence were to open on a new estate, or in a new town, which has no other off-licence.

1. NEW PRODUCT AND NEW MARKET

Estimating the potential market for a completely *new* product or service in a completely *new* market is a daunting task. Any estimates are bound to be highly uncertain. The problem is that there are absolutely no data to go on. Even market research, if you could afford it, would yield estimates with a high error potential. The customer has only the broadest idea of this new product, what it can do, how he can use it. Anyway, his buying intentions will depend on the price of the product, which you will find difficult to establish without knowing how many you can sell. Looking at 'similar' markets might provide you with some limits on the market size. However, at the end of the day your 'guestimate' could be wildly out. For example, the market for personal microcomputers was greatly underestimated, even by established computer manufacturers.

If market research is appropriate, then many small businesses will want to do their own. It is beyond the scope of this book to look at market research in detail, since whole books are written on this subject.[1] Generally, the initial stages of market research would be directed towards defining the customer and his buying characteristics. For example, the buyer might not be the end-user: as might be the case for industrial customers where engineers give product specifications and specialist buyers source the product. The next stage would be to look at the channels of distribution available for the product or service. Market research would probably look closely at 'similar' products both to ascertain the upper limits of spending and to understand buyers' needs and distribution channels.

Once the market is understood, market research would try to describe and quantify it. Initially this might take the form of consulting 'experts' on the market for your new product. Then the customer might be consulted by survey. The survey would be based on a sample, so it is important that the sample is representative of the buying population. Potential customers might be contacted by telephone, post or personal interview, and at the end of the day the market research would provide not only a broad estimate of the market size but also suggestions about how to redesign the product or service so as to better suit the needs of the customer.

If market research can come up with an estimate of the market size, the next question concerns the capturing of it. Of course, if you are the only market entrant, then that question may be straightforward.

---

[1] For further reading in this area look at Derek Waterworth, *Small Business: Marketing for the Small Business*, Macmillan, 1987.

But how long will you remain the only entrant? What will that mean to your sales volume and selling price?

2/3. EXISTING MARKETS

A small business going into an *existing* market has an easier task, since there will be data on the market already available. Some sources of market information are given in Appendix 1 to this chapter. The most prolific of these is the Government Statistical Service, but others include trade associations, banks, stockbrokers, media owners, local authorities and government-sponsored organisations such as the National Economic Development Office. One of the most useful sources is The Economist Intelligence Unit's *Retail Business*, published monthly. It reviews a wide range of markets and condenses information from secondary sources. Most libraries have an index to *Retail Business* and can obtain photocopies of articles. Indeed most of these sources are available at your nearest Business and Statistics Library. Your local library will tell you the nearest one, and many will provide information by post, for a fee.

Kotler lists three approaches to estimating current demand in an existing market.[1]

1 THE CHAIN RATIO METHOD. This is a technique for estimating total market potential whereby the small business uses generally available statistics to estimate demand for a specific product. Kotler uses the example of dietic beer, where a market demand could be estimated as:

> Population × Personal discretionary income per capita × Average percentage of discretionary income spent on food × Percentage of food expenditure spent on beverages × Percentage of beverage expenditure spent on beer × Expected percentage of beer expenditure spent on dietic beer

2 THE MARKET BUILD-UP METHOD. This technique is used mainly by industrial-goods firms seeking to estimate the market potential in a particular territory. It involves identifying the potential buyers of the product and adding together their estimated potential purchases of the product. Their estimated purchases could be based upon published industrial data for product consumption. For example, the straw-box manufacturer could identify potential buyers in an area and apply a ratio of, say, percentage of sales spent on packaging to these firms' sales.

---

[1] Philip Kotler, *Marketing Management Analysis, Planning and Control*, Prentice-Hall, 1980.

3 INDEX OF BUYING-POWER METHOD. This technique is used by consumer-goods firms to estimate market potential in a territory. Since their consumers are so numerous, they cannot list all potential customers and estimate their buying requirements; consequently they assume that market potential is related to some single factor such as population. For example, our off-licence could apply figures for *per capita* expenditure on beer, wines and spirits purchased for home consumption to figures for the number of people using the shopping centre.

Finally, for larger consumer-goods businesses there is the possibility of consulting trend data supplied by the research agencies who operate retail audits and consumer panels and syndicate their results.

Estimating the market size is only the first step, of course. Next comes the question of market share. How much of the market can you capture? How will you capture and then retain it? What actions are your competitors likely to take? Will this affect your sales volume or selling price? Will you have to spend extra money on promotion? Market research can provide some answers to these questions; however, it is expensive. An inexpensive and efficient way of establishing the basic characteristics of your market is to buy into an omnibus survey. The Market Research Society's monthly newsletter carries a regular feature advertising these. The producer of the survey draws the sample, administers the questionnaire, processes the data and reports the results. You take space in the questionnaire, paying according to the questions asked and statistical breakdown required. There are also specialist omnibus surveys which look at particular markets.

The small business must decide whether the exploratory research this provides is sufficient to estimate the sales potential of the business with sufficient accuracy. More detailed market research can be expensive. The small business must decide whether the extra costs are warranted by the more accurate results the detailed research, should provide.

4. EXISTING PRODUCT AND NEW MARKET

A small business selling an existing product or service into a *new* market faces a combination of the problems outlined so far. It could try to apply data on existing markets to the new market. This could work if the two markets are very similar. For example, the off-licence setting up in the new town could apply UK expenditure data to population data for the new town. Since, for the time being, it is the only shop in the town it should be in a good position to capture those sales. However, if the markets are less similar, for example export markets, then estimates of size arrived at in this way can be very inaccurate and full-scale market research is the safest solution to the problem.

However difficult, any new small business must try to estimate the sales it can achieve. Since these are likely to be somewhat uncertain, it is probably a good idea to try to quantify the highest and lowest estimates you would make. If you wish to be more sophisticated, then you might try to allocate probabilities to different levels of sales, as in Table 2.1, and work out the 'most likely' sales outcome by weighting sales by their probability. In Chapter 17 this approach is developed.

Table 2.1 Estimating sales using probabilities

A Sales Estimate	B Probability	A × B Probability weighting
£1,000,000	10%	£100,000
900,000	15%	135,000
800,000	30%	240,000
700,000	20%	140,000
600,000	15%	90,000
500,000	10%	50,000
	Most likely sales estimate	£755,000

Costs and profitability

Whatever the reasons for starting your small business, in the long run it must at least cover its costs, simply to survive. Estimating sales is the first step in evaluating any small business venture. The next step is to estimate your costs and capital requirements and to evaluate the profitability of the venture. There is quite a range of technical skills to gather before this is possible, and subsequent chapters should give you them. This section is intended only to introduce you to these skills and indicate how they may be used by a completely new venture.

Generally, costs fall into three broad categories:

1. DIRECT MATERIAL – the cost of the materials incorporated into the product such as the steel in a manufactured socket wrench, or the cost of food served in a restaurant.

2. DIRECT LABOUR – the cost of the labour going directly into the product or service.
3. OVERHEADS – the other costs of manufacture such as rent, rates, repairs and maintenance, administrative staff, electricity, insurance, depreciation.

If you add to the cost of a product the costs of selling, and delivering that finished product, you will have its total cost, as delivered to the customer. The total costs of the business will depend on how many units it produces and sells.

For a completely new small business, where there is no track record to go back to which will indicate cost behaviour, costs can be estimated using professional evaluations of materials and work requirements. Engineers who are familiar with the technical requirements of a production process will estimate the quantities of materials needed and the labour- or machine-hours required for various operations. Prices and wage rates are applied to the physical measurements to obtain cost estimates. In the preparation of estimates of future profitability the effect of changes in critical factors such as material prices, wage rates or machine-hours of operation must be considered. For service businesses this process is much more straightforward, since probably it will often only involve estimating the level of staff required and their wage rates. However, even restaurants have a material cost – the food they serve.

Overheads for most small businesses are kept to a minimum, but you will have to incur certain expenditures. If you are renting or leasing machinery or buildings, the cost of these overheads is easily verifiable. However, if you purchase these capital items outright, since they will last a number of years it is clearly unfair to allocate their whole cost to any single year. Accountants normally allocate the cost over the life of the asset – this is called 'depreciation'. The easiest way to depreciate an asset is to allocate its cost equally over its lifetime – this is called *straight-line depreciation*. For example, a £17,000 machine which you estimate will last 5 years and then have a resale value of £2,000, will have an annual depreciation cost of £3,000, i.e.

$$\frac{£17,000 - £2,000}{5}$$

At this stage you may have come across two problems. First, some costs will depend upon the volume you produce and sell: for example, material costs. Other costs will not vary in line with the volume produced: for example, rates. This is the basis for economies of scale.

Table 2.2 Rockley Estate off-licence: Profit projection for the year ending 31 October 1988

Profit projection for the year ending 31 October 1988			
Projected turnover (note 1)			£171,400
Projected gross profit (note 1)			26,200
Overhead and administrative costs:			
Wages (note 2)		4,000	
Rent & Rates		2,300	
Electricity		600	
Alarm-system running costs		200	
Insurance		300	
Telephone		300	
Vehicle-running costs		500	
Miscellaneous costs		500	
Depreciation (note 3)			
Vehicle	£1,000		
Till	100		
Fixtures and fittings:	1,000	2,100	10,800
Projected net profit before mortgage repayments and withdrawals			£15,400

Accountants call these *'variable'* and *'fixed'* costs. The higher the level of fixed costs, the greater the potential for economies of scale. Your total costs will vary, to a greater or lesser extent, with the volume you produce and sell. However, they are unlikely to vary proportionately with volume; consequently the cost of one unit of production will be different at different levels of production.

The second problem may be encountered if the small business is producing more than one product and some of the costs are shared by the different products. The problem is how to allocate the costs between the products. A number of techniques can be used to do this. Both these problems are dealt with in subsequent chapters.

It is difficult to know whether to calculate your costs before estimating sales, since your selling price may be influenced by the unit costs you face. However, the unit costs you face will also be influenced by the volume you produce and sell. The problem does not exist to the same extent if you have an existing market with established prices that you will have to charge. However, it is a real problem in new markets.

With estimates of sales and costs you will be able to ascertain whether the project will make a profit or not. An example of a simple profit projection, similar to the off-licence whose sales were estimated earlier, is shown in Table 2.2.

Table 2.2 cont.

Notes to profit projection
1. *Turnover* and *gross profit* are estimated as follows:

	Average household expenditure per week	% of expenditure spent at off-licences	Target penetration (No. of households)	Estimated turnover per week	Profit margin	Estimated profit per week
Beer	£4.46	15%		£ 602	25%	£ 150
Wines and spirits	£2.52	50%		£ 1,134	10%	£ 113
Other	£ .97	50%	900	£ 437	15%	£ 66
Tobacco	£4.42	15%		£ 597	10%	£ 60
Soft drinks	£ .61	50%		£ 275	21%	£ 58
Confectionery	£ .85	50%		£ 383	20%	£ 77
				£ 3,428		524
Weeks trading				50		50
(assume first two weeks, no sales)				£171,400 pa		£26,200 pa

Average household expenditure per week taken from the Department of Employment Gazette, April 1987.
% of expenditure spent at off-licences based upon estimates provided by Retail Business.
Target penetration based upon a potential household market on Rockley Estate of 1,500 families with a target penetration of 60% (1,500 × 60% = 900). It is estimated that the number of households will increase to 2,000 by 1990. There is no competition planned or existing on Rockley Estate.

2. *Wages* are for two part-time employees.

3. *Depreciation*:
   The motor-vehicle and fixtures and fittings have been depreciated over five years.
   The till has been depreciated over ten years.

	Capital expenditure	Depreciation rate	Depreciation
Vehicle	£ 5,000	20%	£1,000
Till	£ 1,000	10%	£ 100
Fixtures and fittings	£ 5,000	20%	£1,000

Capital requirements

The capital needs of the business will stem from two sources. First, there are the major assets needed by the business, such as machinery, plant, vehicles and buildings. The typical small business will rent or lease many of these items, so as to defer any cash expenditure until the business has started generating cash itself. However, inevitably some items will have to be purchased. Second, any small business will invest funds in its working capital, such as stock and debtors, though trade creditors will provide some of the funds by supplying goods on credit. The key to understanding how much you will invest in working capital is to understand that it all depends on *time*: time to turn raw material stock into finished goods, time to sell the finished goods, time to get the cash for the sales and time to pay for the raw materials and labour. Obviously, service businesses invest less in working capital: for example, they could have no stock and provide purely a cash service.

You can arrive at a rough estimate of working capital needs simply by looking at these time spans and relating them to your sales and cost estimates. Although this approach is no substitute for an accurate cash-flow estimate, it is a useful first approximation in estimating the working capital needs of a business.

Look at Table 2.3. Here is a business with estimated monthly sales of £10,000, manufacturing costs of £6,500 and selling costs of £2,500. You decide, for business reasons, that you must keep one month's stock of raw materials and finished goods and offer two months' credit to customers. Fortunately trade creditors do not require payment for three months and the work-force is paid one month in arrears. The stock on the shop-floor at any time represents one-quarter of a month's production, with on average only half completed. In this situation the investment in stock and debtors that you have made represents 1⅛ months of raw material purchases, 2⅛ months of labour costs and ⅛ months of overheads: or £4,500, £3,188 and £125, a total investment in working capital of £7,813. This is the amount permanently tied up in working capital – ignoring inflation and growth in sales – and requires permanent funding. Note that these costs do not include selling costs, since these are only incurred when the stock is sold.

Let us look again at the example of the off-licence used, Table 2.2. This is a cash business with no debtors. If the owner estimates that his minimum stock level is 3 weeks and that, while he must purchase tobacco, soft drinks and confectionery at a cash and carry, he can obtain 4 weeks' credit on purchases of beer, wines and spirits, his working capital requirement will be as follows:

WORKING CAPITAL
Stock: 3 × £ (3,428 – 524)	=	£8,712
less creditors, beer: 4 × £ (602 – 150)	=	(1,808)
creditors, wine & spirits 4 × (1134 – 113)	=	(4,084)
Total working capital		£2,820

If the lease on his lock-up shop cost £2,000 and his other capital

Table 2.3 Working capital requirements

1. **Estimated sales and costs per month**

   Sales (and production)   £10,000

Materials	£4,000	
Wages	1,500	
Overheads	1,000	6,500
		£ 3,500
Selling and delivery costs		£ 2,500
Estimated monthly profit		£ 1,000

2. **Estimated time spans**

Raw materials	1 month's production
Work in progress	¼ month's production (estimated only ½ complete)
Finished goods	1 month's production
Trade creditors	3 months to pay
Wages	1 month to pay
Trade debtors	2 months to pay

3. **Estimated working capital requirement**

	Raw materials	Labour	Overheads	Total
Raw materials	1 month	—	—	
Work in progress	⅛	⅛	⅛	
Finished goods	1	1	1	
Trade creditors	(3)	—	(3)	
Labour	—	(1)	—	
Debtors	2	2	2	
Total time invested	1⅛	2⅛	⅛	
Monthly cost	£4,000	£1,500	£1,000	
Total cost invested	£4,500	£3,188	£ 125	£7,813

expenditure totals £11,000, his total investment in these 'fixed assets' is £13,000.

Thus the off-licence requires a total investment of £15,820 (£13,000 + 2,820) to produce a profit of £15,400 per annum, and that is before his own wage is paid. Is it a worthwhile investment? That answer will have to wait until later. In subsequent chapters we develop a number of techniques to evaluate such investments including *return on capital*, *payback* and *discounted cash flow* criteria. However, the £15,400 profit must cover both the owner's wage and the return (or interest) he would have earned on £15,820 invested elsewhere.

To evaluate any project fully three financial documents are absolutely essential:

1. A PROFIT PROJECTION.
2. AN ESTIMATE OF CAPITAL REQUIREMENTS – PROJECTED BALANCE-SHEETS.
3. ESTIMATED CASH FLOWS.

The final document, the cash-flow estimate or budget, should confirm the capital requirements of the business but it should also tell you about the *timing* of the capital requirements – an invaluable planning tool and essential for supporting requests for short-term finance. It should also give you an indication of the fluctuations in that financing requirement as seasonal trading patterns alter. Again, the analysis of this tool, along with that of the others, will be developed in subsequent chapters.

How will it be financed?

Having found a sound business idea that looks profitable, and established how much capital is required to finance that business, probably the hardest task you will face will be gathering that capital together. Beware of the dangers of launching your business with high hopes but insufficient capital; up to 30 per cent of bankruptcies stem from insufficient capital backing.

The major source of capital for any new business will probably come from two places. First, you will have to find a major part of the funds yourself, and that could mean using your savings, taking out a mortgage on your house or even taking out a personal loan. The second major source will be your trade creditors: suppliers of goods who are willing to wait for payment, as you yourself may have to for payment from your customers.

After that it is a case of borrowing money from banks or other institutions or making use of the various government start-up schemes designed specifically to help small businesses. This section will give you some idea of how much you might be able to borrow and some criteria for deciding what sort of funds to borrow. Chapter 4 will deal with the particular financing characteristics of two fundamentally different types of small businesses: one orientated towards growth, and the other in a more stable commercial environment. Since financing is such an important topic for small businesses, we spend two chapters looking, in detail, at the various financial institutions which might be approached for funds.

How much borrowing?

When you talk to an institution about borrowing money, it will probably immediately start talking about *gearing*. Gearing is a measure of the level of borrowings of a business in relation to its resources. Gearing has traditionally been taken to be the amount of external borrowing divided by the book value of the assets in the business. For example, suppose the business has an overdraft of £15,000 and a mortgage on a premises of £50,000, and that the net assets come to £195,000, then gearing would be 33 per cent:

$$\left(\frac{£15{,}000 + £50{,}000}{£195{,}000}\right) \times 100$$

Often adjustments might be made to the assets of the business to reflect undervaluations of property. Thus gearing is a measure of the security a borrower is offering on a loan. Many lenders use a 50 per cent gearing level as the maximum they will lend. This means half of the business is financed by the lender and half by the owner; but there is really no hard-and-fast rule.

There is also *income gearing*. This is a measure of how well a business can meet its interest payments out of trading income. It is normally taken to be interest payments divided by earnings before interest and tax. For example, suppose interest payments are £10,000 per year and earnings before interest and tax come to £50,000, then income gearing would be 20 per cent:

$$\left(\frac{£10{,}000}{£50{,}000}\right) \times 100$$

Often income gearing is calculated not just on last year's profit but, more importantly so far as new loans are concerned, on future income estimates.

The higher the gearing of a business, the riskier it is seen as being. The lender has less asset security against his loan, and his interest payments are less secure against fluctuations in earnings. Volatility of profit, and hence cash flow, is important – a firm with a volatile pattern of profits should not gear itself too highly, otherwise it may be unable to meet its interest payments. A business can choose the level of gearing it wishes, to suit the degree of risk it is prepared to take. Of course, the lender may not be prepared to share those risks and the firm may find it either very costly or just impossible to borrow funds beyond a certain level of gearing.

A lender of capital will often require security for his investment and will probably have the right to appoint a receiver to look after his interests if the business goes wrong, and interest or capital repayment cannot be met. Often the owner of a small business will be asked to guarantee a loan *personally*.

What type of borrowing?

The basic rule when obtaining and investing capital in a business is to never borrow 'short' and invest 'long'. Always try to match the length of time you have to repay the borrowed funds with the life of the asset you are investing in. Long-term investments (over 5 years) such as buildings, heavy plant and even your base level of working capital, should be financed from long-term funds; funds generated by the business, your own capital or long-term loans or mortgages. Medium-term investments such as vehicles and plant with restricted life are generally suitable for hire purchase, leasing or medium-term loans. The weekly fluctuations in working capital can safely be financed by short-term renewable sources of funds such as bank overdraft. However, in recent years, high rates of inflation have forced businesses to invest more and more in working capital to finance turnover which has not changed in volume terms. This is just as much a long-term investment as buildings, and if financed by overdraft then you face the risk of being called to repay that overdraft whenever bank lending is restricted.

Within these constraints the choice of funds tends to come down to a comparison of interest rates. However, a simple comparison can be misleading. The general rule over recent years has been that interest rates increase with the length of the loan. This is natural enough since the lender has to be compensated for tying up his money for a longer period and loosing the flexibility of deciding to do something else with it. However, the interest rate reflects two elements: first, there is the 'real' element, which is the true cost of borrowing which increases with the length of the loan; second, there is an 'inflation' element to compensate the lender for the decrease in the purchasing power of the capital he has lent. This element must reflect *expectations* of inflation over the term of the loan. Consequently, during periods when current inflation rates are high, but expectations of future rates are much lower, there can be what is called a 'reverse yield gap': when long-term rates are lower than short-term rates. This is due to differences in the expected rates of inflation over the periods.

Most businesses take on medium- or long-term loans at rates of interest which are linked to a fixed percentage above prevailing short-term rates. This means that you are not tied to a fixed interest rate which may appear high in future years. However, short-term rates may rise and overtake the original long-term rate, as they have consistently done over the last 25 years; and in this case the business is faced with increasing interest charges simply to service the same loan. This makes it very difficult to plan borrowing costs with any certainty.

Some small businesses may have the opportunity to obtain fixed-interest, long-term loans. These have the advantage of letting you know well in advance your borrowing costs with absolute certainty. However, the business will be tied to the interest payments on that loan for a long time and the interest rate reflects the lender's expectations about future inflation. You must ask yourself if you agree with the lender. If inflation runs at more than the lender expects, then you will gain: the interest rate you will pay will be low compared with future rates. If it runs at less, you will lose. This decision is more important when considering fixed interest rates because variable rates are constantly adjusting to new expectations of inflation.

Summary

To summarise, short-term loans are generally cheaper than long-term loans. However, they are more risky, since they may have to be repaid on demand, perhaps when the business does not have the funds available. It is safest to match the maturity of a loan to the life of the asset you are investing the funds in.

If fixed-interest loans are available, these will give you absolute certainty about your financing costs. However, be certain you agree with the lender's expectations about inflation, otherwise you could end up with an expensive loan. Most small businesses will obtain loans at a fixed percentage above short-term rates, and the short-term rate will vary.

The more a business borrows, the higher its 'gearing', and the higher its financing risks. If interest and capital repayments cannot be met, it is likely that the bank will call in a receiver to administer the affairs of the business and perhaps start bankruptcy proceedings.

Appendix 1   Sources of market information

A = annual, Q = quarterly, M = monthly, W = weekly

GUIDES TO SOURCES

Guide to Official Statistics (A), Central Statistical Office.
Government Statistics, a brief guide to sources (A), free from the Central Statistical Office, CO: CSO Section, Great George Street, London SW1P 3AQ.
Business Monitors give you the facts about your industry, free from the Central Statistical Office, address above.
Sources of United Kingdom Marketing Information, E. Tupper and G. Wills, (Benn, 1975).
Review of Consumer Research Sources for Products and Media, 2nd edn, Twyman (1976), Institute of Practitioners in Advertising.

GOVERNMENT STATISTICAL SERVICE

Monthly Digest of Statistics (M), and *Annual Abstract of Statistics* (A).
Economic Trends (M).
British Business (M).
Population Trends (Q), England and Wales only. For Scotland and Northern Ireland see estimates of the Registrars-General for Scotland and Northern Ireland.
Population Projections (A).
Business Monitors (prepared by the Business Statistics Office):
 Production Monitors (A, Q, M)
 Service and Distributive Monitors (A, Q, M)
 Miscellaneous Monitors, e.g. *Motor Vehicles Registrations* (M), *Statistical News* (Q), *Cinemas* (A), *Overseas Travel and Tourism* (Q).
Transport:
 Transport Statistics (A)
 National Travel Survey 1975–76.
Family Income and Expenditure (from the Office of Population Census and Surveys):
 Family Expenditure Survey (A)
 General Household Survey (most recent report 1977).
Visit; Government Bookshop, 48 High Holborn, London WC1V 6HB; and the Statistics and Market Intelligence Library, 50 Ludgate Hill, London EC4M 7HU.

COMPANY INFORMATION

KOMPASS Register, companies listed geographically and by Standard Industrial Classification (UK and other countries).
Who Owns Whom (A), Dun & Bradstreet.

Guide to Key British Enterprises, Dun & Bradstreet.
Stock Exchange Yearbook (A), Thomas Skinner Directories.

INTERNATIONAL SOURCES

UN Statistical Yearbook.
Main Economic Indicators (Organisation for Economic Co-operation and Development).
General Statistical Bulletin, EEC.
Overseas Trade Analysed in Terms of Industries (Q).

INFORMATION PUBLISHED BY MEDIA-OWNERS

For example, IPC, *Woman and the National Market* (A); *UK Spending Patterns*, ed. Critchley, 1975.

BANK REVIEWS

Published regularly by Barclays, Lloyds, Midland and National Westminster.

PERIODICALS

Campaign (W).
The Economist (W).
Retail Business (M), a useful source of information about markets and marketing, expert appraisal of 'trade' and published sources, consult the index, photocopies of articles are available.

CHAPTER 3

Setting up a Business

LEGAL FORMS OF BUSINESS	28
Sole trader	28
Partnerships	29
Limited companies	30
OTHER LEGAL CONSIDERATIONS	32
Other forms of business	33
SOURCES OF ADVICE	35
CASH GRANTS	37
Appendix 1 *Sources of advice*	37
Appendix 2 *Cash grants*	39

Legal forms of business

Nothing, in the over-regulated world of today, is ever simple. Before you launch your new business you should give some thought to the legal problems you will have to deal with. The first is deciding what is to be the legal form of the business you wish to launch. Technically there are three major forms of business organisation: the sole trader, the partnership, and the limited liability registered company. About 56 per cent of businesses are operated as sole traders and the balance are fairly equally divided between partnerships and companies.

Sole traders

This is the business owned by one individual. The individual is the business, and the business is the individual. The two are inseparable. It is the simplest of all businesses to start: you simply begin operations. There are fewer government regulations than for the limited company, and there are no major requirements about accounts and audits. Furthermore, it pays no corporate taxes, though all earnings are subject to personal income taxes.

However, the sole trader does face some important limitations. The most significant is that unless the small business incorporates it will find itself unable to obtain large amounts of loan capital. Lending institutions prefer the assets of a business to be placed within the legal framework of a registered company, because of the restrictions then placed on that business. It is quite common for small businesses to start life as sole traders and then to incorporate later in life as larger capital sums are needed.

The second major disadvantage is that the sole trader is personally liable for all the debts of the business, no matter how large. That means that the creditors may look to both the business assets and the proprietor's assets to satisfy their debts. This disadvantage should not be overemphasised, however, because it is a widely adopted precaution to place some of the family assets, such as your home, in the name of your husband or wife, or another relative. Also, it is common practice, even with limited companies, for banks to ask for a personal guarantee before giving the small business a loan.

Finally, the sole trader is limited to the life of the person who created it. Should the proprietor die, the business is deemed to have ceased and this can cause both legal and tax problems.

Partnerships

If two or more individuals start up a business together, they are said to conduct a business as a partnership. That partnership can take the form of an informal oral understanding or a formally drawn up partnership agreement. The partnership has many of the characteristics of the sole trader; ease of formation and running and unlimited liability. Partners are taxed as if the business income were their personal income.

The major advantage of the partnership is that it allows a number of sole traders to pool their resources: some to contribute capital, others to contribute their skills. Also, some professions require their members to form partnerships rather than limited companies, specifically so that they cannot limit their liability for professional negligence: for example, doctors and accountants.

However, there are some severe disadvantages to partnerships. First, each partner has unlimited liability for the debts of the partnership, whether he personally incurred them or not. Secondly, a partnership is held to cease whenever a partner retires or a new partner comes in. Consequently it is normally good practice to set down in a partnership deed the terms on which partnership assets are to be valued and distributed in these events. However, just because the partnership legally ceases does not mean that the business will cease. The other partners may simply buy the assets of the retiring partner. To avoid the problems caused by the death of a partner, it is common practice for each partner to carry life insurance naming the remaining partners as his beneficiaries, and the proceeds of that insurance policy are then used to buy the assets of the dead partner.

Generally any individual considering forming a partnership would be well advised to draw up a formal partnership agreement. It is very easy to go into an informal partnership with a friend, but if you find you cannot work together, or times get hard, you may regret it. Where there is no formal agreement, then the terms of the Partnership Act 1890 are held to apply.

Partnership agreements generally cover the following areas:

1. CAPITAL: How much does each partner put in each year?
2. DIVISION OF PROFITS: What proportion of business profits does each partner receive?
3. INTEREST ON CAPITAL OR DRAWINGS: Are partners entitled to interest on their capital and at what rate? Do partners pay interest on their drawings?
4. LIMITS TO DRAWING: Are there limits as to how much a partner can draw from the business?
5. REMUNERATION OF PARTNERS: Are some partners to be credited with a notional 'salary' to compensate for the extra work they have put into the business?
6. PREPARATION OF ACCOUNTS: How often should they be produced?
7. RETIREMENT AND NEW PARTNERS: What amounts should be paid to a retiring partner? How do you determine that a new partner pays a fair price for his share of the business?

Finally, it is worth pointing out that the Limited Partnership Act 1907 allows a certain class of partner, who provides capital but takes no part in the management of the business, to have their liability for its debts limited to their investment.

Limited companies

A company registered in accordance with the provisions of the Companies Acts is a separate legal entity distinct from both its owners or shareholders, and its directors or managers. It can sue or be sued in its own right and enter into its own contracts. There is a divorce of management from ownership, with a board of directors elected by the shareholders to control the day-to-day operations of the business. In fact, there need be a minimum of only two shareholders and one director, and, usualy with a small business, the owners are also the directors. However, this legal form does offer a number of advantages.

1. The liability of shareholders is limited to the amount they have put into the business, plus any amount unpaid on the shares issued.
2. The company has unlimited life, and shares can be transferred between individuals without affecting the company.
3. There is no limit on the number of shareholders in a company. The maximum number of partners in a partnership business is usually twenty. Therefore, the company can recruit capital from a far wider market.

Nevertheless there are some disadvantages with operating as a limited liability company: Under the Companies Acts a company must maintain certain books of account and appoint an auditor. It must file an annual return with the Registrar of Companies which includes the accounts as well as details of directors and mortgages. Not only does this take a lot of time, it also costs money. It can also mean that competitors have access to information about your company which you might not otherwise wish them to have. The easiest way to form your business into a limited company is to buy one 'off the shelf' from one of the many Company Registration Agents specialising in company formation (Many are listed in the Yellow Pages.) To do so only costs about £150. To register a company yourself requires a tedious filing of a number of documents with the Registrar of Companies, including:

1. A MEMORANDUM OF ASSOCIATION. This is the document that states the objectives of the company and the amount of share capital to be issued. It defines the powers of the company. If a company acts beyond its powers, the directors may be liable for the debts they incur.
2. ARTICLES OF ASSOCIATION. This regulates the affairs of members between themselves and covers such matters as the transfer of shares, the holding of meetings, the powers of directors, the borrowing powers of the company and the audit of the accounts.
3. A LIST OF PROPOSED DIRECTORS, their addresses and details of other directorships.
4. A STATEMENT OF NOMINAL SHARE CAPITAL, plus relevant stamp duty.

5. A DECLARATION that the requirements of the Companies Acts have been met in respect of REGISTRATION.
6. Notice of the ADDRESS OF THE COMPANY'S REGISTERED OFFICE.

In fact there are two types of company limited by shares. The first is the 'public' company, which in its memorandum states it is a 'public' company and has a minimum authorised and allotted share capital of £50,000 (on which stamp duty is payable). This is called a *public limited company* (plc). Any company which is not 'public' is called 'private' and may not invite the public to subscribe for its shares.

Other legal considerations

A newly formed small business must remember to check four areas before getting down to the business of making money:

1. Business names: Any sole trader or partnership may trade under their own names. If they choose another business name then all they have to do is ensure that the name of the owner(s) is stated on all business letters, orders, invoices, receipts or demands for payment together with an address at which all documents relating to the business will be accepted. Also a notice must be displayed at the business premises containing the names and addresses of the owners. A limited company must, however, submit its choice of name to the Registrar of Companies who will only accept it if there is no other company with that name and it is not obscene, offensive or illegal. The Department of Trade has compiled a list of 'sensitive and prohibited names' which require specific approval before they can be incorporated into a business name.
2. VAT. All businesses with VAT rateable turnover in excess of a certain level (see Appendix 1, chapter 9) must register with HM Customs and Excise, and are required to make quarterly returns. It is normally beneficial to register most businesses as soon as they start up, otherwise they must suffer 'input' VAT on all goods or services used, but cannot recharge it to customers.
3. PAYE. Any business with employees, and this includes directors of companies, will have to notify the Inland Revenue and operate the 'Pay-As-You-Earn' scheme for collecting income tax and National Insurance contributions. The Inland Revenue will send the business deduction cards, tax tables, and instructions on how to operate the scheme (see Chapter 9).
4. DHSS. The Department of Health and Social Security will be

helpful in providing information in two areas that will probably affect you: first, the legal rights that your employees will have under the Employee Protection Act 1975, the Trade Union and Labour Relations Act 1974 and Contracts of Employment Act 1972: trial periods, rights to notice, holiday entitlement and the many other areas which should be covered in a contract of employment; and second, any areas of the Health and Safety at Work Act 1974 which might affect your small business.

Additionally, if you are in the retail business, it is as well to check the rights of your customers under The Supply of Goods and Services Act 1982, and remember that if you are going to offer, or arrange, consumer credit, you need to be registered with the Office of Fair Trading.

There are further, more onerous, legal requirements and restrictions on the 'public' company, its members and directors. Generally most companies start life as 'private' and only become 'public' when they need funds from a wider range of shareholders. 'Off-the-peg' companies will be 'private', and generally a small business seeking incorporation should start life as a 'private' company to avoid the additional, onerous requirements.

Other forms of business

Co-operatives

Another form of business organisation is the co-operative. The Co-operative Development Agency (CDA), a body established in 1978 with all-party support, lists about 1,000 active co-operatives. The essential characteristic of an industrial or service co-operative is that it is largely owned, and ultimately controlled, by those working in it. Some co-operatives are simply limited liability companies owned by the 'employees'. The 'true' co-operative is registered under the Industrial and Provident Societies Act 1965 with the Registrar of Friendly Societies. It has limited liability and is taxed as a body corporate. To register under this Act the co-operative must be a 'non-profit' organisation conducted for the 'mutual benefit of members' and 'benefit of the community'. Other rules include:

1. There must be a minimum of 7 members, each with a maximum shareholding of £1,000.
2. There must be equal control of the society by members – not dependent upon funds invested.

3. Distribution of profit must be proportional to the amount traded or taken part in the business by members – not proportional to funds invested.
4. Interest on shares cannot exceed 'the amount required to retain and maintain the capital required to achieve the co-operative's objectives.'

There are a number of organisations set up to encourage the growth of co-operatives (see Appendix 1). Most supply model rules and advice, while some provide consultancy-type services. The CDA cannot offer loans (but can make recommendations to central and local government), however, a number of other bodies can do so. There are also local Co-operative Development Agencies set up with full-time staff and funded by a number of local authorities.

Franchises

An increasingly popular form of business, particularly with those who are less entrepreneurial, is taking up a franchise. A franchise is a business in which the owner of the name or method of doing business (called the franchisor) allows a local operator (called the franchisee) to set up a business under that name. In exchange for an initial fee and a royalty on sales, the franchisor lays down a blueprint of how the business is to be run; content and nature of products/ services on offer, price and performance standards, type, size and layout or business, design of stationery, training and other back-up support. The amount of money needed to take out a franchise varies widely – from £3,000 to over £300,000, plus the royalty on sales.

Since the franchise is usually a tried and tested idea, well known by potential customers, the franchisee should have a far better chance in business. Indeed only about 10% of franchisees fail. There are hundreds of franchises and well over 10,000 franchisees in the UK, but in the USA, where the concept was launched, the number of new franchisees setting up each year is about the same as the total number of franchisees in the whole United Kingdom.

The British Franchise Association was set up in 1977 to establish ethical standards in the industry and disseminate information. Membership is only granted to established franchisers which have been in operation for some time and which have been through a vetting procedure. Franchisers with BFA membership are probably a far safer bet than others without. The address of the BFA is given in Appendix 1. Franchising is dealt with further in chapter 7.

Management buy-outs

In recent years the traditional separation of shareholders and management has been eroded by the growing popularity of 'management buy-outs'. This is where a group of managers pool their resources to buy the business they have been running, usually from a larger, parent company. In legal form it is just another limited company. In 1986 there were some 300 'management buy-outs' to a value of approximately £2 billion.

Rather than the managers buying dead or dying businesses, there is growing evidence that these buy-outs stand a better chance of success than newly-formed companies. Investors in Industry helped finance most of the buy-outs in the UK. They maintain that the mortality rate for them is far lower than for other new companies. Often the larger companies sell off divisions simply because they need the cash, or have decided, for strategic reasons, to vacate a market sector. Sometimes private businesses come on to the market because a founder-owner dies or reaches retirement age. And in these cases the managers of the businesses are in a good position to evaluate their worth and to continue running them profitably. Financial support can also come from some unusual sources. For example, suppliers or customers with a strong interest in maintaining an outlet or source of supply for their own products can sometimes be persuaded to provide funds.

It would seem that managers of existing businesses have a good start in setting up a small business. They already have knowledge of the product and the market, and, since the business has an established track record, they will probably find obtaining capital for the buy-out that much easier than the newly formed small business.

Sources of advice

Many people start up their small business without thinking about these problems, but then many never succeed! It may seem a daunting task to undertake the required analysis, arrange finance and cope with the legal problems; you really do need the information and tools we develop later in the book. Once you have these, then the task, although still hard work, is at least manageable.

Nevertheless, many people will need help and this is available from a variety of sources. Local Enterprise Agencies were set up in the 1980s as a direct response to the need for help and advice on how to set up a business in particular local areas. These are now over 300 such agencies offering free advice on all aspects of business. Sometimes they offer training courses and managed workshops or offices. Frequently they have access to local cash grants and financial institutions. Generally they have a staff of only two or three counsellors, often secondees from banks, firms of accountants or larger companies. The largest is the London Enterprise Agency which has a staff of over 20.

Enterprise Agencies are funded mainly by local authorities, large firms and other organisations. However, the Local Enterprise Agency Grant Scheme which came into operation in 1986 to run for a five-year trial period, will provide a measure of central government support. Their regional spread is good but not comprehensive. Business in the Community is an umbrella organisation for the agencies. It produces a directory of local agencies and will provide you with the name and address of the agency nearest your place of business. Their address is given in Appendix 1.

The government has its own Small Firms Service which in England is run by the Department of Employment, in Scotland by the Scottish Development Agency and in Wales by the Welsh Development Agency. The service also provides counselling and information through over 400 counsellors, all experienced businessmen, and some 100 local offices. Although initial consultations are free, charges are made subsequently. Head office addresses are given in Appendix 1.

The Council for Small Industries in Rural Areas (CoSIRA) provides rural businesses with advice through 32 offices on local opportunities and conditions, business management, marketing and technical advice, skill training and financial services, including loans to attract top-up finance from the private sector. It also makes a modest charge for its services but not for preliminary meetings. Again, the head office address is given in Appendix 1.

There are a range of government schemes to provide free or subsidised commercial consultancy to smaller firms. These cover the areas of marketing, manufacturing, quality assurance, product design, biotechnology, application of microelectronics and certain areas of advanced manufacturing technology. Also the Business Improvement Scheme helps small businesses in areas affected by job losses in the steel, textile and shipbuilding and sea fisheries industries by providing grants to consultancy advice on marketing, financial management, the application of computers and licensing in of products and processes. These schemes are administered by the Department of Trade and Industry. Assistance is also available to the exporting firm through the British Overseas Trade Board (address given in Appendix 1).

Finally, there is a wide range of business start-up courses available through the Manpower Services Commission. In 1986/87 over 59,000 took part in various small business programmes organised by the MSC, at a cost of over £18 million. Most of these courses are free and often training allowances and market research budgets are provided. Details are available from local Job Centres or MSC offices.

Cash grants

There are a plethora of cash grants now offered to business. These are now too numerous to list since whole books are written on the subject.[1] Appendix 2 lists the grants most likely to be of interest to small firms. Interestingly relatively few are directed specifically at small firms. The list includes:

- Grants for small business
- Regional grants
- Grants towards consultancy
- Grants for innovation and investment
- Grants for energy conservation
- Grants for exporting

Further details or these grants should be obtainable from any Enterprise Agency or from local accountants. The contact addresses in Appendix 1 should also be useful.

Appendix 1   Sources of advice

ENTERPRISE AGENCIES

Business in the Community,
227A, City Road,
London, EC1V 1LX   (Tel: 01 253 3716)

Small Firms Service,
Head Office,
Small Firms Division, DOI,
Abell House, John Islip Street,
London SW1   (Tel: 01 211 5345)
(For Regional Office Dial 100 and ask for FREEPHONE ENTERPRISE)

---

[1] See National Westminster Bank, *Official Sources of Finance and Aid for Industry in the UK: A Comprehensive Guide*, September, 1986.

38 *Small business: planning, finance and control*

Council for Small Industries in Rural Areas (CoSIRA),
Head Office,
141, Castle Street,
Salisbury,
Wiltshire SP1 3TP   (Tel: 0722 336255)

Department of Trade and Industry (DOI),
Head Office
1-19, Victoria Street
London SW1H OET   (Tel: 01 215 5544)

Department of Employment (DOE),
Head Office,
Caxton House, Tothill Street,
London SW1H 9NF   (Tel: 01 213 3000)

Manpower Services Commission (MSC),
Head Office,
Moorfoot,
Sheffield S1 4PQ   (Tel: 0742 753275)

British Overseas Trade Board,
Head Office,
1-19, Victoria Street,
London SW1H 0ET   (Tel: 01 215 7877)

British Franchising Association,
75A, Bell Street,
Henley on Thames,
Oxon RG9 2BD   (Tel: 0491 578049)

The Co-operative Development Agency,
Broadmead House,
21, Panton Street
London SW1Y 4DR   (Tel: 01 839 2987)

SCOTLAND

Scottish Development Agency,
21, Bothwell Street,
Glasgow G2 6NR   (Tel: 041 248 6014)

The Highlands and Islands Development Board (HIDB),
Bridge House,
27, Bank Street,
Inverness IV1 1RQ   (Tel: 0463 234171)

WALES

Small Firms Information Centre,
16, St David's House,
Wood Street,
Cardiff CF1 1ER   (Tel: 0222 396116)

NORTHERN IRELAND

Industrial Development Board for Northern Ireland,
IDB House,
64, Chichester Street,
Belfast BT1 4JX   (Tel: 0232 233233)

Appendix 2 Grants

2.1 GRANTS FOR SMALL BUSINESS

There are relatively few national grants directed specifically towards small firms. One such scheme, organised by the Manpower Services Commission (MSC), is Enterprise Allowance. This offers those starting their own business £40 a week for the first 52 weeks trading. Applicants must have been out of work for eight weeks and have £1,000 capital to put toward the business. The MSC also operates the New Workers' Scheme which provides a £15 a week subsidy for up to a year to firms employing people under 21 at rates of pay which reflect their age and lack of experience.

There are, however, a number of local authorities who offer grants to small businesses and new businesses setting up in their areas. A number of the grants towards consultancy services and innovation and investment are also aimed specifically at small firms.

2.2 REGIONAL GRANTS

ASSISTED AREAS

Assisted areas are those parts of the country where the government offers additional incentives to encourage industrial expansion. Certain areas have been designated 'Development Areas' and offer Regional Development Grants (RDG) and Selective Assistance (RSA). Others are designated 'Intermediate Areas' and only offer Regional Selective Assistance. The Department of Trade and Industry produces a list of designated assisted areas, and details of the assistance available.

RDG is the higher of either 15% of eligible capital expenditure towards new assets, or £3,000 for each net new job created. RSA comes in two main forms. First there are project grants, related to the capital costs of a project, which are negotiable and designed to be the minimum necessary for the project to go ahead. Secondly, training grants of 40% of eligible costs, matched by a further 40% from the European Social Fund, are available towards training costs associated with qualifying projects. To qualify, projects must have good prospects for success, create or safeguard jobs and the assistance must be essential for the viability of the project. In addition to RDG and RSA, businesses in Development Areas might benefit from the government's Contract Preference Scheme whereby preferential treatment is given when tendering for contracts placed by government departments, nationalised industries and other public bodies.

SCOTLAND

In Scotland, the Scottish Development Agency has three main forms of cash grants:

(i) LEG-UP (Local Enterprise Grants for Urban Projects) offers 50% funding towards the fixed assets in urban projects which will create jobs or make a positive contribution to the environment.
(ii) PRIDE (Programme for Rural Initiatives and Developments) extends the LEG-UP scheme to rural areas.
(iii) DRAW (Development of Rural Area Workshops) is aimed at rural areas where the population is less than 15,000 and offers 25% grants towards building or expanding premises up to a maximum size of 250 sq. metres and a maximum grant of £15,000.

The Highlands and Islands Development Board offers discretionary grants to supplement other assistance providing up to a maximum of 50% of the cost of a project.

WALES

The Development Board for Rural Wales offers grants to encourage manufacturing and service firms to expand and locate in Wales. It must be demonstrated that a project cannot proceed without a grant. A wage subsidy of up to 30% of basic wages for 26 weeks is also available.

NORTHERN IRELAND

The Industrial Development Board for Northern Ireland offers capital equipment grants of 20%, grants for training personnel at various levels, and substantial relocation grants to encourage key workers to come to Northern Ireland.

Selective assistance is available for employment creating projects. These provide capital grants of up to 50% of the cost of new buildings, machinery and equipment; employment grants related to the number of new jobs created, rent grants of up to 100% for five years; interest relief grants for up to seven years; and grants to help firms attract and recruit good quality management.

Research grants of 40–50% are available towards the labour and material costs of items such as basic research, related design work, making and testing of prototypes, final design and production drawing costs. Market Development grants of up to 40% of approved costs are also available to help firms develop a strategic approach to their marketing, its planning and implementation.

LOCAL AUTHORITIES

There is a wide and diverse range of grants offered by different local authorities. Authorities in inner urban areas may make discretionary grants for environmental improvements, the conversion and improvement of industrial buildings, and up to £1,000 towards the setting up of co-ownership enterprises. They may also make grants towards rents paid by firms taking on new leases of premises, and may also give interest relief grants to small firms employing less than 50 employees for loans on land and buildings.

2.3 GRANTS TOWARDS CONSULTANCY

The government offers a range of grants to subsidise consultancy work in certain areas. These areas include:

- Productivity and quality assurance (directed specifically at small firms).
- Design and development of new products and redesign of existing products to meet market, production or financial needs (directed specifically at small firms).
- Biotechnology.
- Microelectronics and integrated circuits application in industrial products and processes.
- Training in microelectronic applications.
- Advanced Manufacturing Technology Feasibility Studies.
- Support for marketing (directed specifically at small firms).

The extent and conditions for grants relating to each area varies from area to area.

2.4 GRANTS FOR INNOVATION AND INVESTMENT

Again there is a range of grants available. The Department of Trade and Industry offers selective grants of up to 25% of the cost of projects that involve design, development or launching of a new, or significantly modified, product or process. A 50% shared-cost contract may also be arranged.

Grants of up to 20% of the development and capital costs may be available for the construction of up-to-date plant in biochemical engineering. A similar grant of up to 20% of eligible costs may also be available towards investment projects in the microelectronics components industry. Grants of up to 20% are also available, on a selective basis, to help small firms implement consultants recommendations aimed at improving or installing quality assurance systems which meet British Standard (BS) 5750.

2.5 GRANTS FOR ENERGY CONSERVATION

These grants include:

- Energy efficiency surveys – grants towards the cost of short and extended surveys of non-domestic premises by energy consultants.
- Energy efficiency demonstration scheme – grants of up to 25% towards the capital cost of installing innovative energy-saving technology.

2.6 GRANTS FOR EXPORTING

A whole range of exporting support is organised through the British Overseas Trade Board. It offers two grant aid schemes:

- Export marketing research scheme – grants of 50% are available towards the cost of research by consultants into overseas markets. Grants are also available to purchase published studies and to start up new export market research departments.
- Market entry guarantee scheme – grants of 50% of certain overhead costs associated with breaking into a new overseas market or obtaining an increased amount of business in an existing overseas market. The BOTB makes a flat rate 3% of funding fee, plus levy on sales, for the scheme.

CHAPTER 4

Strategy and Planning

THE NEED FOR STRATEGY AND PLANNING	43
Economies of scale	44
Product-market strategies	45
The life-cycle concept	47
Life-cycle crises	50
Managing the life-cycle	52
Financing the life-cycle	55
Diversification strategy	57

The need for strategy and planning

Why do small businesses need to formulate policy and plan for the future? After all, it takes valuable time: time that could be spent selling, or sorting out a production problem, or sending in the VAT return. Anyway the whole business is probably run by only one person. The decisions he has to make are fairly straightforward and major implications can be carried in his head rather than written down. So why waste time and money in moving into this far too sophisticated area of management?

This chapter is intended to show you why setting policy and planning for the future is important, and how to set about it. It highlights the periods in the life of a small business when it is most at risk, and ties in the rest of this book to the policy framework.

Let us start with a simple statistic. About 30 per cent of businesses fail within three years of being set up. In his analysis of the causes of these failures. Douglas Donleary states:

> Most potential bankrupts enter a field where they were once an employee, but do so with no knowledge of selling or book-keeping. They enter as entrepreneurs feeling that they know the business when all they know is the product.[1]

---
[1] Douglas Donleary, 'Causes of Bankruptcy in England' in *Policy Issues in Small Business Research*, ed. Allan Gibb and Terry Webb, Saxon House, 1982.

It is the last sentence we wish to focus on here. Most small businesses are customer-sensitive rather than market-aware. That is, they deal with existing customers and existing products. They are not aware of the market, or indeed the business environment as a whole, and when it changes they are left behind with an outdated product or service or obsolete technology. In today's rapidly changing environment small businesses are crucially vulnerable. They themselves can do little to influence that environment but must react quickly to, or even anticipate, changes in it if they are to survive, never mind prosper. This is why policy and planning are so important.

No business can predict the future with certainty. However, they all must be able to cope with the changes it brings. This requires four things:

1. An understanding of what you, the entrepreneur, want from life and in particular your business.
2. A thorough understanding of the business: its strengths *and* its weaknesses.
3. A thorough understanding of the whole environment: the threats *and* the opportunities if offers.
4. A plan of how the business can survive, or even grow, within this environment.

To do these things we need an essential framework which allows us to understand why small businesses exist, why some grow to become large companies, and why some decline and eventually go out of business.

Economies of scale

The average size of businesses varies from industry to industry. For example, the average size of chemical firms is very large, whereas the average size of retail firms is relatively small. The most fundamental reason for these differences is the extent of economies of scale in an industry: that is, how the total cost per unit produced changes as more units are produced. Generally this can be expected to decline up to some point: for example, as an expensive piece of machinery is used more fully. However, beyond this point unit costs may start to increase: for example as the economies of scale or production become increasingly offset by increasing distribution costs. Thus the potential for economies of scale in a high capital intensity industry like chemicals are great, whereas in retailing the potential savings are much smaller.

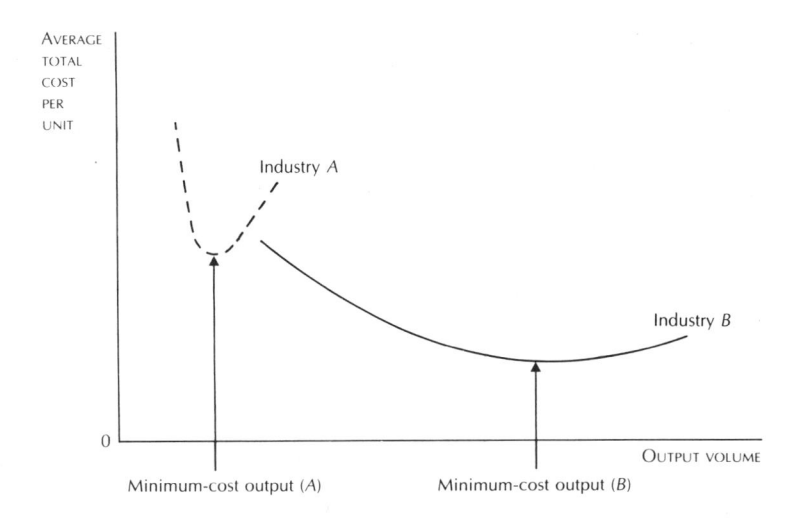

Figure 4.1 Long-run average cost curves

This is shown diagrammatically in Figure 4.1. Total costs include production, selling and distribution costs, and are therefore dependent upon the state of technology, the size of the market and the location of potential customers. The unit costs for industry A turn up at a relatively low level of output, implying that the optimal (that is, lowest unit cost) firm size is relatively small. By contrast, industry B faces considerable economies of scale and therefore the optimal size is much larger.

Product-market strategies

A small business will not be able to survive, in the long run, in an industry where economies of scale are important. If economies of scale are important, then the small business must grow, simply to survive. Equally, any small business in an industry where economies of scale are not important, and the optimal size of firm is relatively small, would be foolish to attempt any major expansion.

This bold statement must, of course, be explained, since we all know of examples where small firms have survived and prospered in industries where economies of scale exist. There are two major reasons for this:

1. The market or product is new and economies of scale are being developed. Firms have not yet had time to grow to their optimal size. In this case small firms must grow and aim to become large firms early in their life cycle . . . simply to ensure their survival. These are the 'big bang' companies – they tend to be the glamorous ones that make the news headlines. However, obtaining market dominance is a high risk strategy and this road to high growth has many casualties on the way.
2. While economies of scale of production exist the *market* for the product is limited, either in total, or geographically, and the theoretical optimal size is not achievable. This happens particularly in highly specialised industries. But specialism can be product or market based. Indeed, having a differentiated, specialist product or service often goes hand in hand with having a well-targeted market segment. This is called following a 'niche' strategy. It is important for small firms since it offers a better chance of selective, sustainable growth than the 'big bang' strategy.

An example of this is the microcomputer industry. Born in the late 1970s with unknown demand for its products and no established producers, it has grown rapidly. However, the industry offers substantial economies of scale, particularly in R & D for hardware and software. Consequently, the market has consolidated with many small firms going out of business. The survivors have been one of two types of firm. First, firms like the Apple Corporation, which recognised that the industry would eventually be dominated by a few large firms offering low cost or premium quality products. Apple grew rapidly, grabbing market share world-wide, so that it is now in a good position to compete with the big company entrants such as IBM. Secondly, the firms like Sun Computers which specialised in CAD/CAM equipment and targeted very specific market segments. As often happens, it has been the middle-sized firm which has pursued neither strategy which has suffered in this industry.

There is a strong element of luck in the 'big bang' strategy or put more scientifically, it is a high-risk strategy. Often firms only realise that it is the strategy they must adopt as the market or technology for the product or service develops. This is because the company needs to establish:

1. That the technology offers the economies of scale (and often cost curves can change dramatically over time).
2. That these economies are in some way important to the customer (through lower price or other advantages).

3. That they are achievable, given the market size.

Certainly, 'niche strategy' offers the better chance of success. It involves filling or creating gaps in the market that big firms find unsuitable for their large investment capacity. It involves specialising in customers or products, not methods of production. It emphasises the non-price elements of the marketing mix, such as quality, and satisfying a small, clearly-defined target market or segment which have these specialised needs. Frequently, small firms stress inherent strengths in innovation, flexibility or personalised service.

One apparent problem with niche strategy is that it is based, by its very nature, on a limited market. However, what might be limited for a large company often offers wide opportunities to the small. Frequently, entrepreneurs pursuing niche strategies find further growth by diversification. This diversification is particularly effective if it pursues further niche opportunities.

One further point needs to be made, and that is that the size of the market, the state of technology and the location of potential customers do change, and with them the importance of economies of scale. For example, in the 1950s and 1960s the rapid growth of towns and cities and the general cheapening of transport costs encouraged the growth of large retail outlets. The rapid rise in transport costs in the 1970s changed that, and customers now face quite high costs in getting to these larger stores. Consequently there has been a resurgence of the smaller local shop.

The life-cycle concept

The life-cycle concept is a relatively simple idea which provides a useful framework for looking at the development of a small business. The idea is that every product or service, and therefore any business tied to just one product or service, faces a life cycle of five stages, shown in Figure 4.2.

STAGE 1: INTRODUCTION. This is the stage where the product or service is introduced and encounters a certain amount of consumer ignorance and resistance. Sales are low and growing slowly and profits are low or negative.

STAGE 2: TAKE OFF. This is the short period when the product or service becomes very popular. Sales and profits grow rapidly, attracting new entrants to the industry.

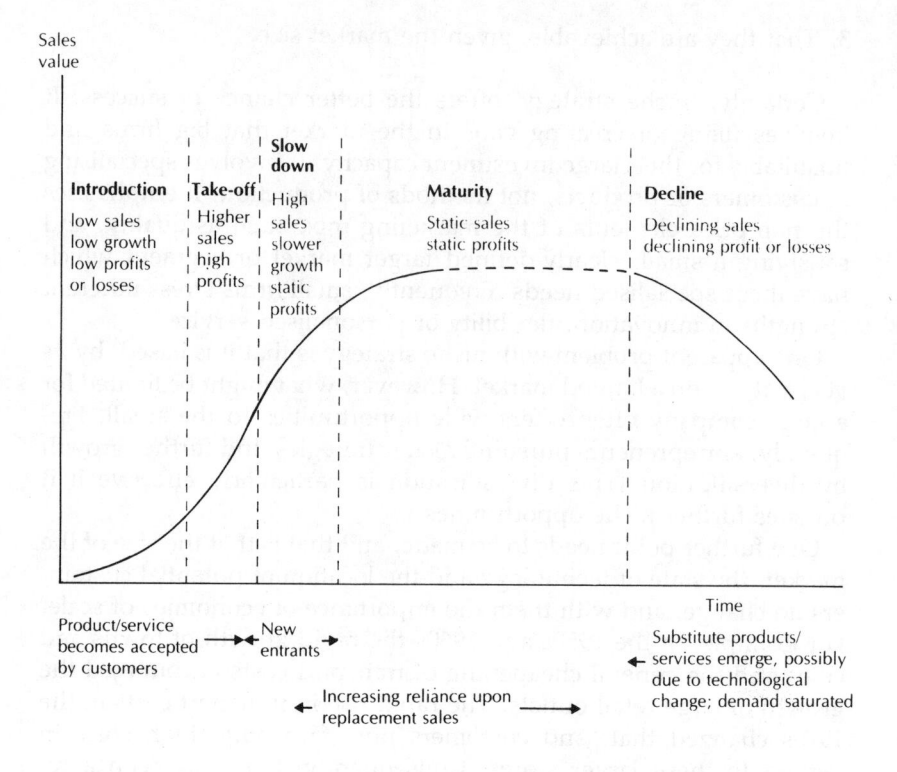

Figure 4.2   The life-cycle curve

STAGE 3: SLOWDOWN. After a while, the rapid growth slows down as competing products or services enter the market and it becomes saturated. Profits might actually dip at this stage.

STAGE 4: MATURITY. Eventually the market becomes saturated and sales are static. Product sales may simply be for replacement. With some products or services this period may be relatively short, for others it can last for years. Often it can be extended by giving the product or service a face-lift, as car manufacturers regularly do.

STAGE 5: DECLINE. After some time, sales will start to decline as substitute, improved products or services become more attractive and the old product becomes obsolete.

Different businesses will face different life-cycle curves. The 'big bang' business, i.e. the one which has entered a new growth market, one which has to expand simply to survive, will experience a rapid

1. The 'stillborn' business   2. The 'meteoric' business

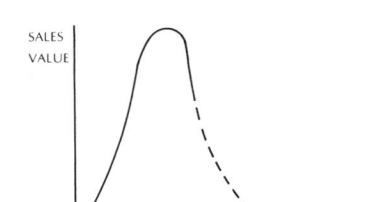

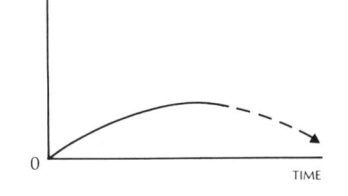

Figure 4.3   Paths to failure

and dramatic take-off stage. The 'stable small business', i.e. the one which has found a niche where economies of scale are not important and growth prospects in the industry are limited, will experience a shallow take-off and achieve maturity relatively quickly and at a fairly modest level of sales.

In his book on corporate failures,[1] John Argenti says that our two types of small business make some predictable mistakes which can lead them into bankruptcy. They have the very short life cycles typified in Figure 4.3. Our 'stable small business' which does not quite make it he calls 'stillborn', since it never even gets to the growth stage and probably never makes a profit. He says that the founder of the 'stillborn' business is typically an expert on the product but knows little about other aspects of the business. The business has no formal accounting system, no budgets, no cash-flow plans, no cost control. The 'big bang' business which goes bankrupt he calls 'meteoric'. It is normally founded by an energetic entrepreneur based upon some product or service innovation. This business experiences such a dramatic growth that it cannot cope with the success. The business has neither the breadth nor depth of management, and the entrepreneur does not find delegation easy. What the business needs is professional managers and formal systems and structures for control. The business cannot handle maturity, so even before it reaches it there is a dramatic failure.

In fact the life-cycle concept tells only part of the story of the introduction of a new product or service. Before it is ever launched the business will have spent a lot of money performing market research, developing the product, installing any new capital equipment

---
[1] John Argenti, *Corporate Collapse – The Causes and Symptoms*, McGraw-Hill, 1976.

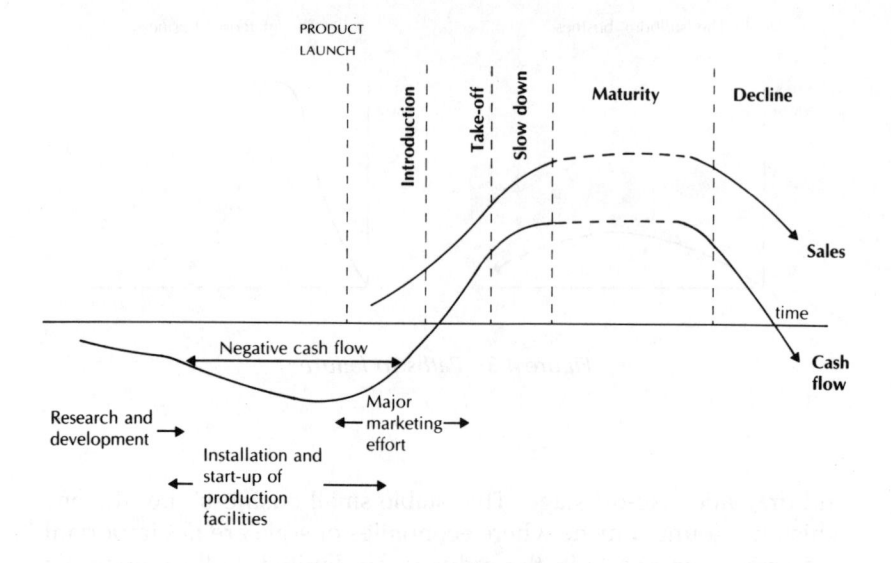

Figure 4.4 The life-cycle curve and cash flows

and training new staff. Perhaps we ought to look at the cash-flow cycle of any product or service alongside the life-cycle curve. This is shown in Figure 4.4. It demonstrates the fact that any new product or service will require adequate funding prior to its launch, and only over the product's life cycle will that cash investment pay itself back and, we hope, with dividends. As we have noted, around 30 per cent of all bankruptcies have insufficient capital as a major cause and it is why we spend three chapters looking at funding. It is no good going into business on a good idea and a prayer. Adequate planning, particularly of the financing required in the early years, is essential.

Life-cycle crises

Businesses can die in many different ways . . . and not always for regrettable reasons. Often entrepreneurs cease trading in one business to pursue another opportunity. Debts may be paid and employees found jobs in the new business. This dynamism is vital. It is evidence of the flexibility that can make small business so market responsive.

However, when the business dies because of insolvency leading to liquidation or bankruptcy, it is likely that creditors will be left unpaid, jobs will be lost and the businessman himself may lose money and prestige, causing hardship to his family. It is this that business analysts try so hard to predict and to prevent. Yet most business deaths do not involve bankruptcy or liquidation. Most businesses simply choose to stop trading, the owners changing to another activity. In the USA and the UK only about 10% of business deaths are due to insolvency.

Various studies give an insight into this process. One by Ganguly and Bannock[1] looks at VAT registrations and deregistrations in the UK over the period 1973–82, which it uses as a proxy for new firm births and deaths. They conclude:

1. 40 – 45% of businesses will still be trading after 10 years.

2. Year in, year out, about 9% of businesses can be expected to die (deregister); varying between 8% and 15%. However, as might be expected, the early years are the riskiest, and 60% of deaths (deregistrations) take place in the first 3 years of existence. Thus, about one-third of businesses cease trading within their first three years of life.

3. This profile of failure is not significantly different between sole traders/partnerships and companies.

4. There are few significant differences between individual sectors. However, the service sector, overall, tends to have a higher failure rate than manufacturing and construction, and within that the retail sector has actually seen a fall in the number of businesses in recent years. Unincorporated businesses tended to have a better survival record in production, constructon, transport, wholesale and motor trades. Companies on the other hand were better in agriculture, retailing, professional and financial services and catering.

Businesses fail, that is, cease to trade against the will of the owner-manager, because of the interaction of the personal characteristics of the entrepreneur with the managerial situation he faces within his business. The personal characteristics of the entrepreneur are particularly important factors in the early period of a business's life – when the failure rate is highest. However, they do not on their own explain the actions of the entrepreneur and his business.

---

[1] P. Ganguly, and G. Bannock. *UK Small Business Statistics and International Comparisons,* Harper & Row (Small Business Research Trust), London, 1985.

The problems facing a small business over its life-cycle were summarised by Buchele[1] as six crises:

1. STARTING UP. This is the difficulty in getting the business started with all the legal, organisational and financial problems. To succeed, the businessman must be an originator or initiator, able to get things done and motivate people.
2. CASH FLOW. This is particularly the problem of the 'big bang' business requiring more and more cash. To succeed at this stage requires careful planning and organisation of financial resources.
3. DELEGATION. As the business grows, the owner must learn to delegate to the managers he recruits. However, he must maintain his supervision of important areas and learn to become a developer or implementer through other people.
4. LEADERSHIP. As the business propers, then the businessman must develop his powers of leadership, learning how to motivate those working for him. Increasingly he will have to change from being an entrepreneur to an administrator.
5. PROSPERITY. Success brings problems for many people. The business should start to run itself and the businessman will often tend to lose contact with its day-to-day running. Often he will miss this. Prosperity often brings with it boredom. The lack of challenge and excitement, the lack of risk-taking can be sorely missed by the businessman.
6. SUCCESSION. Both management and ownership succession can cause a problem for a business. Who will take over the business? Are they capable of doing so? How should the succession be implemented to cause the minimum upheaval in the firm? What are the financial consequences of that succession? There is evidence that, typically, the financial performance of a family business declines with each succeeding generation.

Managing the life-cycle

Most small businesses are set up by one individual, often with a technical or production background, sometimes with a sales background. The business will initially be very dependent upon that one man, since it will look to him to cover the full range of management skills. Typically the skill he has least competence in will be the area of

---

[1] R. B. Buchele, *Business Policy in Growing Firms*, Chandler, 1967.

finance and accounting. Nevertheless the entrepreneur will probably enjoy the challenge of working long hours and the thrill of being the most important person as far as the success of the business is concerned. He will be involved in all aspects of the business and have personal contact with all the employees. This is all part of the enjoyment of a small business.

As the business takes off the owner manager will have to recruit more people. His style of management probably needs to change with the life cycle of the business. The new, growing firm operates in an uncertain, unpredictable and often ambiguous environment. Whilst continuing as the risk-taker, always searching for new market opportunities, the entrepreneur needs to develop his team and delegate more and more. Delegating to those closest to the problem necessitates tolerating mistakes, supporting and protecting staff as they grow into their jobs, encouraging them to experiment and test the market and rewarding their successful initiatives. Inevitably, there will be some confusion and ambiguity of tasks and a certain amount of internal competition. However, organisational structures need to be formalised as the business grows.

As the business approaches maturity the environment should become more stable and predictable and the emphasis probably shifts to control. The owner-manager may well become less of a risk taker as he has more to lose. The emphasis will probably also shift to maintaining stability, fine tuning and structuring the business more tightly; coordination activities, eliminating overlap, careful analysis.

This move towards greater control will necessitate more formal systems. Entrepreneurs start out able to control their affairs by physical and personal discussion, but as the scale of activities increases, they have to rely increasingly on written information supplied on a regular and timely basis. The successful business learns this lesson early in the take off stage.

Too many small businesses rely on the annual visit of the auditors to tell them how they are doing. This delay in information production can be crucial. At the very beginning a growing business must have its own regularly maintained, though simple, book-keeping system. Initially this might not be a full-time job, but it is easy enough to get someone to come in monthly to 'write up the books'. However, the growing business will rapidly find that it does need someone to work full time. Then it will find that it needs a more sophisticated accounting system (microcomputer-based systems are surprisingly inexpensive). We look at some different systems of accounting later in the book.

As with all things, it is essential that the growing business plans ahead. Equally as important as the system is knowledge of how to use it: how to draw up budgets and monitor performance against it; how to use ratio analysis to set the broad framework of that budget and then analyse performance; how to use the data to make decisions; how to control costs and production. If the information you are given tells you that your investment in stock and debtors is too high, what do you do to correct it? All of these issues are addressed in later chapters, but they all stem from the fundamental requirement of a timely, accurate accounting control system. What the Bolton Committee reported is still true:

> It is increasingly important to be able to use systems efficiently, and it appears to us that many running small businesses prefer to emphasise the instinctive element of their work and are unhappy even with simple systems.

As the business develops, a new tier of professional managers must be installed along with more formal, and sophisticated, systems of accounting control. Suddenly the founder of the small business is no longer involved with everything. He needs to delegate. He needs to become a professional manager, probably involved more in policy-setting and administration than the day-to-day activities of the business.

This is a tremendous change in the nature of his work. Not surprisingly many entrepreneurs who successfully launch 'growth small businesses' do not possess the skill to take it into the mature stage of its life cycle: people, perhaps, like John Bloom and Bernie Cornfeld. The founder of a 'growth small business' really must ask himself whether he can, and whether he wants to, take his business into maturity. There are other options, such as selling it as a going concern to a larger company which has experience in putting in professional management and formal control system.

The decision *when* to take on a professional manager is always difficult since there must be both sufficient work for him to do and sufficient cash flow to suport him. The normal situation is to aim eventually to have managers for each of the key areas of marketing, production and finance, reporting to a Managing Director (the organisation shown in Figure 4.5). However, since the founder/Managing Director will probably have skills in the production and sales field, often the first manager he appoints will be an accountant and he will manage the production and marketing areas himself. The only problem with this is that the Managing Director will then be very tempted to get completely immersed in day-to-day management and not concentrate on his role as policy-setter and strategic thinker. If he

Strategy and planning 55

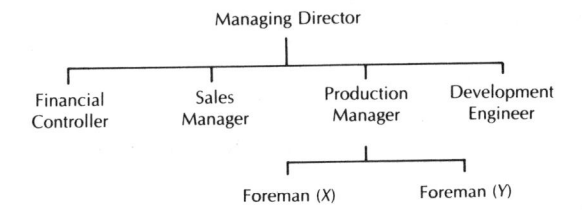

```
                        Managing Director
        ┌──────────────┬──────┴───────┬──────────────┐
    Financial        Sales        Production      Development
    Controller      Manager        Manager         Engineer
                                      │
                              ┌───────┴───────┐
                          Foreman (X)     Foreman (Y)
```

Figure 4.5 A simple organisation structure

does not set policy and plan, nobody else will and in the end there could be no business to manage.

Many small businesses never face these problems simply because they reach maturity at a very modest level of sales. Most small businesses employ only one or two workers. They grow in the first few years after start-up and then stabilise to provide the owner manager with an acceptable, independent life-style. Sales are sufficient to ensure survival and an adequate return on capital and standard of living.

Financing the life-cycle

Initially, when the business was launched, the businessman will probably have turned first to his own resources to set up the small business, for example by taking out a second mortgage on his home. He will probably have leased equipment and possibly rented property so as to minimise the initial financial requirements. If he purchased property, he will probably have done so with the benefit of a mortgage. He may have obtained additional finances from government grants or the growing range of government- sponsored loan schemes. Once the business has survived a while, bank finance may be available on a short-to medium-term basis. The major source of outside funds will probably, initially, come from trade credit: suppliers willing to let you have goods on extended credit terms.

For most small businesses which approach maturity at a relatively modest scale, cash will start to be generated at a relatively early stage. Calls on cash will be relatively low because of the limited investment opportunities within *that* business. However, for many entrepreneurs, once the first business starts generating cash it is simply the signal to start looking for the second profitable business opportunity.

The difference between the 'big bang' business and the 'stable small business' is that after a number of years the 'big bang' business will still not be generating cash. It will probably be making profits, but because of the re-investment required to finance the rapid growth which it needs to survive, the cash will be used up to purchase new plant, hire more people, finance more stocks, and finance more debtors. It will be almost like a treadmill: the faster you run, the faster it goes. This is why cash-flow planning is so vitally important. The small business needs to know its financial requirements well in advance, and then plan to obtain those finances accordingly.

As the 'big bang' business takes off, it will find traditional sources of finance such as overdrafts and term loans both insufficient for the needs of the business and increasingly more difficult to obtain, since the bank manager will probably perceive the business as 'high risk'. This has led to the growth of specialised sources of risk capital, called 'venture capital', such as 3 I (Investors in Industry) (see Chapter 8). These are organisations willing to make a long-term commitment to risky businesses with growth potential. They will generally take an equity stake in the business, so by this stage the business should be incorporated. However, they may also provide debt finance. They will probably intend to liquidate their investment once the business has reached maturity and suitable buyers for the shares can be found. They may even be willing to provide finance for a company from its initial launch.

As the company approaches maturity, it will be looking for further equity funds as it approaches its borrowing limits. First, it may participate in the unquoted securities market and eventually, when the company grows to a suitable size, it might be looking towards obtaining a quotation on the stock exchange and issuing shares to the general public. This is 'going public' and really signals with certainty that the business is no longer 'small'. By this stage the company must have a breadth and depth of professional management covering all major functional areas. It should have sophisticated control systems and an accounting system that is sufficiently good to produce periodic accounts for the general public.

One company to have made it to this stage is Habitat, the home furnishing retailer. It opened its first store in 1964 pioneering a cheap, practical and cheerful mix of home products. It ignored traditional furniture retailing methods and went in for stocking the whole range of things that go into the home: currently some 4,500 different lines from tin-openers to bed linen to furniture. In fact, furniture makes up only 40 per cent of sales; however, the other home products attract customers so they eventually end up looking at the furniture. The furniture itself is based upon cost-cutting exercises like self-assembly sofas or lightweight chairs. In some cases Habitat has entered into almost Marks & Spencer-like relationships with suppliers. Where it felt it was not getting the volume of sales a product warranted, it looked at ways of bringing down the cost and then worked with the manufacturer to achieve this.

The market for the typical Habitat store comprises a catchment area of about 250,000 people, with a high proportion of A, B, and C1 people. Their typical customer is aged 29 with 1 1/2 children and a family income of around £8,000.

By 1980 Habitat had some 53 stores with a turnover of £58 million. In the four years to June 1980 pre-tax profits rose at 34 per cent compounded to nearly £3.5 million. It has experienced a dizzy growth, and has diversified on a number of fronts. Primarily it has diversified its market by opening new stores. It has gone overseas to Belgium, France, and the USA. The 14 stores in Belgium and France were only opened after a lot of market research, but the changes were only in minor details such as the French preference for sheets that need ironing. They have traded at a profit since 1976. The stores in the USA have not been quite so successful and since their opening in 1977 have not yet shown a profit.

Habitat has also diversified into design consultancy, which is not altogether surprising since that is the background of the 73 per cent owner, Terence Conran. Interestingly the business is also 12 per cent owned by the employees through a profit-linked share-ownership plan, started in 1976. Some of them have seen their shares increase in value by a factor of 14 since then.

Although Habitat enjoys an 'arty' sort of image, underneath that exterior there is a highly structured management system with strong controls on store management. Habitat pioneered the use of of computerised cash-tills. Habitat appointed its present financial director in the very early 1970s just before the take-off period really began. He came to them with a background in retailing, the Co-op and Boots, and was responsible for putting in many of the strong financial controls. Habitat has recently 'gone public' and since then 'merged' with the Mothercare chain of stores. It looks very much like the 'growth small business' success story of the 1960s and 1970s, and one where the entrepreneur-owner has adapted to his changing role.

Diversification strategy

As we saw when we introduced the product/market matrix, diversification is possible along two separate paths. First, we can diversify the

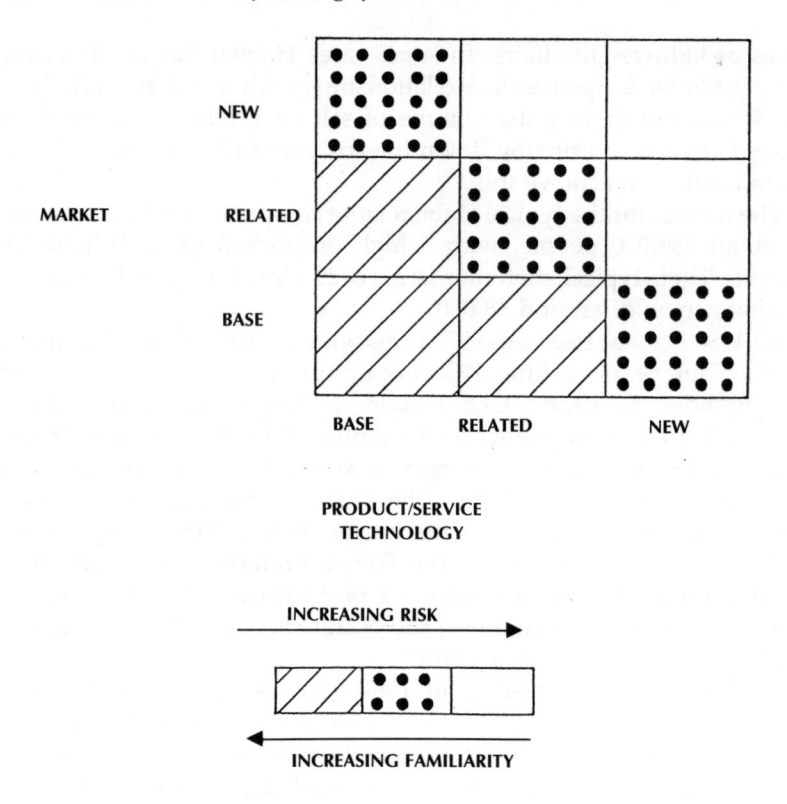

Figure 4.6 Product market matrix

product (that is, introduce new products). Second, we can diversify the market (that is, go into new markets). In so doing it is important to bear in mind the risks involved. For example, we could introduce a new product or service related to our existing product lines; this is a low risk strategy. Similarly, we may decide to diversify into completely new markets, either geographically or by type of customer. For example, a business traditionally selling through wholesalers may decide to sell direct to the public. This would be a major, high-risk, change in strategy, since the business has no experience in this area.

In its search for further growth, a business has four options, illustrated in the product market matrix in Figure 4.6:

1. It can stay with its base product or service, and its existing market, and simply try to penetrate the market further. This is dealing very much with the familiar and is normally the lowest risk option.

Although the point will come when further penetration is not possible or economic.

2. It can develop related or new products for its existing market. For example, an off-licence might start to sell soft drinks or cigarettes. This is called product development.

3. It can develop related or new markets for its existing products. The off-licence might open a new branch in a nearby area of the town, or it might try selling directly to restaurants. This is called market development.

4. It might try moving into related or new markets with related or new products. The off-licence might try selling cigarettes directly to restaurants. Since this strategy involves unfamiliar products and unfamiliar markets it is high risk.

It is generally recognised that, in comparing investment in related and unrelated areas, not only are the risks of the former lower, but also the returns are higher. Market and product development should therefore be incremental from the familiar to the unfamiliar. Further, it is claimed that market developments are to be preferred to product developments because developing new customers is less risky than developing new products.

The strategies discussed above are called 'horizontal' strategies. Two further strategies for growth are open to the small firm. First, 'backward vertical integration' – the firm becomes its own supplier of some basic raw materials or services. Secondly, 'forward vertical integration' – the firm becomes its own distributor or retailer. Both strategies entail new product or service technologies and new customers and are therefore relatively risky.

It is generally accepted that vertical integration is not successful for small firms and that vertical integration should only be a reaction to competitor's activities, for example, to prevent them from controlling raw materials and services. A period of consolidation should follow any growth surge, not because of organisational constraints, but because of financial and entrepreneurial/managerial constraints.

CHAPTER 5

The Business Plan

THE IMPORTANCE OF THE BUSINESS PLAN	60
THE INVESTOR'S VIEW	64
THE FORMAT OF THE BUSINESS PLAN	66
PRESENTING A CASE FOR FINANCE	73
Appendix *A Business Plan for Claridges Restaurant*	77

The importance of the business plan

One of the most important steps in establishing any new business is the construction of a business plan. It can help the owner/manager crystallise and focus his ideas. It can help him set objectives and give him a yardstick against which to monitor performance. Perhaps of more immediate importance, it can also act as a vehicle to attract any external finance needed by the business. It can convince investors that the owner/manager has identified high growth opportunities, and that he has the entrepreneurial flair and managerial talent to exploit that opportunity effectively, and that he has a rational, coherent and believable programme for doing so.

The business plan entails taking a long-term view of the business and its environment. A good plan should emphasise the strengths and recognise the weaknesses of the proposed venture. Above all, it should convey a sincerity of purpose and analysis which lends credibility both to the plan and to the entrepreneur putting it forward.

For an existing business this process involves first, coming to terms with the personal objectives of the owner/manager:

- Do we want income, or capital growth?
- Do we want to sell the business as a going concern when it gets to maturity, or do we want to pass it on to our children?
- Do we want to take risks in the business or do we value security more?

Secondly, it involves coming to terms with the strengths and weaknesses of the existing business, and the opportunity and threats that it faces. This is often called a 'position audit'.

We are seeking to answer the following sorts of questions:

- Where are we and how did we get there?
- What condition are we in?
- What lessons can we learn for the future?
- What threats need to be countered?
- What opportunities are open to us, and how can we exploit them or create new ones?

In other words we need to determine where we *can* go and where we *want* to go.

The in-depth analysis of the business will cover our products or services, finances, personnel and facilities. The sorts of questions we would ask would be:

PRODUCTS OR SERVICES

- Are they quality products or services?
- How do our prices compare with our competitors?
- How much do we spend on promotion?
- Where do we sell the product or service?
- Should we change the product or service in any way?

FINANCES

- What is our current level of profit and cash flow?
- Which products or services does it come from?
- How strong is our balance-sheet?
- What potential sources of capital are available?

PERSONNEL

- Are there gaps in our management?
- Are there gaps in the skills of our workers?
- What do they do best?
- What do they do worst?
- How well do we pay them?

FACILITIES

- How old are our building, machines and vehicles?
- What is their life expectancy?
- How efficient are they?

These questions are by no means exhaustive. They simply illustrate the sort of searching questions that need to be asked and answered truthfully.

As far as the environment is concerned, we also need to ask about four key areas: the customer (the most important person so far as any business is concerned), the competition, the technology, and finally the economy as a whole. The sorts of questions we would ask would be:

CUSTOMER

- Who is the customer?
- What does he want from the product or service?
- How important to him are quality and price?
- Where does he buy the product or service?
- How important is promotion?
- Why do customers buy our product or service, in particular?
- What developments in the product are taking place?
- Can we estimate the size of the market and its future growth?

COMPETITION

- Who are our competitors?
- What size of business are they and where are they located?
- How profitable are they?

TECHNOLOGY

- Is technology changing?
- What are the changes?

ECONOMY

- What are the growth prospects in the United Kingdom?
- Can we sell overseas?
- Will we be affected by any changes in legislation?
- What will happen to the price of our raw materials?

Once we have done this we are in a position to set the basic objectives. These fall into two parts. First, we need a statement of what business we are in. This sounds too simple. But it is needed if a business is to marshall its strengths and not waste its efforts going into areas where it has no experience. The statement should not be too restrictive to prevent development, or so broad as to be meaningless (for example, a coalman might say he is in the business of 'marketing and distributing home fuel requirements'). Secondly, we need a quantified primary long-term objective which reflects what we want as individuals, and what the business can achieve, given the prospects for the environment it finds itself in. This will probably be factors such as profitability, asset levels and growth (for example, an annual real growth in profit after tax of 10 per cent with minimum return on capital of 20 per cent). This objective achieves growth and maintains an asset base for the business.

Of course, setting the objectives is only the first stage, possibly the easiest. How are these objectives to be achieved? Strategies need to be developed in four key areas of production, marketing, personnel and financing.

- Should we develop new products, or go into new markets?
- What happens when the product or service achieves maturity?
- What new buildings or machines are needed?
- What are our manpower needs?
- How do we finance all of these things?

From our strategies come some short-term goals, such as percentage market share, sales margins, number of customer complaints, which allows us to monitor our progress in these strategies towards achieving our objectives. Finally comes the operating needs in terms of products, manpower and finance to achieve these goals.

The final stage is the drawing up of long- and short-term budgets. This is the translation of strategies and plans into detailed estimates of profit, asset investment and cash requirements. The whole process, including the position audit, is shown in Figure 5.1. Of course, at each stage in the process, it is quite possible that changes have to be made in the business objectives, or stategies, because certain aspects of the plan prove to be unachievable. These are shown as feedback loops.

The great advantage of this process is that it means that there must be a thorough understanding of the business and its environment, and this in turn will prepare the business for any changes that may come about in the environment that it faces. That is not to say that the business will always predict the changes: who could have foreseen the dramatic jump in oil prices in 1973? But when changes takes place the business will be in a good position to adjust quickly. It also means that there will be an appreciation of the problems the business will face if it in turn decides to change direction.

Figure 5.1

```
ENVIRONMENTAL ANALYSIS: THREATS AND OPPORTUNITIES
Market       product position and prospects
Competition  traditional, new firms, new industries, profits
Technology   changes and developments
The economy  growth, inflation, law
```

PERSONAL OBJECTIVES → BUSINESS OBJECTIVES → STRATEGIES AND GOALS → OPERATING NEEDS: products, manpower, finance → OPERATING BUDGETS

Feedback loops

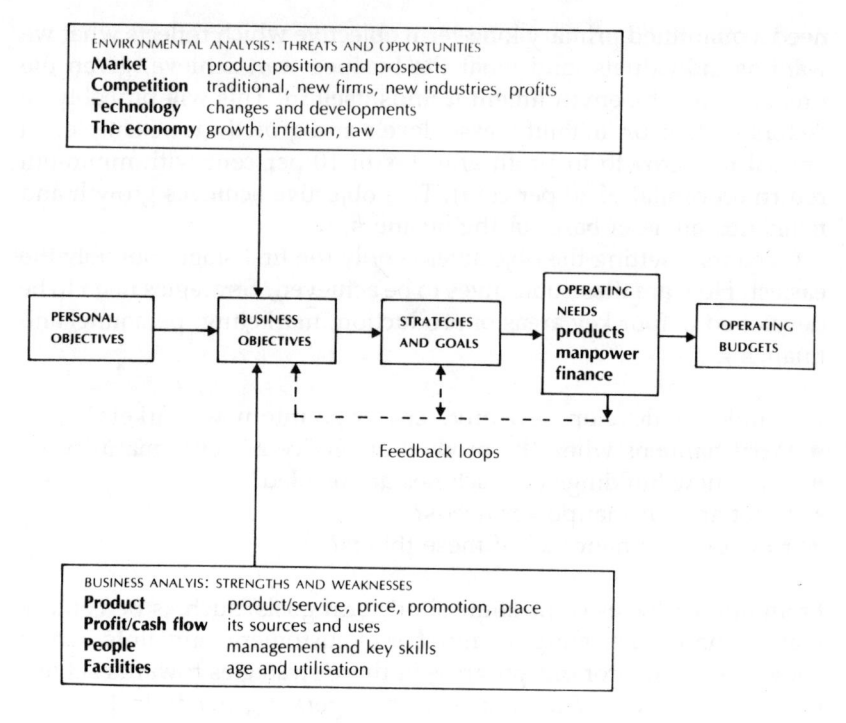

```
BUSINESS ANALYIS: STRENGTHS AND WEAKNESSES
Product          product/service, price, promotion, place
Profit/cash flow its sources and uses
People           management and key skills
Facilities       age and utilisation
```

Figure 5.1 The process of corporate planning

The investors view

The institutions investing in unquoted companies today are becoming highly sophisticated. Most businessmen submit investment proposals to more than one institution for consideration. However, on the other side of the coin, most investment institutions are inundated with investment proposals. It has been estimated that only 1 in 20 of these proposals ever reach negotiation stage. To a very great extent, the decision whether to proceed beyond an initial reading of the plan will depend on the quality of the business plan used in supporting the investment proposals. The business plan is the first, and often the best, chance for an entrepreneur to impress prospective investors with the quality of his investment proposal.

An investor needs to be convinced of two things:

1. That a business opportunity exists which has the potential to earn the investor the high return he demands.

2. That the company proposing to exploit this opportunity can do so effectively.

Any business plan must therefore address both issues. This requires a careful balance between making the proposal sufficiently attractive on the one hand, whilst on the other realistically addressing the many risks inherent in any business venture and showing how they can be acceptably minimised. To do this the business plan should emphasise the strengths of the company, particularly in comparison with its competitors. Behind all the plans and strategies the business plan must demonstrate convincingly the determination and credibility of the owner/manager and other key personnel involved in the business venture. It has been said that the most important factor in the decision whether or not to invest is the credibility and quality of the firm's management.

The most difficult aspect of any deal is deciding upon the split in equity between the various partners involved in a deal. The simple answer is that there are no simple rules and the final result will depend on the attractiveness of the investment proposal and the negotiating ability of the individuals involved. However, the Venture Capital Report, a monthly publication of investment opportunities, suggest the following starting point:

For the idea: 33%
For the management: 33%
For the money: 33%

But it must be stressed that this is only a very rough guide. If an entrepreneur can provide no capital, he may receive less equity. If the idea is a breakthrough, he may receive more, and so on.

It is also advisable to consider the objectives of the investing institution. It will be interested in generating income from its investment by way of dividends or interest and, over the long run, through capital gains. But will the institution take dividends or interest, and when will these be paid? A venture capitalist may require dividends, but it could be in the entrepreneur's interests not to take them because of tax problems. Indeed, it may not be in the interests of the company to pay dividends or interest in its early years. A further issue is how much of the control of the business the owner/manager is actually willing to surrender. Most entrepreneurs wish to part with as little as possible of their business. Indeed, venture capitalists now rarely demand even a 50 per cent stake in the business. At the end of the day, a sensible financing package involving equity and deferred interest terms or convertible loans might be the answer.

The second question is: how will the institution realise its capital gain, and over what period? This issue is frequently called the problem of 'exit routes'. It is a major problem for many investing institutions, since it can often take quite a number of years before it can realise its investment. Related to this is the issue of further funding needs and their availability from the investing institution. Exit routes and their time scale need to be seriously considered and openly discussed. Is the business looking to go on the Unlisted Securities Market (USM) or traded 'Over the Counter' (OTC)? If not, the investing institution might be tempted to promote a merger with a larger company, once the business has taken off. Another possibility is for the owner/manager to 'buy out' the investing institution at a later date.

Also investing institutions have very different ways of operating. Some prefer a 'hands off' approach whereby once they have invested they have little to do with the business, perhaps meeting the owner/manager once a year to review the progress of the business. In contrast, some institutions prefer a 'hands on' approach, insisting on placing a non-executive director on the board and perhaps being in contact with the owner/manager up to eight times a month with at least one visit. They may require consultation on budgets and plans and even changes in senior management.

Finally, it must be realised that funds have different risk/reward profiles. Some specialise, either by size of business or industry sector. Frequently they have minimum investment levels. Certainly obtaining equity funding below £100,000 is still a problem in the UK. Many sound proposals are turned down by particular institutions simply because they do not fit the institution's investment profile. In which case other institutions should be approached. Undoubtedly, deciding upon the appropriate financial structure and choosing the right investors will be a major task for most entrepreneurs. In chapter 6 and 8 we look at these matters from the point of view of the entrepreneur, and in some considerable detail.

The format of the business plan

Any format for a proposed business plan should be viewed as providing general guidance only. Every business is different, and consequently a standard plan is totally inappropriate in every circumstance. Having said that, in Table 5.1 we attempt to outline the bare bones of a business plan. When looking at this it should be noted that it is unlikely that in every circumstance all the items mentioned here will be of sufficient importance or relevance to warrent inclusion in every plan. In particular there is one overriding principle with all business plans:

KEEP IT SHORT!

Any business plan should be sufficiently long to cover the subject adequately but short enough to maintain interest. Some business plans requiring a large amount of venture capital could be well over 50 pages long. However, more normal projects requiring less than, say half a million pounds, should be restricted to 10 to 20 pages.

Clearly Table 5.1 is no more than an outline, and an outline that will have to be judiciously precised. Nevertheless it is an outline that is worth following.

A few comments on the main headings in the plan may be of help:

1. **Overview/Summary**

    The executive summary must be brief – no longer than one or two pages. This should be treated as a stand-alone selling document. It is essential that the highlights of the entire business plan are contained in this summary. For many investors it will be the only part of the plan that they read. Indeed some advisors recommend that investing institutions are only sent this summary initially. Only if they are sufficiently interested should the full business plan be sent.

2. **The company and its industry**

    This section attempts to establish the credibility of the owner/manager and his business in the eyes of potential investors. It is important, as a common way of evaluating future potential is to look first at past performance. If, however, past performance is not a reliable indicator of future potential, then it may be best to leave out this section entirely. Nevertheless, the owner/manager must display a thorough understanding of his own company and the industry in which it is seeking to compete.

3. **The products/services**

    This section should define precisely the products and services to be marketed. Clearly it will vary according to the number and complexity of the products or services to be marketed. Whilst it is important to display a grasp of the technology involved, it is important that this section is written in clear, concise, laymen's

Table 5.1   Outline of business plan

1. **Overview/Summary**
   Purpose of plan
   How much finance is required, and what it is for
   Brief description of business and its market
   Highlights of financial projections

2. **The company and its industry**
   Purpose of company
   History of company
   Past successes of company
   Discussion of industry

3. **The products/services**
   Description of products/services and applications
   Distinctive competences or uniqueness of product/service
   Technologies and skills required in the business
   Licence/patent rights
   Future potential

4. **Markets**
   Customers
   Competitors (strengths and weaknesses)
   Market segments
   Market size and growth
   Estimated market share
   Customer buying patterns
   Critical product/service characteristics or uniqueness
   Special market characteristics
   Competitor response

5. **Marketing**
   Market positioning – critical product/service characteristics or uniqueness in relation to competitors
   Pricing policy
   Selling/distribution policy
   Advertising and promotion
   Product/service support policy
   Interest shown by prospective customers

6. **Design and development** (if appropriate)
   Stage of development
   Difficulties and risks
   Product/service improvements
   Product/service developments in future

7. **Manufacturing and operations**
   Premises location
   Other facilities
   Production/service capacity

Table 5.1 con't

	Sources of supply of key materials or workforce Use of subcontractors Nature of productive process – machinery and critical points
8.	**Management** Owners/directors and other key management Expertise and track record (detail CVs as an appendix) Key management compensation Summary of planned staff numbers and recruitment plans Training policies Consultants and advisors
9.	**Financing requirements** Funds required and timing Deal on offer Anticipated gearing Exit routes for investors
10.	**Financial highlights, risks and assumptions** Highlights of financial plan (sales, profit, return on capital, net worth, etc) Commentary on financial plan Risks and how they will be tackled
11.	**Detailed financial plan** (Quarterly for 3–5 years) Profit and loss Contribution and break-even analysis Cash-flow analysis (monthly in first year) Sensitivity analysis Balance sheets (annual only)
12.	**Items frequently included in appendices** Technical data on products Details on patents, etc. Consultants' reports on products or markets Order and enquiry status CVs of key managers Organisation charts Audited accounts Names of accountants, solicitors and bankers

language. Detailed information can be relegated to appendices. It is important that in this section, and in others, the distinctive competences or uniquenesses of the product/service are emphasised. These can take many forms; new technology, product quality, low production cost or the fit with customer needs. It is also important that the owner/manager demonstrates his ability to develop the product or service beyond its present form. Investors rarely participate in a one product company, without indications of future developments.

4. **Markets**

   Markets and marketing are critical to all companies. Brilliant new technologies are useless without customers. Most institutional investors see this as an area where major mistakes are made by new businesses. It is important to define precisely the market segments that the business hopes to attack. Estimates of market size, growth, share and competitive reaction should be based on the market segment, not on some wider market definition. Having identified the market segment to be attacked, customer-buying patterns need to be understood and, once more, the investor convinced that the product/service characteristics or uniquenesses that the business is offering will meet a ready market. Investors are always interested in the reaction of competition. Any business, particularly one with a good product/service idea, will meet competition sooner or later. It is important to identify current competitors and their strengths and weaknesses. This is especially important in the case of small or new businesses entering markets dominated by larger and more powerful competitors. Every business must develop a strategy for dealing with its competitors.

5. **Marketing**

   Marketing strategy can only be developed based upon a thorough understanding of the market. Often the exact details of the marketing strategy can be complex, covering such areas as market positioning, pricing policy, selling and distribution policy, advertising and promotion, product service support policy, etc. Nevertheless, any business must analyse all of these factors in detail when formulating sales projections. These projections should be built up in as much detail as possible to act as a cross-check against the sales targets developed from the market analysis process outlined previously. Sales estimates based simply on targets without the detailed nuts and bolts of how these targets are to be achieved will inevitably prove unconvincing to a potential investor. Frequently this section can prove to be very lengthy. If this is the case it could, once more, be included as an appendix with only a summary in the main body of the plan.

6. Design and development

Many new businesses that are developing products which have not yet been marketed need to give a potential investor considerable information, not only on the stage of development the project is currently at, but also on the difficulties and risks that it faces, as well as the time scale involved in getting the product into the market. Even existing products and services must look to improvements as well as new developments in the future.

7. Manufacturing and operations

In this section the manufacturing process should be briefly described. The section should highlight any potential problem areas such as new or untried technology or production facilities. It should highlilght the intended use of subcontractors. Investors are very interested in how the business will control the quality of its product and in the case of a service operation it may be necessary to explain how the business is organised and controlled. Premises location and other facility needs should also be discussed. Finally, lead times in crucial supplies, how many sources there are, and how quickly output can be increased or decreased, should also be addressed.

8. Management

The importance of management cannot be overemphasised. In many ways, the development of a coherent business plan simply proves the ability of management. Investors invest in people, not in a business plan. This section is therefore vitally important, particularly for start-up companies. It is worth remembering that for a substantial business to emerge it will be necessary to talk, not about individuals, but about teams of people with complementary skills. Ideally these skills will cover all the functional areas of business. However, it is unlikely that a start-up would be able to bring together a balanced team at such an early stage. It is therefore reasonable to mention both areas of strength and weakness for a start-up business. Weaknesses can often be addressed by using consultants. Key managers should be described in terms of their experience and abilities, together with a statement of their specific responsibilities. Detailed CVs may be included in the appendices. Investors are naturally interested in track record since this gives them some indication about the management's abililty to meet the targets set in the business plan. The summary contained in this section should therefore concentrate on the major achievements and experience of each key manager. Investors will also be interested in the mechanisms for retaining key managers and motivating them to achieve the target set in the business plan.

9. **Financing requirements**

The next three sections of the business plan focus on the translation of these plans and strategies into financial statements and financing requirements. The purpose of this section is to outline the funds that the owner/manager requires and the terms and conditions he is willing to offer to obtain those funds. Invariably, the precise nature of any financial deal will have to be negotiated with the investor. Indeed, investing institutions are frequently expert at constructing financial deals in such a way to meet both their own objectives and those of the owner/manager. It is therefore appropriate simply to set down the skeleton of any deal (total funding required, timing, equity/debt structure) and leave the details for further negotiations. The key is to provide sufficient guidelines to indicate the main features of the financial structure of the business and indicate a fair price for the share of the business on offer, whilst allowing sufficient flexibility, particularly on minor points, to accommodate the wishes of investors. Remember that this is a negotiating situation.

10. **Financial highlights, risks and assumptions**

The purpose of this section is to pull out from the mass of financial data contained in section 11 the highlights for potential investors. For example, the possible worth of the company if forecast results are achieved should be highlighted, as indeed may sales, profit and return on capital targets. However, this section should concentrate not only on the rewards to potential investors, but also on the problems and risks that the business may face. It may be necessary to highlight the cyclical nature of sales or cash flow. It is important that the main risks facing the business are stated simply and objectively. If the owner/manager does not bring them out then it is certain that the potential investor will. Such risks might be, for example, 'that the technology is not protectable', or 'the meeting of sales targets is vitally dependent upon the recruitment of a regional sales force'. However, it is no good simply highlighting risks without stating how those risks will be minimised.

11. **Detailed financial plan**

    A detailed financial plan for at least three years should be included with the business plan. This will include profit-and-loss estimates on a quarterly basis, cash-flow analyses, monthly in the first year but quarterly thereafter, and annual balance sheets. Supplementary to the forecasts should be the assumptions on which they are based, in particular the build up of the sales forecast. Investors are particularly interested in contribution and break-even analysis, since the break-even level is an indication of risk. Forecasts should also be treated to sensitivity analysis. This process involves making different assumptions which would vary the outcome of the financial plans. Typical variations would be based upon changes in sales targets or, for example, timing of cash flows. It is important to choose three or four main variables and to show the effect a variation in these would have on the financial plan. Most sensitivity analyses concentrate on timing, volume, gross margins and credit given.

    The mechanics of financial planning and budgeting is dealt with in Chapter 13.

Presenting a case for finance

The business plan is an essential element in presenting a case for finance. As such it is important that it is well presented. This is not to say that the business plan should be over-elaborate or expensively produced, but simply that it should be functional, clearly set out and easy to use. It is important that the plan has a table of contents. Frequently tabs are used at each section for easy reference. The use of charts, diagrams and graphs frequently make detailed information more comprehensible. Most business plans that contain financial projections use a double-page layout for this information.

However, the business plan is a necessary but not a sufficient condition for obtaining finance for a business proposal. The single most important factor in the eyes of any potential investor will be the personal qualities of the owner/manager and the management team that he brings along. Potential backers are looking for motivation, enthusiasm, integrity, but most of all the managerial ability and competence to make the plan actually happen.

To get a business to grow successfully requires a genuine desire to succeed, amounting almost to a need. The owner/manager must be able to motivate his management team such that they share that desire to succeed. Any entrepreneur must be willing to take risks – but only moderate risks that he believes he can overcome. The technical development engineer who has a good product idea but really only wants to build modified prototypes and is not interested in production and selling will not find any institutional investor willing to back him without teaming up with others who have the qualities that he lacks. Enthusiasm and drive must, however, be tinged with a strong sense of realism in taking a market view of the business and its potential. Arnold Weinstock once said that all successful companies are run by people who understand the market.

Ability is important, and can be demonstrated to a potential backer by track record. Technical ability, along with patents, will protect the project from attempts by competitors to copy it. However, a crucial factor that will convince potential backers that the plan will succeed is the ability of the management team. It is important that the business plan conveys the competence of the management team, not only directly by the inclusion of CVs etc, but also indirectly through the competence of the plan itself.

Once the business plan gets through the initial sifting procedure, the presentation of the plan to backers will act as a further vehicle for demonstrating these qualities and convincing them of the competence of the team. First impressions are important, but demonstrated knowledge of the key areas in the business plan will go a long way towards generating the confidence that is needed.

A leading venture capitalist once admitted that, whilst discussions with the owner/manager centred on the business plan, the final decision whether or not to invest in him really was the result of a 'gut feel', a personal 'chemistry' between the venture capitalist and the owner/manager. At the end of the day that chemistry must lay the foundation for a long-term working relationship – working relationship based upon substance and trust.

Nevertheless, there are many ways of enhancing a presentation. It is always important to rehearse any presentation thoroughly. Among the elements of making the presentation successful it is often said that the owner/manager should manage the presentation with respect to his co-presenters. He should always emphasise market and management team expertise. In terms of style it is important to demonstrate the product or service as far as possible and to maintain eye contact with investors. Notwithstanding this, it is vital that the owner/manager and his team demonstrate a thorough understanding, familiarity, and competence with respect to the business plan. Investors will want to spend some time simply getting to know the team members informally, at further meetings or even over dinner. And if the investment looks attractive . . . well, then it's down to haggling over the price.

An example of a detailed business plan follows in an appendix.

Appendix A Business Plan for Claridges' Restaurant (Partners: S. A. Claridge & C. J. Claridge)

Contents

Executive summary	78
1 The business	79

    1.1 Introduction
    1.2 Business mission
    1.3 Objectives – short term
    1.4 Objectives – long term
    1.5 Key personnel

2 Markets and competition	80

    2.1 Selected market segments
    2.2 Market segments – growth and size
    2.3 Customer benefits
    2.4 Competitors
    2.5 Competitive strategy

3 Selling	86
4 Premises etc	87

    4.1 General
    4.2 Key suppliers
    4.3 Quality control
    4.4 Staffing
    4.5 Wages

5 Financial data and forecasts	89

    5.1 Cash-flow, profit-and-loss accounts and balance-sheets
    5.2 Financing requirements – loans, overdraft

Appendices – Curriculum vitae	98

EXECUTIVE SUMMARY

Claridges Restaurant will be run as a partnership between Caroly Claridge and Susan Claridge.

The 30-seat restaurant will offer a vegetarian menu and a non-vegetarian menu at lunchtimes and in the evenings. At lunchtime a special lunch menu will be provided offering snacks, vegetarian dishes, salads and non-vegetarian dishes for local business people, shopworkers and shoppers. The service at lunchtime will be quick, allowing for a high volume of customers.

In the evening the vegetarian menu will still be offered but a menu including popular dishes such as steak, chicken and fish will be well presented and served with a selection of unusual sauces and dressings. The market aimed for in the evenings will be young professional people between the ages of 18 and 30 years.

All the foods used in Claridges Restaurant will be additive free and natural based. The lunchtime service will enable customers with a limited lunch break to enjoy their meal within the time they have, the restaurant being only a short walk or drive from where they work or shop. Car parking facilities will also be available. A full selection of bar drinks and wine list will also be offered.

The forecast average spend at lunchtime is £2.80; no more than a pub lunch but providing an alternative to the noisy crowded and limited menus of pubs. The forecast spend in the evening is £10.50 including wine, which is well within the range of the young age group. Also provided in the evenings will be some live jazz and blues music such as piano or saxophone to provide fairly sophisticated background music and atmosphere.

In the first year we forecast a loss of £3,962; this mainly due to initial start-up expenses and high advertising expenses in order to attract customers at an early stage. In years two and three we predict a healthy profit due to a 10 per cent increase in sales each year and reduced loan interest in these periods. Due to the healthy cash position at the end of year 3 we would expect to be able to repay the outstanding balance on the loan at the end of year 4.

The overall objectives of the business are firstly to achieve and exceed sales forecasts to enable us to be operating at capacity, so that we can extend our opening hours to include morning coffee and afternoon teas. We would also aim to be able to employ several full-time members of staff and build up a team so that the partners can be clear of routine tasks and concentrate on day-to-day problems, meeting customers, mounting promotions and supervise the general running of the restaurant in order to build up the business further. After five years we would hope to set up a similar operation in another area.

The business will require an initial loan of £20,000 repayable over 5 years to convert the premises, equip the restaurant and pay initial administration fees. An overdraft facility of £3,500 will also be required according to cash-flow forecasts to finance working capital.

By achieving forecasted sales in the first year, we would be able to repay the overdraft by the end of the year, and also pay the interest on the loan, enabling us to start repaying the loan in the second year of trading.

1 THE BUSINESS

1.1 Introduction

Claridge's Restaurant will be run as a partnership between Susan Claridge and Carolyn Claridge.

We have lived in the Beaconsfield area all our lives and through our own experiences and interest in the subject realised that there are no restaurants for young people to eat out at in the evenings that provide a young, lively, fairly sophisticated atmosphere at prices young people can afford, i.e., a meal with wine for £10.00 or under. We also discovered, after conducting some preliminary market research, that there seemed to be a lack of somewhere where people working or shopping in the area could go for a quick lunch or snack spending only a couple of pounds on dishes other than filled rolls or sandwiches or the usual fried bar snacks.

1.2 Business mission

To start up and run a restaurant in the Beaconsfield area providing a menu biased towards healthy eating offering cheap lunches for local business people, shoppers and workers and a varied interesting menu in a young lively sophosticated atmosphere for young professional people in the evenings.

1.3 Short-term objectives

To find and convert suitable freehuold premises to a 30-seat restaurant with adequate kitchen, bar, dining, storage and car parking facilities. To build up a regular clientele and achieve forecasted sales by advertising and promotion and by the product itself, i.e., friendly efficient service and well cooked and presented food, resulting in a meal that is reasonable by being good value for money.

1.4 Long-term objectives

To be able to employ full-time members of staff to build up a reliable and conscientious team working in the restaurant, enabling the partners to concentrate on the day-to-day problems, to meet customers and suppliers, mounting promotions and supervising the general running of the restaurant in order to build and expand the business further. After five years we would hope to purchase a second premises in a different area and set up a similar operation.

1.5 Key personnel

Susan Claridge   Age 24
'O' and 'A' level qualifications in Food and Nutrition BSc Hons Degree in Hotel, Catering and Tourism Management from Surrey University. Practical

experience gained from a variety of establishments including pubs, pub restaurants, À la carte and fast food restaurants. One year industrial experience as management trainee at Portman Intercontinental Hotel, London. Have worked in managerial positions at Wimbledon Tennis Tournament, Paris Air Show and Ascot Races. In April 1986 our business idea was accepted out of several hundred applicants for a place on the Manpower Services Commission-backed Graduate Enterprise Programme held at Cranfield Institute of Technology. This small business programme is sponsored by Arthur Anderson, BP, National Westminster Bank and the British Institute of Management.

Caroly Claridge   Age 21
Catering experience from a variety of catering outlets ranging from institutional catering to pubs, wine bars and restaurants. She has run her own freelance catering business with a partner for the past two years starting on the Enterprise Allowance Scheme. She has a good working experience of local suppliers, professional advisors and book-keeping experience. Her partner, Caroline Burckhardt, Cordon Bleu-trained, will advise on menu planning and food presentation and costing as well as design or layout of kitchen facilities.

John Claridge
Financial advisor. Has run own successful engineering consultancy business for 15 years and has valuable experience in finance, VAT and book-keeping.

Philip Hill
City and Guilds chef qualifications.
Has worked in a 4- and 5-star London Hotel kitchen in all sections.
Has 4 years' experience in assisting in the running of his parents' high class restaurant in London.
Will be advising on general running of restaurant.

Peter Reid
Trained architect and surveyor.
Advisor on property and planning.

2   MARKETS AND COMPETITION

2.1   Selected market segments

Segments aimed for at lunchtime
Shoppers – predominantly housewives aged 30–60 years.
   Socioeconomic groups A, B, C1 and C2 living within a 10-mile radius of Beaconsfield.
Local business people – office workers and employees working locally. All age groups.
Local shopworkers – Any age group.

Segments aimed for in the evenings

Young professional people in full-time employment, for example, bank clerks, office clerks, trainee management, living and working in the area or commuting to London to work. Most have high disposable income to spend on eating and drinking out.

2.2 Market segments – growth and size

According to the Mintel Survey for Leisure Intelligence 1986 on eating out

> restaurant eating has fallen off among those over 45 years old and has conversely risen among the young. The young have now become almost as important a group of restaurant users as their elders. Reasonable prices, nice atmosphere and especially being in the mood for a particular type of food are all in importance among younger adults.

Mintel 'estimates that the market for eating out is worth around £3.5 billion nationwide' and the survey concludes 'the emergence of the youth market, together with the trend to healthier eating presents two potential target markets for eat out operators in the future'.

Population figures for the South Bucks and Chiltern District based on the Registrar General's provisional 1982 mid-year estimate predict that Bucks will remain the fastest growing county in the country, mainly due to Milton Keynes and the Aylesbury Vale, both growth areas. However, in 1982 Wycombe district had the largest population in the county and it is expected to continue to show growth in this area. The total population of 15–19 year olds in the South Bucks and Chiltern District (10-mile radius of Beaconsfield) is 31,498.

We conducted a market research survey on 195 young people between the ages of 18 and 30 who were resident in South Bucks.

Out of 195 people asked, 77.4 per cent said they thought there was a need for a budget-priced restaurant in the area. 33 per cent of this age range regularly eat vegetarian food. The largest percentage, 57.4 per cent, spend between £10–£14 a head on a meal out in a restaurant. The most popular types of restaurant were Steak Houses, closely followed by wine bar bistros. 31 per cent eat out once a month while 30 per cent eat out more regularly (once a week). The most popular socioeconomic grouping for people questioned was C1 – skilled workers; those with highest disposable income. For the lunctime market we questioned 160 shopper resident in the area, shopping at various shopping centres in Beaconsfield and surrounding villages and towns. 58 per cent of those questioned were housewives and 85 per cent said they felt there was a need for a restaurant providing quick snacks and lunches both vegetarian and non-vegetarian. 61 per cent of those questioned ate vegetarian food at some time. 68 per cent said they were concerned about additives in the foods they ate. The most popular range for lunches out was between £2.50 and £3.50 (31 per cent).

We also questioned 72 companies in the area. 75 per cent said their employees ate lunch out at some time, the most popular venue being pubs. 66 per cent said they would use a budget-priced restaurant offering snacks and set lunches.

2.3 Customer benefits

Lunchtime
1. We can offer a snack lunch or a set meal which is an alternative to the usual filled rolls and fried pub lunches.
2. We will also be catering for the ever increasing (see section 2.2) vegetarian and health consumers market by providing foods that are natural based and additive free.
3. Our average spend at lunchtime is forecasted to be £2.80, which is no more expensive than the average pub lunch and considerably cheaper than most wine bar lunches.
4. The service provided will be quick and efficient to accommodate the average businessman's lunch break and for a shopper's snack.

Evenings
1. We will offer the usual popular meat and fish dishes served with varied and unusual sauces, dressings and garnishes.
2. We will provide a fairly extensive vegetarian menu for the health conscious and for those who wish to be a little more adventurous.
3. Our average spend in the evenings is forecasted to be £10.50 including wine, which is considerably cheaper than the majority of restaurants in the area and consequently is good value for money.
4. The atmosphere in the evenings will be lively and sophisticated and this will be achieved by the use of live jazz and blues music and by friendly cheerful service.

2.4 Competitors

Primary competitors
These are restaurants that offer a similar product or service; examples are Browns and Sweeny Todds in Oxford and Maxwells in Covent Garden, the major difference being the lack of vegetarian dishes provided on their menu. Instead they offer a wide selection of salads. The price, atmosphere and markets they serve are similar to those we are aiming for. The nearest outlets of this type are located in Oxford and London, i.e., 30 miles away (see map – *Appendix 3*).

The strengths of these restaurants are that they are well established, large, and usually in prime sites.

Secondary competitors – strengths and weakness
STEAK HOUSES e.g., Beefeater, Berni, Harvester

Strengths
Consistent quality of food and service within a known price bracket. Operate on a tried and tested formula. Branding very notable clientele (Source Mintel) men aged 25–64, mainly C1 socioecon. group and business entertaining and families.

Weaknesses
No variation on menu or service. Limited menu, standardised decor, atmosphere unappealing to youth market.

CHINESE/INDIAN RESTAURANTS

Strengths
Appeal to consumers taste for exotic foods and experiences. Part of the attraction is the feeling of being in a different world. Also meets the changing consumer preference for foreign styles of cooking. Usually late opening hours and takeaway provided.

Weaknesses
Limited menu to country of origin. Mainly meat based. Fairly expensive in Beaconsfield area. Generally unsuitable at lunchtime. Many young people eat there for the late opening hours only.

WINE BAR/BISTRO

Strengths
Often have interesting alternative dishes on the menu, designer decor and a wide range of wines. Generally have a young appeal in the evenings offering an informal atmosphere.

Weaknesses
Widely varying standard of food and service, often expensive for what is offered as food is used to create extra revenue above the sale of wine. Wines are often fairly expensive.

PUB RESTAURANTS

Strengths
Often have much character as part of old pub, reasonably priced, good location.

Weaknesses
Often only an extension of the pub. Food usually plain and simple and unimaginative.

FAST FOOD RESTAURANTS

Strengths
Speed of service, provide miniature meals, strong branding, heavy advertising campaigns. Brand loyalty, clean and fresh appearance. Mainly youth market.

Weaknesses
Limited unvarying menu, standardised product, decor. Short stay only. Unlicensed.

2.5 Competitive strategy

(i) *Price*
Based on market research, we have concluded that there is a gap in the market for a budget-priced restaurant.

Prices are based on a general 30–50 per cent food cost.
Priced as follows:

Starter	–	£1.50
Main Course	–	£4.00
Vegetables	–	£1.00
Dessert	–	£1.50
Coffee	–	50
Wine	–	£2.00
Average food		£10.50

However, it is usual in catering to vary the food cost from one item to another:

Soup, starters, desserts and coffee = 30% food cost
Main course and more expensive items = 50%   "   "
Wine and alcohol = 50% material cost

Therefore price is double the cost.

Dinner

Item	Price £	Materials cost £	%	Gross profit £	%
Starter	1.50	0.45	30	1.05	70
Main Course	4.00	2.00	50	2.00	50
Vegetable	1.00	0.40	40	0.60	60
Dessert	1.50	0.60	40	0.90	60
Coffee	0.50	0.10	20	0.40	80
Wine	2.00	1.00	50	1.00	50
Totals	10.50	4.55	43.3	5.95	56.7

Lunch

Item	Price £	Materials cost £	%	Gross profit £	%
Lunch dish/snack	1.80	0.54	30	1.26	70
Beverage	1.00	0.50	50	0.50	50
Totals	2.80	1.04	37.2	1.76	62.8

(ii) *Promotion*

OPENING PARTY

To include local opinion formers, i.e., councillors, local MP as well as the main potential customers. Also members of the press, senior marketing and sales people, advertising agents, travel and estate agents, bank managers and leaders of industry. For public relations purposes we should also invite our neighbours.

HANDBILLS AND POSTERS

In local shops, offices and industry.

PRESS RELEASE

In local newspapers.

'VALUE ADDED' PROMOTIONS

That is, free glass of wine with a meal during slack periods; one meal in ten free for special groups or complimentary birthday cakes for celebration parties.

SPECIAL PROMOTIONS
Seasonal menu changes and special dishes. Themes to mark dates such as St Valentine's Day, Wimbledon, Hallowe'en, Easter, Mothering Sunday. Themes based on particular types of food, e.g., French.

ADVERTISING
In regional and county magazines and in local papers.

LEAFLET DROPS
Handbills distributed door-to-door by local newsagents with the normal deliveries.

(iii) *Place*
Beaconsfield and the surrounding villages and towns comprise a pocket of wealth in South Bucks.
  The population is mainly made up of:

(a) The elderly and retired
(b) Middle-aged people, socioeconomic groups A, B, C1, C2.
(c) Their offspring who either:

  (i) leave the area at the age of 18 for further education (educational standards being high, 12-plus still operates) and never return to the area for any length of time, or
  (ii) who stay living in the area and work locally or commute to London. A high number live with their parents as property prices are so high. Those that do rent or buy their own homes move out towards High Wycombe or Slough where houses are cheaper.

(d) Young families where the head of the household is a young executive moving up the socioeconomic scale and who will probably stay in the area.

Consequently, the majority of the catering establishments operating at present reflect the affluent nature of the area. There are many high class À la Carte restaurants offering French, Italian and Chinese food, and fairly expensive Indian restaurants and pub restaurants. The Steak Houses are lower priced but have meat-based limited menus, and are very standardised. Other affordable alternatives open to young people are the fast food restaurants, i.e., fish and chip shops, takeaways or pizza and burger restaurants located in the larger towns of High Wycombe or Slough.
  We hope to be located in the Beaconsfield area and research has shown that at present there is no other restaurant offering a similar meal experience in this vicinity.

(iv) *Product*
THE MENU
We will offer a range of interesting starters, both vegetarian and non-vegetarian. The main course will be divided into vegetarian and meat sections. Popular dishes will be included but will be served with a range of different and unusual sauces, accompaniments and garnishes. We also hope to offer a varied selection of salads and home-made desserts. As many as

possible of our dishes will be home-made using natural additive-free ingredients, for example, wholemeal flour, brown rice, wholemeal pasta, vegetable fats.

At lunchtime we will offer a set price lunch with a choice of either starter and main course or main course and sweet, as few people require a three-course lunch these days. Offered also will be salads and snacks such as jacket potatoes with wholesome fillings.

All bar drinks will be available and a selection of wines offering a choice of French, German and Italian wines. We would also like to provide a selection of home-made fruit-based wines.

DECOR

The main colour scheme will be black, cream and green and these colours will be used in the restaurant decor, on the menu, logo, adverts and leaflets.

The black and cream colour scheme will give a sophisticated appearance to the restaurant being neutral colours and thus fairly discreet. The green will add colour, warmth and freshness and will be introduced by the use of plants and greenery.

ATMOSPHERE

Lunchtime

Busy atmosphere with fast service and high volume of customers can be enhanced by the use of fast tempo music playing softly in the background.

Evenings

Slightly more relaxed atmosphere but still lively with live jazz blues piano music or saxophone music as background, also providing a centrepiece attraction.

3 SELLING

In-house sales

(a) *The food* – our most powerful sales weapon will be the food itself; attractively presented and displayed, it should help sell itself, e.g., salad bar, self-service, table or counter
(b) *The menu* – which will be attractive, clear, easy to read and understand and honestly priced with no hidden extras.
(c) *Service staff* – should have friendly, welcoming, helpful attitude – they can boost sales by asking the right questions at the right times. Can be achieved by thorough training and selection.
(d) *Extras* – aperitifs, starters, extra vegetables, desserts, wines, coffees, liqueurs, brandies, cigars are all potential sales and need to be actively sold.
(e) *Service* – this itself can help sell a restaurant; right length of time between courses, efficiency, etc.
(f) *Changes and novelties* – new dishes, new ideas, new table decorations. Point of sale literature to draw attention to changes, e.g., table cards, bulletin boards by the entrace, poster in the window.

4 PREMISES

4.1 General

Type

Preferably a freehold premises with planning permission or already a catering establishment.

Our father will purchase the freehold of a property and will charge us rent for operating our business from there.

Location

SUITABILITY FOR MARKET

In a secondary location, easy to get to with passing traffic and shops and businesses close by. Preferably away from residential areas because of parking and noise constraints. Must be located within a workable distance from suppliers.

ACCESS

The entrance must be clearly visible to encourage 'chance' trade. Rear entrance is needed for deliveries, staff access, refuse removal. Fire regulation authorities require clear access and exit routes. Clear access to car parking facilities for customers and staff is also needed – one space per table plus 2 spaces for staff are generally required.

Size

The four main areas of space needed are:

> Seating of customers
> Food preparation
> Storage
> Other – delivery, guest WCs
> rubbish, office space

For a 30-seat restaurant:

Area	% of Total	Sq. ft
Dining	50	450
Food preparation	20	180
Storage	10	90
Cleaning/wash-up	7.5	67.5
Guest cloaks	7.5	67.5
Staff WC	5	45
Total		900sq. ft.

This is allowing 11–14ft per person for table service at medium price.

A space of 8ft 6in. square is needed for a square table and four chairs in a medium size restaurant. This gives a 2ft 6in. table space for chairs and room to pass. Main traffic routes should be at least 5ft wide – fire regulation authorities specify this.

Design and decor
Ideal shape is rectangular with walls in a ratio of 3:5 and service doors on a long wall.

Attractive features such as fireplaces, natural wood or brickwork are also desirable. Flooring would be carpet tiles, wooden restaurant furniture, lots of greenery and plants. Kitchen – floors tiled. Walls around stoves lined with stainless steel or tiled. Wash up area tiled – easy to clean.

Services
Gas, electricity, water, drainage, sewage, WCs, ventilation, space heating, water heating, refuse collection.

Maintenance
Would largely be carried out by my father, but on leased equipment there is usually a maintenance and service agreement.

4.2 Key suppliers

Butcher – H. A. Price & Sons – good quality butcher, have traded with previously

Dairy goods – local dairy

Fruit and vegetables – local greengrocer

Wholefoods – 'Beans and Wheels' – local wholefood and healthfood co. – free delivery service

Dry goods cleaning materials – Booker Cash & Carry

Equipment – various

4.3 Quality control

(a) *All recipes will be tested initially*
    (i) To give a standard recipe to work to
    (ii) So customers are given a constant product
    (iii) So food costs can be checked exactly
    (iv) Different ingredients and different qualities can be tested
    (v) To enable us to specify accurately the raw materials to be purchased
    (vi) To test one yield of each batch of ingredients
    (vii) To help decide the portion sizes for each item
    (viii) To establish the wate on items in preparation and cooking

(b) *Portion control*
    (i) To help control food costs accurately
    (ii) To enable preparation of portions in advance

    Method
    Use of standard-sized scoops, ladles, serving dishes, plates, bowls, etc. Use of pro-portioned foods, e.g., gateaux

(c) *Checking of deliveries*
Check for – quality
portions
size, e.g., eggs, steaks
damaged goods

4.4 Staffing

Initially my partner and I will be the only full-time staff in the restaurant with perhaps 1 casual staff in the kitchen and 1 in the restaurant. On week-end evenings this may be increased to 2 in each area, depending on trade.

4.5 Wages

£2.00 per hour for 4-hour shift lunchtime and 5-hour shift evening 6.30–11.30 p.m. Plus tips.

5 FINANCIAL DATA AND FORECASTS

5.1 Cash-flow for first year-assumptions

1. Sales forecasts based on a 30-seat restaurant in Beaconsfield area.
   Sales figures high in first month due to opening advertising campaign, opening party and initial curiosity.
   Second month figures lower as traditionally February is a quiet month in catering. Peak time is in 12th month (December) due to Christmas.
2. Drawings @ £50 per week each,
   National Insurance is included in the wages figure.
3. Food and drink purchases @ 40% of sales.
4. Rent is based on our father's mortgage repayment on freehold premises @ 15% interest on £100,000 = £15,000.
5. Rates estimated to be £3,000 p.a.
6. Wages @ £2.00 per hours

    4-hour lunch shift
    5-hour dinner shift

Based on employing part-time kitchen help for the first 6 months on Friday and Saturday evenings and one week-night, also Sunday lunch

= 3 nights	=	15 hours
1 lunch	=	4 hours
		19 hours @ £2.00
	=	£38.00 per week
	=	£152.00 per month

Small business: planning, finance and control

After 6 months we would hope to employ a restaurant helper as well, both kitchen and restaurant staff would be employed for Friday and Saturday nights and Sunday lunch, only cutting out week-night help.

$$
\begin{aligned}
2 \text{ nights} &= 10 \text{ hrs} \times 2 = 20 \text{ hours} \\
1 \text{ lunch} &= 4 \text{ hrs} \times 2 = \underline{8 \text{ hours}} \\
&\phantom{= 10 \text{ hrs} \times 2 =\ } 28 \text{ hours @ £2 per hour} \\
&\phantom{= 10 \text{ hrs} \times 2 =\ } = £56 \text{ per week} \\
&\phantom{= 10 \text{ hrs} \times 2 =\ } = £224 \text{ per month}
\end{aligned}
$$

7. Loan interest on a £20,000 5-year-term loan @ 14% interest = £2,800
8. Loan repayment delayed until 2nd year
9. Overdraft interest worked out on the highest overdraft figure for the quarter @ 15% interest.

Monthly cash-flow statement for first year of trading including VAT excl. income tax

	Mth 1	2	3	4	5	6	7	8	9	10	11	12	Total
Receipts													
Rest. sales	4,830	2,968	4,088	5,096	5,628	6,160	6,902	7,378	7,854	8,064	8,120	8,498	75,586
Total receipts	4,830	2,968	4,088	5,096	5,628	6,160	6,902	7,378	7,854	8,064	8,120	8,498	75,586
Payments													
VAT (payment)			930			1,321			1,732			1,933	5,916
Accountants' fee												500	500
Repair costs						200							200
Petrol/motor expenses	100	100	100	100	100	100	100	100	100	100	100	100	1,200
Drawings @ £50 p.w.	400	400	400	400	400	400	400	400	400	400	400	400	4,800
Food & drink purch. @ 40% of sales	1,932	1,187	1,635	2,038	2,251	2,464	2,760	2,951	3,141	3,225	3,248	3,399	30,231
Heat & light			350			350			350			350	1,400
Rent	1,250	1,250	1,250	1,250	1,250	1,250	1,250	1,250	1,250	1,250	1,250	1,250	15,000
Rates	250	250	250	250	250	250	250	250	250	250	250	250	3,000
Tel. & post.			100			100			100			100	400
Advert. & printing	200	200	200	200	200	200	200	200	200	200	200	200	2,400
Wages gross	152	152	152	152	152	152	224	224	224	224	224	224	2,256
Sundries	100	100	100	100	100	100	100	100	100	100	100	100	1,200
Capital costs						200							200
Loan interest @ 14%	233	233	233	233	233	233	233	233	233	233	233	233	2,796
Overdraft int. @ 15%						247			203				450
Total payments	4,617	3,872	5,700	4,723	4,936	7,567	5,517	5,708	8,283	5,982	6,005	9,039	
Opening bank bal.	1,293	1,506	602	(1,010)	(637)	55	(1,352)	33	1,703	1,274	3,356	5,471	
Surplus deficit	213	(904)	(1,612)	373	692	(1,407)	1,385	1,670	(429)	2,082	2,115	(541)	
Balance c/fwd	1,506	602	(1,010)	(637)	55	(1,352)	33	1,703	1,274	3,356	5,471	4,930	

Balance carried forward 4,930

Profit and loss account for year 1

	£	£
Sales (net of VAT)		65,727
Less cost of sales		
Opening stock	500	
Purchases	26,288	
Less closing stock	(500)	
Cost of sales		26,288
Gross profit		39,439
Less expenses		
Planning permission	50	
Accountancy fees	700	
Solicitors fees	600	
Advertising	3,400	
Printing	200	
Heat & light	1,400	
Insurance	500	
Motor vehicle expenses	1,450	
Sundries	1,400	
Repairs & maintenance	2,347	
Depreciation	2,652	
Telephone	400	
Drawings	4,800	
Wages & N.I.	2,256	
Rent	15,000	
Rates	3,000	
Loan interest	2,796	
Overdraft interest	450	
		43,401
Loss before tax		(3,962)

Opening balance-sheet

	£	£
Fixed assets		13,060
Stock	500	
Cash	1,293	
		1,793
		14,853
Loan		(20,000)
		5,147
Represented by:		
Expenses to date		5,147

Balance-sheet as at end of year 1

	£	£
Fixed assets:		13,260
Less depreciation		(2,652)
		10,608
Stock	500	
Cash	4,930	
	5,430	
Loan creditor	(20,000)	
		(14,570)
		(3,962)
Loss in first year of trading		(3,962)

Quarterly cash-flow for second year assumptions
1. Assume sales increase by 10%
   10% increase in sales = £7,559
   Therefore total sales
   for second year = £75,586
   £83,145

First year quarterly sales figures

Jan. Feb. March	Apr. May. June	July. Aug. Sept.	Oct. Nov. Dec.
Total sales 11,886	16,884	22,134	24,682
22% increase 14,501	30% inc. 19,079	8% inc. 23,905	4% inc. 25,670

= £83,155 = 10% overall increase

2. Assume costs increase by 3% (rate of inflation)
3. Drawings increased from £50 per week each to £60 per week each
   = £480 per month
   = £1440 per quarter
   = £5760 p.a.
4. Capital costs doubles for extra equipment = £400
5. Loan repayment = £20,000 over 4 years
   = £5,000 per year
   = £416 per month
   = £1,248 per quarter
6. Loan interest calculated @ 14% on outstanding loan at end of each quarter.

Cash-flow for third year assumptions
1. Assume sales increase by 10%.

94 *Small business: planning, finance and control*

2. Assume costs increase by 3%.
3. Drawings increased to £70 per week each

$$= £140 \text{ per week}$$
$$= £560 \text{ per month}$$

4. Wages increased by 5%.
5. Capital costs doubled for extra equipment

$$= £800$$

6. Loan repayment still £1,248 per quarter paid at beginning of each quarter.
7. Loan interest calculated @ 14% on outstanding loan at end of each quarter.

Quarterly cash-flow statement for second and third year of trading including

	Q1	Q2	Q3	Q4	Total	3rd year
Receipts						
Restaurant sales	14,501	19,079	23,905	25,670	83,155	91,471
Total receipts	14,501	19,079	23,905	25,670	83,155	91,471
Payments						
VAT (payment)	1,135	1,493	1,871	2,009	6,508	7,159
Accountants' fee				515	515	530
Repair costs		206			206	212
Petrol motor expenses	309	309	309	309	1,236	1,273
Drawings @ £60 p.w. each	1,440	1,440	1,440	1,440	5,760	6,720
Food & drink purchases @ 40% sales	5,800	7,632	9,562	10,268	33,262	36,588
Heat & light	360	360	360	360	1,440	1,485
Rent	3,862	3,862	3,862	3,862	15,448	15,913
Rates	772	772	772	772	3,088	3,183
Telephone & postage	103	103	103	103	412	424
Advertising & printing	618	618	618	618	2,472	2,546
Wages	581	581	581	581	2,324	2,440
Sundries	309	309	309	309	1,236	1,273
Capital costs		400			400	800
Loan repayment	1,248	1,248	1,248	1,256	5,000	5,000
Loan interest	656	613	569	525	2,363	1,663
Total payments	17,193	19,946	21,604	22,927	81,670	87,209
Opening bank balance	4,930	2,238	1,371	3,672		6,415
Surplus deficit	(2,692)	(867)	2,301	2,743		4,262
Balance c/fwd	2,238	1,371	3,672	6,415		10,677
			Balance c/f	6,415		

Profit-and-loss accounts

	Year 2 £	Year 2 £	Year 3 £	Year 3 £
Sales		72,309		79,540
Less cost of sales				
Opening stock	500		500	
Purchases	28,924		31,816	
Less closing stock	500		500	
		28,924		31,816
Gross profit		43,385		47,724
Less expenses				
Accountants' fee	515		530	
Repairs	206		212	
Motor expenses	1,236		1,273	
Drawings	5,760		6,720	
Heat & light	1,440		1,485	
Rent	15,448		15,913	
Rates	3,088		3,183	
Telephone & post.	412		424	
Advert. & printing	2,472		2,546	
Wages	2,324		2,440	
Sundries	1,236		1,273	
Loan interest	2,363		1,663	
Depreciation	2,732		2,892	
		(39,232)		(40,554)
Profit for year		4,153		7,170
Retained earnings b/f		(3,962)		191
Retained earnings c/f		191		7,361

Balance-sheet as at end of years 2 and 3

	Year 2 £	Year 2 £	Year 3 £	Year 3 £
Fixed assets:		13,660		14,460
Less depreciation		(5,384)		(8,276)
		8,276		6,184
Stock	500		500	
Cash	6,415		10,677	
Loan	(15,000)		(10,000)	
		(8,085)		1,177
		191		7,361
Represented by:				
Retained profits		191		7,361

Break-even calculation

Total number of meals sold in 1st year @ average price of £6.65	= 10,660 = £70,889
Cost of one meal Therefore total cost of meals	= £2.90 = £2.90 × 10,660 = £30,914
Therefore gross profit	= £70,889 − £30,914 = £39,975
Gross profit margin	= $\frac{GP}{Sales} \times 100$ = $\frac{£39,975}{£70,889} \times 100 = 56.4\%$
Overheads (fixed costs) for 1st year Therefore break-even turnover	= £23,600 = $\frac{Overheads \times 100}{G.P.\ Margin}$ = $\frac{£23,600}{56.4} \times 100$ = £41,845
Break-even gross profit margin	= $\frac{Overheads \times 100}{Sales}$ = $\frac{23,600}{70,889} \times 100$ = 16.7%

5.2 Financing requirements – loans overdraft

In order to find the initial requirements of the business we would require the following financing:

1. Long-term loan (5 years) £20,000
   This loan will be used for:
   (a) Purchase of restaurant, bar and kitchen equipment
   (b) Initial solicitors and accountancy fees
   (c) Purchase of dry goods and bar stock
   (d) Pre-opening advertising

2. Overdraft facility (short-term) of £1,500
   This facility will only be required for the first six months of trading to finance necessary working capital requirements.

Breakdown of loan expenditure

	£	£	£
Loan			20,000
Expenses			
Planning permission	50		
Solicitors	600		
Accountant	200		
Advertising	1,000		
Printing	200		
Insurance	500		
Tax & insurance	250		
Sundries & extras	200		
Restaurant repairs & maintenance	1,628		
Kitchen repairs & maintenance	519		
Expenditure items		5,147	
Capital additions			
Van	2,000		
Restaurant equipment	7,833		
Kitchen equipment	3,227		
		13,060	
Stock		500	
Cash remaining		1,293	
		20,000	

Curriculum Vitae – Carolyn Claridge

Name: Carolyn Jane Claridge
Home address: 48 Howe Drive, Beaconsfield, Bucks HP9 2BD
Telephone: Beaconsfield (04946) 4924
Date of birth: 09.01.65   *Age*: 21 years
Nationality: British
Marital status: Single
Health: Good
Full Driving Licence since May 1982.

Education: 1978–81   Oakdene School
1981–84   Amersham College of Further Education

Qualifications   7 'O' Levels – Maths, English Literature, English Language, R.E., Political History, Economic History and Sociology.
R S A Grade I – French with Oral.
English Speaking Board – Top Pass.
3 'A' Levels – Communications Studies (B), English (C), Sociology (E).

Employment:

Rushymede Old Peoples' Home, Coleshill, Amersham.
Part-time kitchen assistant – Sept./June 1980.

The Plough, Denham Village.
Kitchen manager – Summer 1982.

The Beech Tree, Beaconsfield.
Part-time function waitress and barperson – Sept./Oct 1983.

Habitat, Guildford.
Full-time sales assistant – Summer 1984.

Perrotts Winebar, Guildford.
Part-time waitress – Summer 1984.

Jolly Woodman, Burnham.
Part-time cook/waitress – Sept/Dec 1984.

C & C Catering Company.
In April 1985 I started my own catering company the 'C & C Catering Company' with the aid of the government-funded Entreprise Allowance Scheme. This company, which has flourised since its outset, deals with function catering both in the private and business sector (e.g. weddings, dinner dances, regular business lunches). It is the success of this company which has further fueled my existing ambition to open a restaurant.

Interests:

Travel.
I have visited the countries of Denmark, Norway, France, Spain, Germany, Luxembourg, Switzerland, Austria and Greece. However, my travels have not been limited to Europe. I have also visited America and Egypt.
   I would like to further my travels as I see it not only as a leisure pursuit but as an important way of broadening my horizons.

Cuisine.
Above and beyond the catering skills I have acquired by running my catering company, I take a great deal of pleasure in studying and experimenting with other nations' cuisines. Through interest acquired through my travels and personal tastes, I have a certain knowledge of French, Italian, Chinese and Greek Cookery.

Sport.
Sport plays a vital role in my life both for pleasure and for maintaining fitness. At school and college I was an active member of several netball teams including the Buckinghamshire County team. Whilst the pressures of 'A' levels curtailed this rewarding pastime, I have not relinguished sport as a valuable leisure pursuit. I play tennis and swim regularly and attend an aerobics/dance class twice weekly – I find these activities very rewarding but flexible enough to be accommodated around my business obligations.

Curriculum Vitae – Susan Ann Claridge

Home Address: 48 Home Drive
BEACONSFIELD
Bucks.
HP9 2BD.

Telephone: Beaconsfield 4924

Personal: *Date of birth*: 10.3.62 *Age*: 24
Nationality: British
Marital status: Single
Health: Good
Full Driving Licence since 1979.

Education: 1974–80 Beaconsfield High School
1978 8 'O' levels including 'A' grades in Food and Nutrition, History and English Literature
1980 'A' level in English (C) History (E) and Food Nutrition (A)
1981–85 University of Surrey – BSc Hons Degree in Hotel, Catering and Tourism Administration Good 2.2 Degree obtained. Chosen option studied Tourism and Travel including marketing in tourism, demand, product and price formulations in tourism, also patterns, regulations and economies of operation of transport for travel and tourism.

Special skills: French to 'O' level standard. Have worked with a computerised reservations system, VDU's and telex. Have experience in man management from industrial year and vacation work at Wimbledon Tennis Tournament.

Employment: Jan. 1981 to May 1981 – Restaurant and bar work at Cricketers Hote, Bagshot, Surrey.
Aug. 1982 to Oct. 1982 – Vacation work, banqueting waitress at The Beech Tree, Beaconsfield.
April 1983 to April 1984 – Management trainee at The Portman Hotel, London W1.
June 1985 to July 1985 – Vacation work:
Waiting – Paris air show
Waiting – Ascot
Management – Wimbledon Tennis Tournament

Interests: Wide range of sporting and leisure interests, for example, I play squash and badminton to a good standard, attend an Aerobics and Stretch Class regularly, and have been shooting with the University Shooting Club. I have travelled widely in Europe and America and toured Egypt last summer. I was an active member of the Oscar Film Unit at university and wrote a social events column for the University Magazine. I was closely involved in departmental social life and have organised many social events in the Department.

CHAPTER 6

Bank Finance

THE IMPORTANCE OF BANK FINANCE TO SMALL BUSINESSES	101
PRESENTING ONE'S CASE FOR MONEY TO A BANK MANAGER	102
AVAILABLE	102
OWN NEEDS	103
BANK LENDING	103
LOAN POWERS OF BANK MANAGERS	104
BANK CHARGES AND INTEREST RATES	108
BANK OVERDRAFTS AND SHORT-TERM LOANS	109
MEDIUM- AND LONG-TERM LOANS	111
THE CHANGING ROLE OF THE BANKS	114

The importance of bank finance to small businesses

It is almost impossible to overrate the importance of bank finance to small businesses. At present some 60 per cent of all the funds needed by small businesses come from the banks. Although the pattern of borrowing by large businesses is changing, and there is some evidence that they are looking elsewhere in their search for funds, this is not true for small businesses. If anything the reverse is the case. Nowadays small businesses turn to their local branch manager, not only for short-term funds but, increasingly, for medium- and long-term funds. It is evident that the relationship that the proprietor or manager of a small business has with his local branch manager is of crucial importance. When he wants money it is to his branch manager that he will almost certainly turn in the first place. It is for this reason that we deal here with the *practicalities* of applying for a bank loan. In Chapter 5 we have already covered the general approach for presenting a case for finance.

Presenting one's case for money to a bank manager

Trying to get an overdraft or a short-term loan – the differences between these two are discussed later in the chapter, and are in any case slight – or an increase or extension of one of these from your bank manager, can be compared with a salesman trying to get an order from a customer. Salesmen sum up the customer and try to work out how he can be impressed by the goods and facilities available.

In an analogous way the proprietor or manager of the small business needs to work out what he has *available* to impress the bank manager, as well as his *own needs*. Let us consider these two in abbreviated note form.

Available

1. YOURSELF. (i) Your physical appearance and whether you seem upright, honest, straightforward and capable. (ii) Your track record as a borrower. In this connection never conceal things from your bank manager to get a temporary benefit. If he finds out, his opinion of you will go down, and for a long while! Managers put most things down in writing at the time of any agreement or transaction, either to you by way of a letter, or by way of a note in their file on you. In other words, they keep a record of you and your performance as a borrower. (iii) The amount of money you are prepared to put in yourself. Very broadly bank managers work on the 50 per cent gearing level discussed in Chapter 2, i.e., they will lend up to about as much as you have yourself in the business.
2. HISTORICAL INFORMATION AND CURRENT INFORMATION. Typically the most recent balance-sheet and profit-and-loss account, together with balance-sheets and profit-and-loss accounts for the preceding years (if available). Audited accounts carry far more weight than unaudited accounts. Details of the business's formation and expansion. Names of legal advisers and accountants or auditors. Any other commitments, charges, etc. The present order book. Trade and other references.
3. If the funds are for some substantial capital investment, for example in new plant and machinery, or for an extension to a factory, a separate CAPITAL INVESTMENT APPRAISAL (see Chapter 18) will be required.
4. A short-term (e.g. month by month for the next year) CASH

BUDGET, and, if possible, a long-term (e.g., year by year for 2 or 3 years) budget. Make sure that bank interest and repayments on the anticipated loan are included.
5. Subsidiary costing and other management accounting figures, if appropriate.

All these will be part of any properly constructed business plan.

Own needs

The reason for needing the funds. For how long they will be required. How they can be repaid. What guarantees, security etc., are available.

Having considered the lending situation from the business manager's point of view, in the next sections we go to the other side of the desk and look at it from the bank manager's seat. We start off by looking at the banks and their lending business.

Bank lending

The bank set-up in the United Kingdom consists of:

1. Four main banks, the 'BIG FOUR' (Barclays, Lloyds, Midland and National Westminster) and the Trustee Savings Bank.

    The two main banks in Scotland are the (rather confusingly named) Royal Bank of Scotland and the Bank of Scotland.

    The Trustee Savings Bank (TSB) has altered the nature and method of operating its business only comparatively recently, and a note here on these changes may be helpful.

    Until the 1970s there were a number of TSBs. These were, in effect, an association of separate savings banks. They were closely controlled by government agencies, and offered only a limited range of deposit taking and related services.

    In the early 1980s a restructuring was proposed. This would bring into operation a new holding company. Shares in this new company were to be offered to the public. The TSB banks were also brought within the supervision of the Bank of England under the Bankers Act 1979 on the same basis as the other banks.

    In 1986 the public issue of shares was successfully made. The TSB now has full clearing bank status, and is broadening its business to include the commercial sector. The TSB is a major UK banking and financial services group. In England alone it has over

1,000 branches: some 300 of these concentrate on corporate business. The TSB's other activities include a unit-linked life company: a substantial general insurance agency business, and one of the largest unit trust management groups in the UK; a major finance house; car rental and leasing, and vehicle distribution. It is evident that the TSB is now a serious competitor to the Big Four in both normal banking and commercial service work.
2. A number of other SMALLER UK BANKS, and certain other organisations which perform many of the functions of the main banks, e.g. the 'Co-op'. There is also Standard Chartered, now nearly as large as Lloyds, except in the main 'high street' banking business.
3. FOREIGN BANKS, typically local branches of American banks, consortium banks, etc.

For the small business only the first two are likely to be relevant, and of these the main banks are outstandingly the most important. In the next chapter the structure and services provided by these banks is analysed more deeply. The main business of the banks is lending money,, though they all accept money by way of deposits and customers' current accounts which are in credit.

Banks long ago realised that they could make bank overdraft, or loan facilities available far in excess of their strict cash resources to meet either these demands or the demands of their depositors if they should wish to draw them out to the full extent that they were 'in credit'. A bank trades with a large number of account customers and only a few are likely to require their money repaid to them at any one time. Over the years the banks have found that they can 'create' deposits and this power exists because bank deposits are always accepted as money by the public.

But will the banks lend to you? As a first step it is likely that you will ask your *own* bank manager. To understand his position and what he can do, we need to look at the banks at local level and the lending powers of bank managers.

Loan powers of bank managers

With some 2,000 or more local branches each, the 'Big Four' banks are too large for these branches to come under the direct control of their head offices in London. All four banks have regional ('district' or 'area' are alternative terms used) offices. Barclays and National Westminster have boards above these regional offices and below head office. These regional offices have control over a varying number of local branches. More details on this point, too, are given in the following chapter.

Each bank manager has a budget given him each year, and a loan limit which applies for every individual application. He will also be given various other targets in terms of numbers of insurance policies, tax work for clients, etc., that he is expected to achieve in a year. However, it is the individual loan limit which is of importance to the small business applicant for funds. This amount varies very much with the size of the branch. Managers' discretions have recently been increased considerably and branch manager's limits will usually be in the range between £15,000 and £100,000. For large branches it can be up to £150,000, or more. Branch managers' discretionary powers will also vary depending on whether the borrowing is secured or unsecured. A typical large branch limit would be about £25,000 unsecured, £125,000 secured. If the loan or overdraft application is above the branch manager's limit, he will refer it to his area or regional manager. Typically these managers will have limits of £700,000 to £1 million, though again the exact amount depends on the size and importance of the region. Above that amount the regional manager must again push it 'up the line' to the next level of authority.

A word or two about the attitude of bank managers to loan applications is apposite here. Bank managers have usually spent all their working lives in their banks, and expect to spend the rest of them there, too. In other words, they are 'company' men. They will be steeped in the traditional approach which is the hallmark of 'British banking'. To that extent their attitude can reasonably be called 'conservative'. However, this cautious approach has proved to be very successful. Before changing it the banks would need to have good reasons. Let us look at the one aspect of this attitude of particular relevance to us here. Consider a first loan application made by an entrepreneur wishing to set up his own business. What we need to consider are the possible benefits and losses both from the position of the loan applicant and the bank manager.

Suppose the new business does not start to get off the ground properly. A further loan will probably be requested. The bank manager will be placed in the unenviable position of either having to foreclose on the business, or sink further funds, with the possibility that later he may have to try and recover these larger amounts, too, if the business never gets going. He will certainly foreclose if pushed to the point, but he will not like to do so; even now, to some extent, banks that do so are seen as the 'villain', and banks are very conscious of their image. He is marginally more likely to foreclose on a small business; closure of a large business by a bank will be nationally reported and will lead to the adverse publicity that banks so wish to avoid.

Suppose, on the other hand, the business is a wild success. The bank manager will, it is true, probably have got himself an important customer (though there is nothing to stop that customer from going at any time to another bank!). The interest on the increased loan amount and certain other ancillary benefits will be important to the bank's business. But the bank will never get more than the fixed rate of interest it has charged on the loan, however much money the business is making. The proprietor will get a share of the benefits of these high profits – the bank no more at all. Therefore, the bank's attitude towards any risky loan (and all first-time loans are risky) must be very different from that of the individual loan applicant. He, the entrepreneur, stands to gain a lot if things go really well; the bank does not.

However, the popular image of a bank manager who does not want to lend (except to large firms whose stability and security are unquestionable) is just not true. It is sometimes believed that a bank manager dare not lend on possibly dubious propositions because he is assessed on the number of successful loans he makes, and each loan that turns bad is seen as a black mark against him – and these black marks may mean a stop to promotion. Again, this is just not true. While too many risky loans would incur adverse comment, an equally likely criticism of a bank manager's performance by his supervisors would be that he was not making enough loans. A cautious policy of never lending except on cast-iron certainties actually would affect his promotion prospects adversely.

So, to sum up, a bank manager will wish to loan i.e., he will wish to loan to your business, provided only that you can convince him that yours is a reasonably good proposition which has been carefully thought through.

Within his loan limits the power of the bank manager is absolute. We have already noted that these are likely to vary at branch level from around £20,000 to many times that figure for large local offices. Most new loans will be within these amounts so, for the first-time applicant, the attitude of his bank manager is crucial to the success of his business.

We earlier noted that bank managers are company men; all their business lives will have been spent with one bank only. But their experiences will be different. Some will have spent most of their time in city offices, others in the country. Over the course of time they will have evolved their own rules for considering loan applications. Because their experiences have been different, the criteria they apply will differ, to some extent, too. Some managers will place heavy emphasis on business security, or personal guarantees from the loan applicant or his wife, others will be more concerned with the prospects of the business, others again with the appearance and attitude of the loan applicant, and the amount he is prepared to put in himself.

Even within these categories the attitude of bank managers will vary. If we consider the one important matter of security, each manager will probably have some basic rule of thumb which he has evolved over the years and come to rely on. A typical rule might be a top loan limit based on 70 per cent of the property available, 50 per cent of all other fixed assets and stock, and 75 per cent of the debtors. However, both the range and the type of security asked for do vary. The Wilson Committee noted that 'Typical security ratios of net assets to borrowing were in the range of 2:1 to 4:1.'

The point we are making here is that bank managers differ in their assessment of a loan risk. They are human, and human beings, even highly respected professionals, dealing with their own speciality, differ. The position is in some ways analogous to that of Inland Revenue officials. Some tax inspectors are rigid on certain aspects; others are more flexible. The remedy is the same when dealing with either intractable tax inspectors or bank managers: change to another one. For tax inspectors dealing with your business affairs, this means changing the registered office of the business, since it is the registered office which determines the tax district. This change is very easy to make: all that is required is that you fill in a form, obtainable from the Registrar of Companies (for limited liability companies). In practice it is common to use the office of your solicitor or auditor for these purposes.

To change to another bank manager is even easier. All you have to do is make an appointment with the local manager of any (or, if necessary, all) of the other banks of the 'Big Four' or TSB. Not that there is any reason why you cannot try branches of banks other than the 'Big Four', but it is simpler to try these first, and it is probably more likely that they will consider a loan for a small business more favourably than the other banks with a less widespread network of branches. If none of these will grant the loan, there is still no reason at all to give up hope. The next step is to try branches other than your local ones. Much as with the tax inspector case, you need some grounds for shopping around outside your local area, so that with your application to a new bank manager you must have a good reason for approaching him. It may be that you are considering setting up a local branch in a new district. That, or any one of a number of similar business reasons, will be good grounds for applying to all the bank managers in that district. One word of caution: when your loan is over the limit that the local branch manager will be able to deal with, it is no good applying to other branches of the same bank in that region. Your original request will have gone up to the regional bank manager for approval. Your second application will also be pushed up the line to him for the same reasons. He is hardly likely to pass the second application having turned down the first one!

Bank charges and interest rates

At branch level the banks in England are truly competitive. Provided the conditions are right, they positively want to lend money to your business. This can be either by overdraft or short-term loan. What do they want from you in exchange for letting you have the funds? Banks make two charges:

1. An ARRANGEMENT OR NEGOTIATION FEE, and (possibly) an annual renewal fee.
2. An INTEREST CHARGE.

An arrangement charge or negotiation fee is generally made for short-term loans; frequently, too, it is made when an overdraft facility is arranged. In either case it is usually a 'one-off' charge made at the time when the overdraft or loan is arranged. It is likely to be of the order of £100 to £300 for loans of, say, £5,000 to £20,000, but the exact charge varies considerably. The amount is at the discretion of the bank manager, and reflects his view of the quantity of work that the bank will be involved in when making the necessary arrangements.

Over the period of the loan the charge made by way of interest will be a much more substantial figure than the arrangement fee. To understand the rate at which interest will be charged we need, once again, to look at the situation from the bank's point of view.

Banks make their money in a number of different ways. However, their main trading activity consists in getting money from lending (i.e., overdrafts, short- and long-term loans), and paying out money for deposit accounts. Both the rates that banks give to depositors, and the rates that they charge for loans, are tied to their own bank base lending rate. In this respect banks operate in a similar way to other financial institutions, such as finance houses, who also relate their lending and borrowing rates to their own base rate.

The base rate for any particular bank is set by that bank itself. The rate is determined by a number of economic factors, such as general money market rates and money supply, and, as well, pressure by the government, mainly through the Bank of England. Although banks do, in theory, determine their own bank rates and the time of any change, in practice they all move more or less in unison: that is, if not on precisely the same day, at least with only a very short period between them. A moment's reflection will show why this must be the case. Suppose three of the 'Big Four' raise their bank base rates, leaving one bank still with the lower rate. Rates paid to depositors, like all rates used by the banks, are, it will remember, directly related to bank base rate. A depositor with this one bank will now be paid a lower rate of interest than those with the other three. If the customer's deposits are large, it will be worth his while to transfer his account to any of the other three banks. The one remaining bank, out of line on bank base interest rates, will therefore lose some of its depositors and this will have a substantial adverse effect on its capacity to lend money. It will be forced to fall into line with the other banks and raise its bank base rate too.

To sum up this section. Changes in general economic money rates, and action by the government, in practice do mean corresponding changes in banks' own base rates. These rates themselves form the basis for determining all interest rates used by the banks and, in particular, the rates paid to depositors and the rates charged for overdrafts and directly or indirectly for all loans.

Bank overdrafts and short-term loans

Overdrafts and short-term loans from joint stock banks have been for many years, and still remain, the main source of outside finance for small businesses. The differences between these two are not very great. A short-term loan is a fixed term commitment by the lender. This term commitment theoretically differentiates a short-term loan from an overdraft, which, technically, is repayable on demand by the bank. In practice, banks do not normally cancel an overdraft facility at short notice; indeed overdrafts frequently remain in existence over many years. In such circumstances it is hard to see that they retain any of the characteristics of short-term borrowing. Indeed, the phrase 'long-term bank borrowing by way of a standing bank overdraft facility' would be far more appropriate, though in fact overdrafts may still be presented as short-term liabilities in balance-sheets.

The other main difference between a bank overdraft and a short-term loan is that interest on the latter is based on the agreed loan amount or on the balance outstanding after scheduled repayments. Interest for an overdraft is always only paid on the amount of money actually borrowed, and this is calculated on a day-to-day basis. Since the amount actually borrowed at some time under an overdraft arrangement is quite likely to be below the agreed limit, it follows that, on this basis, a bank overdraft may well be cheaper than a short-term loan. There is, however, another reason why overdrafts may possibly be cheaper than loans. The interest rates charged for both will, of course, be fixed in relation to the bank's base rate, and will vary with changes in that base rate. However the interest charges for overdrafts normally are of the order of base rate + 2 to 4 1/2 per cent. For short-term loans the interest rates charged are likely to be base rate + 3 to 5 per cent. Fixed rate options are generally available too. At the time of writing the fixed rate is between 13½ per cent and 16 per cent.

Both bank overdrafts and short-term loans may well be secured. This security may be based on the assets of the business; sometimes the security will be a personal guarantee by the proprietor or some other related person. A request for security would not normally be based on whether the borrowing is by way of overdraft or loan but on other factors such as risk and amount.

One other slight difference exists in that overdrafts are more vulnerable to changes in government policy. Instead of forcing changes ment can influence the economy by restricting the amount of money that the banks can lend. Although banks are not obliged to do what the Bank of England asks, in practice they are very responsive to such requests. Alternatively the government may freeze some of the deposits that the banks have with the Bank of England (it can do this very easily, too, since the Bank of England acts as the *bankers' bank*). The effect of these actions is to reduce the amount of funds that the banks have available to lend. If the total amount available is restricted by this government action (or indeed by any change in the banks' own policy towards lending), there is no doubt as to where the first cuts will occur. The banks will see their term loans as contracts already entered into, and hence as ones in duty bound to be observed. However, overdrafts are not obligations in this sense at all. New overdrafts and extensions of existing overdrafts will be the first to be cut. If the overall restrictions were to be severe, the banks might feel themselves forced to reduce or even to cancel entirely an existing overdraft. They would be very unlikely to do this without reasonable warning, except as a last resort, but overdrafts, as we noted, are technically speaking, repayable on demand.
technically speaking, repayable on demand.

What type of borrowing should a small businessman ask for when seeking money from a bank? Should he try for an overdraft facility or a short-term loan? Since overdrafts are slightly cheaper, the simple answer is to try for that form of finance rather than a term loan. In practice, however, the crucial consideration may well turn out to be the attitude of the bank manager. It is he who is lending the money, and it is usually he who is in the position of being able to dictate the terms. If, in the particular situation, he prefers perhaps a secured loan rather than creating a temporary overdraft facility, the businessman will be well advised to accept this and fit in with the wishes of the bank manager. Since the differences between the two are slight, the overriding consideration may be that the bank manager will happily lend under one form of borrowing but be hesitant about the other.

Medium- and long-term loans

At a congress on the future of banking, Sir Harold Wilson stated that private sources of start-up capital for the entrepreneur had been killed off by the British tax system. He said:

> the old sources of finance for the small business have substantially dried up. Not long ago a young man, or not so young man, wanting to set up on his own account had not only his own small personal resource, but there were perhaps one or two relatives around, perhaps his lawyer or his accountant who had faith in him, and were willing to go the first few miles with him. Taxation has sharply reduced these sources of investment. In the phrase commonly used by my Committee, and in evidence produced before us, 'Aunt Agatha is dead'.

The Committee referred to by Sir Harold was the 'Wilson' Committee. The Committee produced an interim report on *The Financing of Small Firms* in 1979. In this interim report the ways for giving tax relief were explored.

Many of these tax reliefs have been implemented. However even the Business Expansion Scheme – the most impressive of these – has not directly solved the problem of private finance for small businesses. The fact is that nowadays 'Aunt Agatha' has available the advice of a number of professional people. These include lawyers, accountants and bank managers. None of these will feel that in today's harsh economic environment he should recommend these ladies to entrust their money to some local young man who is just setting up business. These days, Aunt Agatha may not even ask her bank manager. Anyone can put their available money, whether large or small in amount, into unit trusts or one of the other forms of investment, run by professional managers. These securities are safe, since the trust managers spread their investments over a wide portfolio. Distributions of income are made regularly, and it is easy to put money in or take it out at short notice. In other words, they are ideal for Aunt Agatha. The consequence for small businesses is that they do not now get much direct private investment money; and unit trust managers do not usually include small businesses in their investment portfolios.

Deprived of one of their main sources of long-term finance, entrepreneurs again turned to their bank managers. But banks have traditionally been short-term lenders. The British banking system was founded on the seasonal loan. A local bank would lend to a farmer in the early spring, when he needed supplies of seed, recovering the money from him when he was paid for his harvest. This money, in turn, would be lent typically to a small shopkeeper for building up his stock for Christmas. The money from his Christmas sales would be used to lend to the farmer, and so on. Lending 'long' in any case is against the basic prudent financial doctrine of 'borrowing long and lending short'. That way, of course, there can never be any serious problems about the availability of funds.

Customers' accounts in banks, whether current or deposit, are in theory short term in nature. In practice, because of the wide number and variety of these accounts, they can as we have noted, be relied upon to provide long-term finance for the banks. Because of this, and because of the increasing pressure from entrepreneurs seeking medium- and long-term money from banks, the clearing banks have for many years been widening their loan facilities.

Long-term loans are frequently made by way of a *debenture*. A debenture is a written acknowledgement of the debt, specifying the amount, period, interest rate, fees, security, repayment terms etc., for the debt. Debentures can be unsecured, in which case they are often referred to simply as 'loan stock'. However, they may well be secured on the assets of the business. If interest is not paid. or repayment of the debenture is not forthcoming, the trustee who administers the debenture has the right to take charge of the security and sell it to provide funds from which the debenture-holders will be paid. Often security will be fixed on specific assets, such as land and buildings; and it is these that the trustee can take over to meet the repayment. Sometimes, however, the security is 'floating', so that the trustee can take control of any appropriate assets of the business when the need arises. When this happens, the floating security is said to 'crystallise' on these assets.

Banks frequently use the written form of a debenture when they make a long-term loan. But debentures can also be issued to investors requiring long-term fixed-interest securities on the open market by a business. Sometimes these debentures carry with them the right to convert to ordinary shares at the option of the holders. These are 'convertible debentures'. Conversion rights state the dates on which the option may be exercised, and the number of shares to be acquired for each debenture. Usually fewer shares are offered as succeeding dates are passed. In return for this conversion option, the rate of interest is usually lower than with a normal debenture.

An alternative way of borrowing, much favoured recently, is via a mortgage on the freehold of a property. Essentially this is just a loan secured on that freehold property. Banks, insurance companies, investment companies and pension funds will all lend on this basis. Building societies have been reluctant to lend to companies but are the best source of mortgage for sole traders or partnerships. Repayment of interest and capital can normally be spread over a long period.

All major banks now provide long-term loan schemes generally for amounts between £10-20,000 and £1,000,000. The term is normally in excess of 10 years with a maximum of 30 years. Medium-term loans on a contractual basis are also available for periods of 3 to 10 years. An important feature of many of these schemes is the option of a floating rate (linked to the bank's base rate) or a fixed rate for the duration of the loan, or indeed a loan raised in two parts, one at a fixed and the other at a variable rate. Even when the rate is variable the actual repayments may remain unchanged, with movements in the rate being accommodated by adjustments in the length of the repayment period. Repayment can be made in a variety of ways: for example, equal periodic instalments (monthly, quarterly or yearly) or smaller repayments in early years and larger ones in later years. This stepped repayment option may be the most convenient for many 'start-up' businesses, as the amount paid gradually increases in line with greater cash availability from better trading conditions. Some of these option will only be available for loans in excess of around £20,000. For loans in excess of 5 years to unincorporated customers the fixed rate option is usually not on offer if the loan is for £15,000 or less. Many schemes allow a rest period or 'capital holiday' at the start, during which time no payments (other than for interest due) are made. The capital holiday periods allowed rarely exceed 2 years.

Security, as we have noted, is often required for long-term loans. Security reflects the underlying strength of the existing business and the nature and potential of the new proposition. By its very nature long-term finance is likely to relate largely to fixed-asset formation, so suitable security arrangements in respect of good freehold or long leasehold property are a typical feature of these schemes. Sometimes these loans carry restrictions on certain activities, such as further borrowing, and it is not uncommon for other undertakings (such as maintaining a certain current assets/current liabilities ratio) to be required. This is called a 'negative pledge'.

Security requirements are not usually imposed merely to strengthen the bank's position in the event of bankruptcy or insolvency. It is relatively rare for the banks to realise the security they possess. A more important reason is that security requirements are felt to increase the proprietor's commitment to the health and survival of the business. This is especially true of third party guarantees and pledges on the proprietor's personal assets. The proprietor who lodges his investment portfolio or life policy as security for a loan to his own business, or offers a mortgage on his house, or obtains a guarantee from a friend, is increasing his personal commitment to his business.

The changing role of the banks

Over the years the banks have changed their way of conducting business and the range of the services they have provided. Changes are still in the air. All the main clearers (with the exception of TSB who are building up their network of local branches from a comparatively low base) are continuing with their policy of closing high street branch offices. The present proliferation of bank branch offices in the UK is without parallel in the Western world.

However, closing branches is an exercise which is not without problems. The closure of a local branch has been likened to shutting down a village sub-post office, and all banks already have some staff difficulties with an over supply of staff at manager level. All banks are also tending to split the business they deal with into corporate business and the comparatively unglamorous personal business. It is likely that by the very early 1990s banks will have a number of offices dealing only with corporate clients and a separate network of branch offices catering for personal acounts and the provision of concomitant services.

Banks will continue to expand the range of services they provide. Life assurance, unit trusts, general insurance, investment planning, personal equity plans and personal pensions are examples of these. Competition with the Building Societies seems to have brought considerable advantages to the customer. When the banks moved into home loan provision the cost of mortgages dropped appreciably.

When the 1986 Building Societies Act comes into force in 1988, Building Societies will be in a strong position for attacking the banks in their traditionally dominant fields such as personal loans and credit card borrowing. Banks will have to sell their products and services more professionally. The way they will certainly try to do this is by sprucing up their remaining branch outlets to present a more cosy, less formidable, image. Concentration on new high interest cheque or deposit accounts (rather than the old uninviting deposit accounts) is another. Perhaps above all they will have to train their staff in modern marketing techniques.

All banks now have subsidiaries or associate companies covering a whole range of special financing schemes: credit factoring, leasing, sale and leaseback. Banks can also be particularly useful in supporting export sales. Some indication of the range and nature of these specialist services is given in the next chapter. The banks offer advice on the investment of surplus funds. All have specialist small business advisory units which can help small businesses with particular problems, particularly in the area of financial planning and reporting.

In addition to these formal services the banks can be a valuable source of information. They provide a wide range of material to help the small businessman, including booklets on various aspects of financial management as well as more general management issues. Banks also have 'economic intelligence units' which provide economic and market information for both the United Kingdom and overseas; this can help a small business with its marketing plans.

However, for the small business, money from the local bank by way of an overdraft or a loan has been, and still remains, the dominant factor. That is why this chapter has been devoted to the subject. That is why the following chapter gives detailed information on the structure of banks. It pays to know how your major financial backer operates.

CHAPTER 7

Bank Services for Small Business

THE STRUCTURE OF BANKS	116
The clearing banks	116
Banking organisation	117
THE SERVICES PROVIDED BY BANKS FOR SMALL BUSINESS	119
FINANCING THE BUSINESS	119
Credit factoring	119
Hire purchase, lease purchase, or instalment credit purchase	120
Leasing	121
Sale and leaseback	122
Export finance	122
Franchising	124
Special services for agriculture	127
Loan guarantee scheme	127
INVESTMENT OF FUNDS	128
Deposit accounts, high interest current accounts, etc.	128
Certificates of deposit	129
Stocks and shares	129
Investment services	130
BUSINESS ADVISORY SERVICES	130

The structure of banks

The clearing banks

The Committee of London and Scottish Clearing Bankers (that is 'banks' in the generally accepted use of the term) now includes Barclays, Lloyds, Midland, National Westminster (and its subsidiary Coutts) and the Scottish Banks. The major banks are all public companies quoted on the stock exchange and their shares are held by a very wide range of investors, both individual and institutional.

Traditionally it has been the clearing banks' policy not to operate under their own names in Scotland and Ireland, though all the 'Big Four' banks have now opened a limited number of Scottish branches. The clearing banks have, however, for a long time had shareholdings in the Scottish clearing banks. A series of mergers analogous to those which took place in England around 1968 (before then the main English banking structure was referred to as the 'Big Six' and the 'Little Seven') has reduced the number of Scottish banks from 6 to 3 over the past 20 years. These three are the Bank of Scotland, the Royal Bank of Scotland, and the Clydesdale Bank.

Banking organisation

An overall structure chart for a typical bank (Lloyds) is shown in Figure 7.1. All the banks organise their domestic clearing banks business on a regional basis; this is important for the delegation of lending decisions, as well as for general administration. The exact pattern differs from one to another, and some have stronger traditions of decentralisation than others. It will be seen from figure 7.1 that for Lloyds branch banking there are 16 regions looked after by regional managers, and between them these regional managers control 2,200 branches and sub-branches in the UK. In addition, Lloyds Bank is introducing its Commercial Service. Lloyds Bank Commercial Service (LBCS) managers will be based in main business centres throughout the country, but they will not have the usual administration that an ordinary bank manager has to worry about. Only businesses with a turnover of over £1/2m per annum will be placed under the LBCS control. These managers will have very high discretions and be able respond very quickly to the needs of the small businessman . If they receive requests above their discretion they will pass the request on to the Regional General Manager.

Midland is similarly structured. Any requests for finance above a branch manager's discretionary limit are referred to the appropriate regional authority. Over the past few years, however, a network of area offices has been set up to assist the speed of response. Where geography and other local factors permit, teams of lending managers have been assembled to deal with the majority of business lending from designated branches, with the area manager having a high sanctioning authority.

Both Barclays and National Westminster have additional layers of authority. Barclays has seven regions each with a regional general

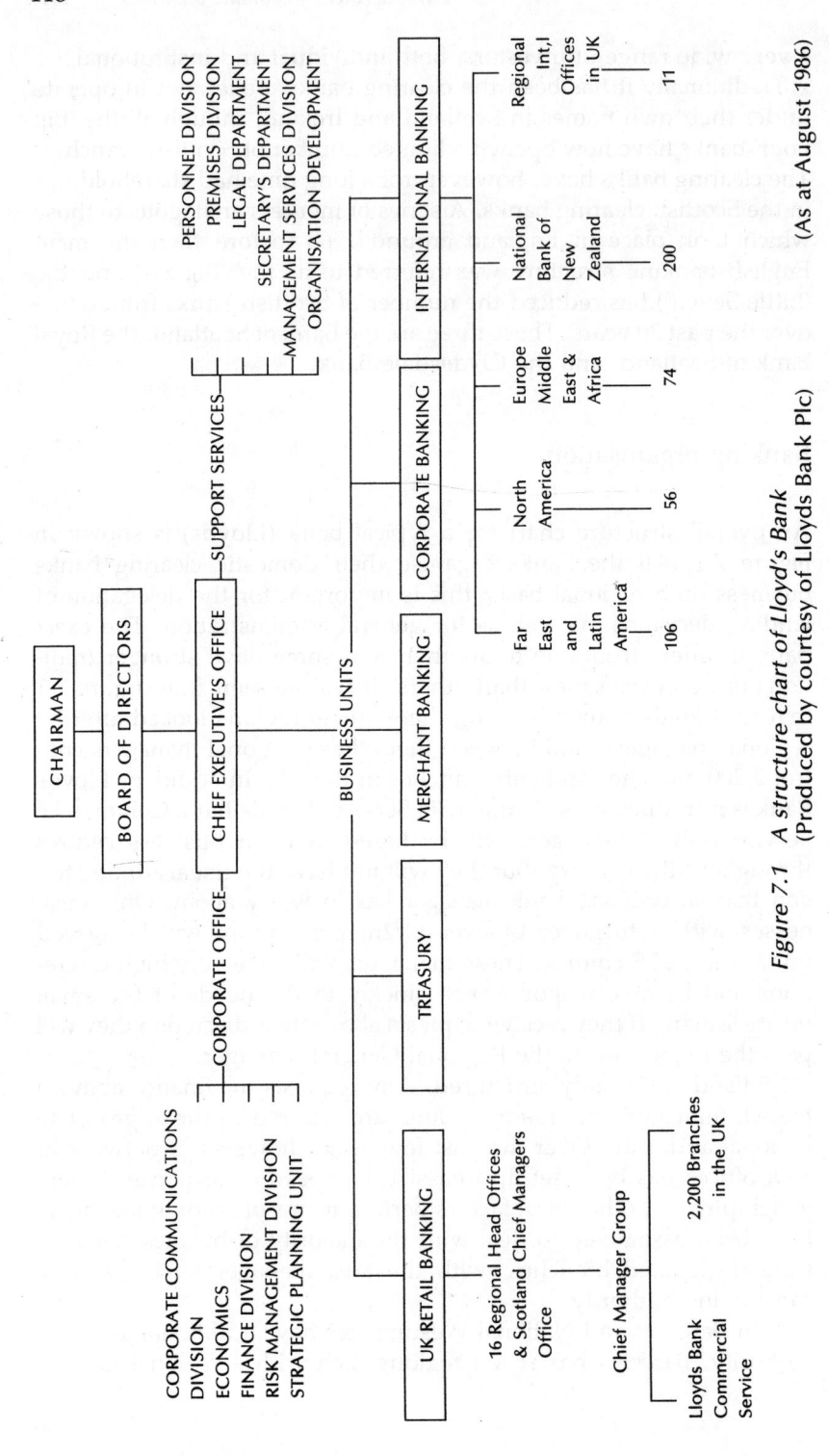

```
                            CHAIRMAN
                               │
                       BOARD OF DIRECTORS
                               │
CORPORATE COMMUNICATIONS ─┐    │         ┌─ PERSONNEL DIVISION
DIVISION                  │    │         │  PREMISES DIVISION
ECONOMICS                 ├ CORPORATE ── CHIEF EXECUTIVE'S OFFICE ── SUPPORT SERVICES ─┤  LEGAL DEPARTMENT
FINANCE DIVISION          │  OFFICE       │         │                                   │  SECRETARY'S DEPARTMENT
RISK MANAGEMENT DIVISION  │               │         │                                   │  MANAGEMENT SERVICES DIVISION
STRATEGIC PLANNING UNIT ──┘               │         │                                   └─ ORGANISATION DEVELOPMENT
                                          │
                                    BUSINESS UNITS
      ┌──────────────┬──────────┬────────────────┬──────────────────┬──────────────────┐
      │              │          │                │                  │
UK RETAIL BANKING  TREASURY  MERCHANT BANKING  CORPORATE BANKING  INTERNATIONAL BANKING
      │                                                │
      │                              ┌─────────────┬───┴─────────┬──────────────┬──────────────┐
16 Regional Head Offices           Far East      North      Europe         National         Regional
& Scotland Chief Managers          and           America    Middle         Bank of          Int.l
Office                             Latin                    East &         New              Offices
      │                            America                  Africa         Zealand          in UK
Chief Manager Group                 106            56         74             200              11
      │
      ├─ 2,200 Branches
      │   in the UK
      │
      └─ Lloyds Bank
         Commercial
         Service
```

Figure 7.1 A structure chart of Lloyd's Bank
(Produced by courtesy of Lloyds Bank Plc)
(As at August 1986)

manager (two RGMs for London). These control some 35 districts, each with executive local directors, who in turn look after some 3,000 branches and sub-branches. National Westminster's domestic banking division comprises 8 regions (executive directors and boards), some 50 areas (with area managers) and again around 3,000 branches.

This completes our survey of the banking structure in the United Kingdom. In the next section we give a summary of the specific services supplied by the banks for small business.

The services provided by banks for small business

The previous chapter provided details of overdrafts, and short-, medium-, and long-term loan facilities offered by the banks. The banks are, however, changing and are now offering a range of other services to their clients. Often these services are also offered by commercial organisations other than banks. These services have been classified as those relating to the financing of the business and those relating to the investment of funds.

Financing the Business

Credit factoring

This is a fast growing form of business. The Association of British Factors reported that its nine members saw a record increase of more than £1 billion in their amount of factoring in 1986. The combined volume of factoring by the nine members reached £5.7 billion. Domestic business showed a 14 per cent increase and international business increased by 19 per cent.

Credit factoring is a form of finance whereby cash is provided against an invoice, normally up to 80 percent of that invoice value. These advances are charged at an interest rate of 2-4 percent above the credit factor's base rate. In the case of 'full' credit factoring, the operation of the business's sales ledger is taken over entirely by the factor, who collects the debts as they fall due. The administrative charge for this is 0.5 to 2.5 per cent of invoice value. It is usual for any bad debts to be covered by the factor. The service is available for both domestic and export sales to most countries of Western Europe, the USA and Canada, where it is necessary to compete on open-market terms.

Clearly the main advantage of this is the direct linkage between sales and credit; it is a very convinient way of financing part of the growth of business. Some of the other advantages which are claimed by credit factors for a business include:

1. Improved credit reputation with suppliers as a result of the ability of the business to establish a pattern of prompt payment.
2. The ability to negotiate cash and trade discounts.
3. The ability to deal with any substantial seasonal variations in sales and cash demands.
4. The ability to plan ahead in the certain knowledge that cash for working capital, etc., will be available.

Finally, credit factors maintain, with some justification, that their expertise in assessing the credit worthiness of both new and current customers, and the complete protection they give against bad debts on all approved sales, are more than worth the charge they make for their services. There are some disadvantages. Some institutions still take this as a sign of weakness and it can lead to a reduction in borrowing capability. Credit factoring also may lead to a loss of contact with customers and generate some bad feeling as the factor presses for payment, unaware of the business's own considerations. As mentioned earlier, keeping in touch with customers is vitally important. Finally, it is quite an expensive form of finance.

There is a comparatively rare variation called 'acceptance credit bill finance', which involves discounting only specific transactions, on a one-off basis. This is operated by *accepting houses*. Your bank manager can arrange this or indeed any credit factoring work. Bank have their own credit factoring subsidiaries.

Hire purchase (HP), lease purchase or instalment credit purchase

This form of finance is used to purchase a wide variety of assets such as plant, machinery and vehicles. The business hires the equipment from a bank or finance house for a fixed period, and has the option to buy the asset at the end of the period for a nominal sum. The initial agreement takes the form of a conditional sale. The asset legally belongs to the business from the outset and hence capital allowances can be claimed by the business.

Depending on possible government regulations, an initial deposit may be required followed by a series of instalments. Interest rates are normally fixed at a premium of at least 4 per cent above the HP company's own base rate. So HP, too, can be an expensive form of finance. Agreement periods are usually from 2 up to 5 years; longer periods can attract a variable rate.

HP is quick and easy to arrange, since security for the agreement is the asset itself. It is well suited to short life, guaranteed return assets, and does not normally affect other bank borrowings. Most managers are keen to arrange this sort of finance.

There are a number of variations. Instalment credit can be provided to retailers, particularly in the motor, caravan and marine trades, to finance their showroom and demonstration stock.

Retailers who enter into HP agreements with their customers can often discount these debts (called 'block discounting') with banks and finance houses, thus releasing capital for use elsewhere. One advantage of the arrangement is that, under normal circumstances, customers are unaware of the arrangement so that the business's relationship with them continues undisturbed.

We can summarise the main features of this form of instalment finance as:

1. Payment is made by instalments. Generally the working life of the asset matches the repayment period.
2. The business has immediate use of the asset.
3. Full capital allowances are available to the business.
4. VAT can be reclaimed on the purchase price.
5. Interest payments can be set against tax.
6. An option to purchase at the end of the 'hire' period is included in the agreement.

Leasing

This is another form of instalment finance. On the face of it, leasing seems very similar to HP. There are, however, two important differences. In contrast to HP, ownership of the asset does not rest with the business that leases the asset until the asset is worthless or is sold. Because of this, taxation capital allowances may be claimed by the lessor, not the business leasing the asset. However, lease payments are, of course, tax-deductible by the business. It is, therefore, particularly appropriate for small businesses whose tax position is such that they cannot benefit from the capital allowance, since these are effectively passed on to the lessee by way of reduced rentals. Also, unlike HP, leasing does tend to affect borrowing capacity, though somewhat marginally, and this is likely to increase if proposals to reflect leasing finance in the balance-sheets of companies are implemented.

Strictly the term 'financial leasing' should be used for this form of credit financing. Where maintenance, service etc., considerations are also included in the lease agreement (this is fairly common for large items of plant and machinery) the term 'operating lease' is correct.

We can summarise the main features of this form of finance as:

1. Payment is made by instalments. Generally the working life of the asset matches the repayment period.
2. The business has immediate use of the asset.
3. Instalment payments can be set against tax.
4. VAT can be reclaimed on the rental sums.
5. At the end of the agreement it is usually possible to extend the lease for a further period by paying a small secondary rental.
6. On final sale it is usual to allow most or all of the sale proceeds to be used as a rebate against the outstanding rental payments.

Sale and leaseback

With this form of finance the business sells an asset, normally a freehold or long leasehold property, to the finance source with an agreement for it to lease back the property over a specified period. The lease terms will usually contain clauses for rent reviews, which may be frequent, and hence increase the cost of raising the initial finance. Rent is tax-deductible, but the business may be liable to capital gains tax on the initial transaction. While the business does secure an immediate inflow of cash with this device, it does remove from its ownership a source of security for future borrowing, and an asset on which there is likely to be substantial capital appreciation.

Export finance

The clearing banks play a major role in helping small businesses to move into overseas markets. Invoices and the bills that the exporter draws on shipment can be discounted through the banks. Facilities for drawing upon the documentary credits established by the importer's bankers can be arranged. The banks also provide their customers with advice on the services available from the Export Credits

Guarantee Department, which guarantee overseas debts, or they will provide such services themselves.

Despite the growth of the commercial insurance market the Export Credits Guarantee Department (ECGD) remains the primary source for exporters of all types requiring insurance for their overseas selling operations. The ECGD's main function is to insure credit by the issue of insurance policies to exporters. These are called 'Guarantees'.

The principal risks covered by the ECGD are:

1. Insolvency of the customer.
2. Customers failure to pay for goods that have been accepted, within six months of the due date.
3. Prevention of payment caused by a general moratorium on external debt by the buyer's country, or by any other similar action, including political events, or economic difficulties outside the UK preventing the transfer of payments.
4. War and other similar events.
5. Cancellation of UK export licence, etc.

The ECGD normally covers 90 per cent of the loss only. This leaves 10 per cent to be met by the exporter. The aim of this policy is to encourage prudent credit management on the part of the exporter.

The ECGD makes two charges. First, an annual premium based on estimated annual export turnover and secondly a risk premium on exports notified to the ECGD, on a monthly basis.

The ECGD is a government-backed agency of long standing. Many small exporters prefer to use the commercial insurance market or give this business to their own bank. The major service that the banks provide in this area is under their own Export Factoring Schemes. These schemes are generally operated through a bank subsidiary. They vary a little from bank to bank but typical features include:

1. All UK goods will be covered, and exports to most countries, including those with difficult trading conditions.
2. Payment will be arranged through Bills or Notes.
3. A maximum credit period of 180 days.
4. Normally a 90 per cent coverage of finance: some schemes give a 100 per cent coverage.
5. ECGD approval for the exporter to join the scheme is required.
6. The goods covered are on selected contracts only: these schemes do not give a general coverage for 'open account' trading.
7. The bank's charge for these services is based on an annual facility fee plus an all-in flat charge, depending on the credit period, and

on a scale valid for a 12-month period. Additionally, an ECGD premium surcharge for foreign currency invoicing, and a flat charge for each buyer limit application.

Export financing is a complicated and rather specialised operation. Unless the small business operator sells mainly in the export market it usually makes more sense for him to go to his bank and use one of the co-ordinated range of export finance schemes, rather than try and make the exporting arrangements directly himself.

Franchising

Franchising almost always requires, initially, the provision of a substantial sum by a start-up business and this sum is generally borrowed from a bank. Franchising is a very fast growing form of business in the UK. It started a little over 20 years ago with businesses such as DynoRod and Wimpey.

Today there are believed to be nearly 200 different types of business being franchised by 250 franchisors through some 9,000 franchise outlets. In other words, around 9,000 people run their own businesses under the umbrella of well-known names.

Total turnover of franchising business in the UK exceeds £1 billion a year. Restaurants, hotels and 'fast food' retailers still form the largest group, but the majority of new franchises have been in the service sector, some with High Street premises (e.g., Prontaprint and British School of Motoring), some direct person-to-person or person-to-business services. Franchise outlets are growing in number and more rapidly than businesses generally.

In the usual form known as 'business format' franchising, the franchisee not only sells the franchisor's product or service, but does so in accordance with laid down procedures. In return the franchisor provides the franchisee with assistance in the organisation and running of the business prior to opening, then continues with further advice and assistance in staff training, marketing, research and development. The franchisee usually trades under the franchisor's tradename and gains the benefit of association with a nationally known product or service.

There are benefits both to the franchisor and the franchisee. The benefits to the franchisee are:

1. It gives the small businessman the opportunity of being the owner and proprietor of a business; and this within the umbrella of an

organisation with an established brand name and proven track record.
2. The franchisor provides for the businessman the necessary business training, marketing, accounting advice and general back up support.
3. A generally shorter pay-back period on the initial capital sum invested by the franchisee.
4. The possibility of generating income and expanding the business with less risk than is usually associated with independent trading.

This risk element is in many ways the most important consideration for an individual proposing to set up a new small business. Estimates of failures within one year for new franchise operations generally range around 8 per cent to 10 per cent. If non-members of the British Franchise Association (the Henley on Thames-based employer's organisation in this field) are excluded, estimates fall to as low as a quarter of these figures. It is evident that franchising substantially reduces the risks inherent in new business venture formation.

The benefits to the franchisor include:

1. An increase in market share with little concurrent capital commitment.
2. Dealing with customers (the franchisees) who, in general, will be highly motivated and hence keen to maximise sales.
3. Lack of union and other associated labour problems.

To purchase a franchise, the franchisee will have to enter into a written agreement on a standard form laid down by the franchisor. The franchisee must examine this document with great care. He should consult a professional advisor such as a solicitor or an accountant who has experience in this field. He should not sign until he is satisfied that the franchisor is a suitable operator for him to be associated with, and that the agreement is reasonable and covers all likely major eventualities.

The following points are relevant:

1. Is the franchisor of good financial standing? This can be determined by looking at his most recently filed company accounts, and by other means (see chapter 20).
2. Has the franchisor produced:
    - a projected cash flow analysis for new businesses;
    - evidence of satisfactory results from existing franchisees?

3. What are the financial considerations in the agreement? It is usual for there to be an initial 3- to 5 year period, automatically renewable if the franchisee is successful. What is the royalty figure? A typical figure is some 10 per cent, but there may be additional (possibly hidden) 'charges', e.g., by way of a mark-up on goods supplied, or as a mandatory management service fee, or even advertising levies in one form or another.
4. Are the market and competitors' conditions satisfactory? Is there a particular area in which the potential franchisee is required to operate?
5. Is the product satisfactory? Will it still be available, and needed, in, say, 5 to 10 years' time?
6. Is there an Operations Manual available?
7. Are premises supplied or leased? If leased do they tie up with the initial period covered in the agreement?
8. What arrangements apply in the event of failure?
9. Is the business entirely ethical, decent, and legal?
10. Are there any special funding facilities available if required, e.g., for seasonal trading?

It is not, in fact, usual for the franchisor to provide temporary finance, let alone permanent finance for the franchisee. What is usual is that the potential franchisee turns to his bank manager for funding. Normally such funding will be in some form such as Business Development Loan. A typical development loan has the following characteristics:

1. It is available in amounts from £2,000 up to £250,000, and for periods of 1 to 20 years (though the smaller sums and shorter periods are more common).
2. It will be for the agreed fixed term. Typically it will have a fixed interest rate option (with consequent fixed repayment sums). This option is likely to prove attractive to the average franchisee since he will then be able to plan in advance.
3. There will be an arrangement fee. This will be of the order of 1 percent or 1 ½ percent of the loan amount (with a minimum fee of £50). This fee, and the interest rate, will depend on the availability of security. If security is arranged by the bank there will be an additional charge for this service.
4. The bank will require life assurance cover for the franchisee, and if applicable, other key management personnel. The bank will also arrange loss of profits insurance to meet loan repayments in the event of fire, accident or illness. All these are charged at commercial rates.

5. Capital Repayment Holidays can be arranged. This is a particularly suitable option if the nature of the franchising operation is such that initially little cash flow is likely to be generated. Under this option only interest repayments are made during the initial period. This initial period can be up to two years in length. The bank will require that the loan is secured.
6. Interest rates for the variable interest rate loan will be linked to the bank's base rate. For both the variable interest rate option and the fixed rate option the rate charged will vary depending partly on the length of the loan, but mainly on whether security is provided. For the fixed rate option current interest rates (based on the loan amount) vary from 7 ½ per cent [1] p. a. to 10 per cent on secured loans, and from 8 ½ per cent to 11 per cent on unsecured loans. The corresponding APR rates are 14.6 per cent to 15.3 percent and 16.5 per cent to 16.6 per cent. Some business loans give the franchisee the ability to change from a bank base rate linked loan to a fixed rate loan, or vice versa, at agreed times.

Special services for agriculture

Farmers look to the clearing banks not only to meet their working capital needs (the classic seedtime to harvest finance) but also for medium-term credit to finance the purchase of machinery and implements. This may take the form of a medium-term loan linked to specific needs or of an instalment credit agreement. Long-term credit, for example to finance the purchase of a farm or of additional land, is generally provided either by the Agricultural Mortgage Corporation (AMC) or by insurance companies. AMC was formed by the clearing banks in 1928 in association with the Bank of England to provide long-term mortgage finance for agriculture. It lends against first mortgages on agricultural land for repayment over as much as 30 years, either at a fixed rate of interest or at variable rates linked to the cost of funds.

Loan guarantee scheme

Under the Loan Guarantee Scheme introduced in 1981, over 16,500 guarantees were issued in the period up to February 1986 in respect of over £538 million in bank loans. The scheme has proved to have a

---
[1] These rates applied when the bank's base rate was 10 per cent.

considerable job creation potential both in numbers and cost effectiveness. The life of the scheme was extended in the 1986 budget and the premium rate halved to make it more popular. Currently the Department of Trade and Industry guarantees 70 per cent of each loan made by participating lenders and in return a premium of 2.5 per cent per annum on the amount guaranteed is paid by the borrower. Appraisal and monitoring requirements have been introduced and better financial management encouraged to improve the survival rate of scheme borrowers. Indeed, in the period of the original scheme, 1981 to 1984, bad debt claims exceeded income by as much as £37 million.

Strictly the provision of loans under the loan guarantee scheme is not the sole prerogative of the clearing banks. In practice a high proportion of loans made under this scheme to small businesses are through the banks. It is for this reason that it has been included here.

Investment of funds

Some businesses, particularly those whose operations are of a seasonal nature, occasionally have surplus funds temporarily available. Banks provide a convenient way of 'investing' these funds. There are, of course, other ways open to the business manager, for instance, he can put them into stocks and shares directly via his broker. However, since the relationship between a small business and its bank manager is so important, it is prudent to use the facilities that the bank provides whenever convenient. This is especially the case when funds are available as opposed to needed. Many banks in the USA require a business to whom they are lending money to keep their current acount always in credit to an agreed level. This is not the case in the United Kingdom. Nevertheless a bank manager is more likely to consider favourably a request for a loan from a customer who has let him have surplus money in the past rather than from one who has put his funds elsewhere.

The facilities available are:

Deposit accounts, High interest current accounts, etc.

Until recently the conventional way to earn interest (typically at 3 to 3½ per cent under bank base rate), and to keep surplus funds readily available, was by way of a 7-day deposit account. In the last few years we have seen the growth of high interest deposit accounts, high interest current accounts and high interest cheque accounts.

The 'HP' subsidiaries of most banks also offer deposit facilities for personal and business customers, paying rates of interest for deposits of up to £50,000. The interest rate received relates to the period of deposit, which can range from 1 week to 12 months.

The money market division of the banks is concerned primarily with larger deposits (e.g., £10,000 minimum) for which competitive rates of interest are offered. These rates, which often vary daily, are available on application to any bank branch. Deposits can be made for fixed periods ranging from a few days to 5 years and, for mutual-notice periods, ranging from 7 days to 3 months. Quotations are also available for 'on-demand', or 2 days' notice, deposits of £50,000 or more.

By comparison with Building Societies the rates offered by banks are not good. Building Societies now pay interest net of tax. Their rates vary depending on the sums involved and whether 'Instant Access' is required, or notice of withdrawal (usually 60 or 90 days), has to be given. However, as we noted, bank managers do tend to favour businesses who keep their spare funds with them.

Certificates of deposit

Another money service offered by banks is the issue of sterling certificates of deposit (CDs). A CD is, as its name implies, just a certificate that a certain sum of money has been deposited with the bank. CDs are issued in denominations of £10,000, with a minimum of £50,000 and a maximum of £500,000 per certificate. Although the certificate shows that the money is on deposit for a fixed period, CDs are negotiable on the money market. Hence, if necessary, it is easy to realise cash before the CDs maturity date.

Stocks and shares

Bank managers do not regard themselves as stockbrokers, though they can buy and sell securities for you. The bank used to split the commission equally with the brokerage firm when the investment was made through them.

Since the 'Big Bang' brokerage rates have altered and the banks have all introduced various schemes. Lloyds Bank's, for instance, is known as the Sharedeal Scheme.

Investment services

Banks will manage investment portfolios. They will either take over the complete administration of the portfolio or they will act as nominee, or attorney, advising you from time to time of changes that could be to your advantage.

Banks will invest in any unit trusts as part of their general investment work. They will also invest funds in their own unit trust(s). All banks, too, have 'off-shore trusts' which take advantage of the favourable tax structures in suitable off-shore islands.

Business advisory services

Most banks have separate departments within their domestic branch business sectors, specifically to advise small businesses on their problems. These departments are usually referred to as the Business Advisory Service (BAS), or some similar name.

The staff of the banks' BAS units will have been carefully selected. Almost certainly they will have had some experience in branch banking themselves, and, in addition, they will have been specially trained in the appropriate small business techniques.

The precise way each BAS, or its equivalent, works varies considerably from one bank to another. Typically, however, a branch manager who feels that the services of the BAS would be appropriate for one of the businesses with whom he deals will apply through the usual bank channels to the appropriate BAS manager. Lloyds Bank, however, have now decentralised their BAS service. They have a BAS manager, attached to each region, who is under the control of the regional general manager.

If the application is successful – and it very often is – one or more of the members of the BAS staff will be introduced, via the branch manager, to the business concerned. The BAS staff will spend one or two days with the business. The points that will be looked into will probably include budgeting, costing, control of working capital and, possibly as well, book-keeping, financial records and estimates of sales and capital expenditure in the future. It all depends on the particular problem. Occasionally branch managers ask for the services of the BAS when they are entering into or increasing an already existing loan; more usually they ask the advice of the unit when a business to whom they have lent money starts to experience financial difficulties.

The services of the BAS unit can be of great help to small businesses who are lacking in financial control expertise. It is the policy of some banks not to charge for the work of their BAS (or equivalent), but if the business requests a repeat visit of the BAS this will be charged – at the rate of around £250 per day. Even so, the business is getting what amounts to first-rate financial management consultancy, and at a very reasonable rate. In practical terms this means that business managers are well advised to accept any offer from their bank manager of a visit from the bank's Business Advisory Service.

CHAPTER 8

Risk Capital

FINANCING METHODS – EQUITY AND OTHER FORMS OF RISK CAPITAL	132
SHARE CAPITAL	142
Forms of share capital	142
Ordinary Shares	142
Preference Shares	143
Sources of share capital	144
VENTURE CAPITAL	147
PRIVATE SECTOR VENTURE CAPITAL INSTITUTIONS	149
APPENDIX FOR THE ENTREPRENEUR ON THE PRACTICAL PROBLEMS OF CHOOSING AND LIVING WITH AN INSTITUTION	151
PRESENTING ONE'S CASE FOR VENTURE CAPITAL	153
Documentation	153
Personal qualities	154

Financing methods – equity and other forms of risk capital

The adequacy of the supply of equity capital to small businesses has long been the subject of debate. The Bolton Report was the first formally to draw attention to this problem (though the special difficulties of these small businesses needing to bridge the gap between private and public sources of equity finance was looked at by the Macmillan Commission just after the war). Almost 10 years after Bolton the Wilson Committee addressed itself to this among other problems in the financing of small firms. The Wilson Committee expressed concern about the lack of suitable data in this area, a difficulty which is not confined solely to the funding of small firms. In its report it gives the results of a survey of some 300 companies for the accounting year 1975. Unincorporated businesses were not covered in this analysis

Table 8.1 is taken direct from the Wilson Report. In this form it is not easy to draw conclusions on owners' capital, funding and gearing. Table 8.2 and 8.3 are extracted from Table 8.1. One obvious conclusion from Table 8.2 is that the percentage of ordinary and preference shares is slightly larger in large companies than small. However, if we include loans from directors, owners' capital, as a whole, is of much the same weight.

There are three possible reasons for the popularity of loans from directors for small businesses. First, funds invested in the business, by way of loans, are more secure than share capital, since in the event of bankruptcy they may rank for repayment even before trade creditors. Therefore, this method of funding by the owners reduces the riskiness of their investment. Secondly, there are possible tax advantages (see Chapter 9). Finally, there is the traditional reluctance of the small businessman to relinquish control) and ownership of his company by bringing in other shareholders. Loans to directors are of course prohibited by see 330 of the Companies Act 1985 (except for loans of small amounts).

The Wilson Committee also noted that small businesses were more dependent upon the banks finance than large companies, particularly in manufacturing industry. However, until fairly recently banks have lent predominantly short-term funds and, even now, do not normally get directly involved in taking an equity stake in a business. This problem is highlighted in Table 8.3 which shows the very low long-term capital gearing ratios of small businesses compared with large companies. The gap narrows when short-term loans and bank overdrafts are included in the definition of external funds. The gap reverses when we include trade creditors in our definition. Similar results were found in a comparison of small business financing in the USA, Japan, France and Israel carried out by Tamari (1980). However, because of 'demarcation' problems between short and long term loans, conclusions must be drawn with care.

More recent figures for the funding of small and medium companies are equally sparse and difficult to come by. The UK government publication *Business Monitor MA3* does give summarised balance sheets and profit-and-loss (income) accounts from a sample of companies of different sizes. There are, however, considerable drawbacks and limitations to these figures. In particular:

1. They relate to limited companies only.
2. The sample for small companies is very limited in scope. At best there are only some 360 companies in these samples.
3. The definitions of sizes for the groups and capital and profit are

Table 8.1 Balance-sheet structure, 1975 (per cent of total assets/liabilities)

	Manufacturing			Non-manufacturing				All small companies				Large companies
	Smaller	Medium small	Total	Smaller	Medium Small	Total	Smaller	Medium small	Total	
Fixed assets													
Tangible fixed assets, net	29.4	26.6	27.4	33.0	34.0	33.5	32.0	30.3	31.1	36.2
Goodwill	0.4	0.6	0.5	0.1	1.7	0.9	0.2	1.2	0.7	3.2
Investment in unconsolidated subsidiaries	—	1.9	1.3	0.2	0.9	0.5	0.1	1.4	0.8	0.3
Total fixed assets, net	**29.8**	**29.0**	**29.2**	**33.3**	**36.7**	**34.9**	**32.4**	**32.8**	**32.7**	**39.7**
Current assets													
Stocks and work in progress	21.5	32.6	29.4	25.7	27.9	26.7	24.6	30.2	27.8	27.5
Trade and other debtors, etc.	34.8	34.5	34.6	28.7	28.2	28.4	30.3	31.3	30.9	23.3
Investments	3.5	0.8	1.6	1.5	1.9	1.7	2.0	1.4	1.6	4.5
Cash and short-term deposits	10.4	3.1	5.2	10.9	5.4	8.3	10.7	4.2	7.1	5.0
Total Current Assets and investments	**70.2**	**71.0**	**70.8**	**66.7**	**63.3**	**65.1**	**67.6**	**67.2**	**67.3**	**60.3**
Total fixed and current assets	**100.0**	**100.0**	**100.0**	**100.0**	**100.0**	**100.0**	**100.0**	**100.0**	**100.0**	**100.0**
Current liabilities													
Bank overdrafts and loans	6.8	10.4	9.4	12.7	16.5	14.5	11.1	13.4	12.4	9.7
Short-term loans	2.6	0.6	1.2	2.9	2.6	2.8	2.8	1.6	2.1	3.0
Trade and other creditors	35.7	29.5	31.3	34.6	29.7	32.3	34.9	29.6	31.9	25.2
Dividends and interest due	0.5	0.9	0.7	0.8	0.6	0.7	0.7	0.7	0.7	1.0
Current taxation	3.8	3.4	3.5	2.3	3.3	2.8	2.7	3.4	3.1	2.3
Total current liabilities	**49.4**	**44.7**	**46.1**	**53.3**	**52.7**	**53.0**	**52.3**	**48.7**	**50.3**	**41.1**
Net current assets	20.8	26.2	24.7	13.4	10.6	12.1	15.3	18.4	17.1	19.2
Total net assets	**50.6**	**55.3**	**53.9**	**46.7**	**47.3**	**47.0**	**47.7**	**51.3**	**49.7**	**58.9**

Capital and reserves									
Shareholders' interest									
Ordinary shares	5.8	10.7	9.3	6.3	9.1	7.6	6.1	9.9	8.3	11.6
Preference, etc. shares	0.6	0.9	0.8	0.3	0.4	0.4	0.4	0.7	0.5	0.7
Capital and revenue reserves	28.8	27.6	28.0	20.9	23.5	22.1	23.0	25.5	24.4	26.8
Total shareholders' interest	**35.1**	**39.2**	**38.0**	**27.4**	**33.1**	**30.1**	**29.5**	**36.1**	**33.3**	**39.1**
Loans from directors	8.3	0.8	3.0	12.3	0.6	6.8	11.2	0.7	5.3	—
Other long-term loans	1.1	6.8	5.1	3.7	6.4	5.0	3.0	6.6	5.0	10.3
Deferred taxation	6.1	8.1	7.5	3.3	7.1	5.1	4.0	7.6	6.0	7.4
Minority interest in subsidiaries	—	0.4	0.3	—	0.1	0.1	—	0.2	0.1	2.1
Total capital and reserves	**50.6**	**55.3**	**53.9**	**46.7**	**47.3**	**47.0**	**47.7**	**51.3**	**49.7**	**58.9**
Total capital and liabilities	**100.0**	**100.0**	**100.0**	**100.0**	**100.0**	**100.0**	**100.0**	**100.0**	**100.0**	**100.0**
£ billion	3.0	7.4	10.5	8.4	7.4	15.8	11.4	14.9	26.3	79.2

Notes:
1. Smaller companies: Capital employed is less than £250,000.
   Medium-small: Capital employed is £250,000 and over, up to about £4m.
2. Capital employed is: Total capital and reserves and minority shareholders interests plus deferred tax plus bank loans and overdrafts, long term and short term loans plus net amount due to other group members.
3. Large companies used for comparison purposes here are: 'Large listed and unlisted companies in manufacturing distribution and certain other services'. Their data were taken from *Business Monitor (Company Finance)* for the same year.

Source: Wilson Report *Interim Report on the Financing of Small Firms*, Cmnd 7503, HMSO, 1979.

Table 8.2 Owners' capital as percentage of total assets, 1975

	Manufacturing			Non-manufacturing			Total		
	Smaller	Medium small	All small companies	Smaller	Medium small	All small companies	Smaller	Medium small	All small companies	Large companies
Ordinary and preference shares	6.4	11.6	10.0	6.6	9.5	8.0	6.5	10.6	8.8	12.3
Total shareholder's interests	35.1	39.2	38.0	27.4	33.1	30.1	29.5	36.1	33.3	39.1
Total shareholder's interests including loans from directors	43.4	40.0	41.0	39.7	33.7	36.9	40.7	36.8	38.6	39.1

Source: Table 8.1.

Table 8.3 Gearing Ratios*, 1975

	Manufacturing			Non-manufacturing			Total			
	Smaller	Medium small	All small companies	Smaller	Medium small	All small companies	Smaller	Medium small	All small companies	Large companies
Long term										
External long-term loans	1.1	6.8	5.1	3.7	6.4	5.0	3.0	6.6	5.0	10.3
Short and long term										
External short- and long-term loans and bank overdraft	10.5	17.8	15.7	19.3	25.5	22.3	16.9	21.6	19.5	23.0
External short- and long-term loans and bank overdraft and trade creditors	46.2	47.3	47.0	53.9	55.2	54.6	51.8	51.2	51.4	48.2

*Expressed as percentage of total assets.
Source: Table 8.1

not quite consistent with those in the Wilson Report. More specifically, for the 1982 *Business Monitor MA3* figures:

Size Large companies: Capital greater than £4.16m
         Medium companies: Capital between £100,000 and £4.16m
         Small companies: Capital less than £100,000

Capital itself is defined as: Shares, reserves, minority interests, deferred tax, all loans and overdrafts (this definition does tie up with the 1975 Wilson figures).

The problems of size notwithstanding, it is still possible to make some useful comparisons between the *MA3* figures and those in the Wilson Report. Tables 8.4 and 8.5 set the latest (1982) figures from the 17th edition of *MA3* against the figures in the Wilson Report for both 'all industries (excluding oil)' and 'manufacturing industries'. A common form basis, with total assets, and total current liabilities and financing, each at 100, is used for ease of comparison.

The 'all industries (excluding oil)' figures show that both *MA3* and the Wilson Report indicate that small companies have, in relation to large companies:

- smaller net tangible assets
- greater debtors
- greater bank loan, overdrafts and short-term loans
- much greater creditors: the *MA3* figures showing a larger gap than the 1975 Wilson figures so that the difference is increasing
- less shareholders' interest – and again the difference is increasing
- less debentures, mortgages and long-term loans: the 1982 *MA3* figures show a clear gap; the 1975 Wilson figures are less clear because of problems in definition and the grouping of these items

The Wilson Report did not include comparable figures for large companies, as such, in manufacturing industries. Table 8.5, nevertheless, does confirm, so far as it goes, that much the same differences apply when the companies in the sample are restricted solely to those in manufacturing. In particular smaller companies show smaller net tangible assets and shareholders interests, and higher debtors and creditors.

From the point of view of the use of funds it is evident that small businesses put a much higher proportion into working capital (mainly stocks and debtors) than do large businesses. They invest a

Table 8.4 Balance sheets – all industries (excluding oil)

	1982 (MA3) Large	1982 (MA3) Small & medium	1975 (WILSON) Large	1975 (WILSON) Small & medium	1975 (WILSON) Medium-small
FIXED ASSETS (FA)					
Net tangible assets	40.1	31.1	36.2	31.1	30.3
Intangible assets	1.1	0.6	3.2	0.7	1.2
Investment in unconsol' subs	0.6	0.3	0.3	0.8	1.4
TOTAL NET FIXED ASSETS	41.8	32.0	39.7	32.6	32.9
CURRENT ASSETS & INVESTMENTS (CA)					
Stocks & work in progress	22.8	26.2	27.5	27.8	30.2
Debtors, prepayments, grants	23.5	30.3	23.3	30.9	31.3
Investments	5.4	1.9	4.5	1.6	1.4
Cash, short-term deposits & tax	6.6	9.6	5.0	7.1	4.2
TOTAL CURRENT ASSETS & INVESTMENTS (CA)	58.3	68.0	60.3	67.4	67.1
TOTAL FA + CA	100.0	100.0	100.0	100.0	99.9
CURRENT LIABILITIES (CL)					
Bank loans overdrafts & short-term loans	13.7	17.7	12.7	14.5	15.0
Creditors and accruals	28.4	40.8	25.2	31.9	29.6
Dividends & interest due	1.0	0.8	1.0	0.7	0.7
Current taxation	2.4	1.5	2.3	3.1	3.4
TOTAL CLs	45.5	60.8	41.2	50.2	48.7
FINANCED by:					
Shareholders' interest	44.5	35.0	39.1	33.3	36.0
Minority shareholders	2.8	0.1	2.1	0.1	0.2
Deferred taxation	1.4	2.9	7.4	6.0	7.6
Debentures, mortgages & long-term loans	5.8	1.2	10.3	10.3	7.3
TOTAL FINANCING	54.5	39.2	58.9	49.7	51.1
TOTAL CL & FINANCING	100.	100.0	100.1	99.9	99.8

Source: *Business Monitor MA3*, HMSO.
Note: There has been some regrouping of figures required for ease of presentation.

Table 8.5 Balance sheet – manufacturing industries

	1982 (MA3) Large	1982 (MA3) Small & medium	1975 (WILSON) Large	1975 (WILSON) Small & medium	1975 (WILSON) Medium-small
FIXED ASSETS (FA)					
Net tangible assets	36.0	28.4		27.4	26.6
Intangible assets	1.2	0.3		0.5	0.6
Investments in unconsol'd subs	0.7	0.6		1.3	1.9
TOTAL NET FIXED ASSETS	37.9	29.3		29.2	29.1
CURRENT ASSETS AND INVESTMENTS (CA)					
Stocks & work in progress	25.6	25.0		29.4	32.6
Debtors, prepayments, grants	25.2	34.8	N/A	34.6	34.5
Investments	5.2	2.0		1.6	0.8
Cash, short-term deposits & tax	6.7	8.9		5.2	3.1
TOTAL CA & INVESTMENTS	62.1	70.7		70.8	71.0
TOTAL FA + CA	100.0	100.0		100.0	100.1
CURRENT LIABILITIES (CL)					
Bank loans, overdrafts & short term loans	13.1	14.4		10.6	11.0
Creditors and accruals	28.0	37.7		31.3	29.5
Dividends & interest due	0.9	1.8		0.7	0.9
Current taxation	2.7	1.6		3.5	3.4
TOTAL CLs	44.7	55.5		46.1	44.8
FINANCED BY			N/A		
Shareholders' interest	44.3	39.5		38.0	39.2
Minority shareholders	3.4	0.1		0.3	0.4
Deferred taxation	1.3	3.7		7.5	8.1
Debentures, mortgages & long-term loans	6.2	1.2		8.1	7.6
TOTAL FINANCING	55.2	44.5		53.9	55.3
TOTAL CL & FINANCING	99.9	100.0		100.0	100.1

Note: There is a small error in one of the figures under Current Assets in the first column. The original figures given in MA3 do not add up. There is no way of telling where the error lies.

Source: *Business Monitor MA3*, HMSO.

correspondingly smaller proportion in net tangible assets (mainly fixed assets).

This situation finds an almost exact parallel in the supply of funds. The 1982 *MA3* figures for 'all industries (excluding oil)' show that small businesses have some 15 per cent more of their total funding from current liabilities (mainly creditors) than large. There is, of course, a corresponding reduction in the funding from other, long-term financing (mainly shareholders' interests). Much the same comments apply when we restrict the firms in the analysis to the manufacturing industry only.

In this chapter we are not concerned with the disparity between the use of funds whether in fixed assets or in working capital. The UK Census of Production figures year after year confirm that the investment per employee in fixed assets rises with size of firm. Many larger firms obviously do have a high investment in plant, machinery and other fixed assets. Only large firms can produce large products such as ships, cars and machinery. To do so they do need to have massive investment in plant. Small firms tend to operate more in the service sector and such firms do not need much fixed asset investment. In saying that small firms' proportionate investment in working capital is high we are merely reflecting this obvious fact. In Chapter 19, on the management of working capital, we go into the operational control of stock and debtors in small firms in some depth.

The disparity between the supply of funds through long-term capital and through creditor financing as between small and large firms is, however, very much a matter to which we need to address ourselves here.

For many years now, small businesses have been the subject of much interest and research. Survey after survey has shown that when small business managers are asked to say what business problems they regard as the most important, they have placed adequate long-term funding very high on their list. At one time the bank manager was seen as the villain: when he did lend them money it was typically at rates of interest some 1 per cent or so higher than for large corporations, and he was often loathe to lend money even at these rates. The *MA3* figures do not show any great disparity between the short-term money (bank loans, overdrafts and other short-term loans) supplied to manufacturing small or large firms. Debenture money is supplied in slightly larger proportions to large firms but the disparity is not great. In our book *Small Business in Europe*, we quoted extensively from the Economist Intelligence Units 10-country survey of small businesses among other sources, and concluded that no longer can small businesses in the UK see themselves as inadequately funded by external bank or equity capital. So for an explanation of the greater creditor financing of small businesses than large we need to look beyond the simple explanation that if small businesses cannot get other adequate external funding it must be from creditor money. Perhaps the corresponding imbalance between shareholders' interest funding of small and large businesses is the reason. Certainly we need to look at the provision of share capital to small businesses. Initially we need to consider briefly the forms and types of share capital and the institutional and other sources of supply of this capital.

Share capital

Any business, whatever its legal form, requires 'permanent capital' of some sort principally to finance its 'permanent assets'. However, as the scale of operations expands, sole traders and partnerships will increasingly be attracted towards the formation of a limited company, not only for the reasons outlined in Chapter 9, but also because most providers of outside finance prefer to lend to companies. This is for two reasons. First, the scope of action of the directors will be restricted by the Companies Acts in the interest of safeguarding all creditors and, secondly, it is a convenient vehicle for lending. It is a legal entity with unlimited life, the liability of whose shareholders is limited to the amount of capital they have subscribed.

Forms of share capital

A limited company, whether 'private' or 'public', will normally have share capital. The amount of share capital that a company is 'authorised' to issue is set down in its Memorandum of Association. The amount of 'issued' share capital is limited to this amount, though even when shares are issued not all of them may be paid for (called 'paid up' or 'subscribed'). It is the issued share capital, whether paid up or not, that is the extent of the shareholders' liability in the event of the company going into liquidation.

There are basically two forms of share capital:

ORDINARY SHARES

These are fixed units or shares of the common fund of the company. They give the holder a proportionate interest in the dividends declared by the directors from the residual profits of the company after paying interest, taxation and any preference dividends. They also give the holder a proportionate interest in the net assets of the business – in a liquidation ordinary shareholders get what is left after all creditors and preference shareholders have been repaid in full. It used to be the practice occasionally to issue non-voting shares, but all shares now will normally carry with them the right to attend and vote at all meetings of the company and, in theory, elect the board of directors, approve the dividends proposed, approve auditors, and even the policies of the board.

PREFERENCE SHARES

These are shares that have a preferential claim on the profits and assets of a business over and above those of the ordinary shareholders. The dividend on a preference share is limited to a fixed percentage of the face value of the share (the amount stated on the share certificate). Preference shareholders have no legal right to a dividend if the directors choose not to declare one, but they always have priority over ordinary shareholders if dividends are paid. Most preference share are 'cumulative', which means that unpaid preference dividends must be accumulated and made good before any ordinary dividends can be paid. Preference shareholders also have priority over ordinary shareholders in the event of liquidation, but they will only be paid the face value of their shares. Some preferences shares are 'redeemable', normally at their face value at a stated date. Others are 'convertible', which allows them to be converted into ordinary shares, normally at the shareholder's option.

There is a hybrid form of share called the 'convertible preferred ordinary share.' This carries the right to either a fixed or a variable dividend and allows a company to pay dividends on this class of share without obliging the ordinary shareholders to take a dividend which might, for tax reasons, be unattractive to them. These shares are most commonly issued to institutions such as Investors in Industry which have special dividend requirements. When converted into ordinary shares, the right to these fixed dividends is lost and the shares become the same as ordinary shares.

Preference shares are legally another form of share capital but, as can be seen, they are very similar to debt or loans. However, unlike interest on loans, the fixed dividend is paid out of 'after-tax' income and therefore suffers a tax disadvantage, making it a relatively expensive form of finance. Large companies no longer issue preference shares to the public: indeed, over the years existing preference shareholders have been offered debenture capital as a substitute. Some institutions such as Investors in Industry are still keen on taking up preference capital, because preference shares normally carry no voting rights unless dividends are in arrears. Thus the institution can obtain a large equity stake without taking control of the business from the hands of the businessman. Of course, it also improves the security of their investment, compared with ordinary shares. However, while ordinary shares are riskier than preference shares, and fixed loans, they are potentially more profitable, generating dividends and capital gains.

Sources of share capital

The first source of any share capital will be the entrepreneur himself and perhaps a friend of his or a relative or both. If the company grows, the shareholders may think about subscribing more capital. This is an obvious first consideration for additional funds since the individuals concerned may well already be heavily committed to the company, and may benefit directly from the investment through salaries, dividends or capital gains on their shares. However, there may be disadvantages. It could mean that the individuals become too tied to the company and its fortunes; if it fails, their wealth could disappear overnight. It could cause capital transfer tax problems.

The next possibility is to seek new shareholders, but since a 'private' company may not offer shares to the general public, this will probably entail approaching relatives or friends. Many of the arguments about spreading risk apply equally to family holdings. We must again bear in mind that much of this family wealth and backing is drying up – the Wilson Committee's 'Aunt Agatha is dead' problem. Also, the problem with friends is that they often don't *remain* friends. As Shakespeare put it in *Hamlet*, 'Neither a borrower nor a lender be: for loan oft loses both itself and friend'. An almost inevitable consequence of getting another backer will be that he will require a seat on the board and a say in the running of the business. He may even require a director's fee, an expense account and a company car!

There are two further possibilities. The first is to sell shares directly to institutions such as venture capital institutions, merchant banks, equity subsidiaries of clearing banks, or insurance companies. These provide long-term loan and equity finance for both start-up and existing businesses. They will normally take a longer-term view than the banks themselves and will be willing to invest in riskier opportunities, if the return is sufficient. We deal with these insitutions in a following section.

The other possibility is to sell shares to institutions or individuals through some form of share quotation or stock marketing listing. Until 1980 this was prohibitively expensive for small businesses. It was reputed to cost at least a quarter of a million pounds for a public company to make a share issue. It had to pay investigating accountant's fees, bankers' fees, underwriters' fees and advertising expenses – and this ignored the cost to the company of its own managers' time. The cost is now likely to be £300,000 or more. Although the stock exchange minimum size for a listing is a market capitalisation of £0.7 million, in practice the economic minimum is over £5 million, equivalent to pre-tax profits of over £1 million. In addition there was, and still is, an accounting requirement of a minimum of five years audited and unqualified accounts. Clearly, a full listing on the stock exchange has never been a serious possibility for a small business.

In November 1980 the Unlisted Securities Market (USM) was set up to allow small businesses access to a method of obtaining a share 'quotation' at relatively low cost. The cost of a USM listing has been around £180,000 for a placing, & some £220,000 for an offer for sale. There are over 350 companies on the USM now. In the USM only 10 per cent (a guideline figure only) of the company's shares needs to be made available to the public (not 25 per cent as with a full listing) and substantial private companies wishing to raise share capital can arrange to place minority stakes with institutions such as investment trusts or pension funds for fees of around 1 per cent of the amount raised. Such institutions are unlikely to interfere in the day-to-day running of the company.

Although there has been no minimum size requirement for the USM, most companies must have had a trading record of three years and no audit qualification. A profit of around £300,000 is usually regarded as a necessary prerequisite. The stock exchange has said that it would also be prepared to accept companies seeking finance to put fully researched projects into production - thus suggesting a limited venture capital role. Once listed, USM companies have had to sign an undertaking, which contains some 20 provisions; these are virtually identical to the standard stock exchange listing agreement, most of which are designed to enforce a minimum standard of regular disclosure of the company's affairs.

Clearly the USM has only been a real option for the larger small company. The Stock Exchange's own idea of a 'small' company is one with a capital of at least £100 million! This neither corresponds to the definitions discussed in this book, or the conventional view held by most people. The USM has had a limited success. For some businesses, however, it has only served as a means by which the proprietors have tried to realise the money tied up in their firms. Many proprietors have become paper millionaires! We use the term 'paper', because the share price, and with it the value of their holding, would fall dramatically if they tried to get their money out by selling all their shares!

The USM has not been of much use for greenfield ventures or very young companies. It has also failed to stop the growth of the Over the Counter[1] (OTC) market. The Stock Exchange has been anxious to curtail the unregulated activities of part of this market for a while. In 1983 the arrival of the Business Expansion Scheme (BES) was another unwelcome factor. A company loses its BES status if it is traded on the USM, but an OTC quotation is, of course, still possible. For some while it had been evident that there was a need for a third tier on the investment market. In January 1987 the Stock Exchange's third market opened.

A company proposing to raise equity capital on the third market requires only one year's accounts (which must not have been qualified). No expected level of pre-tax profits is required. The costs of raising the issue are typically of the order of £50,000–£100,000. However, wide variations in this cost figure do occur. No minimum percentage of equity is currently laid down for a third market company. Since tax relief is available under the Business Expansion Scheme many new investors may find this third market to their liking.

Third market shares are classified as Delta shares by the Stock Exchange. This means that on brokers TOPIC screens no market price is likely to be available for immediate dealing. For the investor it is questionable if the third market provides a genuine forum for trading. One of the main problems of the USM was the lack of an easily accessible market in the shares. The same problem of illiquidity is likely to haunt the investor in the third market. If there is no clearly available exit route the private investor must have many doubts. Institutional investors are unlikely to be much interested in the third market. They do not deal in small amounts of equity and they, too, like to be able to get out fairly quickly if they want to.

The 1986 Financial Services Act requires that share transactions on the open market are carried out by a Recognised Investment Exchange (R.I.E). The Stock Exchange (R.I.E) has, as we have noted, for a long while been concerned to curtail or regulate OTC activities so far

---

[1] See Appendix 1 for some estimates of the costs of an offer for sale and a placing on the OTC market.

as possible. The OTC market in the UK - unlike the corresponding OTC Market in the USA, which is both widespread and, on the whole, well run – does contain some undesirable elements. Private investors can be pushed by unscrupulous operators into buying shares they do not want, and which they then cannot sell. The aim of the Stock Exchange's third market is to provide a genuine market for both the company and the investor. We have already seen that there are some problems for the investor. For the company it is most important to choose the right sponsor. Around 30 to 40 brokers and members of the Stock Exchange are prepared to act as sponsors for new companies wishing to issue new shares in this market. Sponsors have heavy responsibilities connected with the issue. These include:

Assessing the suitability of the company.

Ensuring that the company complies with the advertising and other requirements for entry: one of the main savings in the costs of a flotation in the third market is that only one box advertisement in a national daily paper is required.

Arranging the issuing of a circular to the shareholders with details of directors shareholdings, options and other specified information.

Complying with the legal responsibilities required under the Financial Services Act and making other administrative arrangements.

Maintaining a file on the company.

Ensuring that the spread of ownership of the company's shares continues to be adequate to allow an effective and orderly market in them.

It is evident that for a growing small company requiring equity finance from the third market it is essential to 'shop around' for a suitable sponsor. The costs of a flotation, though less than those for the USM, are still substantial, and may be out of reach of many medium-sized small companies. For such a business, still requiring equity finance, it may still be necessary and desirable to look to venture capital organisations for direct funding.

Venture capital

Venture capital is a term coined in the USA, but its origins are much older. In the fifteenth century Queen Isabella of Spain provided venture capital for Colombus, an investment that paid off handsomely! A century later Shakespeare provided a definition of a venture in his *Merchant of Venice*: 'a thing not in his power to bring to pass, but sway'd and fashion'd by the hand of heaven'. Fortunately, venture capitalists these days are more approachable than the Queen of Spain and do not demand their pound of flesh, at least not in quite the same way as did Shylock! In essence, venture capital is finance for new or relatively new, high-risk, high-profit-orientated projects or companies. Banks, pension funds and investment trusts and other major financial institutions have now all set up their own specialist venture capital organisations.

The market has been dominated by the Industrial and Commercial Finance Corporation (ICFC). Formed in 1945, ICFC is now part of the Finance for Industry (FFI) group, itself renamed more recently as Investors in Industry (3Is). 3Is is owned by the clearing banks and (15 per cent) by the Bank of England. 3Is provides small firms with both equity and loan finance, and though it is prepared to lend between £5,000 and £2 million or more is really looking for growth companies that will earn profits of £100,000 or more. Typically the finance provided takes the form of a package combining equity capital with preference or medium, or long-term loan capital – always at fixed rates of interest, and often convertible into equity. 3Is and its subsidiaries insist on keeping a minority equity stake in the companies they invest in, arguing that to do otherwise would destroy much of the incentive and drive required for the businessmen to succeed. They rarely require a seat on the board but have a network of controllers, normally accountants or business graduates, who monitor client's performance. However, they rarely interfere with a client's business. The redemption of a loan is individually negotiable, as indeed is the particular capital structure provided for individual companies. It is their policy never to require personal guarantees from businessmen. Investors in Industry is willing to consider all high-risk ventures, including start-ups. It is often willing to make a further investment, and is fairly flexible about realising its investment. Indeed, it has been noted that Investors in Industry support companies often have higher than average gearing. Investors in Industry has about 20 offices and, in addition to loan and equity backing, can provide leasing and hire purchase, sale and leaseback, and corporate advisory services.

Investors in Industry has one subsidiary, Technical Development Capital, which specialises in providing capital for new or recently established firms engaged in developing entirely new products. Investors in Industry also manages the Estate Duties Investment Trust, which is a listed public company, whose sole function is to purchase minority stakes in unlisted companies to enable shareholders to raise sufficient cash to meet tax and other personal liabilities without having to relinquish control of their company.

The British Technology Group (BTG) is another similar organisation, formed in 1981 by the merger of the National Research and Development Corporation and the National Enterprise Board. It has the aim of providing finance for innovative investment. Rather than provide start-up capital, it has often encouraged independent innovators to have their ideas accepted for development and exploitation by some larger organisation which has the necessary resources. Not all innovators are happy with this sort of arrangement. However, assistance can often be given as joint venture finance, with repayment by a royalty of sales, and this does not threaten an entrepreneur's independence. About half the companies in which BTG has invested have been small businesses within our meaning of the term.

Private sector venture capital institutions

If the costs of a third market quotation are too high, or a suitable sponsor cannot be found, the small businessman requiring equity finance will probably look first to Investors in Industry or one of its offshoots. If, for some reason, this, too, is not satisfactory, he will need to look at private sector institutions.

Merchant banks have been the traditional suppliers of equity capital. They tend to provide funds for larger private companies: A loan of £200,000 is a common minimum. However, they do provide short-, medium- and long-term finance as well as invoice-discounting services, and they do have stakes in a number of venture capital institutions. They will handle a private placing of shares to a select number of institutional investors. However, the costs are fairly high, and there are many disadvantages in having no issued share capital available to the public.

Insurance companies are a useful source of funds for some sole traders and partnerships. They provide mortgages (loans secured against property), often linked to endowment policies, secured on the lives of the younger partners or directors. Usually such loans are not renewable, and premiums, unlike interest payments, are not tax-deductible and can therefore prove expensive.

All these institutions are really looking for a return of 25 per cent or more and an exit route that allows them to get out in some 5 years or so. Their investment – as they see it – is an investment in management.

All the major clearing banks supply venture capital to growing companies either directly or through some of their many financial subsidiaries. The packages that are offered are wide ranging and flexible. Sometimes the main funding is through a 'capital loan'. Typically loans under such a scheme are available for sums between about £25,000 and £250,000. These loans rank only in front of the shareholders/directors interests. They do not normally require security. The package includes an option for the bank to subscribe for shares in the small business. This option is always for a minority of the shares (usually less than 25 per cent), leaving control of the company firmly in the hands of the proprietor. The option arrangements include provisions for the bank to protect its position as a potential shareholder. Typical provisions provide that:

1. There will be no changes in the capital structure of the company without the bank's agreement.
2. Transfer of shares in the company wil be restricted.
3. The bank will have the right to appoint a director to the board of the company (this right is not usually exercised).
4. Minimum dividends will be paid on the company's ordinary shares under certain conditions.
5. The company will furnish such information as to its affairs as the bank requires.

The bank will maintain a relatively close relationship with the company. For a fee of around 1 per cent of the capital loan it will provide guidance in preparing monthly accounts and financial plans and projections. The bank visits the business regularly and generally takes a much more active part in the affairs of the company than it would do if the funding were solely by way of a traditional medium- or long-term loan.

Many private sector, non-institutional, providers of equity finance (such as Equity Capital for Industry) also now exist. Their aim is capital growth. They invest up to around 45 per cent in the equity of the business. They are even more highly involved in the management of the business. This does not mean a day-by-day interference in management decisions, but does imply a very positive contribution to the development of business strategy, and to medium- and long-term financial planning.

These private venture capital providers have the management expertise and the financial resources required to back a young business requiring its first round of equity capital. Their skills are based on the commercial and industrial background of their investment managers gained from experience in this specialist area of finance. They form close relationships with the management of the companies they back, and are prepared to commit considerable time and effort in helping to resolve the organisational and administrative problems that inevitably occur in an expanding small business.

These venture capital providers do not work on predetermined standard packages for their clients. Each package is tailored to each individual proposal. Within the organisation's own aims of achieving a satisfactory return on capital for the perceived risk, small business proprietors' and managers' personal objectives will be met as far as possible.

As a minority investor in an unlisted company, the venture capital provider will require the inclusion of certain standard protection provisions, either in the companies articles of association or in the form of a written shareholders' agreement. Sometimes board representation for a member of the venture capital providers' team, or, if more appropriate, through an independent, but mutually agreed, appointee, will be required. The aim of this representation is more to assist in helping constructively in long range planning and with major investment decisions than to act as a financial 'watch-dog'.

Venture capital providers have developed recently considerable skills in arranging and financing management 'buy-outs'. A buy-out can give management the opportunity to acquire a significant stake in their own business on realistic terms.

It is evident that there are now many providers of equity capital. Indeed the provision of venture capital is expanding rapidly, particularly since the introduction of the business start-up scheme. It is probably true to say that a suitable project should have no problems finding venture capital backers if it can support the costs of servicing that capital. There are now so many potential backers that a financing package to suit most entrepreneurs can be found if only the trouble is taken to find the right one.

Appendix for the entrepreneur on the practical problems of choosing and living with an institution

We have already talked about the problems of using individuals as sources of finance for the business. However, there are problems in choosing and living with institutions. Which businessman would choose to have only one, exclusive supplier of some vitally important component? Finance is just another, vitally important, component to your business, and if your supplier has problems, whether of his own making or not, he may pass them on to you. The depression of the early 1970s brought this problem home to a number of companies as banks started to decrease the facilities they offered to customers. The moral is to have a diversified range of funding from different institutions.

Some businessmen may have difficulty in finding any backers at all and they will have to approach a number of institutions to obtain any kind of offer. However, with a properly presented case, you ought to be able to shop around and find a 'best buy' to suit your own requirements. Not only do interest rates vary from institution to institution, but so also do lending characteristics. Some institutions have definite policies about how long they wish to be involved with a business. Not all offer equity finance, and those that do have different policies about director representation and intervention. The moral is clear: always shop around.

As we detailed in Chapter 4, the financing requirements of 'stable' and 'growth' small businesses, are likely to be very different. The 'stable' small business will have limited funding requirements, and may never need to seek extra equity or venture capital funds. It will tend to be the 'growth' small businesses that require equity and venture capital funds, and it may be wise for these businesses to approach venture capital institutions at the start-up stage, if the project size warrants it, and build up a good working relationship with them over the years. It is important to remember that, other than for straight loans, long-term venture capital packages can be complicated and difficult to unwind; it is therefore important to choose an institution and a package that you can live with over many years. This involves being clear in your own mind what are your own, personal, objectives and what are the objectives of the venture capitalist – and making sure that the two do not conflict.

You may have strong feelings about sharing ownership and control of your business, in which case it may be wise to promote a venture capital package that involves preference shares. If you wish to regain control of your company at a later date, you may wish to repurchase any shares that you now issue. You could issue redeemable preference shares or come to an agreement over the repurchase of ordinary shares. Often businessmen will not have the personal funds to repurchase shares, but the 1985 Companies Act does allow a company to repurchase its own shares in certain circumstances. If you feel strongly on this point, you will be attracted towards institutions that do not require board representation.

It is well to consider the objectives of the venture capital institutions. They will be interested in generating income from their investment by way of dividends or interest and, over the long run, through capital gains. But will the venture capital institution take dividends or interest, and when will these be paid? Although the venture capitalist may require dividends, it could be in your interest not to take them, because of tax problems. Indeed, it may not be in the interest of the company to pay dividends or interest in its early years. A flexible financing package involving equity and deferred interest terms or convertible loans might be the answer.

How will the venture capital institution realise its capital gain, and over what period? This is a major problem for the venture capitalist, since it may take some time before a company can obtain a quotation, even on the USM or third market. If the institution is not willing to make this long-term commitment, it may be tempted to promote a merger with a larger company once the small business 'takes off'.

Since you will have to live with a venture capitalist for some time, the track record of the institution and the people you deal with are important considerations. The range of additional services that the institution provides might also be important to you. However, there are two sides to any relationship, and you would be well advised to keep the institution informed of the company's progress and problems even beyond the bounds of their written requirements from you. Send them regular financial statements. Meet them regularly to discuss your plans, particularly financing plans. If your business faces problems, let them know.

Presenting one's case for venture capital

In Chapter 6 we discussed the practicalities in the preparation and presentation of a case to a bank manager for overdraft facilities or short-term loans. Much more is expected in presenting a case for long-term capital or equity finance. Your backer must satisfy himself that you have the qualities to make your business succeed in the long run. The more complex the funding proposal, the more detailed the information the institutions will require. As we noted, the institution will not only be interested in the back-up documentation supporting your case, but more crucially it will assess your personal qualities, based upon your own track record, and on how you actually present your case to them.

Documentation

A FULL 'BUSINESS PLAN'. This is always a complex, lengthy document. We develop the accounting skills required to draw up the financial side of the plan in subsequent chapters. It involves undertaking a 'position audit' and translating this into a plan of action for your business. This means, of course, giving details of your company, its products and management, details of your industry, the competition and business risks you face. It involves translating market research into a marketing plan and a manufacturing plan, and bringing this all together into a financial plan which includes projected profit-and-loss accounts, balance-sheets and cash-flow statements. This should demonstrate that your venture is worth while, while also indicating the amount of financial backing required. In particular the venture capital backer will be interested in:

- RECENTLY AUDITED ACCOUNTS, if available. This adds credibility to your case. A backer will think very badly of a business which does not have up-to-date accounts; it is a sign of poor financial control and inadequate auditing. Backers will require to see up-to-date monthly management accounts, if available.
- STATEMENT OF ORDERS ON HAND. Again this adds credibility to your case. Comparisons with past years would be useful.
- DETAILS OF PATENTS, etc. This will demonstrate the extent to which the project is protected from attempts by competitors to copy the product.
- NAME OF ACCOUNTANTS, SOLICITORS, BANKERS involved with the business. Perhaps your business will already have demonstrated its ability to repay loans. All this adds to the credibility of your proposal.

Personal qualities

There is no question but that the most important factor in the mind of a potential backer is the quality of the management of a business, and for most small businesses this means the qualities of one person. Venture capitalists are looking for motivation and enthusiasm, ability and integrity.

To manage a growth business successfully requires a genuine desire to succeed, amounting almost to a need. It is not enough simply to be frustrated at your present workplace, or threatened with redundancy. You must want to be the cause of success. Success in a growing business is obtained through the efforts of others, and you must therefore be able to motivate and lead. You must be willing to take risks – but only moderate risks that you believe you can overcome. The technical development engineer who has a good product idea but really only wants to build and modify prototypes and is not interested in production and selling will not get venture capital backing without first teaming up with an individual with the other qualities necessary for success. Enthusiasm and drive must, however, be tinged with a strong sense of realism in taking a market view of the business and its potential. Arnold Weinstock once said that all successful companies are run by people who understand the market.

Ability is important, and can be demonstrated to a potential backer through your past experience. Technical ability, along with patents and your own know-how, will protect the project from attempts by competitors to copy it. Management ability will help with the implementation of your plans. However, no single person can have all the managerial skills and qualities required, and it is essential to take a realistic view of your own personal weaknesses, and where possible compensate for them.

The presentation of your business plan will serve as a vehicle for demonstrating these qualities and convincing your potential backers of your competence. First impressions are important, but demonstrated knowledge of the key area in your business plan will go a long way towards generating the confidence that institutions need to have before lending money.

Finally, two points to bear in mind. First, institutional investors face many of the same pressures as bank managers, and therefore it is usually better to seek more funds than immediate circumstances call for. Good projections are, of course, essential. While it will be disastrous to underestimate capital requirements, it can be expensive to overestimate them. It is often possible to arrange to 'call down' (use up) finance, as you require it, rather than be given it all at once, thus catering for contingencies while avoiding paying for unnecessary finance.

Secondly, the processing of applications for large amounts of money takes time: not because the institutions are necessarily bureaucratic, but because they need time to investigate your plan, and to go through the same thought process as you have to. Long-term financial needs have to be planned well in advance. Institutions will not be happy with urgent requests for funds.

Appendix 1 Over the counter (OTC) flotations

Rough estimates of minimum capital and cost are as follows:

	Offer for sale	*Placing*
Minimum capital offer	£300,000	£200,000
Cost	£180,000	£ 40,000

CHAPTER 9

Taxation and Allowances

INTRODUCTION	157
TAXATION OF THE SOLE TRADER	158
Income tax	158
Schedule DI and DII income	159
Capital allowances	162
Basis of assessments: tax payments	163
Relief for losses	165
Personal pension plans	165
National Insurance	166
TAXATION OF PARTNERSHIPS	166
Income allocation	166
Relief for losses	167
Change of partners	168
TAXATION OF COMPANIES	168
Corporation tax	168
Basis of assessment: tax payments	171
Restrictions on ACT set-off	171
Relief for losses	172
Business expansion scheme	173
Capital gains and losses on the sale of shares	173
Close and family companies	174
Retirement pensions	175
TAXATION AND BUSINESS	175
Should a business incorporate?	175
Taxation and business decisions	177
Tax-saving hints	178
TAXES BUSINESSES COLLECT FOR THE GOVERNMENT	179
VAT	179
Schedule E: Pay-As-You-Earn	181
National Insurance	183
Appendix 1 Current rates and allowances	185
Appendix 2 Car and fuel benefits	188
Appendix 3 National Insurance contributions	189

Introduction

Often the biggest worry for the small businessman is taxation. Not only must he account for the tax he owes on his own earnings, but he must also act as unpaid collector of taxes from his employees and customers. The sheer complexity of the tax system and the volume of forms that regularly need to be filled in can make him wonder whether he will have any time left for the real business problems he faces.

Most businessmen will have to deal with three separate departments:

- INLAND REVENUE: for income tax, corporation tax and National Insurance payments.
- DEPARTMENT OF HEALTH AND SOCIAL SECURITY for National Insurance matters.
- CUSTOMS AND EXCISE: for value-added tax (VAT).

The national tax-take reflects the importance of these different departments. In 1985 UK tax revenues totalled £135 billion. Table 9.1 shows how this was split between the different forms of taxation. You may draw some interesting conclusions from these figures. First, you may be surprised by the relatively small contribution of corporation tax. In fact, of the £9.1 billion, £3.8 billion (or 42 per cent) represents *advance corporation tax* which is really a withholding tax on dividend payments. So the true tax contribution of incorporated businesses is even less than it appears.

As you will see later in this chapter, the tax allowances and incentive to any form of business are quite generous, so with a little careful tax planning, the financial burden of taxation can be greatly reduced.

Secondly, you may be surprised by the large contribution made by National Insurance. National Insurance contributions are really just another tax. They are compulsory and not genuine 'insurance'. Over the last 20 years the National Insurance revenue has risen considerably, and this tax is now a major burden to any form of business. Not least because the size of the employers' contribution is seen by many as being effectively a tax on employment.

The small businessman has the choice of three major forms of business organisation: sole trader, partnership or limited company. The relative tax advantages of these different trading forms are dealt with later in this chapter. However, the form adopted affects the taxes the small businessman will pay.

Table 9.1 1985 tax revenue

	£ billion	%
INCOME TAXES		
Income tax	35.4	26.2
Corporation tax	9.1	6.7
Petroleum revenue tax	7.4	5.5
NATIONAL INSURANCE	24.1	17.9
EXPENDITURE TAXES		
Value added tax (VAT)	21.0	15.5
Drink and tobacco	8.5	6.3
Oil	6.2	4.6
Miscellaneous customs & excise	3.0	2.2
Motor vehicle duties	2.4	1.8
Other levies	2.1	1.6
LOCAL RATES	13.6	10.1
CAPITAL TAXES (capital gains tax, capital transfer tax)	2.1	1.6
	134.9	100.0

Source: Central Statistical Office, United Kingdom, *National Accounts. 1986* (Blue Book).

As a sole trader, a small businessman is treated as self-employed and liable to income tax on the profits of the business assessed under the rules relating to Schedule DI or DII income. As a partnership, business profits are taxed under the same rules and joint assessment to income tax is raised on the partnership.

As a limited company, the small businessman has to account monthly to the Inland Revenue for the Pay-As-You-Earn income tax due not only on his employee's salaries, but also on his own remuneration. The company must also pay corporation tax on its profits after expenses including salaries or directors' fees.

Taxation of the sole trader

Income tax

The sole trader pays income tax just like any individual. The profits on which income tax is assessed are drawn up on Inland Revenue rules relating to what is called Schedule DI or DII income. The basic rate of income tax is shown in Appendix 1. Because most taxpayers are entitled to some personal relief, such as the single person's allowance or married couple's relief, the average rate of income tax is somewhat less than the basic rate. The personal relief's currently available to individuals are shown in Appendix 1. In addition to these, mortgage interest payable is deductible in full on mortgages up to £30,000.

Taxable income (income after personal reliefs) in excess of a set threshold, usually revised annually, is taxed at a higher rate of tax. Appendix 1 shows this higher rate alongside the relevant taxable income band. It also shows the average rate of tax. As you can see, while the highest UK marginal tax rate on earned income is 40 per cent, the average rate of tax on that income will be considerably less than that. Many argue that higher marginal rates of tax discourage earning additional income (the *price effect*), while others argue that higher average rates merely force people to earn more income in order to maintain their after-tax income level (the *income effect*). The weight of the former argument led the government in 1979 to reduce the highest marginal rate of tax from 83 to 60 per cent.

Prior to 6 April 1984 there was a surcharge above the normal income tax rates on investment income, i.e., income mainly from dividends and interest. For 1983–4 this meant a surcharge of 15 per cent, if gross investment income exceeded £7,100, and thus the top investment income rate was (60+15)=75 per cent. This additional rate no longer applies to individuals.

Schedule DI and DII income

The sole trader may have income from a number of different sources. The following classes of income will be included for each tax year.

Schedule	Source
A	Land and buildings
C	Income from government securities
DI & II	Trades and professions
DIII	Interest
DIV & V	Overseas securities and possessions
DVI	Miscellaneous
E	Earnings from employment (Pay-As-You-Earn: PAYE)

Table 9.2 Schedule DI/II allowable business expenses

1. Cost of goods and materials bought for resale
2. Wages, salaries and pensions paid to employees plus staff welfare costs
3. Running costs of building (rents, rates, etc.)
4. Carriage, packing, delivery and discounts, etc.
5. Printing, stationery, telephone, postage, etc.
6. Insurance, advertising, trade subscriptions
7. Redundancy payments to employees
8. Professional and legal fees of a revenue nature, e.g. audit, bad debt collection
9. Various taxes and National Insurance payments
10. Travel and subsistence expenses for business trips but *not* the cost of travel between home and office (unless you also do business from home)
11. Entertaining staff
12. Gifts incorporating the company name *only* if the value to each recipient is under £10
13. Bad debts and specific bad debt provisions
14. Running expenses of motor vehicles, excluding any proportion for private use
15. Repairs to plant and machinery etc.
16. Interest and hire-purchase costs
17. Pre-trading expenditure of a revenue nature
18. Capital allowances

Each source of income has different rules relating to it. This section concerns only Schedule DI and DII income: the income that the small businessman will generate from his business activity.

The basis for arriving at taxable profits are the accounting profits for a particular year. However, there are certain business expenses which are not allowable for tax purposes. Equally there are certain allowances which are not related to normal accounting measures of income. This is only to be expected since tax officials are trying to enforce statutory regulations with the least possible amibiguity and accounting profit is open to a certain amount of manipulation.

Generally taxable profit takes into account all sales and increases in stock values during a 12-month period. Against this, a business may set all expenses of a revenue nature (as opposed to capital nature) which were incurred *wholly and exclusively* for business purposes, together with capital allowances for capital expenditure. This is considerably more liberal than the expenses allowed against the taxable income of business employees which have to be *wholly exclusively and NECESSARILY* incurred for work purposes. Thus, for example, the

Table 9.3 Schedule DI/II non-allowable business expenses

1. Expenses for private or domestic purposes; where there is an element of business use, then a proportion will be tax-allowable – for example, if a private dwelling is used for business purposes, the allowable proportion will not normally exceed two-thirds*
2. Capital expenditure and depreciation of plant, etc. (there are special rules relating to capital allowances)
3. Loss not connected with the business (there are special rules relating to losses arising from the business)
4. General provisions (e.g. for bad debts); only specific provisions are allowable
5. Drawing from the business
6. Payments of income tax, capital gains tax or corporation tax, etc.
7. Any annuity or other annual payments (other than interest)
8. Professional fees of a capital nature (e.g. relating to a new lease, designing a new building, advising on the purchase of a new business)
9. Any royalty payment from which you deduct income tax
10. Fines and related legal expenses
11. Political donations
12. Charitable donation unless entirely for business purposes
13. Entertaining customers

*However, in this case the dwelling may become liable to capital gains tax on disposal.

cost of travel from home to work is not allowable for employees (taxed under Schedule E, PAYE) but would be allowable for a sole trader if his home was also his 'place of business'. A list of those expenses typically allowable against Schedule DI/II income is given in Table 9.2 and some non-allowable expenses are shown in Table 9.3. Neither list is exhaustive.

Stocks, consisting of raw materials, manufactured components, part-finished products and unsold finished goods, are an important element in the calculation of business profit. Profits are increased by any excess of closing stock over opening stock and decreased by any deficit. It is obvious that stock valuation affects profit. Valuing opening stock more generously than closing stock can therefore decrease profits. Consequently the Island Revenue normally insists that opening and closing stock is valued on the same basis. The normal basis is the lower of cost or net realisable value. Cost is normally taken to ing stock more generously than closing stock can therefore decrease profits. Consequently the Inland Revenue normally insists that opening and closing stock is valued on the same basis. The normal basis is Chapter 12). 'Net realisable value' is what it is estimated would be obtained if the stock were sold in the normal course of business, less any expenses relating to the disposal.

Capital allowances

As already stated, book depreciation charged in the financial accounts and capital expenditures are not allowable expenses for tax purposes. In their place the government has substituted a system of capital allowances which in most cases is more generous than the normal book depreciation accounting treatment. Therefore, in the United Kingdom, unlike many foreign countries, a business's book depreciation policy does not affect its tax position.

The current rates of capital allowances are shown in Appendix 1. The capital allowances are computed according to the assets purchased and used in the annual accounting period. For example, if a sole trader were to purchase £5,000-worth of plant or machinery in the accounting year ending 31 December 1987, he could obtain capital allowances on the £5,000 spent in the tax year when these profits are assessed (see the following section on the basis of assessment). The cost of the plant and machinery purchased in the year is added to the tax written-down value of plant and machinery purchased in previous years (that is, original cost less allowances in previous years). The capital allowance is given on the resulting balance in this 'pool' of assets. The allowance for plant and machinery applies equally to new or second-hand equipment. Vehicles such as lorries and vans designed to carry goods, and those for hire to the public such as taxis, are treated as plant and machinery.

Cars costing under £8,000 receive the normal annual writing-down allowance and are put into their own 'pool' for calculating the allowance. However, tax law discriminates against the extravagant businessman who purchases vehicles costing over £8,000 and the allowance is restricted in any one year on each vehicle to £2,000. If the sole trader uses his car partly for private purposes, the Inland Revenue will probably restrict the allowances, allowing only a certain percentage of the capital allowance to be offset against the taxable profits of the business.

For example, if you were to purchase a car costing £10,000 and the Inland Revenue directed that 20 per cent of the use of the car is for private purposes, then the capital allowance available to the business would be as shown below:

	Year 1	Year 2	Year 3
Total allowance	£2,000 (restricted)	£(10,000–2,000) × 25% = £2,000	£(10,000–4,000) × 25% = £1,500
Available to the business (80%)	£1,600	£1,600	£1,200

Notice the allowances in years 2 and 3 are based upon 25 per cent of 'written-down' value. That is, the net asset value after previous allowances.

When you sell an item of plant or a vehicle, the excess of the sales receipts over the tax written-down value is taxed. Cars costing over £8,000 are dealt with individually. In the previous example, if you were to sell the car for £5,000 in year 4, the tax written-down value would be £4,500 (£10,000 − £2,000 − £2,000 − £1,500), and the total 'balancing charge', as it is called, would be £500 × 80 per cent = £400 (remember private use). Cars costing less than £8,000 and plant and machinery form two separate 'pools' and cash receipts are deducted from the appropriate pool's *total* tax written-down value.

Since the phasing out of 100 per cent first year allowances, a 'balancing charge' is not likely to arise unless all assets in a group are sold, e.g., on cessation of business.

If you buy plant, machinery or vehicles on hire purchase, the business is entitled to the full capital allowance on the capital portion of the total instalments as soon as the asset is brought into use. The interest portion is allowed against business profit as respective instalments are paid. If assets are leased, then only the lease expense is allowed against business profit as paid. Generally the capital allowances on leased assets go to the institution which leases out the asset.

In Enterprise Zones expenditure on industrial and commercial buildings attracts 100 per cent initial allowance although less than the full allowance may be claimed, in which case 25 per cent writing-down allowance is available (straight line basis).

Basis of assessment: tax payments

Employees, paying PAYE tax, are assessed on income in the year in which they receive it. This is called the current-year basis of assessment. *Sole traders and partnerships* are assessed on what is called the preceding-year basis of assessment. This can have important cash-flow implications for a business. On the preceding-year basis a business normally pays tax based upon the earnings during the accounting period which ended during the previous tax year. A tax year runs from 6 April to the following 5 April. Thus the 1987–8 income tax assessment is based upon earnings in the accounting period which ended in 1986–7. This tax would be paid in two equal instalments on 1 January 1988 and 1 July 1988.

For example, if a business has its year end on 5 April (the tax-year end), then the 1987–8 assessment would be based upon the profits for the accounting year ending 5 April 1987. The first payment would be made 9 months after the accounting year end, on 1 January 1988. If a business has its year end on 31 December, then the 1987–8 assessment would be based upon the profits for the accounting year ending 31 December 1986 – a delay of 12 months for the first tax payment.

However, if a business has its year end on 30 April, then the 1987–8 assessment would be based upon the profits for the accounting year ending 30 April 1986 – a delay of 20 months. Clearly the choice of 30 April as an accounting year end has the greatest tax cash-flow advantages. But do remember that other factors need to be considered. For example, you may consider it important to choose a year end when your balance-sheet looks most impressive to your bank manager.

What is clear is that careful choice of accounting year end can yield significant cash-flow advantage to any business. Effectively tax payments will be made in depreciated pounds at a time when income will probably be higher (if only because of inflation). A business can change its accounting year end to take advantage of these provisions, though special rules apply. Special rules also apply to opening and closing year of a business.[1]

---

[1] The special rules that apply on starting a business are:

FIRST TAX YEAR	assessment based upon profits from the starting date to 5 April following
SECOND TAX YEAR	assessment based upon first complete 12-month trading
THIRD TAX YEAR	normally on a preceding-year basis; if a full preceding year does not exist, then profits for the first 12 months, again.

The taxpayer has the option to elect that the assessment for *both* the second and third years be on the actual profits for those tax years (6 April–5 April) rather than on the above basis.

For example, if I start trading on 1 September 1986 and make up my accounts to 30 April each year, my assessment would be:

Tax year	Assessment based on profits	Paid
1986–7	1 September 1986–5 April 1987*	on agreement of assessment
1987–8	1 September 1986–31 August 1987 (1st 12 months)	As above
1988–9	1 September 1986–31 August 1987 (no full preceding year)	January, July 1989
1989–90	Accounting year ended 30 April 1988 (preceding year)	January, July 1990

* This can be expected to be delayed until the first set of accounts has been prepared and my first accounting will end on 30 April 1988.

For the year in which trade is permanently stopped the assessment will be based upon the actual profits from the previous 6 April until the date of cessation. The Inland Revenue will normally exercise its right (if it is beneficial) to make additional assessments to cover any excess of *actual* profits for the two preceding *tax years* over the normal preceding-year basis of assessment.

Relief for losses

Of course everybody, including the taxman, hopes that your business will trade profitably. However, any business can have its bad patches – particularly in the early years as the business is getting off the ground. Also remember that with the generous stock relief and capital allowances it is possible to trade profitably and still end up with a tax 'loss'.

If your business makes a tax loss you may set that loss against:

1. Your other income for the tax year *in which you suffer the loss*. The order of set-off is important. First, it is set against your other earned income, then your unearned income, then your wife's earned income, then her unearned income. For example, if you make a tax loss for the accounting year ending 30 April 1986 (assessed 1987–8) you set it first against other income for 1986–7. This includes business profits in this year.)
2. Your other income for the following tax year. Continuing our example, the following tax year is, of course, 1987–8.
3. Any unrelieved loss may be carried forward indefinitely and set-off against profits from the *same* business.

The above loss relief must be claimed by the business and the claim made within two years.

Special loss relief provisions relate to sole traders or partnerships. First, pre-trading expense of a revenue nature (incurred within three years before trading starts) may now be treated as a loss in the first year of assessment of a new business. Secondly, any losses made in the first year of assessment, or in any of the next three years (after capital allowances and pre-trading expenditure), may be set off against your income for the three years of assessment prior to the year in which the losses were made. Again the relief must be claimed and the claim made within two years.

When you cease trading, and if you make a loss in your last complete year, you may set this loss against your business assessments for the three years prior to your ceasing to trade.

Personal pension plans

Any sole trader will probably be concerned about his pension situation upon retirement. If you make payment to an authorised personal pension plan you may obtain full tax relief in respect of the premiums up to a permitted maximum[1] – that is, up to 40 per cent if your income tax rate is high enough. If you cannot afford to use all this relief in a particular year it can be carried forward to be used within the next six years. As the provisions relating to retirement annuity contracts can be particularly complicated professional advice should always be sought.

National Insurance

A sole trader must pay flat-rate class 2 National Insurance contributions (see Appendix 3). In addition he must pay earnings-related class 4 contributions, which are collected by the Inland Revenue along with Schedule DI/II payments.

Since no additional benefits are offered for the class 4 contribution, this is very much a form of additional taxation. The benefits available through National Insurance are outlined later. It is very noticeable that the self-employed, unlike their employed counterparts, are not as well off. In particular they cannot claim unemployment benefit.

Class 4 National Insurance is paid as a percentage of Schedule DI/II income, after capital allowances and stock relief but with no deduction of personal allowances or pension contributions. Since 6 April 1985 you can claim tax relief on half your class 4 contributions.

Taxation of partnerships

Income allocation

The determination of Schedule DI/II income for a partnership is exactly the same as for a sole trader – as are the provisions relating to capital allowances, loss relief and the basis of assessment. The major difference arises on how the income is allocated to the partners and the determination of the subsequent liability to income tax. The liability to income tax, when determined, is placed upon the partners as a whole – this includes tax at the basic rate and at a higher rate. It is

---

[1] The annual limit of contributions for retirement annuity plans since 1980-1 is 17 1/2 per cent of 'net relevant earnings'. (This means relevant earnings from the business less trading losses, capital allowances, etc.) The limit is increased for taxpayers aged 51 or over.

the responsibility of the 'precedent partner' (normally the senior partner) to make a joint return of partnership income each year.

Investment income is split between the partners in their profit-sharing ratios and they personally must pay the income tax due.

Schedule DI/II income must be allocated between the various partners in their profit-sharing ratios *in the tax year*. These proportions are not necessarily the same as the profit-sharing ratio when the profit was made. Any salaries paid to partners are not normally assessed under Schedule E but are included in the profits liable to Schedule DI/II tax. Interest paid to partners in respect of their capital is also treated as part of the Schedule DI/II profit and is not treated as an annual payment or taxed as investment income.

For example, suppose A and B are in partnership splitting profits equally after interest and salaries. They make up their accounts to 5 April each year.

	Net profit	Loan interest A	B	Salaries A	B	Gross profit
5 April 1986	£15,000	£700	£300	£4,000	£2,000	£22,000
5 April 1987	£18,000	£800	£400	£4,500	£2,500	£26,200

After charging...

The total partnership assessment to tax is shown below:

		Total	A	B
1986–7 TAXABLE INCOME		22,000		
Less Interest	A	(800)	£ 800	
	B	(400)		£ 400
Less Salaries	A	(4,500)	£4,500	
	B	(2,500)		£2,500
Balance split equally		£13,800	£6,900	£6,900
1986–7 income allocation			£12,200	£9,800

Relief for losses

Partnership losses are apportioned between the partners in the same way as profits. Each partner can use his losses as he chooses, as outlined earlier.

Change of partners

If there is a change of partners it will normally be treated as a cessation of trade unless the partners elect to be taxed on the 'continuation basis'. This would mean that the rules relating to cessation of trade apply unless the election is made, in which case the partnership continues to be assessed on the preceding-year basis. Special rules apply to the 'new partnership' from its commencement which differ from the normal rules for the start of a business. The first few years are assessed on an actual basis and thereafter the preceding-year basis applies, unless you elect for the fifth and sixth years also to be assessed on actual profits. On a charge of partners the pattern of recent and projected profits should be carefully considered as the opportunity to alter the basis of assessment to tax can be advantageous in that some high income years may simply 'drop out' of the assessment. The election for the continuing basis does not have to be made for two years from the date of change of partners. A married man should consider taking his wife into partnership in his business: first, because she can make use of the wife's earnings allowance (if she is not already working), and secondly, because (in the case of a couple with high earnings) it might reduce the liability to pay tax at higher rates if coupled with a wife's earnings election. And thirdly, because of the rules outlined above on change of partnership.

Taxation of companies

Corporation tax

Any limited company resident in the United Kingdom is liable to corporation tax on its profits. The rules for computing taxable profit for a *company* are the same as those relating to the various cases of Schedule D income or other Schedules if applicable. In particular, trading income is computed on exactly the same basis as Schedule DI/II, with capital allowances equally available.

The rate of corporation tax, unlike income tax, is fixed by Parliament in the Finance Act for the 'financial year' (1 April to 31 March). For periods from 1 April 1973, a small companies rate has applied for applied for companies with taxable profits below a specified limit (fixed at the same time as the rate). Where a company's taxable profit is between this limit and that at which the full corporation tax rate is payable, marginal relief[1] is given on the tax which would be due at the full rate, based on the following formula:

$$F \times (CT \text{ limit} - \text{'profit'}) \times \frac{\text{'income'}}{\text{'profit'}}$$

where

F is a fraction set by Parliament.
CT limit is the lower limit at which the full rate is payable.
'Profit' is taxable profit including capital gains plus franked investment income.
'Income' is taxable profit *excluding* capital gains.

Appendix 1 shows the rates and limits currently applicable.

The effective marginal tax rate for the example shown in footnote 1 is 42.5 per cent, i.e., higher than the assumed full rate. In the past the effective marginal rate has been as high as 60 per cent. Such a high rate of marginal tax must act as a distinctive to growth for small companies.[2]

However, remember that capital allowances are also available to companies. The *Inland Revenue Statistics* for 1986 reproduced in Table 9.4, show that 96 per cent of companies had taxable profits below £50,000 in 1983. The point to appreciate, once more, is that the profit reported in the financial accounts is not the same as the profit assessed to corporation tax. Capital allowances mean that taxable profit is usually considerably lower than reported profit.

Since the rate of corporation tax relates to 'financial years', if a company accounting year does not end on 31 March taxable profits are apportioned on a time basis between financial years. This is only important when the rate of corporation tax changes. For example, for the financial year 1986–7 the lower rate was 29 per cent and for

---

[1] For example, suppose the rates and limits were:
  Taxable profit below £100,000: 30 per cent
  Taxable profit above £500,000: 40 per cent
  Fraction for tapering relief: 1/40
(note: based on actual 1985 rates)

For a taxable income of £300,000 with no capital gains or franked investment income, tax payable would be:

£300,000 × 40% − 1/40(500,000−300,000) = £115,000

[2] There are provisions which make it impossible to subdivide a company into smaller units each paying the lower rate of corporation tax.

Table 9.4 Net income chargeable to corporation tax, 1983

Chargeable amount £	Number of assessments (thousands)	Cumulative (%)
0– 499	379.1	65
500– 999	23.1	69
1,000– 1,999	34.4	74
2,000– 2,999	20.3	78
3,000– 4,999	19.6	81
5,000– 9,999	35.0	87
10,000– 19,999	27.2	92
20,000– 29,999	12.6	94
30,000– 49,999	10.3	96
50,000– 99,999	10.4	97
100,000–199,999	6.1	98
200,000–499,999	4.0	99
500,000 and above	4.9	100
	587.0	

Source: Board of Revenue, *Inland Revenue Statistics*, 1986.

1987–8, 27 per cent. Thus for the accounting year ending 31 December 1987 one-quarter of income would be taxed at 29 and three-quarters at 27 per cent.

Corporation tax is also paid on any capital gains. Until 17 March 1987 a fraction of any capital gains was added to the income liable to taxation and always taxed at the higher rate, thus effectively making the rate 30 per cent, as for individuals. From 17 March 1987 a company's capital gains have been taxed at a rate applying to its income, rather than 30 per cent. Chargeable gains are thus added to income to find the total profit chargeable to tax and could mean that, for example, the marginal rate will apply rather than the small companies' rate.

Corporation tax was first introduced in the United Kingdom in 1965. In 1973 the method of taxation was changed to what is called an 'imputation system'. This system is designed to be 'neutral' as far as dividend payments are concerned. This means that high dividend distribution companies should not be unnecessarily penalised. Under the imputation system, if a company pays dividends, they are paid net of tax at the basic rate of tax (see Appendix 1) to the shareholder, and the deduction is paid over to the Inland Revenue. This is called 'advance corporation tax' (ACT) and it may be deducted from the company's overall corporation tax bill, so that effectively a lower rate of tax is paid.

ACT is, in effect, just a dividend-withholding tax. If the shareholder does not pay tax at the standard rate the tax may be reclaimed by the shareholder, and if the shareholder pays tax at higher rates, then he will have to account personally to the Inland Revenue for that.

For example, let us suppose for simplicity that the basic rate of tax was 30 per cent and corporation tax was 40 per cent, and suppose a company earning taxable profits of £50,000 *pays* a net dividend of £14,000. This is equivalent to a gross dividend of £20,000 on which income tax of £6,000 would be due (£20,000 × 30%). The corporation tax legislation would refer to an ACT rate of 3/7 to be applied to the net dividend, but this is the same as 30 per cent on the gross dividend (3/7 × £14,000 = £6,000). The company's total corporation tax bill would be £20,000 (£50,000 × 40%). However, the ACT would have to be paid over first and the balance of £14,000 (£20,000 − £6,000), which is called mainstream corporation tax (MCT) would be paid later. Notice the ACT to be offset against the total corporation tax bill is the amount on dividends actually *paid* in that year, not only on dividends declared. See Appendix 1 for current tax and ACT rates.

Basis of assessment : tax payments

Corporation tax is charged on the basis of the actual income assessable for each accounting period.

MCT is generally paid nine months after the accounting year end. Companies trading before 1 April 1965 have been able to retain their payment period at that date, but the Finance Act 1987 provided for this privilege to be phased out over three years.

ACT withheld must be paid to the Inland Revenue within 14 days of the following quarter days: 31 March, 30 June , 30 September and 31 December. In addition, if a company's accounting period does not end on one of these dates, the period of three months during which it ends is divided into two periods for which returns must be submitted.

Restrictions on ACT set-off

The amount of ACT which can be offset against a company's tax bill ('mainstream' corporation tax) is limited. The maximum amount is the ACT which would be paid if the company's taxable income was fully distributed. Thus, assuming the same simplified rates as in the previous example, if a company earns £50,000 it can only offset £50,000 × 30% = £15,000 of ACT. If it pays a dividend of £42,000 in that year (remember that payment could relate to the previous year's profits), then it must pay ACT of £42,000 × 3/7 = £18,000. The MCT to be paid will be (£50,000 × 40%) − £15,000 = £5,000. Hence the total tax.paid (ACT + MCT) will be (£5,000 + £18,000) = £23,000. In other words, the company has been unable to offset £3,000 of ACT and its effective tax rate is 46 per cent (£23,000/£50,000).

Recently the small companies rate of tax has been reduced, and as it approaches the basic rate of tax the amount of unrelieved ACT will decline.

Unrelieved ACT may be carried *back* and set off against corporation tax payable for any accounting periods beginning in the six years (prior to 1 April 1984 only two years) preceding that in which the distribution was made. In most cases this will result in a tax repayment. Any ACT not set off in this way may be carried *forward* for set-off indefinitely.

Restrictions on ACT set-off arise primarily when taxable profits are low compared with reported profits. As long as reported profits are high, shareholders may expect high levels of dividends, but if tax allowances are high, e.g., in the past capital allowances have included 100 per cent first year allowances, taxable profits are reduced and the ACT which can be set off is restricted. The problem also occurs when a company faces fluctuating profits and high dividends, relating to the previous year's good trading results, are actually paid in a year when profits are lower.

If a company pays a dividend it must pay ACT − even if taxable profits are zero. The dividend policy of a small company, where the manager is also probably the principal shareholder, requires careful planning so as to minimise the total tax liability the business faces, and to gain the maximum delay for those payments. Generally, dividends are not an attractive way of getting profits out of a company.

Relief for losses

Any adjusted loss arising for a company can be carried back for one year and set against taxable profits from the preceding year. Tax repayment may result. Any remaining losses may be carried forward indefinitely to be set off against future profits. Expenditure incurred in the three years before trade commenced can be deducted from trading income in the year trade is first carried on. As with sole traders, when a company ceases to trade, it may set any loss in the last year against profits for the preceding three years.

Business expansion scheme

Introduced originally as the business start-up scheme for three years from 6 April 1981, the scheme, now known as the business expansion scheme, was designed to encourage investment in small businesses by private individuals. Relief from income tax is obtained in respect of amounts subscribed for shares in a qualifying company. There are a number of detailed restrictions on what are qualifying trades, but generally included are manufacturing, retailing and wholesaling. The companies issuing the shares may be new companies or certain established unquoted trading companies.

The amount invested must be at least £500 and the limit for relief in any tax year is £40,000. Excluded from the scheme are employees, paid directors, and shareholders owning more than 30 per cent of the company. The shares on which relief is claimed must be held for five years, otherwise the relief will be clawed back.

Relief has been given in the tax year in which the shares are issued and there has been a tendency for investment to be concentrated at the end of the tax year – probably because of tax planning considerations. To alleviate this problem the Finance Act 1987 allowed a part of the relief on shares issued in the first 6 months of the tax year to be carried back to the previous tax year. The amount which can be carried back is limited to £5,000, or half the relief on the shares issued (whichever is lower), and is subject to the overall annual relief limit.

Capital gains and losses on the sale of shares

If a businessman sells his shares in the company, he must pay capital gains tax on the profits of the sale, even though the accumulated profits of the company will already have suffered corporation tax. poration tax.

The Finance Act 1980 introduced an important relief for disposals of shares in small businesses. Individuals who were original subscribers for shares in an unquoted company can elect to relieve any loss on disposal of shares against income tax. Previously, the loss had to be set against capital gains only. There are a number of stringent conditions which must be satisfied to obtain this relief but it is a considerable advantage for small businessmen.

Close and family companies

Potentially one of the major problems facing incorporated small business has been the special provisions enacted by Parliament in 1972 relating to what are termed 'close companies'. Close companies are broadly speaking those under the 'control' of 5 or fewer people and their 'associates'.[1] Hence the provisions apply to most small businesses. The majority of family businesses are also 'close'. The provisions are intended to inhibit the use of a company as a tax shield.

The close company provisions are designed to inhibit the three most common ways of using a company to avoid paying tax. These possibilities are:

1. Disguising a payment to a shareholder as an expense of the business. This makes the payment both tax-deductible for the company and tax-free in the hands of the shareholder.
2. Disguising a payment to a shareholder as a loan. This would mean that a shareholder might not pay tax on what it is, in effect, a dividend.
3. Not paying any dividend at all, thus using the company as a tax shield for individuals in years when their tax rates might be high.

The first possibility was dealt with by extending the meaning of distributions (dividends) for close companies. These are now held to include all 'benefits in kind' (such as living expenses and accommodation) provided for participants (shareholders or loan creditors) or their 'associates'. There are two important exceptions. If the recipient is a director or an employee, or if the benefit is the provision of a pension, then the benefit is not regarded as a distribution and is thus probably allowable against corporation tax, and ACT need not be accounted for on the benefit. Remember, however, that the benefit may still be taxable in the hands of the recipient under Schedule E income rules.

Prior to the Finance Act 1980 certain interest payments to directors were also treated as distributions. This is no longer the case.

The second possibility was dealt with by requiring close companies that make loans to participators or their 'associates' to pay a withholding tax on the loan at the current rate of ACT (see Appendix 1) – this is repaid if the debt is repaid.

---

[1] 'Associates' include close family such as husband, wife, child, father, mother, brothers, sisters, etc.

However, if the debt is relinquished, the participator may also be required to pay higher rate tax on the gross amount.

Finally, the possibility of holding funds in a company, which was being taxed at a lower rate than the shareholder, was dealt with by some fairly extensive legislation allowing the Inland Revenue to apportion among shareholders the excess of 'relevant income' over the distributions, and tax them accordingly. These provisions have been considerably diluted: first, it was always fairly easy to convince the Inland Revenue that the funds were actually required for business purposes, including expansion or repayment of loans originally obtained for the purpose; secondly, the Finance Act 1980 narrowed the definition of 'relevant income' to include only investment income and 50 per cent of property income. Thus companies with only trading income can now retain as much money in the business as they please.

Retirement pensions

As a director of a company, a businessman can participate in what is termed as 'exempt approved company pension scheme' and there can be considerable advantages related to this. The company's contributions to such a scheme are tax-deductible for the company, and the directors and employees can obtain relief on their contributions of up to 15 per cent of their emoluments, the relief for regular personal contributions being at the highest tax rate paid by the businessman. The benefits of such a pension scheme can include:

1. Pension of up to two-thirds the final emoluments.
2. Part of the pension may be paid as a tax-free lump sum.
3. Widow's pension of up to four-ninths the final emoluments.
4. Life assurance of up to four times the final emoluments on death in service.

From 1 July 1988, directors should be able to take out their own personal pensions and still obtain tax relief following the provisions of the Social Security Act 1986.

Taxation and business

Should a business incorporate?

Probably the first question a small businessman asks his accountant is whether he should form a company. From a tax point of view there used to be a major advantage in not incorporating until a fairly high level of taxable income was earned. Since the small companies rate of corporation tax has been reduced to fall in line with the basic rate of income tax it is clear that there are tax advantages in forming a company. Furthermore, the rate of corporation tax on higher profits is now lower than the higher rate of income tax (see Appendix 1).

The major disadvantage of incorporation is probably the fact that the company generally has to pay its taxes earlier than the unincorporated business – 9 months instead of up to 20 months after the accounting year end. This is equivalent to an interest-free loan for 11 months from the Inland Revenue.

Also the special rules which apply to the beginning and ending of a Schedule DI/II business, which means that the first year's profits can be doubly and trebly assessed, and on cessation one or two of the last year's profits can drop out of assessment, allow businessmen to organise cessation (for example, by changing a partnership), so as to ensure that high profit years drop out of assessment. This freedom does not exist for the company.

Further disadvantages of the company become apparent when the businessman tries to get his money out. The rules relating to close companies restrict the freedom of small incorporated businesses regarding expenses and loans to shareholders. If the businessman simply decides to leave the profits in the company, having suffered corporation tax, and, at some further date, to dispose of the company as a going concern, he faces capital gains tax on any profit on the sale of those shares, despite the fact that those profits have already been taxed.

Normally, the director of a company will want to pay himself a salary, After all, even a director must eat. This also has its disadvantages. First, although the salary is a deductible expense for the company, the director must pay Schedule E (PAYE) tax on the salary and other taxable benefits such as a car (see Appendix 2). This must be paid when the salary is paid. Contrast this to the treatment of Schedule DI/II income. Secondly, PAYE must be paid whether the business is making a profit or not.

Probably the least attractive and most expensive way of getting money out of the company is to actually pay a dividend. The shareholders may have to pay higher-rate tax on top of the basic rate withheld at source. Again, ACT must be paid over on designated quarter days, a problem the unincorporated business does not face. Luckily the Finance Act 1980 relaxed 'close company' rules regarding dividends, and the pressure to pay them no longer exists.

Also it is worth repeating that a company may still have to pay tax (income tax on the director's salary and ACT) even though it is making a loss. That loss can then only be set off against profits made by the company. For the sole trader he may set it against other *personal* income.

The situation regarding National Insurance must also be considered. As we saw, the sole trader pays a flat-rate class 2 contribution and a graduated class 4 contribution. However, directors are personally liable to class 1 contributions, and furthermore, the company must also pay the employer's contribution, which is considerably greater. All in all, the director (and his company) will pay more but he will obtain better benefits. The sole trader is well advised to make use of personal pension plans to improve his pension rights. However, even with these, unlike the director, he will not be able to claim unemployment benefit if his business collapses.

This chapter has steered clear of the very complex provisions of inheritance tax (IHT), formerly capital transfer tax (CTT). After 17 March 1986 lifetime transfers between individuals are only taxed if death occurs within seven years. There is specific relief against inheritance tax in respect to business property transferred. However, companies are generally a more flexible trading medium for minimising IHT. For example, partners will normally have the business valued as a whole based on underlying assets on any transfer, whereas it is possible to have shareholdings valued on a dividend yield basis, thus reducing their value appreciably.

In conclusion, from a tax-minimisation point of view, incorporation is probably worthwhile now that corporation tax rates are low, but bear in mind other considerations covered elsewhere in this book.

Taxation and business decisions

Chapters 17 and 18 examine the financial criteria on which to base decisions. Incremental analysis is used to examine the effects on business profit or cash flow of a particular business decision. Frequently such decisions involve consideration of the tax consequences, and in these situations businesses need to consider the incremental or marginal tax effect of the decision. This can be very difficult, since it involves 'guessing' the tax situation a business will face in the future, 'guessing' the future rates of tax, and then estimating the incremental effects of the decision on the tax situation. Clearly this involves a lot of crystal ball gazing. Yet large companies spend considerable sums on sophisticated tax planning, so they must think it worthwhile.

While sophisticated tax planning must remain an area for experts, all businesses need to have some ground-rules for evaluating the tax consequences of any decision.

Only the Chancellor of the Exchequer knows with any certainty what the rates of tax will be in any future period. Consequently businessmen can only base their decisions on current tax rates.

In assessing the incremental tax effect of any decision, marginal tax rates are of far more relevance than average average tax rates. The marginal tax rate faced by a business indicates the proportion of any *extra* £1 of income that will go to the government. Sole traders and partnerships who pay tax face the marginal tax rates shown in Appendix 1 (headed 'Tax rate'). As proposals yield greater additional profits, so the marginal rate of tax faced by the business will increase.

Companies with taxable profits below £100,000 face a marginal tax rate equal to the small companies rate for projects taking income up to £100,000. A company which undertakes a project raising its taxable profits into the range £100,000 – £500,000 faces the company's effective marginal rate (this is greater than higher rate corporation tax). Bear in mind that if the company faces ACT set-off restrictions, any extra £1 of income is available to set against ACT, thus reducing the marginal tax rate to the difference between the applicable corporation tax rate and ACT rate (see Appendix 1 for current rates).

Although these rates are no more than the broadest indicators of the potential complications which can affect the incremental tax charge a business may have to face, they do provide a simple framework to assess the tax effect of any business decision.

Tax-saving hints

To evade paying tax is completely illegal. However, an individual is free to minimise his tax bill. Be warned the tax planning is very complicated and professional advice is normally a sound investment. However, there are some simple points worth bearing in mind. The most important of these is never to do anything that saves tax at the expense of business benefits or which jeopardises the business in any way. Always remain as flexible as possible since tax rates and the tax system can, or do, change.

SOLE TRADERS AND PARTNERSHIPS

1. Obtain the maximum possible pension cover (remember personal pension plans).

Taxation and allowances 179

2. Claim all possible business expenses. (Your car may be allowable for capital allowances and running costs.)
3. Have an accounting year end of 30 April.
4. Plan changes in partnerships to make the most of starting-up and cessation rules.
5. Consider taking on your wife as a partner, if she can do some of the work – you can use up her personal allowances at the very least.
6. Make the most of losses.
7. Plan your capital purchases to gain the tax advantages as soon as possible. Generally make the expenditure towards the end of the accounting year.

COMPANIES

1. Set up a company pension scheme and join it.
2. Give yourself a company car[1] and other assets.
3. It may benefit you to give yourself an interest-free loan.
4. Plan your salary and dividends to minimise your tax liability.
5. Consider making your wife a director.
6. Plan your capital purchases and dividend payments to gain the tax advantage as soon as possible. Generally, make the expenditure towards the end of the accounting year.

Taxes businesses collect for the government

VAT

Value-Added Tax (VAT) was introduced to the United Kingdom in 1973. All other EEC countries have VAT, though the rates are not harmonised. Since its introduction VAT has been a constant irritant to businessmen. It now seems to take up more time than dealing with the Inland Revenue. Indeed the Customs and Excise, who administer the scheme, seem to have, and to exercise, considerably greater powers than the Inland Revenue.

VAT is payable whenever goods or services pass from one business

---

[1] The tax liability raised on the individual on the provisions of a company car is laid out in Appendix 2.

or person to another. Even the import of goods suffers VAT, though when goods are exported no VAT is charged and any VAT paid may be reclaimed. The current rate of VAT is 15 per cent.

Generally a business must charge VAT on all goods or services it supplies (called 'outputs') and against this it may offset the VAT it has been charged on any goods or services (called 'inputs'). Unlike income or corporation tax, no distinction is made between capital and revenue items. Normally a business must pay over the difference between its 'outputs' and 'inputs' to the Customs and Excise at the end of every three months. Should 'inputs' exceed 'outputs', a repayment of VAT may be claimed after only one month. A typical return to the Customs and Excise will show:

Total outputs during the period	£80,000	
VAT thereon		£12,000
Total inputs during the period	£40,000	
VAT thereon		£ 6,000
Balance payable to Customs and Excise		£ 6,000

All invoices supplying goods or services must show the VAT charged. Since each business gets a credit for the VAT it suffers, only the ultimate consumer actually bears the tax. A business merely acts as a collecting agent for the government.

All businesses with taxable turnover in excess of the limit shown in Appendix 1 must register with the Customs and Excise and are required to make these returns every three months. Any small business not registered must bear the 'input' VAT on all goods or services it uses, but does not charge VAT to its customers. Deregistration is allowed under certain circumstances (see Appendix 1).

The Finance Act 1987 provided for the introduction of regulations which will allow small business to account for VAT on the basis of cash received and paid rather than relating it to invoice dates. This will require EEC approval. Small businesses will also be able to elect to make one VAT return annually (instead of every three months) although tax would have to be paid during the year in nine equal instalments with a final balancing instalment to accompany the annual return. Both schemes should help to relieve some of the VAT accounting burden currently falling on small businesses.

Because retailers cannot possibly account for each sale separately, special schemes exist for them.

Not all goods and services suffer VAT. Some goods are 'exempt', which means that no VAT needs to be charged on their supply. However, no credit is given for the 'inputs' to the business, and in this situation the business is forced to bear the costs of VAT. Typical 'exempt' goods and services include: land, education, banking, insurance, betting and gaming, health services, postal services, burial and cremation.

Some goods and services are called 'zero-rated'. This is probably the most beneficial status available because not only is no VAT chargeable on the supply of the good or service, but also any VAT charged on 'inputs' may be reclaimed. Typical 'zero-rated' goods and services, include: all exports, most foods, books and newspapers, construction of new buildings, transport, drugs and medicines, clothing for young children, large caravans and houseboats, and many fuels.

There are a number of special situations which need to be mentioned. VAT is chargeable on most second-hand goods, other than those where there are special provisions.[1] VAT on business entertainment is not deductible (as in Schedule DI/II tax rules). Input VAT is not deductible on cars acquired for business use (again a special case in Schedule DI/II tax rules). These do not include vans or commercial vehicles, nor does it affect car dealers.

The provisions relating to VAT can be complex, and the amount of record-keeping required is certainly time-consuming. Strict provisions have been introduced to deter businesses from evading or delaying VAT payments. Penalties for overdue returns and payments may be imposed. For example, the Finance Act 1985 introduced a 'default surcharge' of up to 30 per cent of the VAT involved which could be imposed from 10 October 1986. The Customs and Excise issue over 20 special booklets which give details of the various provisions and how they relate to particular types of business. These can be obtained free of charge from any Customs and Excise VAT office.

Schedule E: Pay-As-You-Earn

Any business with employees, and this includes directors of companies, will have them taxed under Schedule E income tax collected under the 'Pay-As-You-Earn' system. The employer is responsible for administering the PAYE system: deducting the correct amount of tax from employee's salaries and paying it over to the Collector of Taxes

---

[1] Cars, motor-cycles, caravans, boats and outboard motors, original works of art, antiques over 100 years old, aircraft, electronic organs, have VAT charged only on the dealer's mark-up.

on a monthly basis. Statutory sick pay and maternity pay are also now handled by employers instead of the DHSS. Amounts paid are taxed and are reclaimed by the employer from the DHSS.

Employers may use their own records (including computerised records) to maintain particulars for each employee and calculate amounts due. The official Deductions Working Sheet (form P11(87)) may be used. These show:

- Personal details, e.g. National Insurance number, tax code, date of birth
- National Insurance contributions
- Maternity pay and sick pay
- Gross pay for the period
- Cumulative gross pay for the tax year to date
- Total 'free pay' pay to date (Table A)
- Total taxable pay to date
- Total tax due to date (Table B)
- Tax to be paid for the period

Total 'free pay' to date is found by reference to Table A in the tax tables provided by the Inland Revenue. Total tax due to date is normally found by reference to Table B in the tax tables (Tables C and D relate to higher-rate taxpayers) and the tax due is found by subtracting the total tax due to date for the previous period from that due for the current period.

Each employee is given a code number by the Inland Revenue based upon the total allowances the taxpayer is due, calculated from his annual tax return. To convert your code number into allowances simply multiply by ten. For example, a code of 440 means the taxpayer has allowances of £4,400. A suffix H or L refers to the married or single status of the taxpayer.

At the end of each year the employer must complete a form (P35) showing total tax due and total tax collected for the year and return it to the Inland Revenue together with an end of the year return (P14) for each employee. The P14 is basically a summary of the information shown on P11(87) or other record, including the National Insurance number, date of birth, final tax code and totals of pay, National Insurance and tax deducted. The employer should also issue a form (P60) to each employee, this is a copy (part of the set) of the P14.

When an employee leaves, the employer must issue him with another form (P45) and send another copy to the Inland Revenue. This form gives details contained on the taxpayer's deduction card which allows the new employer to prepare a new tax-deduction card in the normal way.

For directors and higher-paid employees (over £8,500) a further form (P11D) must be completed and sent to the Inland Revenue. This gives details of expenses and benefits in kind such as company cars or car expenses, entertainment, travelling, subsistence, company accommodation, subscriptions paid, medical expenses paid, educational assistance paid, beneficial loans[1] and many other categories. Against this is set the amounts repaid to the employer and the amounts from which tax has already been deducted under PAYE.

Generally the tax rules regarding expenses and benefits in kinds are comparatively less favourable for P11D employees. Directors are taxed on premiums for sickness insurance schemes, on the annual value of any company house, on the personal benefit from a company car (although the assessments are not excessive - see Appendix 2), and on 20 per cent of the market value when first used of any other assets (such as suits and furniture) given to the director (a point worth remembering).

The PAYE system is designed to ensure that at each point in the tax year the correct proportion of an individual's liability for the whole year has been paid. It is an ingenious system which operates with the minimum of involvement from the taxpayer. However, it is basically run by employers, and it is an expensive administrative operation – for all employers. The system works less smoothly when there are changes in taxpayers' personal allowances. If they go up during the year, the taxpayer must inform the Inland Revenue and it will refund the tax he has overpaid, up to his change his coding. If allowances go down, the taxpayer will generally be credited with the tax he should have paid up to the change of coding, and the deficiency collected in the subsequent tax year by reducing his allowances.

National Insurance

National Insurance contributions are paid by virtually all working people. The self-employed pay flat-rate class 2 contributions and earnings-related class 4 contributions. Employees must pay earnings-related class 1 contributions and their employers pay the employers' portion. Current rates are shown in Appendix 3.

At present, employers may be contracted in or out of the state earnings-related pension scheme (SERPS). Contracted out employees usually belong to an approved pension scheme provided by the company.

---

[1] A beneficial loan is one to a director or higher-paid employee or relative which bears interest at a rate lower than 12 per cent.

The Social Security Act 1986 introduced the necessary legislation to enable individuals to leave their employer's pension scheme and take out personal pension from 1988. There are two basic aims behind these provisions. First, it is now acknowledged that SERPS will cost more in the next century than originally anticipated and the country can afford. It is actually paid for out of the current working population's contributions rather than beneficiaries' past contributions. The percentage of salary that will be provided through SERPS for pensioners is therefore being reduced and the basis of calculating this contribution will be altered to further reduce its value. Secondly, it is hoped that individuals will be able to benefit from more flexible pension arrangements, for example, not losing future benefits if they change employment.

Any real pension scheme should have contributions related to the benefits obtained from the scheme. In the case of class 1, contracted-out, class 2 and class 4 contributions, this is not the case since the benefits from the scheme are not at all related to the payments individuals make. Only class 1, contracted-in to SERPS, employees receive an element of earnings-related benefits. National Insurance is far more of an additional tax, on both employer and employee, than anything else, and it is a very expensive tax.

In return for the payments ot National Insurance, contributors are eligible to such state benefits as retirement pensions, unemployment and sickness benefit and supplementary benefit. People who have not contributed to National Insurance are still eligible for supplementary benefit. The self-employed are not eligible for unemployment benefit, but they can claim supplementary benefit.

Unlike the PAYE scheme, National Insurance contributions are charged on a non-cumulative weekly basis, and therefore the weekly charge depends solely upon earnings in that week. It is not affected by earnings in earlier or later weeks. Therefore, it is quite possible for a casual worker not to pay income tax, because his annual earnings are so low, but still to pay National Insurance contributions on a week-by-week basis.

Class 4 National Insurance contributions are paid, by the self-employed, along with their Schedule DI/II income tax to the Inland Revenue. Class 2 National Insurance contributions are paid over each month to the Department of Health and Social Security. Class 1 National Insurance contributions are paid over each month by employers, along with the PAYE deducted, to the Inland Revenue.

Appendix 1 Current rates and allowances

Tax year commencing 6 April 1987

Sole traders and partnerships

Tax rates

Taxable income	Tax rate	Average rate[1]
1st £19,300 @	25%	20.6%
Over £19,300 @	40%	

Main tax Allowances

Personal reliefs

Single person	:	£2,605
Married rate*	:	£4,095
Wife's earned income*	:	2,605
Additional personal allowance for children	:	£1,490[2]
Blind person	:	£ 540
Age allowance[3] 65–79 Single	:	£3,180
Married	:	£5,035
80+ Single	:	£3,310
Married	:	£5,205

(handwritten notes: 1991, 3295, 60, 3295)

Limited companies

Corporation tax
Taxable profit less than £100,000 rate is:
  Year ending 31 March 1988 : 27%
  Year ending 31 March 1989 : 27%
Rate for taxable profit over £500,000 : 25%
Marginal relief on profits between £100,000 and £500,000
Marginal relief fraction:
  Year ending 31 March 1988 : 1/50
  Year ending 31 March 1989 : 1/40
Effective marginal rate:
  Year ending 31 March 1988 : 37%
  Year ending 31 March 1989 : 37½%

Advance corporation tax (ACT) rates
  Tax year to 5 April 1988 : 27/73 × dividend paid
  Tax year to 5 April 1989 : 25/75 × dividend paid

* From 6 April 1990 wives will be taxed independently. In addition to alterations to allowances this will have implications for business tax planning.

continued on page 176

Appendix 1 con't

Tax year commencing 6 April 1987	Sole traders and partnerships	Limited companies
Capital allowances	Plant and machinery Cars Industrial buildings Enterprise zones: Industrial and commercial buildings, shops, offices and hotels Hotels Agricultural buildings Patent rights and 'know how'	: 25% on reducing balance : 25% on reducing balance (max. £2,000) : 4% on original cost : 100% allowance : 4% on original cost : 4% on original cost : 25% on reducing balance
Capital Gains Tax	Capital gains tax is levied on gains upon the disposal of chargeable assets. Chargeable assets include all forms of property, stocks and shares, land and buildings, goodwill, certain debts, options and currency other than sterling.	
	Gains in excess of £5,000 @ 25% or 40% depending on income ie: if taxable income plus gains (over £5,000) exceed £19,300 rate is 40%.	Capital gains added to taxable trading income and taxed at appropriate corporation tax rate. Trading losses can be set off against capital gains of the same or previous period.
	Assets have their cost increased by reference to the increase in the retail prices index between acquisition (or March 1982) and disposal. Indexation may create or increase a capital loss.	
	Losses may be carried forward to set against future capital gains.	Losses may be carried forward to set off against capital gains of the company.

Subject to certain conditions, gains (up to £100,000 for those aged 60 and over) on the disposal of a business or shares in a family trading business are exempt from capital gains tax.

Losses on the disposal of shares in unquoted companies may be set against income tax, subject to conditions.

Value Added Tax

The annual registration limit for VAT is £22,100 from 5 March 1988 (quarterly limit £7,500). Deregistration is allowed if future supplies will not exceed £21,100 (this limit operates from 1 June 1988).

Standard rate of VAT is 15%, all other supplies are either zero rated or exempt.

---

[1] For a married couple with no allowances other than the £4,095 personal allowance. Calculated by taking total tax payable and dividing it by the income at top of the band plus £4,095. Thus for the range to £19,300 the calculation is:

$$\frac{4,825}{19,300+4,095} = 20.6\%$$

[2] Subject to certain conditions
[3] Reduced by £2 for every £3 of excess income over £10,600 down to personal relief level.

Appendix 2 Car and fuel benefit scales

Car benefit	Cars under 4 years old 1987/88 (£)	Cars under 4 years old 1988/89 (£)	Cars over 4 years old 1987/88 (£)	Cars over 4 years old 1988/89 (£)
Original market value up to £19,250 with cylinder capacity:				
1400cc or less	525	1,050	350	700
1401cc – 2000cc	700	1,400	470	940
Over 2000cc	1,100	2,200	725	1,450
Original market value:				
£19,250 – £29,000	1,450	2,900	970	1,940
Over £29,000	2,300	4,600	1,530	3,060

Fuel benefit 1987/88 and 1988/89 (£)

Cylinder capacity:

1400cc or less	480
1401cc – 2000cc	600
Over 2000cc	900

Appendix 3 National Insurance contributions, 1987–8

	Total weekly earnings	Contracted-in Employee	Contracted-in Employer	Contracted-out Employee	Contracted-out Employer
CLASS 1	Up to £41.00	NIL	NIL	NIL	NIL
	£41.00–£69.99	5%[1]	5%[1]	3.00%[2]	1.20%[2]
	£70.00–£104.99	7%[1]	7%[1]	5.00%[2]	3.20%[2]
	£105.00–£154.99	9%[1]	9%[1]	7.00%[2]	5.20%[2]
	£155.00–£305.00	9%[1]	10.45%[1]	7.00%[2]	6.65%[2]
	over £305.00	[3]	10.45%[1]	[4]	[5]

[1] On all earnings.
[2] On earnings over £41.00. The first £41.00 is charged at the contracted in rate appropriate to the level of earnings.
[3] Employee's maximum contribution is 9% of £305 (i.e., £27.45).
[4] Employee's maximum contribution is 9% on first £41.00 plus 7.00% on earnings between £41.00 and £305 (i.e., £22.17).
[5] 10.45% on first £41.00 plus 6.65% on earnings between £41.00 and £305 plus 10.45% on excess over £305.

CLASS 2 (self-employed)
(not payable by male over 65 or female over 60)
£4.05 per week on earnings above £2,250 per annum

CLASS 3 (voluntary contributions)
(the benefit of which is mainly entitlement to basic retirement pension)
£3.95 per week

CLASS 4 (self-employed)
(not payable by male over 65 or female over 60)
6.3% on profits assessable to tax between £4,750 and £15,860 per annum (maximum £699.93)

CHAPTER 10

An Introduction to Accounting and the Companies Acts

ACCOUNTING INFORMATION: A PRACTICAL SECTION	190
Understanding the balance-sheet	190
Understanding the income statement/profit-and-loss account	193
Generally accepted accounting principles	196
THE ACCOUNTING REQUIREMENTS OF THE COMPANIES ACTS	199

Accounting information: a practical section

Understanding the balance-sheet

The problem with accounting and finance is that it is full of mumbo-jumbo! Many of the ideas and notions are really quite simple and straightforward. Over the years accountants have managed to shroud their profession in the blanketing fog of technical jargon. As soon as the accountant starts talking this foreign language, eyes cloud over, minds turn off and the financial information he is talking about manages to retain that somewhat mystical and unreal quality of a DHSS handbook. Unfortunately for the businessman a lack of understanding of basic accounting and finance is a sure recipe for bankruptcy. Balance-sheets and income statements can become fascinating reading if they relate to *your* money and *your* business.

In fact a business is essentially a very simple thing. A business collects money and pays money out, not necessarily in that order. And this is all that the balance-sheet tries to tell you about: where the money came from and where it went to – as simple as that.

An introduction to accounting and the companies acts   191

Table 10.1 A very simple balance-sheet

IN		OUT	
Share capital	£1,000	Fixed assets	£1,100
Loans	500	Stock	550
Creditors	200	Cash	50
	£1,700		£1,700

When you start up a business you will obtain money from a number of sources. There will be the money you put into the business yourself. This will be the permanent long-term capital of the business; for a company this would be the share capital. You might borrow someone else's money, or loan capital or bank overdrafts. And finally, you might obtain credit from suppliers of raw materials or merchandise – creditors.

The next thing that happens is that you will start to do things with the cash you have collected. (Accountants would call this cash 'funds', but there is little difference.) You might buy fixed assets such as land, buildings, plant, machinery, desks, typewriters. These are the long-term assets of the business that you mean to keep. Then you will start to purchase stocks of raw materials or merchandise that you wish to sell. You will start to pay people for their work on the raw materials. This is all expenditure of your initial capital and it goes into creating the stock (of raw materials, work-in-progress and finished goods) that you intend to sell. Any cash left over may just sit in your bank account.

So that, very simply, is a balance-sheet: where cash comes from and where it goes to. Take the simple example in Table 10.1. Notice that the cash in *equals* the cash out; that is why it is called a balance-sheet, because it ought to balance.

Once you start to sell things you will probably not obtain cash straight away but will sell on credit. Customers who owe the company money are called *debtors*, or *accounts receivable*, and the net current assets of the business (stock + debtors + cash – creditors) are called *working capital*.

Once the business starts making profits it will plough back some of these. Confusingly many terms are used for these, such as 'reserves', 'retained earnings', 'undistributed profit', 'accumulated profit', 'profit-and-loss account'. All this represents is the funds that the business has retained itself. Those funds could take the form of cash or more stock or more fixed assets or indeed any asset. For example, suppose the business in Table 10.1 sold stock costing £200 for £500 on credit; a

Table 10.2 A simple balance sheet

IN		OUT	
Share capital	£1,000	Fixed assets	£1,100
Loans	500	Stock	350
Creditors	200	Debtors	500
Profit-and-loss account	300	Cash	50
	£2,000		£2,000

profit of £300. The new balance-sheet is shown in Table 10.2. Notice that total assets have grown to £2,000, and this growth in assets is represented by retained profit, shown in the profit-and-loss account. These retained profits belong to the shareholder.

That, very simply, is what a balance-sheet is: a snapshot at a point of time telling you what the assets of the business are and where they came from. The accountant does manage to complicate this by showing the balance-sheet in many different ways. A common format is shown in Table 10.3. The figures are exactly the same as in Table 10.2, just rearranged. The emphasis has altered so as to show the total funds that the *shareholder* has put into the business (£1,300) rather than *total* funds. One area of confusion is that the term 'capital' is sometimes used on its own to mean *shareholders' capital* (also sometimes called *equity*) and sometimes to mean *total capital*. Total capital normally only includes long-term loan capital, but it can include any of the other sources of funds: bank overdraft and/or creditors. So when presented with the term 'capital' it is essential to ask for a definition!

The next thing to notice is that the assets are listed vertically in increasing order of liquidity. By this we mean that fixed assets are relatively illiquid in that it would take some time to turn them into cash, whereas cash is obviously your most liquid asset. Stocks probably become debtors before turning into cash. Working capital is shown by deducting creditors due within one year from the current assets. The distinction between long- and short-term assets or liabilities tends to be very simple. If the asset will, in the normal course of business, generate cash within one year, or the liability requires payment within one year, it is called 'short' term. Once more, the balance-sheet 'balances' in that the shareholders' capital of £1,300 is shown as being invested in the list of assets less the short- and long-term liabilities of the business.

Having explained what the balance-sheet *is*, it may be an idea to emphasise what it is *not* and dispel some popular misconceptions. It does not tell you much about the *value* of the business. The business

Table 10.3 Balance-sheet format complying with 1985 Companies Act

	£
FIXED ASSETS	1,100
CURRENT ASSETS	
Stock	350
Debtors	500
Cash	50
	900
CREDITORS DUE WITHIN ONE YEAR	
Trade creditors	(200)
NET CURRENT ASSETS (WORKING CAPITAL)	700
TOTAL ASSETS *less* CURRENT LIABILITIES (NET ASSETS)	1,800
CREDITORS DUE AFTER MORE THAN ONE YEAR	(500)
	1,300
CAPITAL AND RESERVES	
Share capital	1,000
Profit-and-loss account	300
	1,300

might well be of far greater value if offered for sale as a going concern because of its potential for growth. Anyway, that value is the result of negotiations between buyer and seller. Nor is it a measure of the scrap or disposal value of the business. You may have extreme difficulty in selling your stock or your fixed assets if the firm goes out of business. In fact you are unlikely to realise the amounts shown in the balance-sheet.

Understanding the income statement/profit-and-loss account

The terms 'profit-and-loss account' and 'income statement' are identical when referring to the current year's activities. However, as mentioned earlier, the term 'profit-and-loss account' is also used, confusingly, for the accumulated profit shown in the balance-sheet in the 1985 Companies Act formats. Profit represents the natural growth in business assets from trading activities. Funds can increase and assets can grown for a number of reasons: more share capital, more loan capital, more creditors. However, the increase in profit represents the growth in assets due to the trading and business activities of the firm.

The income statement gives you the detail of how the profit was arrived at. In the simple example we used the income statement would show:

	£
Sales	500
Cost of sales	(200)
Profit	300

However, as we shall see later, generally much more detail is shown for a normal business.

The income statement is therefore a record of how the assets of the business have grown over a certain period. Normally that period is one year for tax purposes. However, a well-run business will produce balance-sheet and income statement information far more frequently than that: often once a month, and at least quarterly. Without that information the business does not know how it is doing or what assets it has at its disposal for its future activities.

As usual, it is important to understand what the income statement does not tell you. It does not tell you if you have any spare cash. Profit is not the same as cash. It could be cash, but it could be represented by increases in stock, debtors or fixed assets. The income statement does not tell you what you did with the funds that you generated. Nor does your income statement tell you anything about what will happen in the future – you might guess that, next year, profit will be the same as last year, but you would be better advised to prepare a budget to find out. Nor does the income statement tell you whether your fixed assets need replacing next year, or what major capital expenditure you might be committed to.

Fixed assets last a number of years and it is clearly unfair to allocate their whole cost to any single year. The cost of fixed assets is shown in the income statement by a 'depreciation' charge. This charge is designed to allocate the cost of the asset over the years of its useful life. The problem with the fixed asset is that it will last for more than one year, and therefore you must decide on a method of cost allocation. Using the 'straight-line' method outlined in Chapter 2, if the estimated life of the fixed assets in our example was 10 years, the annual depreciation charge would be £110 (£1,100/10). This is the amount that we write off the cost of fixed assets each year, in which case the income statement would show:

	£
Sales	500
Cost of sales	(200)
	300
Depreciation	(110)
Profit	190

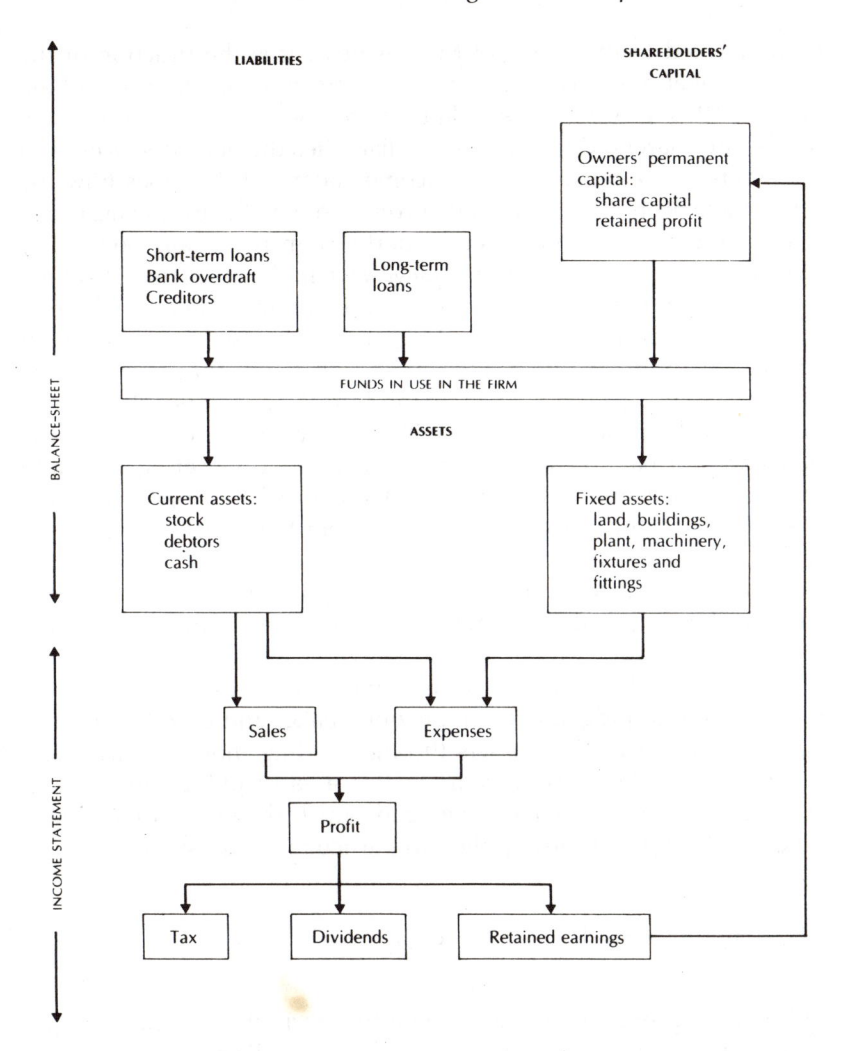

An introduction to accounting and the companies acts

Figure 10.1 Business transactions and their relationship in the balance-sheet and income statement

The fixed assets in the balance-sheet would be shown at £990 (£1,110–£110). If you construct the balance-sheet, you will see that it balances again. The linkage between the balance-sheet and income statement is shown in Figure 10.1. The diagram summarises the essential functions of the business: the translation of funds from various sources into assets, which are expended in generating sales revenue. The resulting profit will determine the tax liability for the year and influence the dividends that will be paid; anything left will be reinvested in the assets of the business. It is the function of the balance-sheet and income statement to try to describe different aspects of this process. The balance-sheet describes the sources of funds, the shareholders' capital, the liabilities the business faces, and the assets of the business. The income statement describes how the assets have been used to generate profit and how the profit was used.

The problem of depreciation underlines an important point. The calculation of profit is a matter of *judgement*: in the estimated life of the fixed asset; and in the amount of depreciation to write off each year. There are other areas where judgement is exercised in deciding on profit. For example, often a business will know that some of the debtors will not eventually pay up, and therefore will not show these debtors in the balance-sheet or will set up a 'provision' in case the debts are not paid. (That is, simply a liability to be set against, and therefore cancel out, the asset. The advantage of this approach is that it emphasises the uncertainty of the debt.) Similarly judgements regarding the quality and quantity of stock must also be made, and some old, damaged or useless stock might not be shown in the balance-sheet or, again, a 'provision' might be set up in case the stock proves unsaleable.

The point is that financial measurement is not exact. Profit is the result of certain judgements that people make, and therefore it is an *estimate* of the growth of assets through trading, not an exact calculation of it. To help accountants in this area of judgement, certain accounting principles have developed which themselves have been modified by conventions applied to particular circumstances.

Generally accepted accounting principles

Methods of preparing accounts were first formulated centuries ago. However, it was not until an Italian monk, Luca Pacioli, wrote a book in 1494 that any comprehensive system of accounting was documented. Since then, the principles involved have been handed down through generations, though it was not until the 1930s that any serious attempt to formalise them was made. Collectively they are called 'generally accepted accounting principles'. Briefly, the principles and terms are:

BUSINESS ENTITY

Accounts only show transactions affecting the *business*. This means that how they affect the persons who manage or are employed by the business is not relevant. While this distinction can easily be drawn for a limited company, with an existence of its own, the distinction between business and personal transactions is more difficult to define for a sole trader or partnership.

Going concern

Unless there is good reason to believe otherwise, it is assumed that the business will continue to operate for an indefinite period in the future. If the business is expected to cease, then its assets would often not fetch what was paid for them.

Money measurement

Accounts only measure transactions recorded in money terms. They do not record the goodwill built up with customers by a company as a result of successful trading. (The goodwill you see in the accounts is something different, as we shall explain later.) Nor do they measure industrial relations. They only measure financial transactions.

Realisation

Profit is only taken into account when the goods or services are passed to the customer and he incurs liability for them (i.e. realised). Therefore, stocks of finished goods are normally valued at cost, rather than at their selling price.

Historic cost

Assets purchased by a business are shown at their historic cost: the amount paid to purchase them. Real worth can vary for any number of reasons, but accounting measurement normally recognises only the historic cost paid for an asset. It is assumed that this is equal to value. This rule is simple and easy to apply, but it has been severely criticised in times of high inflation, as giving misleading information, and as a result alternatives, called methods of 'inflation accounting', have been developed by the accounting profession.

Matching

This matches the costs of resources used in the creation of the goods sold against sales revenue, for the purpose of profit calculation. If an item of stock is purchased, its cost is not necessarily charged against profit in the month it was bought, but rather in the month it was sold.

DOUBLE-ENTRY

As you noticed in the case of the balance-sheet example, accounts balance: that is, shareholders' capital *equals* the total assets of the business *less* all liabilities. In the practice of recording transactions, this is achieved by a method called *double-entry book-keeping*. This is a simple process: every time an additional asset is created or purchased for the business, recognition of where it came from must also be made. For example, if you subscribe £1,000 cash to your business, recognition of its source must also be made, let us say by showing £1,000 share capital. The idea is that, at all times, the following accounting equation is maintained:

$$\text{Shareholders' capital} = \text{Assets} - \text{Liabilities}$$

If, for any reason, the accounts of a business do not 'balance', then some aspect of the transactions has been incorrectly recorded.

MATERIALITY

Often there is a 'correct' accounting treatment for an asset which would cost more to implement than it would have influence on the financial statements. For example, that kettle purchased last year for £15 could be depreciated over its useful life of 10 years, but is it worth it? Why not just treat it as an expense in the year you purchased it? The convention of materiality allows you to do that by recognising that accounting only concerns itself with events which have significant bearing on the finances of the business. What is 'material' does, however, depend upon individual circumstances and is, of course, another matter of judgement.

CONSERVATISM

This is sometime known as *prudence*. It means that if there is a choice between two different valuations of an asset, the accountant will always choose the most conservative figure. For example, stock is always valued at the lower of its cost or what it might realise in an orderly sale (net realisable value). This approach might not always give the most accurate picture, but it does have less severe economic consequences for decision-making, as many ex-owners of bankrupt companies can testify.

Consistency

As we have seen, there are many alternative ways of recording transactions, and accountants recognise that there is no single 'correct' way. However, they do require transactions to be recorded consistently from one period to another, since to do otherwise can cause distortions in reported profit figures.

The accounting requirements of the Companies Acts

How sole traders and partnerships prepare accounts and who they distribute them to is a matter for the business to decide. However, limited liability companies must distribute accounts to all shareholders and file a set of acounts with the Registrar of Companies. The 1985 Companies Act in Schedule 4 also lays down standard balance-sheets and income statement formats to be used by them. These formats are not quite as straightforward as the ones developed in this chapter so far. A full, unabridged, balance-sheet for a manufacturing company is shown in Table 10.4. The values shown in certain accounts are not related to the previous example, and will be used in chapter 16 to develop your understanding of financial information. As you can see, there is considerably more detail than we have so far considered and also some terms that might be unfamiliar.

Notice that the amount unpaid on share capital is shown as an asset (line A) of the company since this defines the full extent of the shareholders' liability. The term 'called-up' refers simply to the process of share issue. The company is said to 'call up' any remaining capital after initial application and allotment monies have been collected.

Fixed assets are divided into three main categories: intangible assets, tangible assets and investments. Tangible assets are the physical assets of the business and are usually shown at cost, *less* depreciation. However, some assets such as land are shown at valuation, if this is significantly higher than historic cost. In fact the Companies Acts (there are six relevant Acts: 1948, 1967, 1976, 1980, 1981, 1985) require extensive further disclosure of these assets, including separate details of historic cost, depreciation, revaluation, additions and disposals by asset category. Intangible assets include patent costs, development costs, royalty agreement costs and other 'soft' assets. Really they are just costs that have been deferred and placed in the balance-sheet. Goodwill represents the excess paid for another company over the historic cost of its assets purchased. It does not represent the 'true goodwill' of the whole business as a going concern, as noted in the previous section. Goodwill must be written off over a suitable period. Bankers tend not to trust these 'soft assets' and normally deduct them when appraising a balance-sheet. Investments in private companies are usually shown at cost, but when the holding becomes large enough so that the company is classified as a 'subsidiary' or an 'associate', then it must be treated in a particular way. Generally a company is a 'subsidiary' if the holding is not less than 50 per cent and an 'associate' if not less than 20 per cent. Small investments in listed companies are, however, usually categorised as current assets because of the ease of realisation, and, while still listed at cost, market value is normally also disclosed.

Provisions (line I) are liabilities of 'uncertain' amount. For example, the business might have a liability for taxation that is uncertain as to amount because a point of tax law is in question. Prudence would dictate that a provision be set up to recognise the liability even though the actual amount is uncertain.

In the capital and reserves section (line K), a number of terms need to be explained. Share premium is the amount paid for a share in excess of its face-value. For example, if a £1 share is issued by the company for £1.50, the share premium would be 50p. Generally the only allowable source of dividends is accumulated profit in the profit-and-loss account, and the share premium account is therefore not available for distribution; after all, it is really the same as the ordinarily subscribed capital. The amount recorded for the revaluation of any fixed assets is shown in the revaluation reserve. This is not normally distributable unless the revaluation is realised by the sale of the asset, in which case the amount would be transferred to the profit-and-loss account.

Table 10.4 shows the full balance-sheet as specified by Format 1, the Companies Act 1985. The headings or sub-headings may be deleted if there is no amount to be shown in respect of the financial year in question and the previous year. Also, those items preceded by arabic numbers may be combined if they are not material, and, even if material they can be combined, provided that the individual amounts are disclosed in the notes of the accounts, in which case only those items preceded by letters or roman numbers would be shown. Last year's figures must also be shown.

The 1985 Act also lays down standard income statements or profit-and-loss account formats as shown in Table 10.5. Notice the use of the word 'turnover' rather than sales. The Act requires a considerable amount of disclosure. Of course, the company itself will have far greater detail about the amounts making up these figures. For example, the account for 'distribution costs' might be presented, within the company, by separate accounts for packaging costs, van depreciation, van running costs, and drivers' wages. However, this would represent the minimum number of accounts that any business would have to keep.

'Extraordinary' income and charges come from events or transactions 'outside the ordinary activities of a business', and are both material and expected not to recur frequently. They do not include items that are simply large. An example of an extraordinary charge would be redundancy costs in closing a factory.

While 'full' accounts must be sent to shareholders, small businesses need not file all this information with the Registrar of Companies. The amount of disclosure required for public filings depends upon whether the company is classified as 'small' or 'medium' by the 1985 Act (see Chapter 1). If the company is 'small', then an income statement is not required at all. The balance-sheet need only show those items preceded by a letter or roman numeral. In addition, certain notes about accounting policies, share capital, loans to directors, aggregate debtors and creditors falling due after more than one and five years respectively, secured creditors, investment in other corporate bodies and details of any ultimate holding company must also be appended to the accounts. If the company is classified as 'medium', then items 1, 2, 3 and 6 in the income statement may be combined to give the one heading of 'gross profit'.

The Companies Acts require extensive additional disclosure. All companies must provide a statement of their accounting policies. Large companies need to disclose turnover, and profit before tax, substantially different classes of business, and provide geographic analysis. All companies other than 'small' ones need a director's report covering a number of specified areas. These include a review of the year's activities, recommended dividends, certain personnel policies, lists of directors and their share dealings, details of any of its own shares purchased by the company and a review of future developments. The Acts also require certain other specified disclosures such as selected expenses (e.g. audit fees, directors' remuneration, charitable and political donations, hire charges and depreciation) and the number of employees and their aggregate remuneration.

The Companies Acts require a company to prepare and file audited accounts annually, and the small businessman will rely heavily on the auditor to prepare the accounts in such a way as to comply with the Acts. The auditor is required to sign the accounts as representing a

Table 10.4 Balance-sheet in accordance with the 1985 Companies Act
(unabridged) (Format I)

A	CALLED-UP SHARE CAPITAL NOT PAID			£ —
B	FIXED ASSETS			
	I Intangible assets			
	1 Development costs	£ —		
	2 Concessions, patents, licences, etc.	—		
	3 Goodwill	—		
	4 Payment on account	—	—	
	II TANGIBLE ASSETS			
	1 Land and buildings	£500,000		
	2 Plant and machinery	£400,000		
	3 Fixtures, fittings, tools and equipment	—		
	4 Payments on account and assets under construction	—	900,000	
	III INVESTMENTS			
	1 Shares in group companies	£ —		
	2 Loans to group companies	—		
	3 Shares in related companies	—		
	4 Loans to related companies	—		
	5 Other investments other than loans	—		
	6 Other loans	—		
	7 Own shares	—	—	£900,000
C	CURRENT ASSETS			
	I Stocks			
	1 Raw materials and consumables	£100,000		
	2 Work-in-progress	75,000		
	3 Finished goods	100,000		
	4 Payment on account	—	275,000	
	II Debtors			
	1 Trade debtors	£265,000		
	2 Amounts owed by group companies	—		
	3 Amounts owed by related companies	—		
	4 Other debtors	—	265,000	
	III Investments			
	1 Shares in group companies	£ —		
	2 Own shares	—		
	3 Other investments	—	—	
	IV Cash at bank and in hand		60,000	
			600,000	
D	PREPAYMENTS AND ACCRUED INCOME		—	
			600,000	

Table 10.4 cont't.

E	CREDITORS: AMOUNTS FALLING DUE WITHIN ONE YEAR			
	1 Debenture loans	£ —		
	2 Bank loans and overdrafts	—		
	3 Payments received on account	—		
	4 Trade creditors	(147,500)		
	5 Bills of exchange payable	—		
	6 Amounts owed to group companies	—		
	7 Amounts owed to related companies	—		
	8 Other creditors	(102,500)	(250,000)	
F	NET CURRENT ASSETS			£350,000
G	TOTAL ASSETS *less* CURRENT LIABILITIES			£1,250,000
H	CREDITORS: AMOUNTS FALLING DUE AFTER MORE THAN ONE YEAR			
	1 Debenture loans	£(200,000)		
	2 Bank loans and overdrafts	—		
	3 Payments received on account	—		
	4 Trade creditors	—		
	5 Bills of exchange payable	—		
	6 Amounts owed to group companies	—		
	7 Amounts owed to related companies	—		
	8 Other creditors	—		£(200,000)
I	PROVISIONS FOR LIABILITIES AND CHARGES			
	1 Pensions	£ —		
	2 Taxation	—		
	3 Other provisions	—		—
J	ACCRUALS AND DEFERRED INCOME			£
				—
				£1,050,000
K	CAPITAL AND RESERVES			
	I Called-up share capital			£800,000
	II Share premium account			—
	III Revaluation reserve			£ 55,000
	IV Other reserves			
	1 Capital redemption reserve funds	£ —		
	2 Reserve for own shares	—		
	3 Reserve provided for by Articles of Association	—		
	4 Other reserves	—		—
	V Profit-and-loss account			£195,000
				£1,050,000

Table 10.5 Profit-and-loss account in accordance with the 1985 Companies Act (Format I)

1	Turnover		£1,825,000
2	Cost of sales		£(1,375,000)
3	Gross profit		£450,000
4	Distribution costs		(£110,000)
5	Administrative expenses:		
	Audit fee	£ 3,000	
	Director's remuneration	£ 11,200	
	Directors' commission	£ 7,800	
	Other costs	£125,000	(147,000)
6	Other operating income		—
	TRADING PROFIT		193,000
7	Income from shares in group companies		—
8	Income from shares in related companies		—
9	Income from other fixed asset investments		—
10	Other interest receivable		—
11	Amounts written-off investments		—
12	Interest payable		(18,000)
	PROFIT BEFORE TAX		175,000
13	Taxation		(70,000)
14	PROFIT ON ORDINARY ACTIVITIES AFTER TAX		105,000
15	Extraordinary income	£ —	
16	Extraordinary charges	£ —	
17	Extraordinary profit		—
18	Tax on extraordinary profit		—
19	Other taxes not shown above		—
20	PROFIT FOR THE FINANCIAL YEAR		105,000
	Dividends		(42,500)
	Retained profit for the year		£62,500

'true-and-fair' view of the affairs of the company or state his reasons for not doing so (such accounts are said to be 'qualified'). To do so he needs to verify independently all the items in the accounts. He will attend the stock count, verify debtors and creditors and check other assets and liabilities.

However, the auditor can provide a far greater service to the small business. Many small businesses get the auditor to prepare the accounts, since they consider themselves not to have the time or expertise to do so. If this is the case, it is imperative to prepare accounts regularly, say monthly or quarterly, rather than waiting for the annual visit required by the Companies Acts. However, if the business prepares its own accounts, the auditor will take an interest in the accounting system of the business and the control the business has over its assets. He will be an invaluable source of advice on this, and indeed other financial matters. The auditor will also prepare a computation of the business's tax liability for submission to the Inland Revenue and can provide worthwhile advice on this complex area. In short, the auditor can provide the small business with the sort of expert financial advice that it will find invaluable. Through specialists in his firm, he can be a source of expert knowledge on areas which most businesses could never hope to know in depth.

The auditor will himself be a qualified accountant and a member of one of the professional accounting bodies whose members are qualified for appointment as auditors in Britain. These are the Institute of Chartered Accounts in England and Wales, in Scotland, in Ireland, and the Association of Certified Accountants. These bodies, together with the Chartered Institute of Management Accountants, have issued a number of *Statements of Standard Accounting Practice* (SSAP) for application to all financial statements intended to give a 'true-and fair' view, and the auditor must also comply with these. These statements regulate ways of accounting for certain transactions or events, and also impose certain additional disclosure requirements, the major requirements relating to a 'source and application of funds statement.' We shall deal with these later. The modified disclosure requirements for 'small' and 'medium' companies mean that the accounts filed with the Registrar will not comply with those SSAPs and therefore will not give a 'true-and fair' view. However, shareholders' accounts must still comply with the requirements of the SSAPs.

The Companies Acts require that all companies keep certain accounting records 'sufficient to show and explain the company's transactions'. These are developed in Chapter 15.

CHAPTER 11

Costs and Profit

COST DEFINITIONS AND USES	206
COST-VOLUME-PROFIT BEHAVIOUR	210
Cost Behaviour	211
Breakeven point	213
Calculating breakeven	215
Using contribution analysis	217
Target income calculations	219
The risk-return trade-off	220
Limiting factors	222
Multi-product analysis	223
Costs and selling price	224
Determining fixed and variable costs	225

Cost definitions and uses

Everybody knows what costs are until they try to define them. That is not altogether surprising because there are many different kinds of cost, and one cost concept may be suitable for a given purpose while another might not. In other words, there is no such thing as *the* cost of a good or service. The appropriate cost depends on the purpose to which it will be put.

A working definition of cost is the sacrifice required to obtain something. Costs are normally expressed in money. Thus you may pay £4,500 for a second-hand car; however, you are unlikely to value that car at £4,500, since you might have been willing to pay £5,000 for it. Nor is £4,500 necessarily the price you would get if you were to sell the car tomorrow; you might only get £4,200 for it. Equally if you were to replace the car tomorrow with an identical one, you might have to pay £4,800 because you got such a bargain in the first place.

The *historic cost* of the car was £4,500: the amount of money it actually cost when it was purchased. The *opportunity cost* is £4,200: what the car could now be sold for. This is the amount forgone by not selling, and is the notion of cost that is relevant to decision-making.

Costs and profit   207

The *replacement cost* is £4,800: the cost to replace it with an identical vehicle. The balance-sheets of large companies often show fixed assets and stock at their replacement cost as well as their historic cost.

This chapter will focus on historic cost. Later chapters will use the notions of cost developed here, but will focus on the use of costs in decision-making. Many of the concepts developed here will, however, be equally relevant for *cost prediction*. Historic costs are often a good basis for prediction, but can rarely be used as a measure of predicted costs without being altered in the light of other factors. To understand these factors we have to understand how costs behave with changes in the volume of goods or services that we produce and sell.

Two words commonly used to describe cost behaviour are 'fixed' and 'variable'. A *fixed cost* is one that does not vary with changes in output. For example, if a factory is not being fully used, no additional expenditure will be necessary on factory rent and rates, or managerial salaries, to increase output. These costs are fixed with respect to an increase in production. A *variable cost* is a cost that does change with output. For example, additional expenditure would be required to provide the extra materials or the wages of workers directly involved in manufacture, or even the additional electricity to power the machines. The distinction is not always clear cut. For example, your electricity bill consists of a fixed charge for your meter and a variable charge according to usage of electricity.

Fixed costs are frequently described as either *discretionary* (costs that *can* be altered at the discretion of management, e.g. advertising), or *committed* (costs that management *cannot* alter and are therefore fixed over a wide range of activity, e.g. factory rent or rates).

When trying to predict future costs, knowledge of cost behaviour patterns allows you to predict how these costs are affected by changes in output. What it does not tell you about is the effect that inflation will have on those costs, and a further allowance for anticipated inflation will have to be made.

There are other cost terms commonly used by accountants, particularly in relation to manufacturing businesses. These are summarised in Figure 11.1. *Direct costs* are those costs that can be directly identified with a product or job (or alternatively in larger organisations, a cost centre). The two most obvious examples are materials and labour. It should be relatively easy to identify the materials going into a product, as indeed it should be relatively easy to identify which products or jobs an employee works on. Direct costs tend to be mainly variable costs, but not exclusively so. Factory *overhead costs* or *indirect manufacturing costs* are all those other factory manufacturing costs which are not directly attributable to a particular job or product

```
                        TOTAL COSTS
                             │
          ┌──────────────────┴──────────────────┐
          │ Manufacturing or production costs   │
          │                                     │
   ┌──────┴──────┐                              │
   │ Prime costs │                              │
   │             │                              │
┌──┴──┐ ┌─────┐ ┌─────┐   ┌──────────────┐  ┌──────────────┐
│Direct│ │Direct│ │Direct│  │Factory overhead│ │Selling, distribution│
│materials│ │labour│ │expenses│ │costs or indirect│ │and administration │
│     │ │     │ │     │   │manufacturing │  │costs         │
│     │ │     │ │     │   │costs         │  │              │
└─────┘ └─────┘ └─────┘   └──────────────┘  └──────────────┘
```

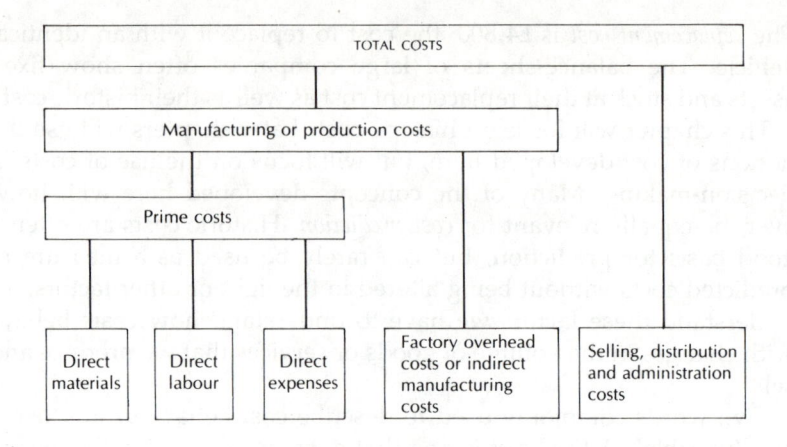

Figure 11.1   Manufacturing cost terminology

(such as the cost of indirect materials or labour, repairs and maintenance, depreciation of factory or general heat and power). *Prime costs* are simply the total of all direct costs, and *manufacturing or production costs* are simply the total of prime costs and factory overhead costs. The *total costs* a business faces will be the manufacturing costs, plus all other costs such as selling, distribution and administrative costs.

The terms *direct* and *indirect* have no meaning unless they are related to an object of costing such as a job or product. Traceability is the essence of the distinction. The word 'direct' refers to the practical, obvious, physical tracing of cost as incurred by the given cost object. There is almost always some sort of observable physical identification with the cost object. Because of this, direct costs are the most reliable costs when attributing costs to one of a number of products or departments.

Let us take an example to bring home the differences in this terminology. If the car in the previous example has a life expectancy of 5 years, straight-line depreciation would yield a depreciation charge of £900 per year. Suppose insurance costs £120 per year, the road fund license fee £80, and the car is housed in a garage with one other vehicle at an annual rental of £200 for the two. Suppose the car is expected to travel 12,000 miles in a year and does 30 miles to the gallon, petrol costing £1.80 a gallon. Maintenance costs are 2p per mile. The operating costs for the year should be as shown in Table 11.1.

Table 11.1

	Variable costs (£)	Fixed costs (£)	Total costs (£)
Direct costs			
Petrol, oil (6p × 12,000)	720		
Maintenance, etc. (2p × 12,000)	240		
Insurance		120	
Road fund licence		80	
Depreciation		900	2,060
Indirect costs			
Garage rent		100	100
TOTAL COSTS	£960	£1,200	£2,160

Thus we can analyse costs in two ways:

	£		£	(p per mile)
Direct costs	2,060	Variable costs	960	8
Indirect costs	100	Fixed costs	1,200	10
TOTAL	2,160		2,160	18

Notice that £960 of the direct costs were variable (with respect to mileage) and £1,100 were fixed costs.

Thus *average cost* per mile of running the car is 18p per mile (£2,160 *divided by* 12,000 miles), while the *marginal cost* per mile, the cost of travelling one extra mile, is only 8p (£960 *divided by* 12,000). This example illustrates the sort of confusion that cost classifications can cause. What is the cost of running the car? If you had the car anyway, and were offered 13p per mile to use it to collect somebody from the station, would you take it?

This example also illustrates how different costs are relevant to different purposes. Generally, costs are important for three purposes:

1. INCOME DETERMINATION. In order to determine income you need to have an accurate measure of costs. We shall see later in the chapter that this is not as straightforward as you might think, since expenditure does not necessarily represent a cost immediately. For example, the car was purchased for £4,500, but the allocation of that expenditure to cost was in five equal depreciation instalments of £900. If the car in fact lasted for only four years, our 'cost' should have been £1,125 per year.

2. CONTROL AND PLANNING OF THE BUSINESS: This involves controlling the costs of various activities – departments or cost centres – as well as product costs. If you could only get 13p per mile for hiring out your car, you would realise income of only £1,560 per year and would therefore be making a loss of £600 each year. You might decide to look at ways of cutting those costs, or getting rid of the car and going out of the car-hire business altogether. Planning and control activities are continuous and interrelated. Information derived from the control of a business will be used to plan for the future. These plans will, in turn, influence how you control the business. During the course of operations, many factors may alter the original plan and some of these factors will come from the information derived from controlling the business.
3. DECISION-MAKING. In choosing between alternative courses of action, cost will be an important element in the decision. But which cost? In the example, the hire offer yielded a marginal benefit of 5p per mile (13p–8p), so as a one-off opportunity it would be worthwhile taking. But in the long run, of course, any business must cover all its costs, not just its variable costs.

Most accounting systems will provide data for all these purposes. It is just a question of being able to disentangle the information and find the costs that are relevant to almost all organisations: manufacturers, retailers or service businesses. However, the case of the manufacturing company is probably the most comprehensive and general. It embraces production, marketing and general administration functions, and if we can develop an understanding of cost accounting in this sort of organisation it can readily be applied to any organisation.

Cost-volume-profit behaviour

Cost-volume-profit analysis gives a very broad overview of the planning process and develops an understanding of the key element in any business decision: the trade-off between risk and return. However, it is worth stating at the very beginning that we shall be considering very simplified versions of the real world. Whether these simplifications can be justified depends upon the facts of a particular case and the relative accuracy of those simplifications compared with the costs of a more complex model.

Cost behaviour

We shall build upon the concepts of *fixed* and *variable* costs by making further simplifying assumptions. Let us assume that over the range of output being examined the fixed costs stay fixed and the variable costs vary directly and proportionately with output. This is the case in the example used in the previous section. Variable costs were 8p per mile and fixed costs £1,200 up to 12,000 miles per year. These fixed costs were £1,200 whether 2,000 or 12,000 miles were covered. Insurance, licence and garage rent were completely unaffected by mileage, though in practice depreciation might be affected if annual mileage were significantly higher or lower than 12,000 miles. The variable costs vary directly and proportionately with mileage covered: at 12,000 miles variable costs are £960 (8p × 12,000 miles); at 2,000 miles they are £160 (8p × 2,000 miles); at zero miles variable costs are zero. These cost relationships are shown in Figure 11.2.

Of course, the assumptions we have made are not completely true. As we have seen, the fixed costs are only fixed in relationship to a given period of time and a given range of activity (or mileage), often called the 'relevant range'. The 'activity' of a business is normally measured by the volume of goods sold (in units) or its sales value. As activity increases, at some stage the fixed costs will also increase. In our example the depreciation may increase. More generally as the

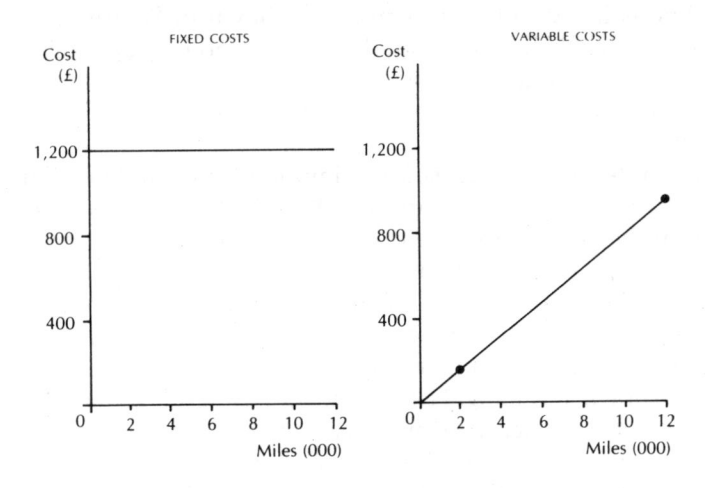

Figure 11.2 Cost variability

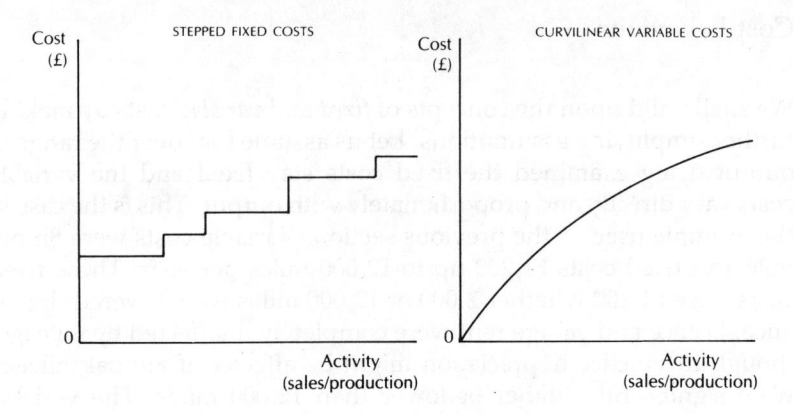

Figure 11.3 Cost variability over a wide range of activity

activity of production increases we may have to purchase additional machinery, and eventually the factory building itself may have to be expanded. This results in fixed costs exhibiting the 'stepped' characteristic shown in Figure 11.3, as the 'relevant range' is increased. Variable costs also do not necessarily increase linearly with output. For example, we may be able to obtain quantity discounts on material purchases or reorganise production so that the workers are more efficient. This will mean that, over a large enough range, the variable cost line is likely to be curvilinear, as shown in Figure 11.3. These features of cost behaviour underline the importance of specifying the 'relevant range' and they also underline the fact that our assumptions about linearity are only likely to be true over a restricted range of activity.

In Chapter 4 we discussed the importance of understanding the average cost curve for a particular business. From the information given in the car example we can derive this curve. The variable cost per mile is 8p, but as more miles are driven the fixed costs are spread over a greater number of miles and therefore the averaged fixed cost per mile will decrease. Therefore average cost per mile will be as shown in Table 11.2. The average cost curve that we get from these data is shown in Figure 11.4. It shows how average costs per mile decline as more miles are driven. From the information available, we have not yet arrived at the point where costs per mile start to increase, but economists tell us that at some point diseconomies of scale will set in.

Table 11.2

Miles	Average fixed cost per mile £	Variable cost per mile £	Average cost per mile £
1,000	1.20	↑	1.28
2,000	0.60		0.68
3,000	0.40		0.48
4,000	0.30		0.38
5,000	0.24		0.32
6,000	0.20	0.08	0.28
7,000	0.17		0.25
8,000	0.15		0.23
9,000	0.13		0.21
10,000	0.12		0.20
11,000	0.11		0.19
12,000	0.10	↓	0.18

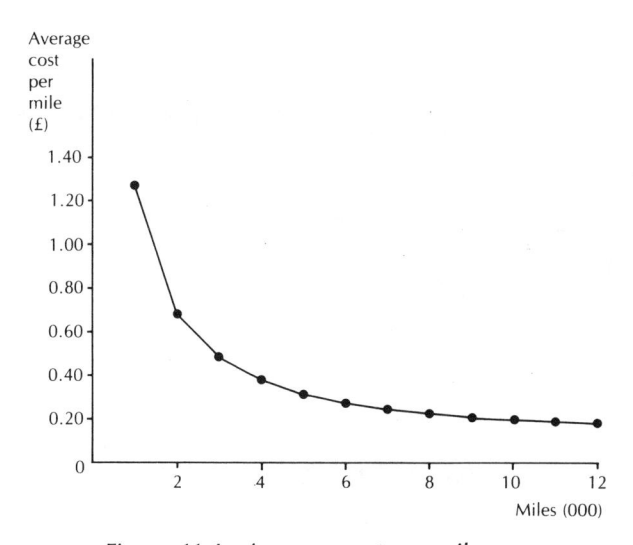

Figure 11.4 Average cost per mile

Break-even point

The analysis of costs become more relevant when income considerations are introduced. Suppose that in our previous example you were able to hire out the car for 20p per mile. In that case, if the car

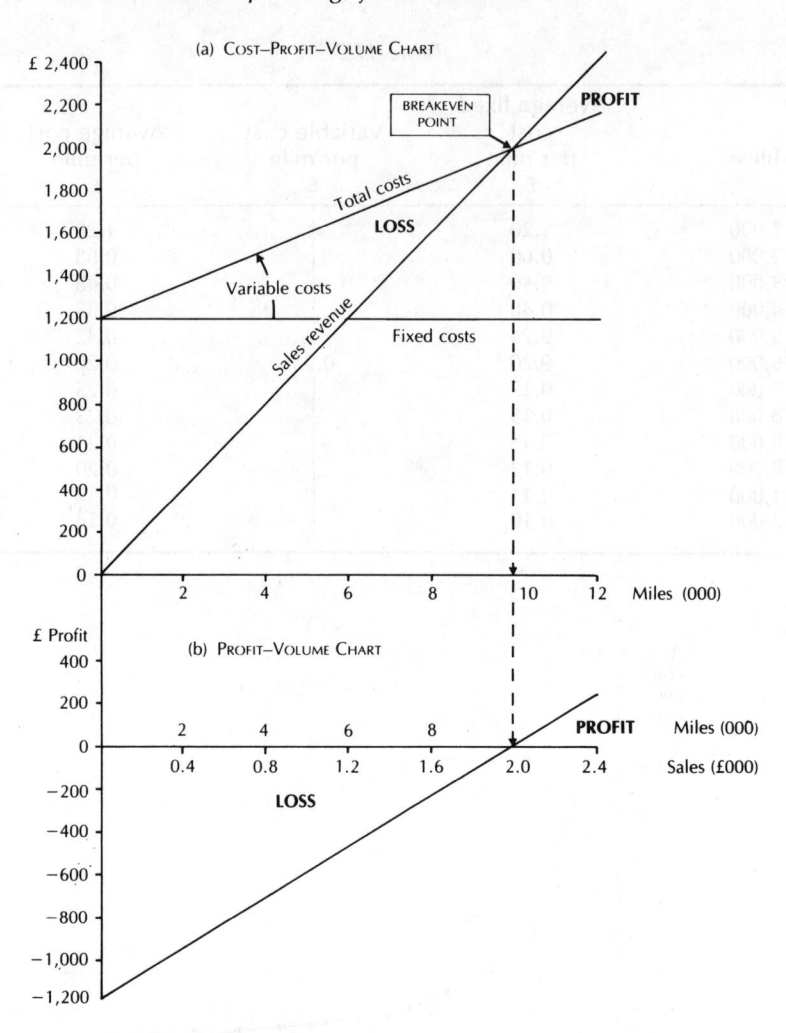

214   *Small business: planning, finance and control*

Figure 11.5   Break-even charts

were driven 12,000 miles, it would generate £2,400 of revenue (20p × 12,000 miles) and a profit of £240 (£2,400 − £2,160). If the car was not used at all during the year, it would generate no revenue and make a loss equal to the fixed costs of £1,200.

These relationships are shown in Figure 11.5 in the form of a cost-volume-profit chart and a profit-volume chart. To arrive at the cost-volume-profit chart the total cost line must first be plotted. This is simply the fixed cost line with the variable costs added on to it. As you can see, at 12,000 miles there are £1,200 of fixed costs and £960 of variable costs. Next the sales revenue line must be plotted. Since revenue is generated at a constant 20p per mile, this is also a straight line, but through the origin. At 12,000 miles revenue is £2,400. Profit is £240 (£2,400 − £2,160).

The *break-even* point is the point at which the sales revenue and the total cost lines cross each other: that is, at 10,000 miles. It is the point of zero profits: the point at which the venture starts to generate profit. Below 10,000 miles per year a loss will be made; above 10,000 miles a profit will be made. Since marketing analysis is often such a difficult thing for a small business, particularly a new start-up small business, the break-even point is an essential piece of information, around which marketing plans can be built.

This information can be translated on to the simpler profit-volume chart. To draw any straight line only two points are needed. The maximum loss the car business faces is at zero miles per year when the total fixed costs of £1,200 represent the maximum loss. The break-even point (zero profit) we know is at 10,000 miles. We also know that, at 12,000 miles, profit is £240. Notice that the profit-volume line can also be specified in terms of sales *value* as well as *volume*. Thus the break-even point of 10,000 miles represents total sales of £2,000 (20p × 10,000 miles).

The difference between sales revenue and variable costs is called *contribution*. This is the contribution towards the fixed costs which are incurred anyway: the contribution towards achieving profitability. The contribution per mile in our example is 12p per mile (20p–8p). The total contribution towards fixed costs at 5,000 miles is £600 (12p × 5,000).

Calculating breakeven

The break-even point can be calculated rather than derived from graphs. At the break-even point there are no profits. Thus:

Total contribution − Fixed costs = 0

If

Q = number of units produced/sold to break even
P = selling price per unit
V = variable cost per unit
F = total fixed costs

$P - V$ = contribution per unit

then

$$(P - V)Q - F = 0$$

Therefore

$$Q = \frac{F}{(P - V)}$$

This equation gives us the general formula:

$$\text{Break-even point (in units)} = \frac{\text{Total fixed costs}}{\text{Contribution per unit}}$$

If we wished to find the break-even point in the sales value terms, all we have to do is multiply by the unit selling price.

Let us apply the formula to the car hire example:

$$\text{Break-even in units} = \frac{£1,200}{(20p - 8p)} = 10,000 \text{ miles}$$

$$\text{Break-even in value} = 10,000 \times 2p = £2,000$$

Often the contribution is expressed as a percentage of sales, called the contribution margin percentage, or profit-volume ratio. For the car hire business this is 60 per cent (12p/20p × 100%). The advantage of this is that the break-even point in sales value terms is given directly by dividing fixed costs by the profit-volume ratio. For example,

$$\frac{£1,200}{60\%} = £2,000$$

At this point it is worth repeating the simplifying assumptions made in calculating the break-even point:

1. Sales = production, so stocks remain unchanged.
2. Sales price is constant throughout the 'relevant range'.
3. Variable costs vary linearly with activity throughout the 'relevant range'.
4. Fixed costs are absolutely fixed throughout the 'relevant range'.
5. In any multi-product operation, the sales mix remains unchanged.

It must be remembered that the division of costs into their fixed and variable components is dependent upon the time scale involved. For very short time periods even labour costs can be fixed, but in the longer term few costs are completely fixed. Despite these simplifying assumptions this 'contribution' approach to looking at business decisions has the major advantage of being easy to understand and crystallising the choices available to the decision-maker.

Using contribution analysis

Consider the problems to be faced if you were only able to hire out that car at 13p per mile. Should you close down the business? What options are open to you? You would be making a loss:

			£
Sales revenue	13p × 12,000 miles		1,560
Costs:			
Variable	960		
Fixed	1200		2,160
		Loss	£ 600

However, if you look at it from a contribution approach, at least you are making a contribution to your fixed costs of £600 (£1,560 – £960). Therefore there are some other options open to you other than just closing down the business.

- INCREASE SALES REVENUE
  (a) *By increasing mileage (volume).* Your new break-even point is 24,000 miles (1200/(13p–8p)) and you would have to exceed this to go into profit.
  (b) *By increasing mileage charge (selling price).* Every penny added to the mileage charge is an extra penny contribution to fixed costs and will bring down your breakeven point accordingly:

Mileage charge (p)	Break-even (miles)
13	24,000
14	20,000
16	15,000
18	12,000

- REDUCE VARIABLE COSTS
  This is often very difficult to do. Essentially it entails doing the same job more efficiently – in this case, driving more economically

to save petrol or cutting down on maintenance costs, perhaps by doing the maintenance yourself.
- REDUCE FIXED COSTS
  Reducing overheads is the first thing most businesses that find themselves in trouble will do. In our case, we could stop keeping the car in a garage, or buy a new, cheaper car.

Contrast your problem with that faced by your friend, who, say, bought a cheaper car whose depreciation charge was only £280 per year. He found he could only hire out his cheaper car for 7p per mile, but, because he faces the same other costs as yourself, he too is making a loss:

			£
Sales revenue	7p × 12,000		840
Costs:			
Variable	960		
Fixed	480		1,440
		Loss	£ 600

What options are open to him other than closing down the business? If you look carefully at the figures you will see that there is one important difference. He is not even making a contribution to his fixed costs. His contribution is negative: − £120 (£840–£960). He can never hope to break even until his mileage charge (7p) exceeds his variable costs (8p). He has two options: increase his mileage charge (selling price), or decrease his variable costs. You can see how a knowledge of cost behaviour has demonstrated the courses of action open to you and your friend.

One final concept is that of the *cash break-even point*. This is the point where cash inflows equal cash outflows. The cash breakeven point is usually lower than the profit breakeven point since most businesses have some non-cash expenses. Returning to our car-hire example, the only non-cash expense is depreciation (£900). If the hire charge were 20p per mile again, the cash breakeven point would be only 2,500 miles ((1200 − 900)/(20p −8p)). After 2,500 miles, the business is at least generating positive cash flows.

Cash is the essential lifeblood of any business. Bills are paid with cash, not profit. In this case, once the car has covered 2,500 miles, each additional mile will yield 12p cash in excess of the fixed cash outgoings. This can be invested so it will be available to replace the car at some future date, or it may be used for other things, such as

Target income calculations

The break-even formula can be adapted to allow the calculation of the level of activity required to generate a certain target income. Let us assume that, in the previous example, you required a 10 per cent return on your investment of £4,500: that is, £450 per year. In that case:

Total contribution − Fixed costs = Target income

The necessary level of activity to generate this income will be given by

$$Q = \frac{\text{Fixed costs} + \text{Target income}}{\text{Contribution per unit}}$$

Thus

$$Q = \frac{1{,}200 + 450}{0.12}$$
$$= 13{,}750 \text{ miles}$$
$$= £2{,}750 \text{ sales}$$

If your target income were expressed as a percentage of sales, say 15 per cent, this would be only slightly more difficult. In this case 15 per cent of sales revenue is 3p per mile (20p × 15%). Hence:

$$Q = \frac{1{,}200 + (0.03 \times Q)}{0.12}$$
$$Q(0.12 - 0.03) = 1{,}200$$
$$Q = \frac{1{,}200}{0.09}$$
$$= 13{,}333 \text{ miles}$$
$$= £2{,}667 \text{ sales}$$

The break-even equation can be used in a similar way to examine the effects of cost changes on the break-even point. Let us assume insurance costs go up by £100. The new break-even point would become:

$$Q = \frac{\text{Fixed cost} + \text{Additional fixed cost}}{\text{Contribution per unit}}$$

$$= \frac{£1{,}200 + £100}{0.12}$$

$$= 10{,}833 \text{ miles}$$
$$= £2{,}167 \text{ sales}$$

However another way of looking at the problem is to ask how much extra sales is required to cover the increase in fixed costs. This is given by the formula:

$$\text{Additional } Q = \frac{\text{Additional fixed cost}}{\text{Contribution per unit}}$$

$$= \frac{100}{0.12}$$

$$= 833 \text{ miles}$$
$$= £167 \text{ sales}$$

This is a particularly useful way of looking at decisions to increase discretionary fixed costs, such as advertising, because it tells you the additional sales required to recover that investment.

The risk-return trade-off

The profit-volume chart allows us to understand the nature of most financial decisions quite clearly: that is, the trade-off between risk and return. Generally the higher the fixed costs in any business, the higher its risk. Similarly the higher the breakeven point, the higher the risk. However, as volumes increase, the fixed costs do not change and the profit potential generally increases.

Let us illustrate with another example. Suppose an engineering company can produce an additional 1,500 units of either valve A or valve B per year. The additional fixed costs to be invested to achieve this production would be £15,000 for A and £20,000 for B. Valve A sells for £35 and variable costs total £15. Valve B sells for £36 and variable costs total £11. The breakeven point for A is 750 valves (£15,000/(£35 − £15)) and for B is 800 valves (£20,000/(£36 − £11)). If the

Costs and profit 221

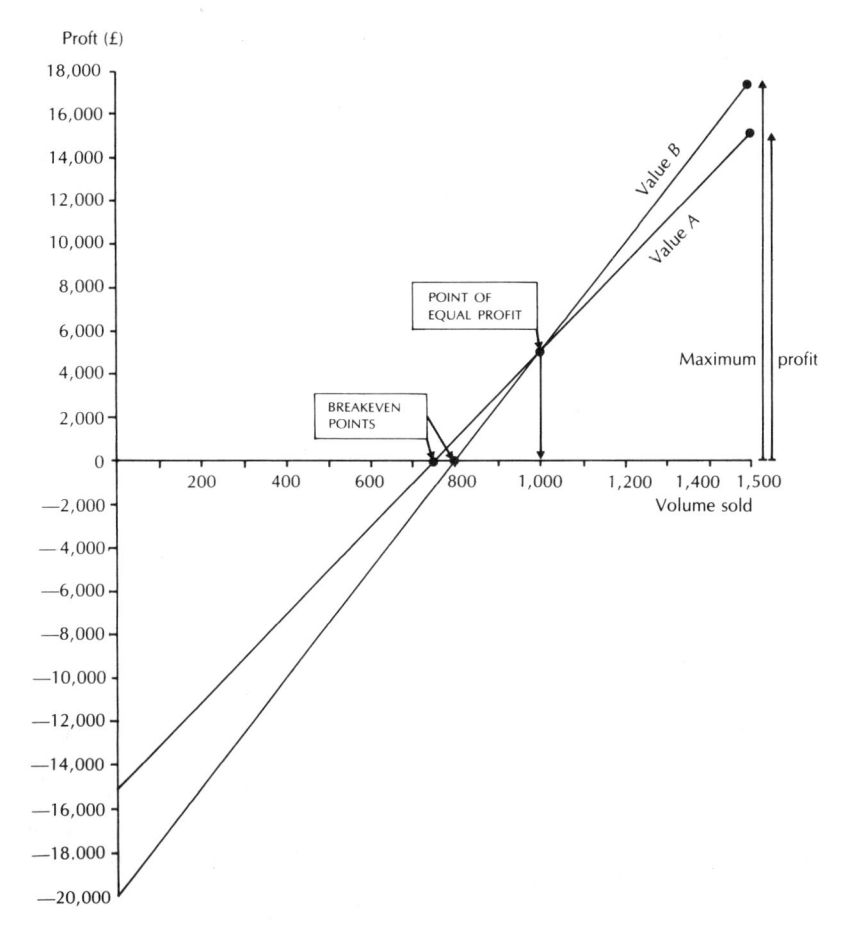

Figure 11.6

company can sell all its production of 1,500 valves, valve A would generate profit of £15,000 ((£35 − £15) × 1,500 − £15,000)) and valve B a profit of £17,500 ((£36 −£11) × 1,500 − £20,000)). The profit-volume charts for A and B are shown in Figure 11.6. Since the business can invest in either valve A or valve B, but not both, the decision depends critically upon the estimate of sales. If sales are above 1,000 per year, valve B yields more profit. If sales are below 1,000 per year, A yields a higher profit (or a lower loss). In other worlds valve B offers the chance of a higher return, but this has to be set against the risk of a greater loss, and losses occurring when sales fall below only 800 valves.

It is often possible to substitute variable cost for fixed costs; for example, when a company invests in labour-saving machinery it might substitute higher depreciation charges (a fixed cost) for lower labour costs (a variable cost). Rather than A and B representing different valves, consider the decision if A were to represent a labour-intensive way of producing a valve and B a capital-intensive way of producing the same valve. The capital-intensive way offers higher returns, but only if high volumes can be achieved. Generally small businesses are more labour-intensive than larger companies.

A final point to consider is that the largest non-operating fixed cost a small business faces is often interest on debt. This has to be paid whether sales are high or not. The higher this fixed cost, the higher the risk of the company, and the higher will be its breakeven point. Dividends, on the other hand, are totally discretionary costs. If sales are low, dividends do not have to be declared. This is why equity finance is generally considered to be less risky than debt finance.

Limiting factors

Often a small business will face restrictions on the alternatives open to it because of shortages of working capital, production facilities, raw materials or skilled labour. These shortages may occur because the small business cannot obtain additional funds to invest or because the businessman does not want to invest additional funds. Whatever the reasons, these restrictions, called 'limiting factors', can cause problems for the businessman who wishes to maximise his profits. The framework developed so far can be used to solve this problem.

Given a range of manufacturing possibilities, all with unchanged fixed costs, profits will be maximised when contribution is maximised. The maximum possible contribution will be restricted by the limiting factor and will be obtained when the contribution per unit of the limiting factor is maximised.

For example, suppose a company can manufacture four products, A, B, C, and D, and faces shared fixed costs of £45,000. The limiting factor it faces is the number of press-hours available, restricted to 2,000 per year. Cost, revenues and other details are set out below:

	A	B	C	D
Maximum sales (units)	250	1,000	750	500
Press-hours per unit	2	1	4	2
Selling Price	130	100	100	100
Variable costs	68	49	66	68
Contribution	62	51	34	32
Contribution per press-hour	31	51	8.5	16

As can be seen, product B generates the maximum contribution per press-hour, followed by A, D and C, in that order. Thus the company should produce as much as possible of the products in that order (B, A, D, C) until all available press-hours are used up.

This would generate the following levels of production and resulting income:

		Press-hours	Contribution £
B	1,000 units @ £51 per unit	1,000	51,000
A	250 units @ £62 per unit	500	15,500
D	250 units @ £32 per unit	500	8,000
	TOTAL	2,000	74,500
Fixed costs			45,000
Profit			29,500

Any combination of sales other than this would generate a lower profit so long as the restriction of press-hours remains.

If there is more than one limiting factor (for example, press-hours and raw materials available), the problem is far more complex and cannot be solved simply by calculating contribution per limiting factor for each of the scarce resources, since the ranking this would give for each resource could be different. To obtain a solution all possible contributions of production, and their effect on profit, must be considered. This is best achieved using linear programming techniques, beyond the scope of this book. However, linear programming packages are now available for most microcomputers and these can be relatively simple to operate.

Multi-product analysis

Many businesses, like the one in the preceding example, will sell a number of products. These products will share facilities, and it will often not be possible to split off fixed costs and allocate them to particular products. It is still possible to use profit-volume analysis in a multi-product business. What is required is an estimate of the mix of sales, i.e. we need to know in what proportions the different products will be sold. Once this is known, the average contribution per unit sold can be calculated, and this, when divided into the fixed costs, will give the breakeven point.

Let us return to the example in the last section. If we remove the restriction on press-hours, but accept the sales mix as we calculated it, we can work out the average contribution per unit sold:

	B	A	D
Units sold	1,000	250	250
therefore, sales mix	4/6	1/6	1/6
Contribution per unit	51	62	32
Average contribution per unit (sales mix × contribution)	34	+ 10⅓ +	5⅓ = 49⅔

Since fixed costs are £45,000 the breakeven point is 906 units (45,000/49⅔).

These units would be sold in the standard mix indicated above, which represents 604 units of B (4/6 × 906) and 151 units of both A and D (1/6 × 906). The problem with this approach is obvious. What happens when the mix of sales changes? The only solution is to repeat the calculation using a new sales mix.

In this particular case, with the restriction on press-hours removed, it would benefit the company to sell all it can produce of A, which has the highest contribution of the three products. Once it has satisfied this demand, product B gives the next highest margin.

Costs and selling price

Any marketing man would tell you that the selling price of any good or service should be dictated by the customer and the market. However, costs are a constraint on setting that selling price. In the long run any business will want to make a profit, and that entails meeting all the costs of the business. However, as we have seen, as volume increases, average cost per unit produced will probably fall as fixed costs are spread over more and more production (see Figure 11.4). Since the lower the selling price, the more a business is likely to sell, the two sides are indeed very much linked. A £1 drop in selling price is £1 less contribution to fixed costs, but if sales volume increases sufficiently then the drop in selling price might be worth while.

To illustrate this, let us return to the earlier car-hire example and the breakeven data. If we add some market estimates of the mileage you might cover, given these different mileage charges, we can determine the charge that would yield the highest total contribution to fixed costs of £1,200, and thus yield the highest profit: see Table 11.3.

Charging 18p per mile would yield the highest profit, although the breakeven point is now 12,000 miles. In choosing between the 20p and 16p per mile options, both yielding the same profit, the lower

Table 11.3

Mileage charge	Contribution per mile	Breakeven point (miles)	Estimated mileage covered	Total contribution	Profit
13p per mile	5p	24,000	22,000	£1,100	Loss £100
14p per mile	6p	20,000	20,000	£1,200	Nil
16p per mile	8p	15,000	18,000	£1,440	£240
18p per mile	10p	12,000	15,000	£1,500	£300
20p per mile	12p	10,000	12,000	£1,440	£240

breakeven at 20p (therefore lower risk) would indicate that this is the most sensible choice.

We have assumed so far that only one price can be charged for a good or service. This is not always the case. In our car-hire example suppose you had covered your estimated 12,000 miles, at 20p per mile for the year, and were offered one special journey of 100 miles which you could take because you had no other work. However, you were offered only 13p per mile. Would it be worth taking the job?

The job offers a mileage charge (selling price) below normal, but it is still above your variable costs and offers an additional contribution of £5 ((18p – 13p) × 100 miles)) that you would not otherwise have. Your fixed costs are covered, and even if they were not it is still £5 towards them that you would not otherwise have, since there is no work available at your normal mileage charge. On the face of it, as a one-off job when the business has the spare capacity the job is worth taking. However, the question is whether the one-off job will stay just that. If your other customers get to know about this 'special deal', will they not want to be charged 13p per mile also? 'You did it for a stranger so why not do it for a friend?' If you are forced to charge 13p a mile to all your customers, you will make a loss of £100 in the year. The only way you can charge this 'differential price' is if your existing customers will not find out or if you can claim you gave some kind of inferior service. British Rail charges differential prices by having two classes and a complex fare structure, offering special deals (Senior Citizens, Student Rail Cards, Day Returns, etc.) and many manufacturing companies price their exports differentially on the basis that the home market will not find out about it.

Determining fixed and variable costs

There are two methods of determining which costs are fixed and which are variable. Only the first method is suitable for start-ups, and in fact this method is far more commonly used then the second.

(1) INSPECTION OF COSTS CLASSIFICATIONS. The most intuitive way of determining whether a cost is fixed or variable is by inspection. Some costs are fixed or variable by their very nature, and their behaviour patterns are readily determined. For example, depreciation is normally fixed for any one year. Costs such as materials and piecework labour costs are variable. For situations where the subsequent analysis is not very sensitive to errors in classification, this method is quick and inexpensive. Often costs are partly fixed and partly variable. Also a little special thought is required since *all* depreciation charges are not necessarily fixed and *all* wages are not necessarily variable, particularly downwards.

(2) EXAMINATION OF PAST COST-BEHAVIOUR PATTERNS. When past data are available they can provide empirical evidence of cost-behaviour patterns. Any analysis of past behaviour can then be used to estimate the future, assuming future behaviour will be like that in the past. If we were to plot the behaviour of a particular cost against sales activity, we might arrive at a graph similar to one of those in Figure 11.3. However, it is unlikely that the straight line would be a perfect fit, and it is possible that the cost will be partly fixed and partly variable. Also past cost behaviour will be affected by both the factors we are trying to isolate and by the effects of inflation.

The first task is to adjust the cost data to eliminate the distortions caused by inflation. The £1 recorded in 1980 would purchase more than £1 today. To distinguish the effects of volume changes on our costs we must allow for this distortion. The problem is to find just what £1 in 1980 represents today. The easiest way to do this is to use an appropriate inflation index. The government publishes indices for all sorts of industrial costs. Let us assume we choose the simplest of all, the Retail Price Index. In 1980 this averaged 263.7, and in 1981 it averaged 295.0. Thus to purchase £1.00 of goods in 1980 required £1.12 (1 × 295.0/263.7) in 1981. By using an appropriate cost index we can adjust our cost data so that they are all in current £ and are not distorted by the effects of inflation.

Now we may plot the adjusted data and fit to it the line shown in Figure 11.7 as *AB*. We could do this in one of two ways: first, by simply drawing the line from visual inspection – however, a mistake in drawing such a line could result in a large error; second, we could employ statistical regression analysis, which would allow us to determine the line of 'best fit' – the one that minimises the sum of the squared deviations of the data points from the fitted line. It is beyond the scope of this book to explain how this line is arrived at. However, fixed and variable cost elements (called the 'intercept' and the 'slope' respectively) can be calculated using many pre-programmed calculators or by applying the following formula:

Costs (£)

Total fixed costs = OA

Variable cost per unit of activity = $\dfrac{BC}{OD}$

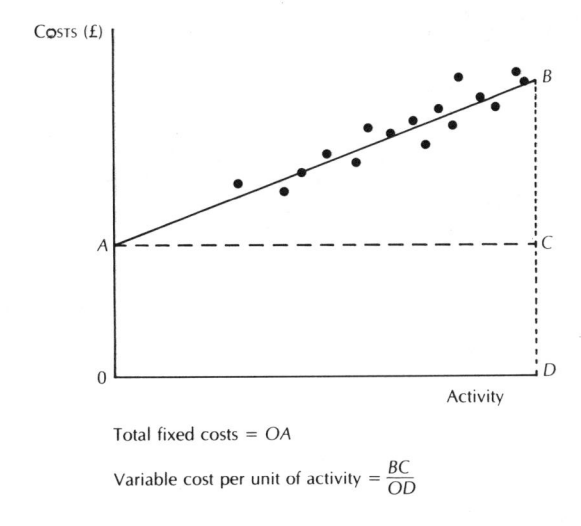

Figure 11.7 Scatter graph to determine fixed and variable costs

$$\text{Variable cost per unit of activity} = \frac{n(\Sigma xy) - (\Sigma x)(\Sigma y)}{n(\Sigma x^2) - (\Sigma x)^2}$$

$$\text{Total fixed costs} = \frac{(\Sigma y)(\Sigma x^2) - (\Sigma x)(\Sigma xy)}{n(\Sigma x^2) - (\Sigma x)^2}$$

where

Σy = total costs (sum of all cost observations)
Σx = total volume (sum of all activity level observations)
n = number of time periods
Σxy = sum of each product of cost and activity level (sum of each cost × activity level)

This technique looks complicated. However, it can be applied to the total costs of a business rather than each individual cost element, thus saving considerable time.

CHAPTER 12

Controlling Costs

JOB AND PROCESS COSTING	228
VALUING DIRECT MATERIAL COSTS	230
VALUING DIRECT LABOUR COSTS	231
OVERHEAD COSTS	231
FLOW OF COSTS	233

Job and process costing

Any business must control all its costs if it wishes to remain competitive. A large business needs to control costs in total as well as the costs of particular departments or activities. It also needs to control the costs of particular products or services. A small business will probably not have separate departments until much later in its development. Its major problem will be controlling costs in total, as well as individual product costs. We have already noted that total costs comprise direct costs, indirect manufacturing costs and administrative costs (see Figure 11.1). The problem, then, is to *value* these costs and then to assign them to individual products.

If the small business is producing only one product, then the average cost of each product over a period of time is simply total costs divided by total production. If it costs a total of £80,000 (£50,000 direct costs and £30,000 indirect, overhead costs) to produce 4,000 standard valve units, then the average total cost is £20 per unit. This is called *process costing*, and is fairly straightforward unless you are trying to determine the costs at various stages of the process or are producing more than one standard product using shared facilities. We shall deal with this problem later.

Many small businesses produce a large number of different products: for example, a general engineering company manufacturing to special order. Assigning costs in this sort of business is called *job*

Controlling costs

JOB DESCRIPTION: Switch Box					DATES			
JOB NUMBER: 5432					STARTED	DUE		FINISHED
QUANTITY ORDERED: 1					5 Oct	26 Nov		12 Oct

DIRECT MATERIALS					DIRECT LABOUR			
DATE	REFERENCE	QUANTITY	PRICE	VALUE £	DATE	OPERATOR	HOURS	RATE	VALUE £
5/10	64	1	100	100	5/10	32	6.5	2	13
	86	3	5	15	6/10	52	14	2.5	35
	87	3	22	66	6/10	53	12	2.5	30
	92	2	15	30	4/10	9	9	2.5	22.5
9/10	180	2,000	0.02	40	11/10	7	2.5	2	5
	181	150	0.01	15					
	190	500	0.01	5					
		TOTAL		271		TOTALS	44		105.5

SUMMARY

	£
DIRECT MATERIALS	271.00
DIRECT LABOUR	105.50
OVERHEAD APPLIED	

LABOUR HOURS	RATE £
44	2.50

110.00

TOTAL MANUFACTURED COST   £ 486.50

Figure 12.1   Job card

costing. Jobs will be assigned a number and then direct costs recorded under that number on a job card. Figure 12.1 shows a typical job card. In a small business, employees or supervisors might complete the card themselves. Normally direct materials are recorded from materials requisition notes issued by stores. Employees normally keep some sort of job time ticket showing the time spent on particular jobs and it is from these that the direct labour details are entered. An addition will be made for factory overheads (explained later) and the total will give the manufactured cost of a particular job.

Valuing direct material costs

Direct costs are by their very nature the easiest costs to assign to a product. However, the valuation of these costs is possibly not as straightforward as you might think.

Often it is not practicable, or desirable, to identify the cost of a particular part when the cost has varied with each delivery. Accountants use a number of conventions to get over this problem. For financial reporting and tax purposes, only the first is still acceptable.

1. FIFO: FIRST-IN, FIRST OUT. This method assumes that the earliest stock is issued first and therefore any remaining stock is valued at its most recent price.
2. LIFO: LAST-IN, FIRST OUT. This method is the opposite of FIFO. It assumes that the latest stock is issued first and any remaining stock is therefore valued at its older price. This method is popular in the USA.
3. AVERAGE OR STANDARD PRICE. Here an average or standard cost of the stock is calculated and used for all issues. The problem with this is that unless the average or standard is recalculated after each addition to stock, it can soon become very unrealistic and inaccurate.

There are drawbacks with all methods. While FIFO values the remaining stock at near to market prices (replacement cost), it values the issues at older and therefore inaccurate prices. LIFO reverses this. For example, look at the following issues and receipts and the way FIFO and LIFO value them:

Date	Receipt	Issue
January	2,000 @ £1	
February	800 @ £0.90	
March		2,400
April	400 @ £1.10	
May		600
Total receipts	3,200 = value £3,160	

	FIFO		LIFO	
March	2,000 @ £1	£2,000	800 @ £0.90	£ 720
	400 @ £0.90	360	1,600 @ £1	1,600
ISSUES	2,400	£2,360	2,400	£ 2,320
May	400 @ £0.90	£ 360	400 @ £1.10	£ 440
	200 @ £1.10	220	200 @ £1.00	200
ISSUES	600	£ 580	400	£ 640
REMAINING STOCK p. 250	200 @ £1.10	£ 220	200 @ £1	£ 200

It is important to remember that these are different ways of *valuing* issues of stock and not ways of actually dealing with stock issues. Actual issues should be on a FIFO basis to avoid accumulating old stocks.

Valuing direct labour costs

The cost of employing someone is not just his basic salary. The employer has to pay employers' contributions to pension schemes and National Insurance, holiday pay and bonus and overtime payments. If an employee gets four weeks' paid holiday a year, this and National Insurance will add almost 25 per cent to the cost per working hour of an employee. It is this true gross cost which should be recorded on job cards. Bonus and overtime payments are often recorded separately on a job card, though sometimes only normal rates are charged and any overtime or bonuses are treated as part of overheads. It is common practice not to charge jobs directly for workers' idle time. Normally this is charged to a separate account, which can then be controlled, and included in a job cost as part of overheads.

Overhead costs

Overhead costs have to be apportioned to jobs or to products if they are sharing production facilities. Large companies also have the problem of apportioning them to departments or activities. If the only objective is to apply actual overheads to actual production for the year, then the most accurate apportionment would be made at the end of the year, when actual results are determined. However, this would be too late for many of the day-to-day decisions businessmen have to make, and overhead rates often have to be determined in advance of production. This involves estimating or budgeting the overhead costs in advance as accurately as possible and apportioning these to production. We deal with the process of budgeting in the next chapter. Obviously estimates will never be completely accurate, and adjustments will have to be made at the end of any accounting period to reflect these differences.

The next problem is deciding on a basis for apportioning these estimated overheads to jobs or products. What is needed is a measure of activity that realistically causes that overhead to be incurred. Commonly used bases of activity are:

- Direct labour-hours
- Direct labour costs
- Units of output
- Machine-hours

No measure is totally satisfactory, and it is impossible to generalise since it depends on the nature of the overhead costs, It is also important to have an eye on practicability, cost and the accuracy required, since these factors would influence your decision whether to adopt an 'ideal' method. On the job card in Figure 12.1, overheads are apportioned on the basis of labour-hours. But if these overhead costs were predominantly machine depreciation and power, would it not have been more accurate to apportion overhead costs on the basis of machine-hours since not all labour time is spent on machines? Of course, it would be possible to go through each of the overhead costs and decide on a different measure of activity, and then allocate the cost on the basis of its separate measure of activity. This would be time-consuming and expensive. The problem is that it does matter, since the cost that you come up with influences your pricing policy and decisions on resource allocation. So, inevitably, you will be forced to compromise on accuracy and the time spent on cost apportionment.

Unfortunately, there is still one final problem. Having decided on a suitable measure of activity, as with costs, actual results are only available at the end of the year and this is probably too late for the businessman. We might try for a period shorter than a year, but activity levels do fluctuate greatly because of many factors outside the control of the business. We are forced, once more, to use estimates of activity for the year. This will probably be based upon the budgeted or expected activity levels. Theoretical plant capacity is not a useful measure since it is rarely achieved.

The overhead rate of £2.50 per labour-hour used on the job card in Figure 12.1 is the result of the following calculation:

$$\frac{\text{Total budgeted or estimated overhead costs}}{\text{Total budgeted or estimated activity expressed in direct labour- hours}}$$

Both the numerator and denominator are estimates. Therefore, the result is likely to be somewhat inaccurate. The issue of an unrealistic measure of activity simply compounds a problem to which there is no completely satisfactory solution. Even at the end of the year, when we know our overhead costs and our activity level accurately, we cannot apportion overheads 'accurately' because the measure of activity we decide upon will inevitably involve something of a judgemental compromise. As you will appreciate, this is an extremely complex problem for large companies with multi-product lines, shared facilities and many different overhead costs. The scale of the problem is altogether smaller for the small business, with fewer overhead costs and perhaps only one product, and the resulting overhead rate is probably more accurate. However, it is just as well to treat the notion of 'cost' with some scepticism.

Flow of costs

Costs are an integral part of profit determination and stock valuation. In any service business costs go straight to the profit-and-loss account as incurred. Only in certain consultancy-type businesses will they form part of any unbilled work-in-progress. The distinction is clear here. If services have been billed to a client, they are costs; if not, they are work-in-progress stock.

In a retail business stock comprises all bought-in goods. If the goods are sold, the cost of them becomes the cost of goods sold in the profit-and-loss account. If the goods are not sold, then they are part of stocks. Any overhead costs of the business are treated as costs that go straight to the profit-and-loss account and not into stock valuation.

In a manufacturing business the process is more complex and is represented diagrammatically in Figure 12.2. Prime costs and factory overhead costs are part of the cost of the goods that the business

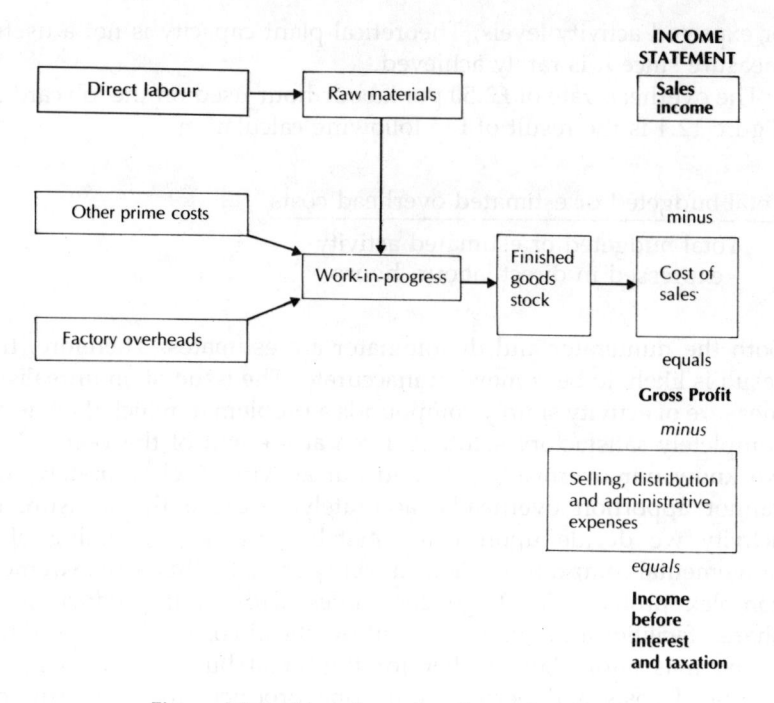

234 *Small business: planning, finance and control*

Figure 12.2 Manufacturing flow of costs

produces. As these goods are sold, these costs are taken to the profit-and loss account as cost of goods sold.

In a job-costing system the job cards will form the basis for the valuation of work-in-progress and finished-goods stocks. Raw material stock records will form the basis for the valuation of raw-material stocks. Cost of sales can be calculated by either identifying the individual jobs sold and their related cost, or by applying the following formula, familiar from the previous chapter:

	Opening period stocks:		
	Raw materials	X	
	Work-in-progress	X	
	Finished goods	X	XX
plus	Prime costs for the year	X	
plus	Factory overheads for the year	X	XX
minus	Closing period stocks:		
	Raw materials	(X)	
	Work-in-progress	(X)	
	Finished goods	(X)	(XX)
	Costs of goods sold		XX

Of course, the application of this formula requires an amount of work in stock valuation which, although essential for year-end accounts preparation, is time-consuming. For periodic income-reporting purposes it is far easier simply to identify particular jobs completed and sold. However, if this is done, it is essential that the costing system and the stock control and reporting system are both accurate and reliable.

If the overhead rate used during the year is inaccurate, then an accurate one, using actual overhead costs and actual activity levels, may have to be calculated and used to value closing stock levels at the year end.

In a process-costing system individual job cards are not used, but average product costs can be determined in the way outlined and stock records of raw materials and finished goods form the basis for stock valuations. Work-in-progress is more problematical, and frequently an estimate of the percentage of completion is applied to products' final cost. The cost of sales can then be determined using the previous formula. The only way to determine periodic income quickly and easily is to use the estimates of the costs of the products, called *standard costs*, and apply this to the quantity sold. Again, accurate stock records are essential.

CHAPTER 13

Financial Planning and Budgeting

THE ROLE OF BUDGETS   236
A practical example   239

The role of budgets

Chapters 4 and 5 highlighted the importance of forward planning in small businesses. These plans are usually summarised and quantified in what is called a 'master budget'. However, budgeting has a number of roles to play for a small business. Not only is it a tool for planning ahead and co-ordinating those plans, but it also provides a framework for controlling the business and allowing the owner to delegate authority and responsibility as the business grows.

Budgets are only part of the overall 'business plan'. They are the result of a careful look at the business and its future and summarise the planned activities of selling, producing, distributing and financing. Budgets co-ordinate these activities, ensuring consistency in the plans for different segments of the business: for example, that productive capacity is sufficient to meet sales estimates and, if it is not, that suitable plant and machinery is purchased at the appropriate time, if this proves a sound financial investment. Budgets therefore co-ordinate many of the decision-making aspects of financial management. They quantify expectations about the future in three major documents:

1. BUDGETED INCOME STATEMENT.
2. BUDGETED CASH-FLOW STATEMENT.
3. BUDGETED BALANCE-SHEET (which highlights estimates of capital expenditure and sources of finance).

Financial planning and budgeting 237

```
┌─────────────────────────┐   ┌─────────────────────────┐   ┌─────────────────────────┐
│ MARKET RESEARCH AND     │   │ DESIGN AND DEVELOPMENT  │   │ FINANCING PLAN          │
│ EVALUATION              │   │ PLAN                    │   │                         │
│ Customers               │   │                         │   │ Desired financing       │
│ Market size, trends     │   │ Development status      │   │ Security offerred       │
│   of segments           │   │   and tasks             │   │ Capitalisation          │
│ Competition:            │   │ Difficulties and        │   │ Use of funds            │
│   strengths             │   │   risks                 │   │                         │
│   weaknesses            │   │ Product improvement     │   │                         │
│ Estimated market        │   │ New product             │   │                         │
│   share and sales       │   │   development           │   │                         │
│ Ongoing market          │   │ Costs                   │   │                         │
│   evaluation            │   │                         │   │                         │
│ Economics:              │   │                         │   │                         │
│   margins               │   │                         │   │                         │
│   costs                 │   │                         │   │                         │
└─────────────────────────┘   └─────────────────────────┘   └─────────────────────────┘

┌─────────────────────────┐   ┌─────────────────────────┐   ┌─────────────────────────┐
│ MARKETING PLAN          │   │ PRODUCTION PLAN         │   │ FINANCIAL PLAN          │
│                         │   │                         │   │                         │
│ Overall market          │   │ Geographic location     │   │ Budgeted income         │
│   strategy              │   │ Facilities and          │   │   statements            │
│ Pricing                 │   │   improvements          │   │ Budgeted cash-flow      │
│ Sales tactics and       │ → │ Strategy and plans      │ → │   statements            │
│   distribution          │   │ Work-force              │   │ Budgeted balance-       │
│ Service and warranty    │   │                         │   │   sheets                │
│   policies              │   │                         │   │                         │
│ Advertising and         │   │                         │   │                         │
│   promotions            │   │                         │   │                         │
│ Breakeven and           │   │                         │   │                         │
│   profitability         │   │                         │   │                         │
└─────────────────────────┘   └─────────────────────────┘   └─────────────────────────┘
         Feedback loops
```

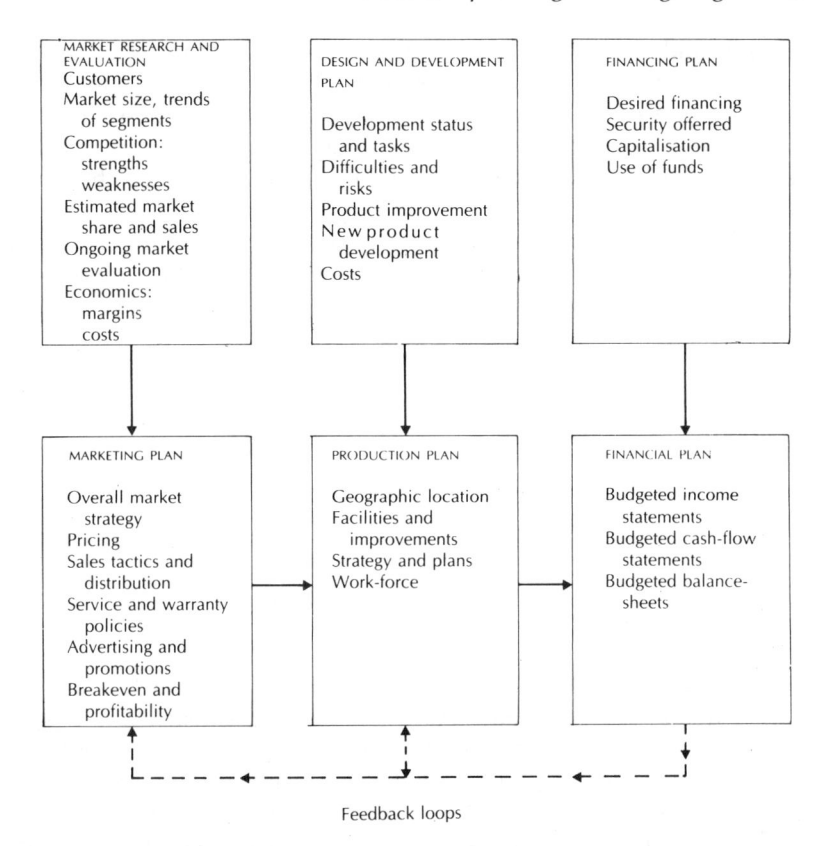

Figure 13.1   The planning process

The business plan involves taking a long-term view of the business and its environment. Accordingly, it tends to cover a period of three to five years. Usually the plan for one year ahead is in considerable detail, and for the periods after that tends to be set in broader terms. An outline of the planning process is shown in Figure 13.1. It emphasises the co-ordination of sales, production and financing plans.

The marketing plan quantifies estimates of sales and sales revenue as well as selling, advertising and distribution costs. To back up and justify these estimates the plan will set down the overall marketing strategy to be followed: pricing, sales tactics, advertising and promotion, service and warranty policies, and distribution. Breakeven and profitability information will be used to support this strategy. However, any marketing plan must be based very firmly on market research and evaluation. This involves identification of customers, market size, trends and segments, as well as the competition faced. This should support the market-share target that the business has set. Market research should provide an ongoing evaluation of market trends identifying potentially profitable opportunities for the business.

The production plan is obviously related to the marketing plan, but it may be somewhat different. For example, sales may include factored goods so that production will be only part of the sales targets. Alternatively, it may be planned to increase or decrease levels of finished goods, in which case production will be higher or lower than sales. Production can normally be calculated using the following equation:

$$\text{Units to be produced} = \begin{array}{l}\text{Desired stock of finished goods at end of period} \\ + \text{ Budgeted sales} \\ - \text{ Stocks of finished goods at beginning of period}\end{array}$$

Stocks of finished goods form a cushion between fluctuations in market demand for a product and the need to stabilise the use of manpower and production facilities. The production plan would be supported by an analysis of the productive facilities and manpower to ensure that they are sufficient to meet the sales plan. If they are not, then either the sales plan will have to be altered or new equipment purchased. Such purchases would have to be justified and co-ordinated on a capital expenditure budget. The production plan would be supported by a design and development plan which would identify product improvements and new product developments. These would be quantified into estimates of research and development expenditure and lead to further capital expenditure requests.

Once the level of production has been determined in physical units, material usage and purchases can be determined:

$$\text{Purchases in units} = \text{Desired material stock at end of period} + \text{Usage} - \text{Material stock at beginning of period}$$

This information can now be included in the financial plan by applying estimated material costs. Direct labour costs will depend upon type of products and wage rates for the period, as well as methods to be used to obtain the desired production. Factory overhead costs will depend upon the behaviour of the individual items of cost in relation

Financial planning and budgeting

to anticipated levels of production. The cost of sales can now be determined in the normal way:

$$\text{Cost of sales} = \begin{array}{c}\text{Finished-goods stock}\\\text{at beginning of period}\end{array} + \begin{array}{c}\text{Materials +}\\\text{usage}\end{array} \begin{array}{c}\text{Direct}\\\text{labour}\\\text{costs}\end{array}$$

$$+ \begin{array}{c}\text{Factory}\\\text{overhead}\\\text{costs}\end{array} - \begin{array}{c}\text{Desired stock of}\\\text{finished goods at}\\\text{end of period}\end{array}$$

The information generated by the marketing plan and the production plan will be combined with estimates of administrative and other expenses to form the *budgeted income statement*. Decisions on stock purchases and estimates of payment of creditors and collection of debtors will be combined with capital expenditure proposals and information on other cash payments to generate a *budgeted cash-flow statement*. This shows the timing of cash receipts and disbursements, and from it will come any financing requirements a company might face. This information is in turn used to produce the *budgeted balance-sheet* for the business.

In many respects the planning and budgetary process is relatively easy for a small business. The owner should know his products very well, how much he can produce, how much he can sell, and the capabilities of the people working for him. Often this planning is done in his head. What is needed is the more formal approach of writing it all down and comparing it with actual results. The problems of budgeting are greater as the business expands. However, as it expands budgeting will become the only effective way of controlling the business and the manager to whom the owner is forced to delegate authority.

One final point to note about Figure 13.1 concerns the feedback loops. At all stages of the preparation of the plan constraints may occur which render previous plans unattainable. This means that the original plans must be modified. For example, sales estimates may be unattainable because of production bottlenecks. The bottlenecks may not be curable in the short term because of either logistic constraints or financial constraints (limiting factors).

A practical example

To clarify this process we shall go through the mechanics of budgeting and generate the three essential financial planning documents:

Table 13.1 Balance-sheet, 31 December 1988

			£
FIXED ASSETS			484,000
CURRENT ASSETS		£	
Stock			
Finished goods: valve A (400)		30,400	
valve B (360)		19,800	
		50,200	
Raw materials base stock		10,000	60,200
Debtors	£	VAT	
estimated payment January	66,000	9,900	
estimated payment February	78,000	11,700	165,600
			225,800
CREDITORS DUE WITHIN ONE YEAR			
Overdraft			(30,000)
Creditors			
due for payment January	20,880	3,132	
due for payment February	20,880	3,132	(48,024)
Corporation tax (due September)			(27,500)
			(105,524)
WORKING CAPITAL (NET CURRENT ASSETS)			120,276
NET ASSETS (TOTAL ASSETS *less* CURRENT LIABILITIES)		604,276	
CREDITORS DUE AFTER MORE THAN ONE YEAR			
Long-term loan			(100,000)
			504,276
CAPITAL AND RESERVES			
Share capital			10,000
Profit-and-loss account			494,276
			504,276

the budgeted income statement, cash-flow statement, and balance-sheet. The example is one for a manufacturing company which is already in business, producing two specialist valves (*A* and *B*). The year-end (31 December 1988) balance-sheet for the company is shown as Table 13.1. We shall prepare the budget for 1989 only. The budgeting process would be easier for a start-up company, since there would be no balance-sheet at the beginning of the period, and easier for a service business, since there would not be a manufacturing process to complicate the costing. In other words, the example is intended to be fairly comprehensive, though certain simplifying assumptions have been made to ease exposition.

The company has been fairly successful so far and the owner is looking for a return (profit before interest and tax) on his net assets of 15 per cent per annum. So far he has funded his fairly rapid expansion by a long-term loan of £100,000, which is not due for repayment until 1994, and an overdraft which, this year, reached its maximum permissible level of £30,000. Because of the highly cyclical nature of demand, the company has experienced difficulty with supply of valves at certain times of the year. Since the valves are always required for immediate delivery, if an order cannot be met within a few days, it will be lost. The company would like to rectify this problem by increasing its stock of finished valves.

SALES BUDGET

The sales manager sees the 1989 market as continuing to be extremely good for the company. He wishes to increase the company's share of this expanding market and therefore suggests that if selling price is only increased in line with inflation (12 per cent), then sales volume should increase some 20 per cent. Looking at the pattern of last year's sales and noting the requirements of existing major customers, he arrives at his first estimate of sales, broken down by month, as shown in Table 13.2. Since he knows that his budget exceeds the productive capacity of existing plant, before proceeding further he passes it on to the managing director and the production manager for consideration.

Table 13.2 Sales budget (units) Mk 1

	Jan	Feb	Mar	Apr	May	June	July	Aug	Sep	Oct	Nov	Dec	Total
Valve A	400	400	440	280	100	100	80	80	200	360	360	440	3,240
Valve B	600	660	520	320	160	160	120	120	360	660	780	780	5,240

PRODUCTION BUDGET

The company would like to be able to meet both the tentative sales budget and to build up finished valve stocks. However, demand is cyclical, whereas production needs to be kept fairly stable throughout the year, since skilled labour cannot be hired and fired at will. Also, even if new machinery were to be purchased in January, it could not be installed and working effectively until March. An added problem is works holidays: one week in December and January and two weeks in August. In those months production is always down, *pro rata*.

Capital investment appraisal techniques (to be developed later) are used to decide how many new machines to purchase. These machines will cost £120,000 (+ VAT @ 15%: £18,000) and can be installed in January. Like all creditors, payment can be delayed two months. These machines will increase production of valve A from the normal 240 to 320 per month and of valve B from 400 to 520 per month from March onwards.

The budgeted production schedule is shown in Table 13.3. Opening stocks of valve A were 400 and of value B 360. The new production schedule will indeed result in higher year-end stocks of 640 and 830 respectively. The lower production in January, August and December reflects the works holidays. Monthly stock levels were computed to compare with the provisional sales budgets to ascertain whether demand will be met. Unfortunately this is not always so, and it is estimated that sales of 100 A valves and 200 B valves will be lost in March and February respectively. However, our investment appraisal tells us it is not worth installing extra productive capacity to satisfy demand in these months. Thus budgeted annual production, sales and stock figures are agreed:

	Units	Valve A	Valve B
	Stock 31 Dec. 1988	400	360
plus	Production	3,380	5,510
minus	Sales	–3,140	–5,040
	Stock 31 Dec. 1989	640	830

The costs of production, after taking into account inflation in material prices and wage increases, are shown below. These are derived from the company's detailed costing records.

Cost per unit	Valve A £	Valve B £
Direct labour (fixed cost)	24	15
Direct materials (variable cost)	22	18
Variable factory overheads	15	12
Fixed factory overheads (depreciation)	15	10
	76	55

Workers are on fixed weekly wages. The current wage bill is £10,290 per month. With wage increases due in March and the new operatives needed in that month, this will jump to £14,319 per month (a total of £163,770 for the year). Direct material and variable overheads are paid under normal trade terms, on average delaying payment by two months. Fixed factory overhead is depreciation of plant and

Table 13.3 Budgeted production schedule (units)

	Jan**	Feb	Mar	Apr	May	June	July	Aug***	Sep	Oct	Nov	Dec**	Total
Valve A													
Stock b/f	400	180	20	—	40	260	480	720	800	920	880	840	
+ production	180	240	320	320	320	320	320	160	320	320	320	240	3,380
– sales	(400)	(400)	(340)*	(280)	(100)	(100)	(80)	(80)	(200)	(360)	(360)	(440)	3,140
stock c/f	180	20	—	40	260	480	720	800	920	880	840	640	—
Valve B													
Stock b/f	360	60	—	—	200	560	920	1,320	1,460	1,620	1,480	1,220	
+ production	300	400	520	520	520	520	520	260	520	520	520	390	5,510
– sales	(600)	(460)*	(520)	(320)	(160)	(160)	(120)	(120)	(360)	(660)	(780)	(780)	5,040
stock c/f	60	—	—	200	560	920	1,320	1,460	1,620	1,480	1,220	830	—

* lower of budgeted sales or stock on hand.
** ¾ production.
*** ½ production.

243

244 Small business: planning, finance and control

equipment. This totals £105,800 (£15 × 3,380 + £10 × 5,510). These unit costs give the following estimates of production costs, cost of sales and stock costs:

		Valve A		Valve B	
		Units	£	Units	£
	Stock 31 Dec. 1988	400	30,400	360	19,800
plus	Production (costs)	3,380	256,880	5,510	303,050
minus	Sales (costs)	−3,140	−238,650	−5,040	−277,200
	Stock 31 Dec. 1989	640	48,640	830	45,650

The company keeps a tight control over raw material stocks, and the current base stock of £10,000 will be maintained in value terms.

PURCHASING BUDGET

The next task for the company is to prepare the monthly purchasing budget. This is shown in Table 13.4. The unit variable costs of direct material and overheads and fixed direct labour costs are applied to the production schedule shown in Table 13.3 to arrive at estimated purchases each month.

Notice that VAT at 15 per cent has been added to purchases of materials and overheads, assuming all purchases are chargeable. A company acts as a collector of VAT for the Customs and Excise. Although it will have to pay VAT on purchases and charge VAT on most sales, it can reclaim the VAT paid and must repay the VAT it collects to the Customs and Excise on a quarterly basis. Therefore, while VAT does not affect a business's profitability (except in so far as it may deter customers) it can cause cash-flow problems, as the business pays and collects VAT at different times from its payments to the Customs and Excise.

REVISED SALES BUDGET

The original sales budget could not be met and therefore it will have to be revised, in line with Table 13.3. The revised sales budget is shown in Table 13.5. Valve A is priced at £90, and valve B at £75, excluding VAT. Notice that, once more, VAT chargeable is shown separately. This will only affect the cash-flow budget.

To achieve this level of sales it is estimated that selling, distribution and general costs will have to rise to £24,000. Let us assume, for

Table 13.4 Budgeted schedule of purchases, overheads and wage payments

	Jan	Feb	Mar	Apr	May	June	July	Aug	Sep	Oct	Nov	Dec	Total
Valve A													
Production (units)	180	240	320	320	320	320	320	160	320	320	320	240	
Direct Materials @ £22	£ 3,960	5,280	7,040	7,040	7,040	7,040	7,040	3,520	7,040	7,040	7,040	5,280	
Variable overheads @ £15	£ 2,700	3,600	4,800	4,800	4,800	4,800	4,800	2,400	4,800	4,800	4,800	3,600	
Labour @ £24	£ 4,320	5,760	7,680	7,680	7,680	7,680	7,680	3,840	7,680	7,680	7,680	5,760	
Valve B													
Production (units)	300	400	520	520	520	520	520	260	520	520	520	390	
Direct materials @ £18	£ 5,400	7,200	9,360	9,360	9,360	9,360	9,360	4,680	9,360	9,360	9,360	7,020	
Variable overheads @ £12	£ 3,600	4,800	6,240	6,240	6,240	6,240	6,240	3,120	6,240	6,240	6,240	4,680	
Labour @ £15	£ 4,500	6,000	7,800	7,800	7,800	7,800	7,800	3,900	7,800	7,800	7,800	5,850	
Totals													
Direct materials and Variable overheads	£15,660	20,880	27,440	27,440	27,440	27,440	27,440	13,720	27,440	27,440	27,440	20,580	£290,360
Related VAT @ 15%	£ 2,349	3,132	4,116	4,116	4,116	4,116	4,116	2,058	4,116	4,116	4,116	3,087	£ 43,554
Quarterly VAT totals			9,597			12,348			10,290			11,319	
Labour	£10,290	10,290	14,319	14,319	14,319	14,319	14,319	14,319	14,319	14,319	14,319	14,319	£163,770

245

Table 13.5 Sales budget Mk 2

	Jan	Feb	Mar	Apr	May	June	July	Aug	Sep	Oct	Nov	Dec	Total
Valve A: units	400	400	340	280	100	100	80	80	200	360	360	440	3,140
£(@ £90 each)	36,000	36,000	30,600	25,200	9,000	9,000	7,200	7,200	18,000	32,400	32,400	39,600	£282,600
Valve B: units	600	460	520	320	160	160	120	120	360	660	780	780	5,040
£(@ £75 each)	45,000	34,500	39,000	24,000	12,000	12,000	9,000	9,000	27,000	49,500	58,500	58,500	£378,000
Total	£81,000	70,500	69,600	49,200	21,000	21,000	16,200	16,200	45,000	81,900	90,900	98,100	£660,600
Related VAT @ 15%	£12,150	10,575	10,440	7,380	3,150	3,150	2,430	2,430	6,750	12,285	13,635	14,715	£ 99,090
Quarter VAT totals			33,165			13,680			11,610			40,635	

simplicity, that these costs incur VAT at 15 per cent (£3,600), they accrue evenly over the year, and that they are paid monthly.

BUDGETED INCOME STATEMENT

The budgeted income statement is shown in Table 13.6. Sales are as shown in Table 13.5 and cost of sales was calculated from the costing records detailed previously. The budgeted profit before interest and tax payments is £120,760: a margin of 18 per cent on sales.

Table 13.6 Budgeted income statement, 1989

	Valve A £	Valve B £	Total £
Sales	282,600	378,000	660,600
Cost of sales	238,640	277,200	515,840
GROSS PROFIT	43,960	100,800	144,760
Selling, distribution and general costs			24,000
PROFIT BEFORE INTEREST AND TAX			120,760
Estimated corporation tax			48,000
Profit before interest but after tax			72,760

BUDGETED CASH-FLOW STATEMENT

The budgeted cash-flow statement is shown in Table 13.7. This shows the cash-flow surplus or deficit each month and the resulting effect on the cash balance or overdraft of the business. The format has been adopted so that it is suitable for general use, in that it includes captions for sale of assets, dividends, loan repayments, etc.

Sales receipts and related VAT are lagged by two months. In other words, sales in January (per Table 13.5) do not generate cash receipts until March. Obviously this means sales in November and December will not have been collected by the year end. Similarly, purchases and related VAT are lagged by two months. January purchases (per Table 13.4) are not paid until March, and November and December purchases are not paid for by the year end. Selling, distribution and general costs and related VAT are paid in the month incurred, as are direct labour costs. The capital expenditure and related VAT is paid in March, and the corporation tax bill shown in last year's balance-sheet is paid in September.

Table 13.7 Budgeted cash-flow statement 1989

	Jan	Feb	Mar	Apr	May	June	July	Aug	Sep	Oct	Nov	Dec	Total
RECEIPTS													
Sales receipts	£ 66,000	78,000	81,000	70,500	69,600	49,200	21,000	21,000	16,200	16,200	45,000	81,900	615,600
Related VAT	9,900	11,700	12,150	10,575	10,440	7,380	3,150	3,150	2,430	2,430	6,750	12,285	92,340
Sales of assets													
Loans received													
Total receipts (A)	£ 75,900	89,700	93,150	81,075	80,040	56,580	24,150	24,150	18,630	18,630	51,750	94,185	707,940
PAYMENTS													
Purchases													
Direct materials and overheads	20,880	20,880	15,660	20,880	27,440	27,440	27,440	27,440	27,440	13,720	27,440	27,440	284,100
Related VAT	3,132	3,132	2,349	3,132	4,116	4,116	4,116	4,116	4,116	2,058	4,116	4,116	42,615
Selling, general, etc.	2,000	2,000	2,000	2,000	2,000	2,000	2,000	2,000	2,000	2,000	2,000	2,000	24,000
Related VAT	300	300	300	300	300	300	300	300	300	300	300	300	3,600
Direct labour	10,290	10,290	14,319	14,319	14,319	14,319	14,319	14,319	14,319	14,319	14,319	14,319	163,770
Capital expenditure			120,000										120,000
Related VAT			18,000										18,000
VAT payments to C & E			4,668			432			420			28,416	33,936
Corporation tax									27,500				27,500
Dividends													
Interest payments													
Loan repayments													
Total payments (B)	£ 36,602	36,602	177,296	40,631	48,175	48,607	48,175	48,175	76,095	32,397	48,175	76,591	717,521
SURPLUS (DEFICIT) (A) – (B)	£ 39,298	53,098	84,146	40,444	31,865	7,973	(24,025)	(24,025)	(57,465)	(13,767)	3,575	17,594	(9,581)
CASH (OVERDRAFT) b/f	(30,000)	9,298	62,396	(21,750)	18,694	50,559	58,532	34,507	10,482	(46,983)	(60,750)	(57,175)	(30,000)
CASH (OVERDRAFT) c/f	9,298	62,396	(21,750)	18,694	50,559	58,532	34,507	10,482	(46,983)	(60,750)	(57,175)	(39,581)	(39,581)

Table 13.8 VAT quarterly returns summary

	March £	June £	Sep £	Dec £	Total £
VAT receivable	33,165	13,680	11,610	40,635	99,090
minus					
VAT payable					
Materials and overheads	− 9,597	−12,348	−10,290	−11,319	−43,554
Selling and general	− 900	− 900	− 900	− 900	− 3,600
Capital expenditure	−18,000				−18,000
Quarterly payments	4,668	432	420	28,416	33,936

VAT payments to the Customs and Excise are quarterly, at the end of March, June, September and December. These are based, not as you might expect, upon VAT received *less* VAT paid, but instead upon the VAT you have charged *less* the VAT charged to you during the period, irrespective of whether or not you have received or paid it. Budgeted VAT payments have been calculated in Table 13.8. VAT receivable is taken from Table 13.5 and VAT payable on materials and variable overheads from Table 13.4. Selling and general costs and capital expenditures are as detailed. This complication is unfortunate, but essential, since VAT can make an enormous difference to the cash flows of any business and often a small business can experience difficulty meeting these quarterly bills.

The budgeted cash-flow statement is essential for short-term planning. The business started the year with an overdraft of £30,000, which was the maximum facility offered by the bank. This overdraft limit will not be exceeded until September, when an overdraft of £46,983 will be required. This will increase to £60,750 in October, and even at the end of the year will be £39,581. Obviously the business must either arrange to increase its overdraft facility in advance for these months or arrange for a term loan to inject the needed cash. But would the banks lend to the business? To find this out, we need to look at the business's profit and its balance-sheet.

BUDGETED BALANCE-SHEET

The budgeted balance-sheet is shown in Table 13.9. Debtors and related VAT represent November and December sales, and creditors and related VAT represent November and December purchases of materials and overheads. Finished-goods stock was calculated in the production schedule and the raw materials base stock is maintained

Table 13.9 Budgeted balance-sheet, 31 December 1989

			£
FIXED ASSETS (NET)			498,200
CURRENT ASSETS		£	
Stock			
Finished goods: valve A (640)		48,640	
valve B (830)		45,650	
		94,290	
Raw material base stock		10,000	104,290
Debtors	£	VAT	
November sales	90,900	13,635	
December sales	98,100	14,715	217,350
			321,640
CREDITORS DUE WITHIN ONE YEAR			
Overdraft			(39,581)
Creditors			
November materials and			
overhead purchases	27,440	4,116	
December materials and			
overhead purchases	20,580	3,087	(55,223)
Corporation tax (estimate)			(48,000)
			(142,804)
WORKING CAPITAL (NET CURRENT ASSETS)			178,836
NET ASSETS (TOTAL ASSETS less CURRENT LIABILITIES)			677,036
CREDITORS DUE AFTER MORE THAN ONE YEAR			
Long-term loan			(100,000)
			577,036
CAPITAL AND RESERVES			
Share capital			10,000
Profit-and-loss account		£	
brought forward 1988		494,276	
1989 profit		72,760	567,036
			577,036

at £10,000. The overdraft was calculated from the budgeted cash-flow statement. Corporation tax is estimated at 40 per cent of profit from Table 13.6.

Fixed assets are calculated below:

	brought forward 31 Dec. 1988 (net)	£484,000
plus	purchases	120,000
minus	depreciation	−105,800
	carried forward 31 Dec. 1989 (net)	£498,200

Financial planning and budgeting 251

Table 13.10 Analysis of accounts

Debtors			
brought forward 1988	£144,000		
+ sales	660,600		
– cash received	–615,600		
carried forward 1989	£189,000		

Creditors		**Stock**	
brought forward 1988	£ 41,760	brought forward 1988	£ 60,200
+ purchases	290,360	→ + purchases	290,360
– cash paid	–284,100	+ depreciation alloc.	105,800
carried forward 1989	£ 48,020	+ labour costs	163,770
		– cost of sales	–515,840
		carried forward 1989	104,290

VAT			
brought forward 1988	debtors	£21,600	
	– creditors	6,264	£ 15,336
– collected from sales			– 92,340
+ paid on purchases (materials and overheads)			42,615
+ paid on selling and general costs			3,600
+ paid on capital expenditure			18,000
+ VAT paid quarterly to C & E			33,936
carried forward 1989	debtors	£28,350	
	– debtors	–7,203	£ 21,147

Depreciation is calculated by writing off assets over an estimated 10-year life. The company does this by charging depreciation of 10 per cent on the gross cost of the asset over a 10-year period.

Net assets for the company total £677,036, an increase of £72,760 over last year, which represents the profit the business has made this year, since our budget shows no increase in share or loan capital. For those readers with a more detailed knowledge of accounts, Table 13.10 analyses the movement on key balance-sheet accounts.

The business is making a return on net assets of 17.8 per cent:

$$\frac{120,760}{677,036} \times 100$$

well above the target set by the owner, and above current interest rates. However, this return does exclude interest and taxation.

The capital gearing is 21.9 per cent:

$$\frac{39,581 + 100,000}{677,036 - 39,581} \times 100$$

well below the maximum level of security that Chapter 2 noted many lenders require.

That maximum gearing level of 50 per cent would be reached with outside loans of £318,728 on net assets of £(677,036 – 39,581). In other words, the business would probably be able to support more loan capital to enable it to meet the cash-flow deficit, if the bank manager will not increase the overdraft facility. The owner now has all the information he requires either to approach the bank manager or another source of funds.

CHAPTER 14

Control and Delegation through Budgets

CONTROL THROUGH BUDGETS	253
Variable budgets	255
Setting standards and monitoring variances	257
Overhead standards and variances	260
Delegation through budgets	265

Control through budgets

Once plans have been made and budgets prepared, they can be used to control and monitor the performance of the business. They allow the owner to adopt 'management by exception' by comparing actual results to his budgets on a timely basis, and investigating the reasons for deviation from the budget. This can save him time and allow him to concentrate his effort in the areas where there are problems, where things are not going according to plan. The differences between actual results and the budget, called 'variances', can be analysed in such a way as to give indications of the causes of these deviations from plan. In short, the budget provides a framework for controlling the running of a business in an efficient way. It also acts as a better basis for judging actual results than past performance. The fact that sales are better than last year might be encouraging, but it is by no means conclusive as a measure of success, since inefficiencies can be hidden in past performance or factors outside the control of the business might have changed.

The budget provides the framework against which the performance of the business can be judged. It is therefore important that the budgeting process follows the accounting classifications used by the business for regular reporting, so that actual results can be compared directly with budgeted results. Consider the example in the previous chapter. The classification 'selling, distribution and general costs' could include all sorts of accounts, such as salaries, commissions, rent and rates, insurance, travelling, entertaining, printing, publicity, etc. The budgetary process should include estimates of each of these accounts separately, so that the actual expenditure can be compared with the budget.

Monitoring performance of the business alongside the budget or plan allows you to manage by exception. That is, so long as actual results correspond to the plan, then *prima facie* no corrective action, or indeed further investigation, is needed. Of course, it is extremely unlikely that actual results will agree exactly with the budget, since a certain degree of inaccuracy is inevitable. Judgement must be used in deciding whether the variance is sufficiently large to justify further investigation and action. Nor should the budget necessarily be changed. The budget is an estimate of the outcome of certain proposed actions. It gives the logically thought-out conclusions to a whole series of assumptions, and many of these assumptions will prove not to be correct. It should only be changed if actual practice has changed so radically from the budget as to render it useless: for example, when major changes in policy are made. Minor changes can be either reflected as variances or else reflected as lump-sum adjustments to the budget.

Not all variances are under the control of the business. For example, wage rates may be set by national negotiations and property rates are set by the local authority. To save time it is wise to segregate costs into two categories: 'controllable' and uncontrollable'. The business can then ignore variances on uncontrollable costs and concentrate upon the variances on controllable items.

The comparison of actual with budgeted results is an essential task, to be carried out on a timely and regular basis. Most businesses review their results monthly. This is best achieved using some form of *budget comparison statement*. This statement could show actual results for the month alongside budgeted results and then the variances. It would also give cumulative results for the year to date. An example of such a statement is given in Figure 14.1. There is no single best form of comparison statement. Some businesses may require information on their performance in the same month last year. Others may dispense with the monthly information and concentrate on the cumulative figures. It depends upon the nature of the business.

A/C no.	Account	COST CLASSIFICATION: Selling, distribution of general costs			MONTH		
		This month			Cumulative this year		
		Budget	Actual	Variance	Budget	Actual	Variance
	Wages and salaries						
	National Insurance						
	Commission						
	Rent and rates						
	Insurance						
	Travel						
	Entertainment						
	Publicity						
	Telephone						
	Freight						
	Printing						
	Postage						
	Professional fees						
	TOTAL						

Figure 14.1 Budget comparison statement

Variable budgets

So far we have talked about budgets as 'fixed' and 'static' plans for the future. In the example we used the company's plan was to produce 3,380 *A* valves and 5,510 *B* valves, and all costs were calculated based upon these production volumes. But what would happen if those increased production targets were not achieved. Production costs might well be down, but would this be good or bad?

'Variable' or 'flexible' budgets are an attempt to reflect the effect of changes in volume on the budgeted costs. They are an attempt to tailor a budget to a particular volume, not vice versa. The approach is based on our knowledge of cost-behaviour patterns developed in the preceding chapter.

Let us take as an example the budget for valve *A* prepared in the preceding chapter. Suppose the actual results detailed below were achieved, but the company only produced 3,150 valves instead of the

256   *Small business: planning, finance and control*

3,380 budgeted. Are these results good or bad? What action should be taken?

	Budgeted £	Actual £	Variances £	
Direct labour	81,120	80,020	1,100	F
Direct materials	74,360	72,100	2,260	F
Variable factory overhead	50,700	46,900	3,800	F
Fixed factory overhead	50,700	50,800	100	U
Total production costs	256,880	249,820	7,060	F

(where F = favourable, U = unfavourable variance)

Simply looking at the variances tells us very little. All, other than fixed factory overheads, are favourable.

Let us analyse the budgeted costs of valve *A* into their variable and fixed elements:

		Valve A £
Variable costs (per valve):		
materials		22
overheads		15
Total		37
Fixed costs (total):		
labour		81,120
overheads		50,700

A variable budget for the production costs of valve *A* would tell a different story:

	Budget	Variable budget based on actual production	Actual	Variance	
Units produced	3,380		3,150	230	U
	Per valve £	£	£	£	
Variable costs:					
materials	22	69,300	72,100	2,800	U
overheads	15	47,250	46,900	350	F
Fixed costs:					
labour		81,120	80,020	1,100	F
overheads		50,700	50,800	100	U
		248,370	249,820	1,450	U

We can now see that materials have cost us £2,800 more than we budgeted for, at that level of production. Is this because of inefficient use of materials or wastage, or was it because their cost increased more than budgeted? Conversely variable overheads were less than we budgeted for at that level of production.

Since wages are 'fixed', the favourable variance on labour would seem to have little connection with the production level. It may be due to the wage rise being less than budgeted, or fewer new operatives being hired. However, there could be a connection since the availability of skilled workers is essential for machine operation. Suppose we could not hire the extra skilled operatives as expected in March, and it was not until May that all the new men were recruited. This could cause both our production to be lower than budgeted and our labour costs to be lower than budgeted. In the circumstances this variance may be favourable but it certainly was not desirable. Of course that unfavourable production variance may be due to a number of other factors, including inefficiency. The point is that further investigation is needed and that there may be a link between it and some of the financial costs we are trying to control.

The variable budget gives a better idea of how *efficiently* a business has produced a given output. However, the issue of achieving the budgeted output level must also be addressed. Consequently, if variable budgets are to be used, information on production *levels* must also be included in the budget comparison statement. Deviations from the production budgets must be investigated *as well as* deviations from the financial cost budgets.

Setting standards and monitoring variances

The variable budgetary technique can be further developed to provide more information on the causes of variances. This involves setting 'standards' for constituent elements of the budgeted cost and then reporting on the variances for the constituent elements.

The costs of many purchased inputs to a business may be expressed simply as the product of quantity and price. Consequently many variances are the result of variances in the quantity used or the cost per unit paid for the input. Take the example of valve *A*. Suppose each valve contains 4 special washers each costing £1.50, and this is included in the material cost of £22 per valve. At the actual production level of 3,150 valves we should use 12,600 washers, and the budgeted cost for washers would be £18,900 (£1.50 × 12,600). Suppose the actual cost of these washers is £1.55 each and that we actually used 14,000 washers, thus yielding an actual cost of £21,700

(£1.55 × 14,000). What caused the unfavourable variance of £2,800 (£18,900 − £21,700)?

Part of the variance was caused by the increase in the quantity of washers used: called the 'volume variance'. The volume variance was 1,400 washers (14,000 − 12,600) at £1.50 per washer (= £2,100). Part was caused by the increase in the price of washers: called the 'price variance'. The price variance was 5p a washer (%1.50 − £1.55) over 14,000 washers (= £700). The total variance is equal to the sum of the volume variance plus the price variance (£2,100 + £700 = £2,800: unfavourable).

The general rule for calculating the variance of a variable cost is:

Volume variance	= Variance in volume × Standard price
Price variance	= Variance in price × Actual volume
Total variance	= Volume variance + Price variance

This analysis may be extended to many other costs which have inputs of quantity and price per unit, and certain terminology has developed to describe particular variances. In the case of material cost variances, the volume and price elements are often called 'usage' and 'price' respectively. These relationships are shown in Figure 14.2.

It is apparent that in order to establish a budgeted or standard cost for the washers, we established both standard price and a standard for usage. The standard price may be based upon historic costs but would essentially be an estimate of the cost of the washer in the future. The usage standard may be based upon technical specifications and wastage rates and involves certain policy decisions about the efficiency of usage.

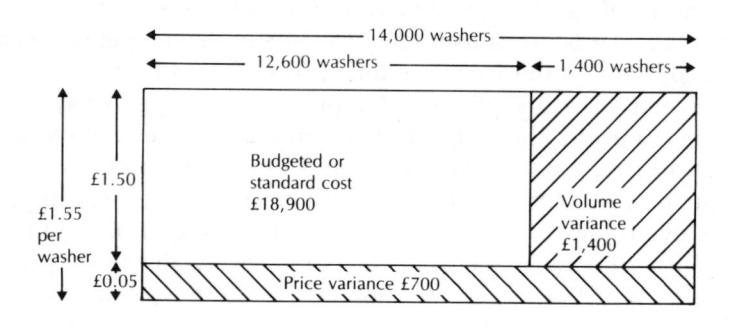

Figure 14.2 Graphical analysis of variances

Control and delegation through budgets

In the case of labour cost variances, the volume and price elements are called 'efficiency' and 'rate' variances respectively, but they are calculated in the same way as material cost variances. We shall not use our valve example at this stage because labour costs there were a fixed cost and, as we know from the previous chapter, the apportionment of fixed costs to products causes added complications. Suppose that another valve manufacturer has variable labour costs, with his workers being paid an hourly rate. In all other respects his costs are surprisingly similar to those of valve A. He budgets for an hourly rate of £2 and, while he also plans to produce 3,380 valves, he only succeeds in producing 3,150 valves. He budgets that each valve takes 12 hours of labour. In fact his labour rate is only £1.97 per hour and he pays for 40,619 hours worked. Thus:

Budgeted variable labour costs
(using variable budgeting)
£24 per valve

$\overbrace{3{,}150 \times 12 \times £2}$ = £75,600

37,800 hours budgeted

Actual variable labour costs
40,619 × £1.97 = £80,020

TOTAL VARIANCE £ 4,420 U

Variance in 'volume' of hours worked
37,800 − 40,619 = 2,819 U

Variance in 'price' of labour
£2.00 − £1.97 = £ 0.03 F

Therefore

'Efficiency' (volume) variance	= 2,819 × £2	= £5,638	U
'Rate' (price) variance	= £0.03 × 40,619	= 1,218	F
	TOTAL VARIANCE	4,420	U

In the case of labour costs the standards consist of the labour rate per hour and the hours spent producing the valve. There is obviously scope for setting tough efficiency standards. However, essentially we are talking about the standards being realistic and attainable, allowing for the ordinary machine breakdowns and idle time, perhaps set with the aid of work-study techniques. In this case standard setting is just part of the ordinary budgeting process. If we deviate from this, setting tough standards with a view to improving motivation, then any budget set using these standards cannot be used for planning and control. The resulting budget could probably not be attained, and the variances would be so large as to be meaningless for control purposes. Anyway, such large variances are themselves likely to have a demotivating effect.

Interpreting the actual meaning of variances takes a little practice and an understanding of their causes. Variances often highlight questions rather than answers. Why was the labour rate only £1.97? If this in some way reflects the quality of the workers, then this might reflect itself in the poor efficiency variance. Perhaps by paying a higher rate we could have improved efficiency. However, the unfavourable efficiency variance might just reflect a tight standard. All that the variance does is to focus our attention on the questions; it does not provide the answers.

Overhead standards and variances

The variable overhead variance can also be analysed in the same manner as these other variable costs variances. The analysis depends critically upon the constituent elements of the variable overhead cost and how it is allocated to the product. In the example of valve A the variable overheads were £15 per valve, and using variable budgeting the budget for 3,150 valves was £47,250. The actual variable overhead cost of producing 3,150 was £46,900, giving a favourable variance of £350. By definition, this variable cost varies directly and proportionately with volume and allowance has therefore already been made for the present level of activity, and consequently there can be no volume variance. The £350 is all 'price' variance (often called 'expenditure' variance):

> Budgeted variable overhead costs
>   3,150 × £15   = £47,250
> Actual variable overhead costs
>   3,150 × £14.89   = £46,900 (approx)
>   Total variance (= price variance)   350 F

There is no conceptual reason, assuming sufficient data are available, why a price and volume variance cannot be calculated. What is required for a volume variance to exist is for these costs not to vary *directly* with volume but for them to vary *indirectly*, via some other measure of activity such as machine or labour-hours. The relationship between machine or labour-hours and volume then depends upon the efficiency of the machine or work-force. Suppose, as is quite normal, these costs varied with labour hours, rather than volume. In this case part of that £350 might have been due to the efficiency of the work-force in completing their job and part to 'price' variance. Let us translate that variance into labour-hours, using the information for the variable labour cost used previously:

Budgeted variable overhead costs
37,800 hours × £1.25 = £47,250

3,150 × 12
Actual variable overhead costs
40,619 × £1.155 = £46,900 (approx.)
350 F

In other words, the variable overhead rate of £15 per valve translates into £1.25 per budgeted labour-hour, and, to achieve our actual costs of £46,900, given the labour-hours of 40,619, the hourly rate must in fact has been £1.155. Therefore:

Variance in 'volume' hours worked
37,800 − 40,619 = 2,819 U

Variance in 'price' of variable overheads
£1.25 − £1.155* = £0.095*
(*There is a rounding error here.)

'Efficiency' (volume) variance = 2,819 × £1.25 = £3,524 U
'Expenditure' (price) variance = 0.095* × 40,619 = 3,874 F
TOTAL VARIANCE = 350 F

This means that if the variable overhead costs varied, and were apportioned, based on hours worked, then that £350 favourable variance would have been due to two factors: first, a £3,874 favourable expenditure variance, implying costs per hour were kept below budget: and second a £3,524 unfavourable 'efficiency' variance due to the work-force not completing their job in the budgeted or standard time.

So far we have dealt with variable costs and their variances. Fixed costs pose added problems which, conversely, make the analysis of variances simpler. As we know, the apportionment of fixed costs to products involves the calculation of 'overhead rates', which requires estimates of both production levels and the fixed costs. Both estimates can be inaccurate.

Consider the problem posed by the original fixed labour costs for valve A. The budgeted rate of £24 per valve will result in apportioned costs of only £75,600 (£24 × 3,150). If these were variable costs, this figure would be the variable or flexed budget for labour. The previous variable labour cost example was carefully constructed to demonstrate this. Instead the budgeted fixed costs were £81,120. The difference between this and actual costs of £80,020 is a £1,100 favourable variance, and this is called the 'expenditure' variance. However, accountants often wish to highlight the difference between the fixed budget of £81,120 and the fixed costs apportioned to the product of £75,600. This unfavourable variance of £5,520 is called the 'volume' variance. Notice that the expenditure variance, plus the volume variance, equals £4,420, unfavourable (£1,100 F + £5,520 U), which was the difference between actual costs and those apportioned to the valve.

The unfavourable fixed overhead cost variance of £100 in our valve example is an expenditure variance. If we wished to calculate the volume variance, we would apply the fixed overhead per valve (£15) to actual production (3,150 valves) and compare this with our budget. Thus the favourable volume variance is £3,450 (£50,700 − (3,150 × £15)).

It is obvious that the volume variance is of limited use since it is not really controllable. However, it does highlight the cost of operating under the budgeted level of activity. Figure 14.3 shows these variances in diagrammatic form and Figure 14.4 summarises the formulae for these different standard costing variances.

Standard costing information is often used as an approximation to actual costing data, to enable financial information to be produced quickly. With standards established, they can be used for the amounts going into the work-in-progress and finished-goods stock accounts shown in Figure 12.2. The variances will go directly to the profit-and-loss account. If the variances are large, then the value of stocks at the year end, which would similarly be valued at standard cost, might need to be adjusted.

Variance analysis can also be applied to sales revenue to ascertain whether deviations from budgeted sales revenue are due to variations in sales price or in sales volume. Sales price variance is the difference between budgeted and actual selling price, multiplied by the actual sales made. Sales volume variance is the difference between budgeted and actual sales volume multiplied by the standard selling price. This is all very much like material cost variances.

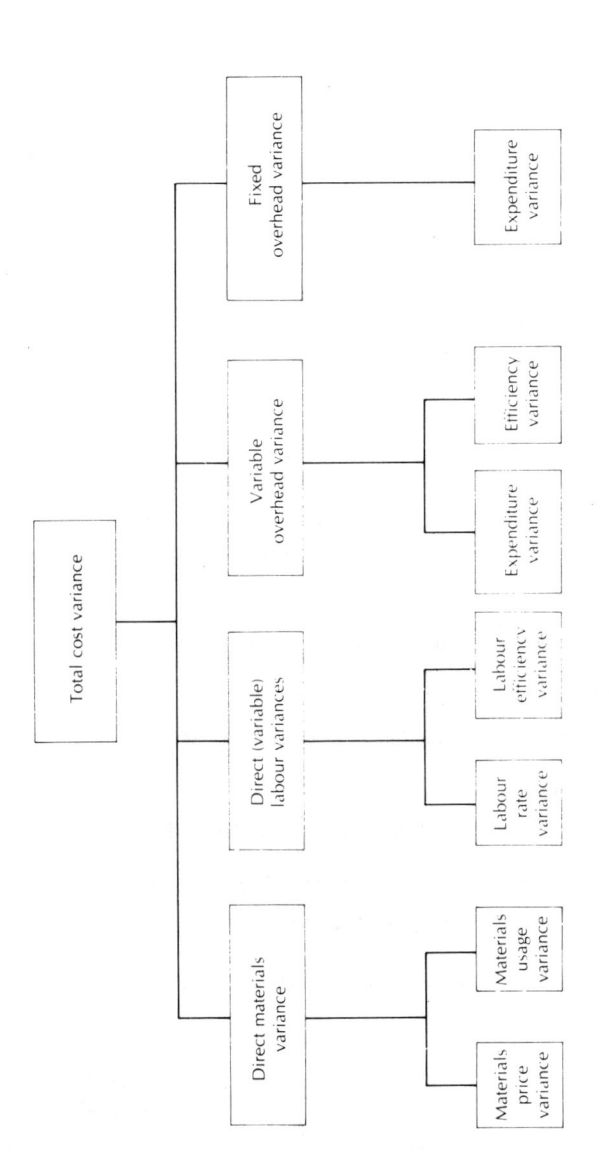

Figure 14.3 Standard costing variances for budget

Materials price variance

(Standard price — Actual price) × Actual quantity

Materials usage variance

(Standard quantity — Actual quantity) × Standard price

Labour rate variance

(Standard rate − Actual rate) × Hours paid for

Labour efficiency variance

(Standard hours for job — Actual hours worked) × Standard rate

Variable overhead expenditure variance

(Standard rate per hour − Actual variable cost per hour) × Actual hours worked

Variable overhead efficiency variance

(Standard hours for job − Actual hours worked) × Standard rate

Fixed overhead expenditure variance

Budgeted fixed overheads − Actual fixed overheads

Fixed overhead volume variance

Fixed overheads applied to products − Budgeted fixed overheads

Sales price variance

(Standard selling price − Actual selling price) × Actual quantity

Sales volume variance

(Standard quantity − Actual quantity) × Standard price

Figure 14.4 Variance formulae

For example, if 3,000 A valves were sold at £92 each rather than 3,200 at £90, as budgeted:

Budgeted sales	3,200 × £90	= £288,000	
Actual sales	3,000 × £92	= £276,000	
	TOTAL VARIANCE on turnover	£ 12,000	U
Sales price variance	(£90 − £92) × 3,000	= £ 6,000	F
Sales volume variance	(3,200 − 3,000) × £90	= £ 18,000	U
	TOTAL VARIANCE on turnover	£ 12,000	U

Delegation through budgets

For the very small business budgets will only be prepared at the company level. However, as the small business grows, budgets can be prepared for each department or division. This has the advantage of allowing the owner to delegate responsibility for planning to others further down the management line. This can be essential for the 'growth small business', where the owner will frequently not have the time, or indeed the expertise, to deal with all aspects of the plan himself. If he simply delegates work to assistants but makes all the decisions himself, it can lead to bottlenecks and delays in making decisions; indeed, wrong decisions can be made. If he simply rubber-stamps other people's decisions, he is wasting time. Budgetary control can be adopted in such a way as to encourage delegation of responsibility and decentralisation of decision-making, while at the same time providing the owner with sufficient information to satisfy himself that everything is running as planned. The budgeting process can then be used as a tool for communicating and co-ordinating the activities of responsible managers. It can become a systematic tool for establishing standards of performance, providing motivation and assessing the results managers achieve. Indeed, as a business grows in complexity and size, budgetary control becomes increasingly important. What was primarily a planning tool for a small business becomes equally important as a control tool as the small business grows.

An essential element in the delegation of responsibility is that each manager knows exactly what he is responsible for, and that he does in fact control the items for which he is held responsible. It must be emphasised that responsibility cannot be assigned without authority. A fundamental necessity is to have a clear-cut, known organisation structure. A typical organisation chart was shown in Figure 4.5. This should be accompanied by written definitions of authority and responsibility for everybody who appears on the chart. Only if managers have clear lines of authority and responsibility can they be held accountable for their actions. Often a manager cannot control all elements affecting his department's results. It will therefore be difficult to balance the need for fairness in dealing with uncontrollable items with the possible motivational benefits from regarding the manager as if he were in control.

If budgets are to be used as a delegation tool, each item of income or expenditure needs to be the direct responsibility of a named individual. The key in allocating responsibility is to decide who *controls* that item of expenditure. In many businesses the manager allocated responsibility will, in turn, delegate responsibility further down the line. For example, the production manager would be delegated responsibility for direct labour costs, and he, in turn, might delegate responsibility for direct labour in producing valve A to foreman X, and for valve B to foreman Y (see Figure 4.5), each being responsible for, and having authority in, organising the work-force in that department.

Of course, if managers are going to be held responsible for budgeted items of income and expenditure that they control, then they must have a say in the budgetary process. There is the obvious reason that they all probably know more than the owner about certain aspects of the business. However, budgets also act as ways of motivating managers. If they know that their performance is going to be judged against standards set in advance, then they will normally try hard to meet those standards. However, they will also want to know how the standards were set. It is now widely accepted that people tend to accept standards more readily if they themselves participate in setting them. Imposing budgets from above will cause resentment, and a feeling of lack of commitment and responsibility.

The sales and production targets are the first things to be decided upon by the owner and his departmental heads. These will, in part, be what the business would *like* to achieve, consistent with its long-term objectives, but in the end will be fixed according to what it thinks it *can* achieve. After this process the detailed budget will start to be drawn up, first being prepared at the lowest possible level of control, and then being submitted to the next level up the hierarchy for approval. The budgets will often not be accepted immediately. Items of expenditure will be modified, after discussion between the persons involved. It is important, from a motivational point of view, that all modifications are explained and agreed upon, rather than being imposed upon responsible managers.

When the owner receives the overall budget from his departmental mangers, he also might like to see modifications. Perhaps there will be inconsistencies between departments. Perhaps the profit or cash flow will not be sufficient. Perhaps the budget is not entirely consistent with the long-term objectives of the business. The process can therefore be lengthy, with the lowest level of management submitting plans up the hierachy, being consulted about change, and then the modified plan being submitted upwards until it finally gets to the managing director and board level.

The process has a very beneficial side-effect in a business of any size. It communicates information from one manager to another. It gets people to talk and argue about the future. When the small business was really small, the owner did this all himself. Now he needs a formal process to achieve the same result. At the end of the process all managers have the final full budget statement circulated to them.

Once the budget is prepared, there is the task of monitoring and controlling performance. The first issue is to decide into what periods the elements of the budget should be broken down. Information varies in significance over time, so intervals for budget reports should be carefully chosen. There is no point in sending monthly reports when action is required weekly. This is very important for small businesses, which often prosper because they can react very quickly to changing events.

It is often better to have approximate figures soon, rather than accurate figures later. This is where standard costing can be particularly useful. As you will now appreciate, the production of accurate cost information can be a complicated and time-consuming affair.

Budget comparison statements (Figure 14.1) should be sent to each manager controlling items of expenditure. Items not under the control of the manager should not be included in this. Some costs will be under the control of more than one person. However, if the business uses standards and reports variances, it is possible to allocate responsibility for the different variances to different managers. For example, material cost variance can be split between *price variance*, which is the responsibility of the material buyer, and *usage variance*, which is the responsibility of the production manager and his foreman. With costs controlled by more than one person, the cost would be included on a manager's budget comparison statement, but it would be made clear that he was only responsible for one element of the variance.

In the case of the material usage variance, both the production manager and his foreman are responsible for the variance, and therefore both people will have the item included in their budget comparison statements. The difference lies in the degree of aggregation shown in that statement. The foreman requires information on usage for each item of raw material. The production manager, to whom the foreman is responsible, may only require aggregate data on usage variances. This build-up of detail into aggregate information will continue up the organisation hierarchy, like a pyramid of information. The owner/manager may only be provided with the broadest of aggregate financial information. This allows him to control the business without being overwhelmed by the detail he would require if he did not delegate his authority.

Therefore, as the small business develops, the budgetary process can also be developed to enable the owner to delegate responsibility. It allows him to assign responsibility to his managers and then control and monitor their performance. It acts as a mechanism for communicating information within the business and can also serve to motivate the managers under him. It should allow him to control the business on an exception basis, intervening only when things go wrong and the business deviates from the planned path. This should leave him free for the very important process of strategic planning, i.e. thinking about the long-term prospects for the business.

CHAPTER 15

Accounting Systems

THE NEED FOR AN ACCOUNTING SYSTEM	269
A SIMPLE CASH BOOK/OPEN-INVOICE ACCOUNTING SYSTEM	270
THE FINCO SYSTEM	279
COMPUTERISED ACCOUNTING SYSTEMS	279
SPREADSHEET PACKAGES	289

The need for an accounting system

The Companies Acts require that all companies keep certain accounting records 'sufficient to show and explain the companies' transactions'. The following records should be kept:

1. A record of day-to-day cash receipts and expenditures.
2. A record of assets and liabilities.
3. A statement of stock at the end of each financial year, and a statement of stock-taking from which it was prepared.
4. Except for ordinary retail trade, statements of all goods sold and purchased showing the goods and the buyers and sellers.

Whilst sole traders and partnerships are not required to keep these records they would be well advised to copy their corporate counterparts. Without adequate accounting information it is impossible to monitor the performance of the business and, if you have got this far in the book, you will know where that will lead! However, any business registered for VAT is required to keep adequate accounting records.

It is reckless to run a business without any accounting records. Nevertheless, even today many accountants make a living from the annual visit of clients with cheque book stubs, bank statements and bags of invoices asking them to 'write up the accounts' and 'deal with the taxman'.

Owner/managers start by keeping records themselves. The simplest accounting systems can be very cheap and relatively easy to operate. They can provide regular and timely financial information without that visit to the accountant. Later on, as the owner/manager starts to think his time might be more usefully spent helping the business expand, he might employ a book-keeper, perhaps initially on a part-time basis. He could, on the other hand, use an outside book-keeping service, but information must then be sent regularly and frequently. As the size of the business grows, so too does the complexity of the task of controlling it. However, microcomputers have come to the rescue providing an increasingly cheap way of processing a lot of data. Nevertheless, any system is only as good as the information entered into it. If you put garbage in, then you will get garbage out.

Remember that the prime objective of producing accounting information is to enable you to compare what has actually happened with *your budgets and plans*. If you are not performing according to budget then appropriate action should be taken. To help with this comparison it is important that your accounting information is produced in the same format as your budgets and plans.

A simple cash-book/open-invoice accounting system

The simplest cash-book/open-invoice system requires only a cash book and four boxes or files. A cash book is simply a book in which cash receipts and payments can be entered and analysed. The system is shown in Figure 15.1. Sales invoice are kept in box A until paid, when they will be transferred to box B. Similarly purchase invoices for goods and services are kept in box C until paid, when they are transferred to box D. It is all very simple. Invoices in box A represent unpaid sales invoices, and, if kept in chronological order, customers can be chased for payment as invoices become due. Similarly, box C represents unpaid purchase invoices. The total of boxes A + B invoices gives the total sales for the period and the total of boxes C + D gives total purchases.

Cash receipts and payments are entered in the cash book and analysed according to the accounting equation. Let us develop the simple example used in Chapter 10 and itemise a number of transactions:

Accounting systems

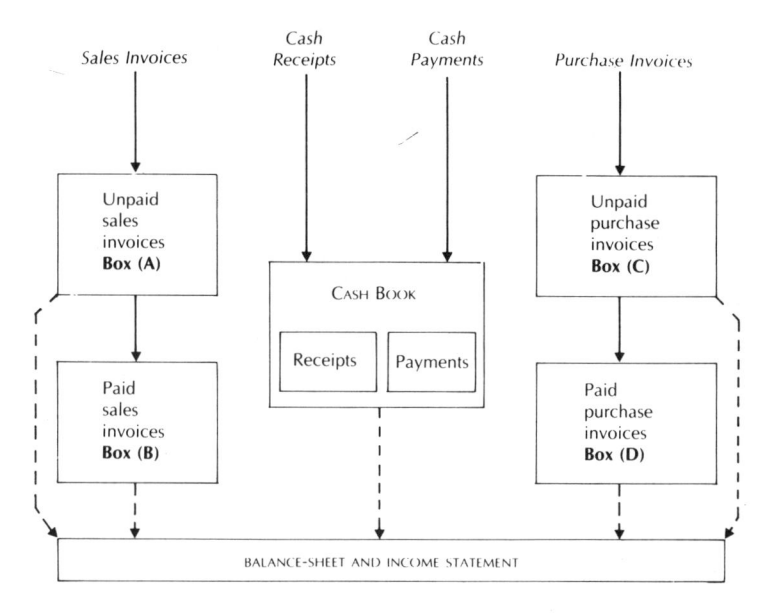

Figure 15.1 A simple cash-book/open-invoice accounting system

1. Receive cash from share capital £1,000
2. Receive cash from loan capital £500
3. Pay creditors £1,250
   (*Transfer invoices from box C to box D*)
4. Receive payment from debtors £200
   (*Transfer invoices from box A to box B*)
5. Pay cash expenses (no invoices) £30

These transactions are shown, as they would appear in the cash book, in Figure 15.2. The accounting equation is shown at the head of the account columns. Each transaction has a dual effect on the equation. For example, transaction 3 represents a payment of £1,250 to creditors; cash is decreased £1,250, as is creditors. Thus:

Assets	–	Liabilities	=	Shareholders' capital
(–1,250)	–	(–1,250)	=	0

At suitable times (say monthly) the cash book can be totalled (line I). Normally this will represent the cash the business has in the bank, and it is important to check that this agrees with the bank statements.

The next thing to do is to total up the invoices in the boxes. The total purchase invoices in boxes C and D come to £1,650. However, only £550 represented purchases of stock and £1,100 represented purchases of plant and machinery. We can now start to adjust the cash-book totals to represent this transaction. Creditors have increased £1,650, stock £550 and fixed assets £1,100.

The total sales invoices in boxes A and B come to £500. Sales increase the shareholders' capital by increasing debtors. Thus both profit and assets are increased, maintaining the accounting equation.

At the same time, the cost of the stock that you have sold should be shown. Let us assume the cost of the stock is £200. This is deducted from stock, and is shown as the cost of the sales you have made. Calculating the cost of stock is often problematical and we shall return to the topic in the next chapter.

Depreciation is the amount that we write off the cost of those fixed assets each period. Let us assume it is £110. This decreases the cost of the asset in the balance-sheet by writing off the charge to profit as an expense.

These figures can now be totalled again (line II). This gives what is called the 'trial balance totals' and corresponds to the totals that would be shown in proper accounts, if we were keeping a full set of books of account (called a *general ledger*). It is called a trial balance because it should balance, maintaining the accounting equation. Unfortunately, if you have made a mistake, it may not. The totals in the trial balance for debtors and creditors should correspond to the total invoices in boxes A and C respectively.

Finally, we might wish to make some adjustments to the trial balance. For example, we may know that we are about to receive a repair bill for £40 for work done on the machines during the period. What we do is raise an 'accrual' for that amount. This is a device which allows us to recognise the expense without including the creditor in the trial balance and purchase invoices boxes – after all, we shall receive an invoice in due course and do not want to pay twice. If the £40 were for stock, then it would be written to the stock account rather than the expense account. Similarly, we may realise that part of that £30 cash payment in transaction 5 was for goods or services that we have not yet received. Let us assume £10 was an advance payment of rental on some office equipment. Clearly, we do not want to recognise the expense in this period, though the advance payment was made in this period. The device that allows us to recognise this good or service we have not yet received as an asset is called a 'prepayment'. We reduce expenses by £10 and increase debtors since we are 'owed' that service in the next accounting period.

The balance-sheet totals can now be extracted (line III), and a

273

Figure 15.2 A simple cash-book/open-invoice accounting system

CASH BOOK	ASSETS	−	LIABILITIES	=	SHAREHOLDERS' CAPITAL

	Cash			Debtors	Stock	Fixed assets		Creditors	Loans		Shares	Past periods' profit	Profit and Loss	
	Receipts	Payments											Sales	Costs
1. Share capital	+ 1,000									=	+ 1,000			
2. Loan capital	+ 500								+ 500					
3. Creditors paid		− 1,250					−	− 1,250						
4. Debtor receipts	+ 200			− 200			−							
5. Cash expenses		− 30												− 30
I CASH BOOK TOTALS	+ 1,700 − 1,280			− 200	0	0	−	− 1,250	+ 500	=	+ 1,000	0	0	− 30
	+ 420													
Balance-sheet from previous period	0			0	0	0	−	0	0	=	0	0	0	0
Reverse adjustments														
Total purchase invoices received (Box C + D)					+ 550	+ 1,100	−	+ 1,650						
Total sales invoices issued (Box A + B)				+ 500						=			+ 500	
Cost of sales					− 200									− 200
Depreciation						− 110								− 110
II TRIAL BALANCE TOTALS	+ 420			+ 300	+ 350	+ 990	−	+ 400	+ 500	=	+ 1,000	0	+ 500	− 340
Adjustments:														
Accruals							−	+ 40						− 40
Prepayments				+ 10			−							+ 10
III BALANCE-SHEET TOTALS	+ 420			+ 310	+ 350	+ 990	−	+ 440	+ 500	=	+ 1,000	+ 0	+ 500	− 370

balance-sheet and income statement drawn up (Figure 15.3 and 15.4). The total in the stock account should correspond to the cost of the stock physically on hand, and it is good practice to perform a stock count at the end of the period. It is of course possible that the costed-out value of stock on hand will not agree with the stock account. This could be due to stock losses or just your inaccurate calculation of cost of sales. However, any discrepancy would require investigation and could mean a further revision of the accounts.

If, for some reason, it is not possible to calculate cost of sales accurately as the sales are made, then the figure, we know, can be calculated using the costed-out values of stock on hand at the beginning and end of the period. The calculations would be given by:

	£
Stock beginning of period	—
plus Stock purchases	550
	550
minus Stock end of period	(350)
Cost of sales	200

This is a simple system to maintain records which comply with the Companies Acts. However, so far we have only considered a business which is just starting up. There are one or two minor complications when we set up the system for the next accounting period. Notice that in Figure 15.2 there was a line for 'balance-sheet from previous period' which had zeros in it because the business was just starting up. In the next period this line would have the balance-sheet total (line III) entered in it. Next, we have two simple tasks:

(1) GET NEW BOXES. If you just continue using the same boxes, you would of course, start to doublecount sales and purchases. What we are doing is labelling these invoices with the period when we recognised the income or expense (e.g. September sales or purchases), so do not know them away, because it could be that some of the unpaid invoices will still be unpaid at the end of the next period – in which case the debtors are still assets (unless they are bad debts), and the creditors are still liabilities. In this situation the 'trial balance' totals (line II) for debtors and creditors will be equal to the invoices in boxes A and C for this period, plus those from previous periods.

(2) REVERSE THE ADJUSTMENTS. Last period you added £40 to your creditors and £10 to your debtors. This period you should receive the £40 invoice and the £10 service. To avoid doublecounting you must take these liabilities and assets out of the balance-sheet by reversing the adjustments. Thus the 'reverse adjustments' line in Figure 15.2

Balance Sheet

FIXED ASSETS	£ 990
CURRENT ASSETS	
Stock	350
Debtors	310
Cash	420
	£1,080
CREDITORS DUE WITHIN ONE YEAR	£ (440)
NET CURRENT ASSETS	£ 640
TOTAL ASSETS *less* CURRENT LIABILITIES	£1,630
LOANS	£ (500)
	£1,130
CAPITAL AND RESERVES	
Share capital	£1,000
Profit-and-loss account	130
	£1,130

Table 15.3 Balance-sheet

Figure 15.3

Income Statement

Sales	£ 500
Cost of sales	(200)
	300
General expenses	(170)
Net profit before tax	£130

Figure 15.4

would show debtors −10, creditors −40 and costs −30 (+10 − 40). The system is now ready for the next accounting period.

Many small retail businesses will not have the problem of maintaining the sales invoice boxes (A and B) because their business will be mainly cash sales. This makes the process in some ways easier. However, because detailed sales invoices are not kept, there is no record of what stock is being sold, and therefore no way of costing it. The essential requirement for a retailer is a modern, efficient, cash register or till. Apart from the obvious advantages, particularly with sales assistants, in monitoring and controlling cash received over the counter, it allows you to analyse your sales by category. These categories would be relatively homogeneous goods with a similar mark-up. For exammple, the Rockley Estate off-licence of Chapter 2 purchased a till which allowed sales to be analysed into the six categories of beer, wines and spirits, other drinks, tobacco, soft drinks, and confectionery, which were known to have certain standard profit margins. In this way, by applying the standard margin to the different categories of sales analysed on the till roll, the cost of sales can be calculated. Of course, this will only be an estimate of the cost of sales, and therefore a regular count of stock is absolutely essential for a retailer and will be the only way he could determine his profit accurately.

Larger retailers often have more sophisticated cash registers which are in fact more like small microcomputers. They allow the recording of the actual item of stock being sold so that the cost of sales can be accurately determined. For example, the item sold might have a magnetic label on it detailing its stock number and selling price. When a light-sensitive pen is run over this, the cash register will show the correct selling price and store details of the stock being sold. This is then used to calculate cost of sales accurately and to control and re-order stocks.

More sophisticated manual systems

The operation of any system of accounting which is more complicated than the simple cash-book/open-invoice system will require a better knowledge of the mechanics of book-keeping than this book is designed to give. Anyway, if the volume of transactions is sufficient to warrant a more complicated system, then the small businessman will probably have to hire a book-keeper or accountant for the day-to-day operations of the system. Nevertheless, it is as well that the businessman is familiar with the outline of an accounting system since he will be the principal user of the information produced by it.

The basic ideas from the previous section are still present in any more complicated systems. However, the major difference is that the volume of transactions is such that the sales and purchase invoices have to be summarised and analysed and are then recorded regularly in the books of account, often referred to as 'posting' to the books of account. A typical system is shown in Figure 15.5. The sales day book is written up daily from the sales invoices, and the sales for a period (say a week) are totalled and entered into the general ledger account for debtors. The general ledger, sometimes called the *nominal ledger*, is a record of all the accounts making up the balance-sheet. The book-keeper maintains the dual aspect of accounting by posting a corresponding entry to the general ledger account for sales. This is called double-entry book-keeping. Individual items are also posted to the personal account of the customer in the debtors' ledger (sometimes called the *sales ledger*). This should show the amounts due for each customer, giving details of invoices and payments.

The purchase invoices are written up in a similar fashion in a purchase day book. This normally has a number of sub-columns so that the nature of the purchase may be classified (stock, fixed assets or one of the various expense categories). The column totals are posted to the general ledger account of creditors and the appropriate corresponding account. Individual items are also posted to the personal account of the supplier, kept in a creditors' ledger (sometimes called a *purchase ledger*).

The cash book acts as a book of prime entry for posting to almost all the accounts of the general ledger. Cash receipts in payment of sales invoices will be recorded in it and also entered in the personal account of the customer in the debtors' ledger. Column totals for sales receipts would be posted to the cash and debtors' accounts in the general ledger. Cash sales would, of course, go directly to the sales account in the general ledger. The debtors' ledger should agree, in total, with the amount in the debtors' account of the general ledger, and any difference would indicate that mistakes have been made in postings to these records.

Similarly, cash payments on purchase invoices are recorded in the cash book and also in the personal account of the supplier in the creditors' ledger. Column totals would be posted to the cash and creditors' accounts in the general ledger. Any cash purchases would be posted to the appropriate general ledger account directly. Once more, both the creditors' ledger and the cash book should agree with the appropriate general ledger account.

Outside the system shown in Figure 15.5, wages of production workers would be posted from a wage sheet to the cash book and then to the cash account and stock account of the general ledger. Wages of those not directly involved in production would go directly to the appropriate expense account. The method for posting cost of sales depends upon the stock costing system that the business uses.

The balance on each of the accounts in the general ledger makes up what we have called the trial balance, and the trial balance provides us with the basis for the information required to draw up a balance-sheet and income statement.

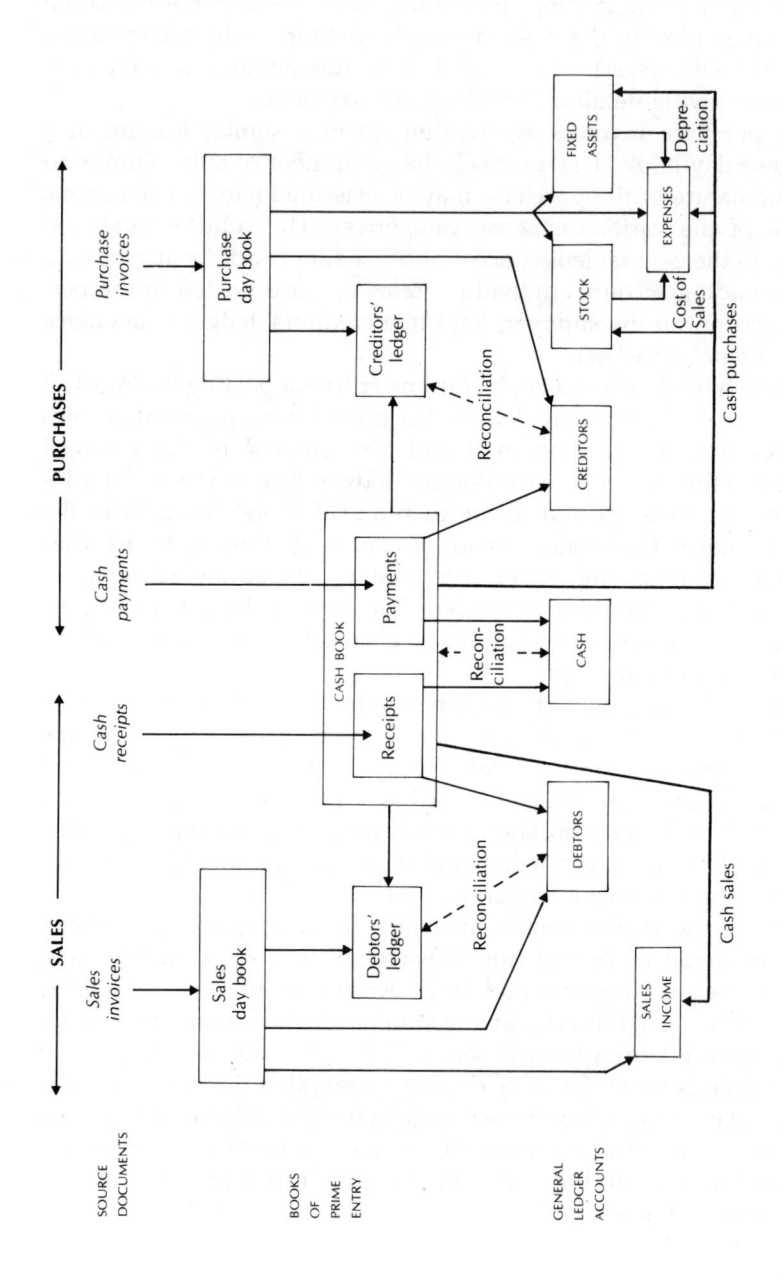

Figure 15.5 Manual accounting system

Computerised accounting systems

As the business grows more sophisticated, analysis of accounting information may be required more frequently and more speedily than previously provided. At the same time, the volume of transactions will be growing. Any manual system would start to groan under the strain of such demands, particularly if the speed of required change is quite rapid. This is a particular problem for 'growth' small businesses.

Sophisticated computer-based accounting systems are now within the budget of small businesses, thanks to the advent of the microcomputer. There are a large number of very adequate proprietary systems of accountancy software on the market. One – typical of the better systems – and very good value – is FINCO (available from Casdec Ltd. Broadward View, Chester-le Street, County Durham, DH3 3NJ). This system is based upon six 'working pads':

A Bank record
B Cash record
C Sales record
D Purchase record
E Payroll record
F VAT computation

The interrelationship between these 'working pads' is shown in Figure 15.6 and Figures 15.7, 15.8, 15.9, 15.10, 15.11, 15.12 show the detailed information contained on them. The system allows the small businessman to record cash, sales, purchase and payroll transactions clearly and simply. It also allows VAT liabilities to be computed quickly.

The microcomputer system itself can cost anything between £1,000 and £10,000. This amount buys the basic computer, visual display units, disk storage and printer. The amount depends upon the type of equipment purchased, but more importantly upon the storage capacity required. Information is stored both in the computer itself and, generally for business systems, on magnetic disks. The more information you require to store, the more expensive the microcomputer system will be. The storage requirement is largely dictated by the volume of transactions handled by the microcomputer. A second consideration is the speed of access of the information stored, and, as you would expect, the quicker the access time, the more expensive the equipment. It is beyond the scope of this book to look in detail at how to choose a microcomputer and the best ways of using it. Whole books have been written on the subject.[1]

280

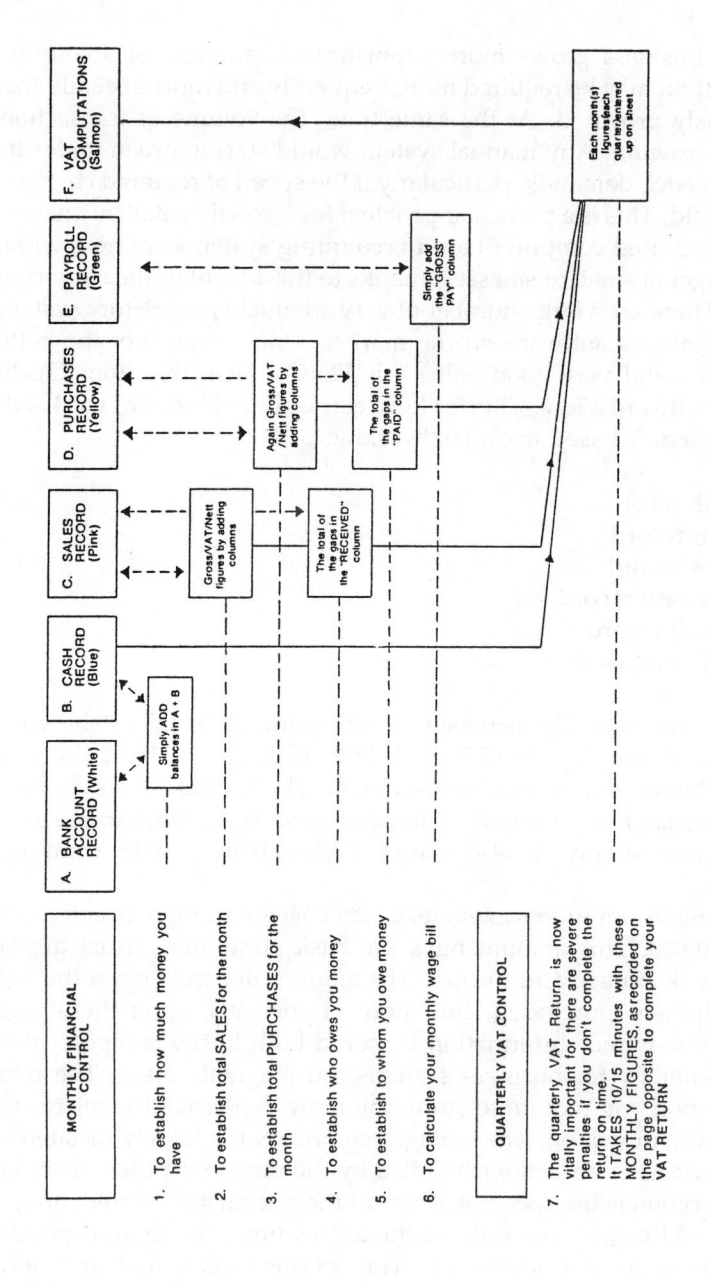

```
                                                                    ┌──────────────┐
                                                                    │ Each month(s)│
                                                                    │ figures each │
                                                                    │quarter)ntered│
                                                                    │ up on sheet  │
                                                                    └──────────────┘
                                                                           ▲
┌────────────┐                                                             │
│F. VAT      │─────────────────────────────────────────────────────────────┤
│COMPUTATIONS│                                                             │
│ (Salmon)   │                                                             │
└────────────┘                                                             │
┌────────────┐         ┌──────────┐                                        │
│E. PAYROLL  │◄───────►│Simply add│────────────────────────────────────────┤
│   RECORD   │         │the "GROSS"│                                       │
│  (Green)   │         │PAY" column│                                       │
└────────────┘         └──────────┘                                        │
┌────────────┐   ┌─────────────┐  ┌──────────┐                             │
│D. PURCHASES│◄─►│Again Gross/VAT│►│The total│─────────────────────────────┤
│   RECORD   │   │/Nett figures by│ │of the gaps│                          │
│  (Yellow)  │◄─►│adding columns │ │in the    │                           │
└────────────┘   └─────────────┘  │"PAID" col│                            │
                                  └──────────┘                             │
┌────────────┐   ┌─────────────┐  ┌──────────┐                             │
│C. SALES    │◄─►│Gross/VAT/Nett│ │The total │─────────────────────────────┤
│   RECORD   │   │figures by adding│ │of the gaps│                         │
│   (Pink)   │◄─►│columns       │ │in the    │                            │
└────────────┘   └─────────────┘  │"RECEIVED"│                            │
                                  │column    │                             │
                                  └──────────┘                             │
┌────────────┐                                                             │
│B. CASH     │─────────────────────────────────────────────────────────────┘
│   RECORD   │
│   (Blue)   │
└────────────┘         ┌──────────┐
                       │Simply ADD│
                       │balances in│
                       │A + B     │
                       └──────────┘
┌────────────┐              ▲
│A. BANK     │──────────────┘
│  ACCOUNT   │
│  RECORD    │
│  (White)   │
└────────────┘
```

┌─────────────────┐
│ MONTHLY FINANCIAL│
│   CONTROL   │
└─────────────────┘

1. To establish how much money you have
2. To establish total SALES for the month
3. To establish total PURCHASES for the month
4. To establish who owes you money
5. To establish to whom you owe money
6. To calculate your monthly wage bill

┌─────────────────┐
│QUARTERLY VAT CONTROL│
└─────────────────┘

7. The quarterly VAT Return is now vitally important for there are severe penalties if you don't complete the return on time.
   It TAKES 10/15 minutes with these MONTHLY FIGURES, as recorded on the page opposite to complete your VAT RETURN

Figure 15.6

FINCO
© Casdec Limited 1981

Business Name: EGG, SAMPLE & Co

BANK ACCOUNT RECORD

Period From 1 · 1 · 81 To 31 · 1 · 81

Serial No. A

DATE		DESCRIPTION	Cheque No.	RECEIPTS Total	Sales	Cash	Misc.	Details	PAYMENTS Total	Cash	Purchases	Payroll	Drawings		Misc.	Details	Acc'ts use only	BALANCE
Jan	1	Balance b/f																- -
"	5	Cash Banked	-	600 00		600 00												600 00
"	6	D. Egg	-	700 00			700 00	Capital										1300 00
"	6	Echo Papers	14231						60 00		60 00							1240 00
"	8	Carter & Co	-	100 00	100 00													1340 00
"	10	S. Sample	-	700 00			700 00	Capital										2040 00
"	21	Blank Ltd	14232						460 00		460 00							1580 00
"	21	Cash	14233						50 00	50 00								1530 00
"	21	Playfair Ltd	14234						320 00		345 00				(25 00)	Discount		1210 00
"	28	Wages	14235						1400 00			1400 00						(190 00)
"	29	White Ltd	-	1050 00	1150 00		(100 00)	Discount										860 00
"	30	D. Egg	STO						400 00				400 00					400 00
"	30	S. Sample	STO						250 00				250 00					210 00
TOTAL (c/fwd) (Month January)				3150 00	1250 00	600 00	1300 00		2940 00	50 00	865 00	1400 00	650 00	- -	(25 00)			210 00

Example Entries

Shows just a few of the types of entry for which the flexibility of the system caters.

Figure 15.7

CASH RECORD

FINCO — © Casdec Limited 1981

Business Name: E.G. SAMPLE & CO.

Period From 1.1.81 To 31.1.81

Serial No. B

DATE	DESCRIPTION	Vchr No.	RECEIPTS Total	Sales	Bank	Misc.	Details	PAYMENTS Total	Postage	Petrol	Stationery	Bank	VAT	Misc.	Details	Acc'ts use only	BALANCE
Jan 1	Balance b/f	–															1 –
" 1	Sales	–	115 00	115 00													115 00
" 2	Sales	–	230 00	230 00													345 00
" 3	Sales	–	276 00	276 00													621 00
" 4	Postage	–						10 00	10 00								611 00
" 5	Banking	2						600 00				600 00					11 00
" 15	Sales	–	172 50	172 50													183 50
" 16	Big Top F/S	3						23 00		20 00			3 00				160 50
" 17	L. Petrn & Co	4						34 50			30 00		4 50				126 00
" 19	Big Top F/S	5						46 00		40 00			6 00				80 00
" "	Big Top F/S	6						23 00					3 00	20 00	Motor Repair		57 00
" 20	D.I.Y. Ltd	7						28 75					3 75	25 00	Tools		28 25
" 21	Bank	–	50 00		50 00												78 25
TOTAL (Month January)			843 50	793 50	50 00			765 25	10 00	60 00	30 00	600 00	20 25	45 00			78 25

Example Entries

Shows just a few of the types of entry for which the flexibility of the system caters

Figure 15.8

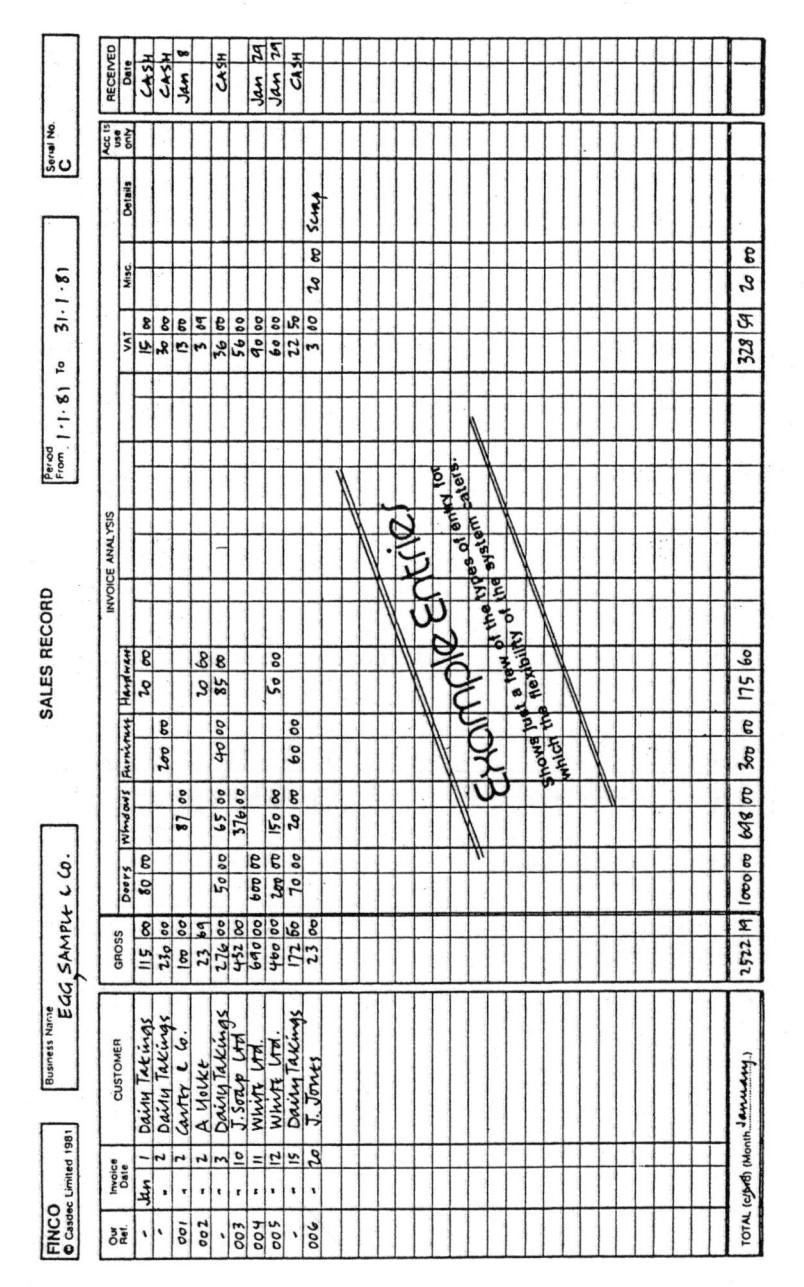

Figure 15.9

FINCO
© Casdec Limited 1981

Business Name EGG SAMPLE & Co.

PURCHASES RECORD

Period From 1.1.81 To 31.1.81

Serial No D

Our Ref.	Invoice Date	Invoice Ref.	SUPPLIER	GROSS	INVOICE ANALYSIS: Stock	Printing	Adverts	Vehicle Hire	P.H. & L.			VAT	Misc	Details	Acc is use only	PAID: Date	Cheque No
1	Jan 1	4321	ABC Ltd.	201 25	175 00							26 25					
2	" 4	A43	Playfair Ltd.	115 00	100 00							15 00				Jan 21	14234
3	" 4	4C42	XYZ Co. Ltd.	172 50		150 00						22 50					
4	" 6	8994	Blank Ltd.	460 00	400 00							60 00				Jan 21	14232
5	" 6	A44	Playfair Ltd.	230 00	200 00							30 00				Jan 21	14234
6	" 6	93	Echo Papers	60 00			60 00					- -				Jan 6	14231
7	" 14	A61	Playfair Ltd	483 00	420 00							63 00					
8	" 20	1243	Rolls Rental	115 00				100 00				15 00					
9	" 22	03-06	British Telecom	80 50								10 50	70 00	Telephone			
10	" 25	14762	N.E. Electricity	123 00					123 00			- -					
TOTAL (c/fwd) (Month January)				2040 25	1295 00	150 00	60 00	100 00	123 00	- -	- -	242 25	70 00				

Example Entries

Shows just a few of the types of entry for which the flexibility of the system caters.

Figure 15.10

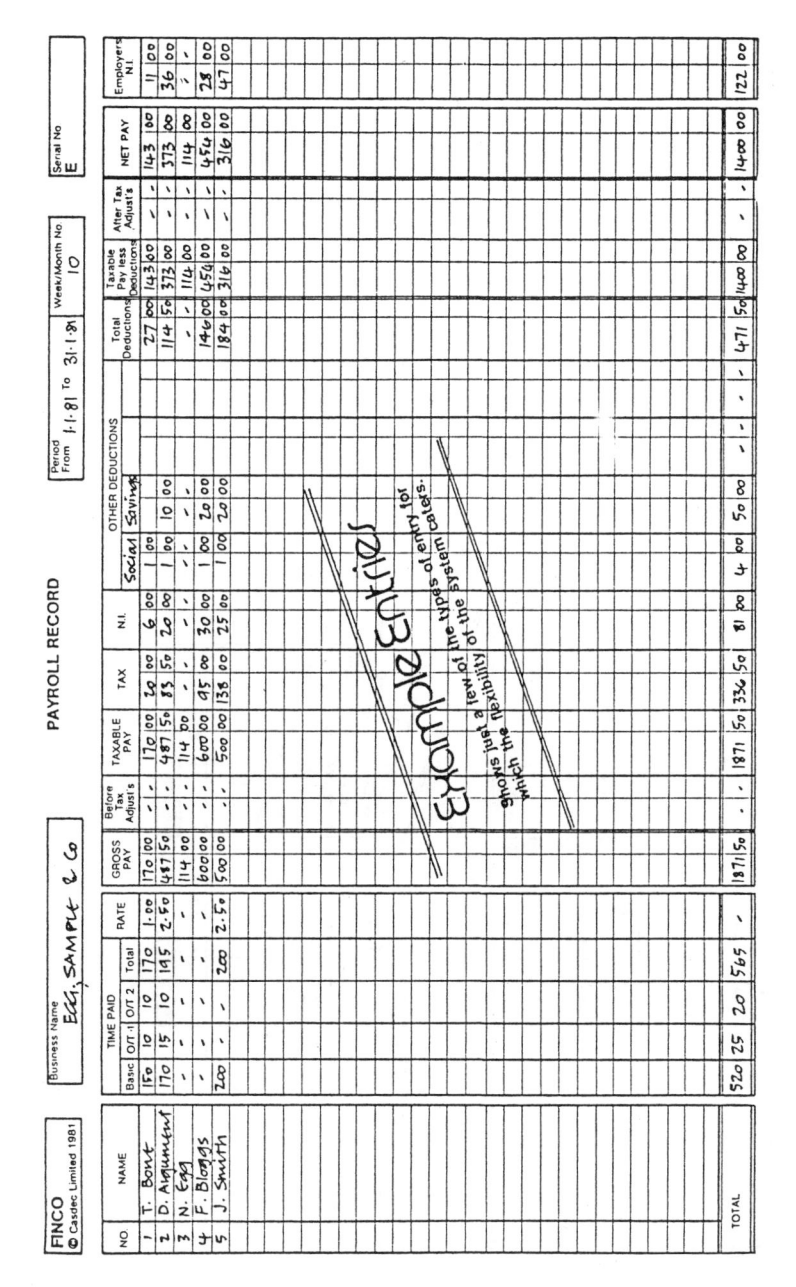

Figure 15.11

286

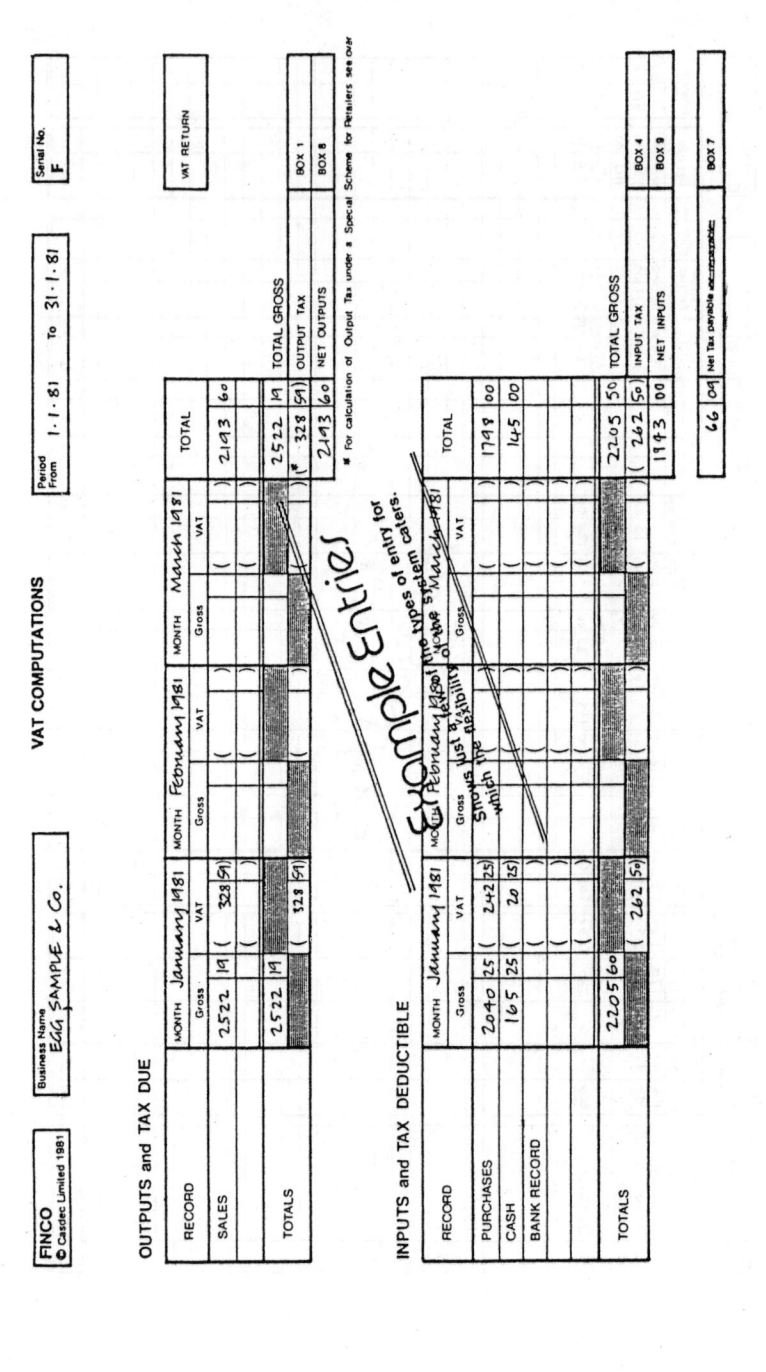

FINCO © Castdec Limited 1981 | Business Name: EGG SAMPLE & Co. | VAT COMPUTATIONS | Period From 1·1·81 To 31·1·81 | Serial No. F

OUTPUTS and TAX DUE

RECORD	MONTH January 1981		MONTH February 1981		MONTH March 1981		TOTAL		VAT RETURN
	Gross	VAT	Gross	VAT	Gross	VAT			
SALES	2522 19	(328 91		(		(	2193 60		
TOTALS	2522 19	(328 91		(		(	2522 19	TOTAL GROSS	BOX 1
							(* 328 91)	OUTPUT TAX	
							2193 60	NET OUTPUTS	BOX 8

\# For calculation of Output Tax under a Special Scheme for Retailers see over

Example Entries — MONTH February 1981 Shows just a list of the liability of the system caters. MONTH March 1981

INPUTS and TAX DEDUCTIBLE

RECORD	MONTH January 1981		MONTH		MONTH		TOTAL		
	Gross	VAT	Gross	VAT	Gross	VAT			
PURCHASES	2040 25	(242 25		(		(	1749 00		
CASH	165 25	(20 25		(		(	145 00		
BANK RECORD		(		(		(			
		(		(		(			
TOTALS	2205 60	(262 50		(		(	2205 50	TOTAL GROSS	BOX 4
							(262 50)	INPUT TAX	BOX 9
							1943 00	NET INPUTS	

66 09 Net Tax payable or repayable BOX 7

Figure 15.12

and, as you would expect, the quicker the access time, the more expensive the equipment. It is beyond the scope of this book to look in detail at how to choose a microcomputer and the best ways of using it. Whole books have been written on the subject.[1]

The accounting systems that run on microcomputers (called the 'software') are of two types. The first are systems which are tailor-made for a particular business. That is, a computer programmer has written a suite of programs specifically for the business, for the particular applications that the business has in mind. These are expensive and generally outside the budget of most small businesses. It is the second type of program, the 'off-the-shelf' program such as FINCO that has made computerised accounting systems accessible to all businesses. In fact, simply to label them as 'accounting systems' is to do them a disservice, because they often comprise a full system of business control, with the accounting system integrated into other aspects. As well as an accounting system, they offer programs for controlling stock in quantity terms (Chapter 19), job costing (Chapter 12), budgeting (Chapter 13), and the ubiquitous word processing, possibly linked to mailing lists compiled from the debtors' and creditors' ledgers. Such 'integrated business systems' can cost under £1,000.

Most systems are 'modular' so that different processs in the business control program can be run separately, but are also 'integrated', so that one module passes information on to another. For example, items invoiced to customers in the debtors' ledger will deplete stock in the general ledger, as well as in the records of stock quantity. Most systems are 'parameter-driven'; this means that the business has some flexibility in the hardware that the programs can be used with. It also means that items like discount rates or VAT rates can be altered to suit the individual business.

An actual 'integrated business system' is shown in Figure 15.13. Perhaps, surprisingly, the system is not so different from the manual one shown in Figure 15.5, and indeed the principles involved are exactly the same. The obvious difference is that the computer automatically completes the double-entry book-keeping from initial input of information. It will also produce standard format invoices, payroll slips and other such paperwork automatically. Clearly this alone can save considerable time for a small business.

In fact the major differences lie in the areas of control that we cover in later chapters of the book. The stock-control program allows the business to control the physical stocks it holds. Purchases and sales of stock would be recorded automatically, and costing information from

---

[1] See, for example, Khalid Aziz, *So You Think Your Business Needs a Computer?*, Kogan Page, 1986.

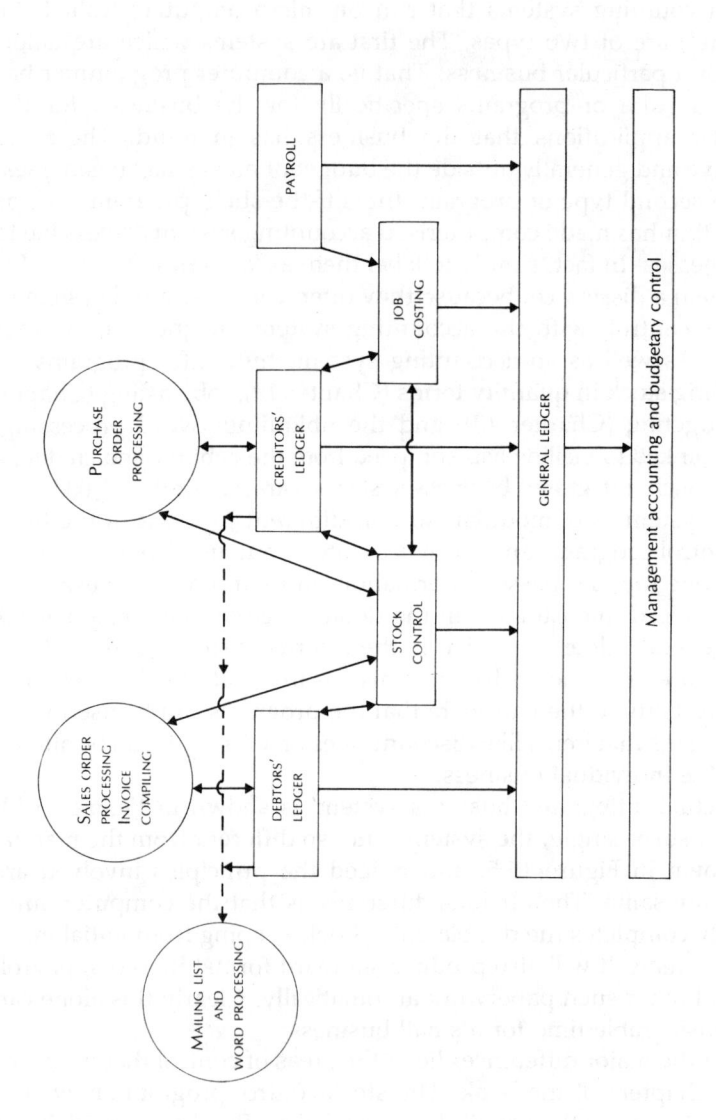

Figure 15.13 An integrated computerised business system

the creditors' ledger would allow the stock and cost of sales accounts in the general ledger to be posted. The program would allow the small business to obtain a print-out of stock, showing individual parts, quantity and prices. To facilitate the control of that stock many programs give details of purchases and uses of stock over a period, as well as lead times, minimum stock levels and minimum re-order quantities (all terms that will be explained in Chapter 19). The job-costing program would allow a manufacturing small business to calculate the cost of a job, made up from raw materials, labour and some overhead costs. Of course, the job, once completed, becomes part of the stock of finished goods before being sent to the customer, at which point the stock and cost of sales accounts in the general ledger would be entered.

Sales ledgers are frequently fully open, allowing incoming cash to be fully or partly posted to an outstanding invoice whilst not allowing an invoice to be cleared until it has been settled in full. Settlements can take early payment dates into account and penalties can be imposed on late payers. Credit control is now very important and most systems allow:

A. Credit information to be stored on customers and displayed at order input stage.
B. Slow payers to be automatically chased each time balances outstanding exceed a given level.
C. The production of aged debtors listing (Chapter 20)

Purchase ledgers can offer similar facilities, including analysis by invoice or due date, and ledger listings showing detailed statements of all accounts, including both open and closed items. Settlements can frequently be in full or in part, with payments being allocated to a specific item or a whole account.

Spreadsheet packages

One of the biggest success stories of microcomputers is the spreadsheet package. These are essentially flexible worksheets where the user defines the structure of the output, its format and related narrative, and the arithmetic functions to be performed on various lines of the worksheet.

On the screen the user sees an electronic spreadsheet with rows and columns into which figures can be placed. Once the functions have been defined and the data put into the microcomputer, the

CASHFLOW FORECAST (£ '000) >>>> Y/E 30th SEPTEMBER 1987

MONTH	1 OCT	2 NOV	3 DEC	4 JAN	5 FEB	6 MAR	7 APR	8 MAY	9 JUN	10 JUL	11 AUG	12 SEPT	SEPT 87 YTD
RECEIPTS													
Sales – Cash													0.00
Sales – Debtors	0.00	0.00	0.00	24.00	30.15	20.55	31.90	38.80	36.50	0.00	0.00	0.00	181.90
Loans Received				0.00									0.00
Capital Introduced													0.00
Disposal of Assets													0.00
Other Receipts	0.12	0.12	0.12	0.12	0.12	0.12	0.12	0.12	0.12	0.12	0.12	0.12	1.44
A. TOTAL RECEIPTS	0.12	0.12	0.12	24.12	30.27	20.67	32.02	38.92	36.62	0.12	0.12	0.12	183.34
PAYMENTS													
Cash Purchases													
Payments to Credit	0.00	0.00	0.00	0.00	(30.00)	(30.00)	0.00	(30.00)	(60.00)	0.00	0.00	0.00	(150.00)
Wages & Sals. (ne	(0.10)	(0.10)	(0.10)	(0.10)	(0.10)	(0.10)	(0.10)	(0.10)	(0.10)	(0.10)	(0.10)	(0.10)	(1.20)

PAYE/NIC													
Office Equipment	(0.05)	(0.05)	(0.05)	(0.05)	(0.05)	(0.05)	(0.05)	(0.05)	(0.05)	(0.05)	(0.05)	(0.05)	(0.60)
UK Delivery Costs	0.00	0.00	(0.10)	(0.10)	(0.10)	(0.10)	(0.10)	(0.10)	0.00	0.00	0.00	0.00	(0.60)
Rent/Rates													(0.60)
Telephone	(0.04)	(0.04)	(0.04)	(0.04)	(0.04)	(0.04)	(0.04)	(0.04)	(0.04)	(0.04)	(0.04)	(0.04)	(0.50)
Telex	(0.03)	(0.03)	(0.03)	(0.03)	(0.03)	(0.03)	(0.03)	(0.03)	(0.03)	(0.03)	(0.03)	(0.03)	(0.40)
Loan Repayment													0.00
Interest													0.00
Insurance	0.00	0.00	0.00	0.00	0.00	0.00	0.00	0.00	0.00	0.00	0.00	0.00	0.00
Travel Expense	(0.02)	(0.02)	(0.02)	(0.02)	(0.02)	(0.02)	(0.02)	(0.02)	(0.02)	(0.02)	(0.02)	(0.02)	(0.24)
Advertising	(0.02)	(0.02)	(0.02)	(0.02)	(0.02)	(0.02)	(0.02)	(0.02)	(0.02)	(0.02)	(0.02)	(0.02)	(0.24)
VAT													
Corporation Tax etc.													0.00
Dividends													0.00
B. TOTAL PAYMENTS	(0.27)	(0.27)	(0.37)	(0.37)	(30.37)	(30.37)	(0.37)	(30.37)	(60.27)	(0.27)	(0.27)	(0.27)	(153.78)
Balance (A – B)	(0.15)	(0.15)	(0.25)	23.76	(0.09)	(9.69)	31.66	8.56	(23.65)	(0.15)	(0.15)	(0.15)	
Balance b/fwd	0.00	(0.15)	(0.29)	(0.54)	23.22	23.13	13.43	45.09	53.64	30.00	29.85	29.71	
Balance c/fwd	(0.15)	(0.29)	(0.54)	23.22	23.13	13.43	45.09	53.64	30.00	29.85	29.71	29.56	

Figure 15.14 Example of a spread sheet cash flow

machine automatically performs the computations at a press of a button. Change a figure and the machine will perform the computation again at the press of the same button.

Spreadsheets are particularly useful for:

A. Cash flow projections.
B. Profit-and-loss account projections.
C. Capital investment appraisal (Chapter 18).

An example of a spreadsheet cash flow projection is shown in Figure 15.14.

Following the success of these products there has been a logical move to packages which offer many 'add-on' extras such as word processor, database and graphics, all integrated into the one package. An integrated package follows figures from a spreadsheet to be fed directly into a graphing facility which produces a variety of graph formats. Often the graph can then be placed inside a word-processed document. The word-processed document can be mailed to clients selected from a database on the basis of some predefined criteria. For example, with a list of clients, their addresses and account values, new lists could be selected of people living in a certain area whose account exceeds a certain figure.

There are a wide variety of packages now on offer. Probably the most popular is still Lotus 1.2.3 but others include Symphony and Framework; all cost less than £600.

It is therefore worth remembering when you read subsequent chapters that computer programs are now readily available to perform many of these analyses. This means that many of the so-called 'sophisticated techniques' which have been dismissed in the past by small businesses as time-consuming or too expensive to undertake are now far more relevant because the microcomputer has dramatically altered the cost-benefit equation. Small businesses will use the techniques far more in the future. It is important for the small businessman to understand them.

CHAPTER 16

Understanding Financial Information

INTRODUCTION	293
ANALYSING THE ACCOUNTS OF A BUSINESS	294
RATIO ANALYSIS OF 'PUBLISHED' ACCOUNTS	295
ANALYSING THE COMPLETE ACCOUNTS OF A SMALL BUSINESS	306
FUNDS-FLOW ANALYSIS	307
VALUE-ADDED STATEMENTS	310
INFLATION ACCOUNTING	311

Introduction

In many of the earlier chapters (particularly Chapters 10 and 15) we have been concerned to show the types of financial accounts that a small business will keep, and how these accounts should be prepared. When the term 'the financial accounts', or more simply 'the accounts', is used it is usual to assume that it refers to the *balance-sheet* and the *profit-and-loss account* for the year, and we shall continue to use it in this sense. The technique most frequently employed in understanding these accounts is *ratio analysis* and in the main part of this chapter we shall be concerned in applying this approach to the historical balance-sheet and profit-and-loss account of a business. We shall build on the example given in Chapter 10 (Tables 10.4 and 10.5).

The word 'historical' has a special significance in accounting. Its significance can best be explained by way of an example. Let us assume that we purchased an asset (freehold property, machinery, vehicle) some years ago for a sum of £10,000. In the book of accounts it is this £10,000 figure which will be recorded. It is usually referred to as the 'input' figure. In normal historical accounting the input figure will be the basis for all accounting records relating to the transaction. Depreciation will always be based on this figure, as will profit and loss on sale of the asset, and so on. In general no account will be taken of any increase in the replacement cost of the asset. Years ago with high inflation rates, the correctness of accounts prepared on these lines had been called into question. 'Inflation' accounting therefore needs to be discussed, as well as the relevance of accounts prepared on these new bases to small businesses.

Although the ratio analysis of an historical balance-sheet and profit-and-loss account is still the technique most used in analysing the financial performance of a business, we shall consider two others – funds-flow statements and value-added statements. Both have rather limited relevance to small businesses.

Analysing the accounts of a business

In analysing the balance-sheet and profit-and-loss account of a business a distinction needs to be made between those accounts which are prepared in accordance with the requirements of the Companies Act 1985 (and preceding Acts) and other accounts.

We noted earlier that the requirements of the 1985 Act apply to every set of accounts laid before the members in general meeting by every Company registered in England and Scotland. This is the case whether the company is large or small, public or private. There are exemptions for 'small' and 'medium' companies but *only* in respect of the version that they need to file with the Registrar of Companies. Many of these companies will not prepare new sets of accounts taking advantage of these exemptions because of the extra time and trouble involved. The 1985 Companies Act version has to be prepared for the shareholders: why bother about additional versions? The terms 'small' and 'medium' are defined in the Act. We introduced these definitions in Chapter 1.

Many small businesses will be sole traders or partnerships. The accounts of these businesses do not have to be in accordance with Companies Acts. The owners, proprietors and partners of these businesses will require *complete* accounts, i.e. with all the expenses in the profit-and-loss account shown in great detail. The directors and senior executives of *all* companies will also have access to *complete* accounts. We have to deal, therefore, with two main types of accounts:

(a) those prepared in accordance with the Companies Act 1985.
(b) complete accounts

and with the difference between the two mainly lying in the limited information given in a profit-and-loss account prepared under (a). Our ratio analysis approach will concentrate initially on the first of these two. It is common to refer to accounts prepared on this basis as 'published' accounts. The earlier 1981 Act in fact defined 'publishing' in a slightly different, rather specialised (and somewhat misleading!) way, no doubt to conform with the *Fourth Directive* of the EEC. However, 'published accounts' is a well-recognised term for accounts which are prepared in accordance with the Companies Acts and are publicly available, and we too shall use it in this sense. Since the published accounts of a company are the only accounts that will be available to an 'outsider', ratio analysis of these accounts will cover analysis from the points of view of investors, lenders and creditors. Ratio analysis of published accounts is much the same whether the company is large or small, so that section will be of a fairly general nature. Later we shall extend our analysis to complete accounts. These are the detailed accounts available to those managing the business, and that analysis will therefore concentrate on assessing accounts from the managerial efficiency point of view. In that section we shall concentrate very much on small businesses.

The next section, therefore, deals with ratio analysis of published accounts. We begin by considering some general rules and then we give a comprehensive example of the application of the ratio analysis approach to a company's accounts.

Ratio analysis of 'published' accounts

In Chapter 10 a clear distinction was drawn between cash and historical profit. For a long while the latter was the accepted measure of the gain that a business had made within a period. For quite a while now – particularly since the advent of high rates of inflation – doubt has been cast on exactly what reported profit is or should be. By contrast cash is simple, exact and much more useful! Since the reason for working out ratios is to understand and analyse the performance of a business, many ratios are based quite directly on these two measures, i.e. profit and cash.

In the analysis of a business cash is divided into long-term cash, which traditionally should be concerned with the financing of fixed assets, and short-term cash, which is necessary for working capital management, i.e. for the day-to-day operations of the company. In practice the precise point of separation between these two is often difficult to establish. Nevertheless this broad division between the two types of cash is widely recognised.

Ratios based on profit, short-term cash and long-term cash are therefore the main divisions when analysing the performance and financial status of a business. There are other ratios *indirectly* concerned with performance, e.g. stock turnover, and these form a fourth group which can be classified as asset efficiency, indirect, coverage or service ratios. 'Indirect' here means that improvement in these ratios is likely to lead in turn to better figures for profit or cash.

We have already noted that published accounts are of particular interest to investors, i.e. those buying or selling shares (or considering doing so), in the company. In that section we need to look at the market price and discuss whether that price indicates a good 'buy' and possibly whether a controlling interest could be built up.

Finally, employees are another group with a special interest in a company. Since the performance of employees is of concern to the management of the business and contributes towards profit, some of these ratios could be seen as forming part of the first group. Profit per employee – usually regarded as the financial definition of 'productivity' – is one of these. However, for simplicity, we have kept all ratios relating to employees separate. Our groups are therefore:

Principally for

(a) Profitability ratios   ⎫
(b) Short-term cash ratios   ⎬ Direct   ⎫ Management
(c) Long-term cash ratios   ⎭   ⎬
(d) Asset efficiency ratios   Indirect ⎭
(e) Investors' ratios   Investors
(f) Employees' ratios   Employees

What should one think of the following statement? 'Our accounts are just out. We have made a profit of £202,011. Didn't we do well!?'

Did the business do well? Clearly a lot more information needs to be supplied before we can answer this with any authority. There is the matter of size. If the business is an alpha stock near the top of *The Times* list of the largest companies, then it is not doing at all well. If, on the other hand, the year's work just consists of the proprietor building toys in his own backyard every other weekend, then he's on to a pretty good thing!

It is a matter of size, and the two principal measures of size of a business most used are capital and sales turnover. In the management sections we therefore relate profit both to capital and to sales turnover, and express each of these as a percentage. But the matter is not ended there; there are further problems. What, for instance, is menat by 'profit'? Is it profit before tax or profit after tax?

To decide, as between these two, which is the right measure to use in ratio analysis, we have to remind ourselves that the main purpose of this group of ratios is to assess the management, trading, and operating efficiency of a business. Taxation rates are decided by the government; they cannot be controlled by the managers of the company. Profit on ordinary trading activities *before* tax is therefore the right measure.

We now have two ratios in which we relate profit to invested capital and to sales turnover. The first is the ratio most widely used of all in assessing the performance of a business. It represents the profit made per pound (or other unit of money) invested in the business. It is variously referred to as *return on invested capital* (ROI), *return on capital* and *return on net assets*. Table 16.1 gives the balance-sheet and profit-and-loss account used in Chapter 10. These accounts are still in the form required by the Companies Act 1985, though some of the less important items which have no figures against them have been (as they would be in the presentation of actual accounts) omitted. Figures for the previous year have been included. A glance at the balance-sheet demonstrates the indentity of net assets (total assets *less* current liabilities) and invested capital (capital, reserves and debentures). The word 'return' is synonymous with profit.

The return on invested capital ratio can be expanded as follows:

$$\text{ROI} = \frac{\text{Trading profit}}{\text{Invested capital}} = \frac{\text{Trading profit}}{\text{Sales}} \times \frac{\text{Sales}}{\text{Invested capital}}$$

Cancelling out sales from the top and bottom on the right returns it to the original ROI ratio, so the statement is nothing more than an identity. Nevertheless it can be of great use. It is the basis of a very detailed application of ratio analysis first developed by the American chemical giant Dupont.

Since invested capital is equal to net assets we can write the identity as:

ROI = Margin on sales × Asset turnover

If we wish to increase ROI, we can do so by either increasing margin on sales or by increasing asset turnover. Since net assets, in the short run at any rate, are fixed, this means it can be done either by increasing the profit on each pound of sales, or by increasing the sales turnover. So which should a business concentrate on? High profit margin, or high turnover? The answer presumably is 'whichever it can', and this answer will vary with the business and the trade or industry within which it operates. A high-class antique furniture

Table 16.1
A Balance-sheet

		£	Previous year £
FIXED ASSETS			
Tangible assets		900,000	950,000
Trade investments in related companies		—	—
		900,000	950,000
CURRENT ASSETS	£		£
Stocks	275,000		250,000
Debtors	265,000		220,000
Investments (listed government securities)	—		—
Cash	60,000		17,500
	600,000		487,500
CREDITORS: AMOUNTS FALLING DUE WITHIN ONE YEAR			
Trade creditors (147,500)			(130,000)
Taxation (60,000)			(70,000)
Proposed dividend payable (42,500)			(50,000)
	(250,000)		(250,000)
NET CURRENT ASSETS		350,000	237,500
TOTAL ASSETS less CURRENT LIABILITIES[1]		1,250,000	1,187,500
CREDITORS: AMOUNTS FALLING DUE AFTER MORE THAN ONE YEAR			
9% debenture loans		(200,000)	(200,000)
PROVISIONS FOR LIABILITIES AND CHARGES		—	—
ACCRUALS AND DEFERRED INCOME		—	—
		1,050,000	987,500
CAPITAL AND RESERVES[2]	*Authorised*	*Issued*	
Ordinary shares of £1	1,000,000	750,000	750,000
10% preferences shares of £1	50,000	50,000	50,000
		800,000	800,000
Revaluation reserve		55,000	55,000
Profit-and-loss account		195,000	132,500
		1,050,000	987,500

[1] Alternatively net assets or invested capital.
[2] Alternatively equity capital or net worth or shareholders' funds.

B Profit-and-loss account

	£	Previous year £
Turnover	1,825,000	1,660,000
Cost of sales	(1,375,000)	1,251,000
Gross profit	450,000	409,000
Distribution costs	(110,000)	(100,000)
Administrative expenses	(147,000)	(133,700)
Trading profit	193,000	175,300
Income from fixed asset investments	—	—
Other interest receivable	—	—
Interest payable	(18,000)	(18,000)
Profit on ordinary activities before taxation	175,000	157,300
Tax on profit on ordinary activites	(70,000)	(70,000)
Profit on ordinary activities after taxation	105,000	87,300
Extraordinary items	—	—
Profit for the financial year	105,000	87,300
Dividends paid and proposed		
Preference	(5,000)	(5,000)
Ordinary	(37,500)	(45,000)
Retained profit for the year	62,500	37,300

ADDITIONAL INFORMATION
Market price (ordinary share of £1)	£1.20
Total wages expenses	£450,000
Depreciation expense	£ 50,000
Number of employees	100

RATIOS

PROFITABILITY

(a) Return on invested capital or return on capital (see notes 1 and 2)

$$\frac{\text{Trading profit}}{\text{Invested capital}} = \frac{193,000}{1,250,000} \times 100 = 15.4\%$$

(b) Margin on sales

$$\frac{\text{Trading profit}}{\text{Sales}} = \frac{193,000}{1,825,000} \times 100 = 10.6\%$$

(c) Return on ordinary shareholders' funds (see note 10)

$$\frac{\text{Profit after tax and preference dividend}}{\text{Net worth}} = \frac{100,000}{1,000,000} \times 100 = 10\%$$

B Ratios

SHORT-TERM CASH

(d) Current ratio (see note 8)

$$\frac{\text{Current assets}}{\text{Current liabilities}} = \frac{600{,}000}{250{,}000} = 2.4$$

(e) Liquidity ratio (acid test) (see note 8)

$$\frac{\text{Current assets, } less \text{ Stock}}{\text{Current liabilities}} = \frac{325{,}000}{250{,}000} = 1.3$$

LONG-TERM CASH

(f) Gearing (see note 9) ratios
  (i) Traditional gearing

$$\frac{\text{Long term debt and Preference Shares}}{\text{Capital employed}} = \frac{250{,}000}{1{,}250{,}000} \times 100 = 20\%$$

  (ii) Debt to net worth

$$\frac{\text{Total debt}}{\text{Net worth}} = \frac{500{,}000}{1{,}050{,}000} \times 100 = 47.6\%$$

Interest cover (income gearing)

$$\frac{\text{Trading profit}}{\text{Interest}} = \frac{193{,}000}{18{,}000} = 10.7$$

ASSET EFFICIENCY

(g) Day sales outstanding (see note 5)

$$\frac{\text{Debtors}}{\text{Sales per day}} = \frac{265{,}000}{5{,}000} = 53 \text{ days}$$

(h) Stock turnover (see note 6)

$$\frac{\text{Cost of sales}}{\text{Stock}} = \frac{1{,}375{,}000}{275{,}000} = 5 \text{ times a year}$$

B Ratios

(i) Asset turnover

$$\frac{\text{Sales}}{\text{Net assets}} = \frac{1{,}825{,}000}{1{,}250{,}000} = 1.46 \text{ times}$$

INVESTORS

(j) Earnings per share (EPS)

$$\frac{\text{Profit after tax and preference dividend}}{\text{Number of ordinary shares issued}}$$

$$= \frac{100{,}000}{750{,}000} \times 100 = 13.3\text{p}$$

(k) Price-earnings ratio (P/E ratio)

$$\frac{\text{Market price}}{\text{Earnings per share}} = \frac{1.2}{0.133} = 9$$

(l) *Times* dividend covered (dividend cover)

$$\frac{\text{Profit after tax and preference dividend}}{\text{Dividend}}$$

$$= \frac{100{,}000}{37{,}500} = 2.7 \text{ times}$$

(m) Dividend yield (yield)

$$\frac{\text{Dividend per share}}{\text{Market price}} = \frac{0.05}{1.2} \times 100 = 4.2\%$$

EMPLOYEES

(n) Wages per employee

$$= \frac{450{,}000}{100} = £4{,}500$$

(o) Sales per employee

$$= \frac{1{,}825{,}000}{100} = £18{,}250$$

(p) Profit per employee

$$= \frac{193{,}000}{100} = £1{,}930$$

(q) Net assets per employee

$$= \frac{1{,}250{,}000}{100} = £12{,}500$$

Notes to Table 16.1

[1] The return on invested capital (ROI), or return on capital, which should be achieved by a company depends very much on the industry in which the company is operating.

[2] Investment analysts use trading profit or PBIT rather than profit before tax (PBT) for ratios (a), (b) and (p). PBIT (a term widely used pre-1981) stands for net profit before deduction of interest and taxes. It is arrived at, arithmetically, by adding back interest to the net profit before tax figure. PBIT, it is argued, is a better figure to use since it excludes *both* the cost of equity capital (i.e. dividends) and the cost of debt (i.e. interest). Hence fair comparisons can be made as between companies with differing capital structures. EBIT (earnings before interest and taxes) is synonymous with PBIT. See also notes 7 and 9 for comments on long-term and short-term debt.

[3] The term equity capital means capital and reserves.

[4] A fair case can be made out for excluding listed investments from the bottom of ratio (a). Deducting investments in related companies is not so satisfactory. Although these assets, too, are employed outside the business, they are necessary for its successful running. Usually the effect of making the deduction is not material. (If either type of investment is excluded from the denominator, then the interest or dividend from that investment must be excluded from the numerator (top) of the ratio.)

[5] Theoretically the sales figures in days sales outstanding, ratio (g), ought to be restricted to credit sales, i.e. cash sales should be excluded. Most credit sales are made on a 30-day basis, but actual 'days sales outstanding' is usually much more than this. The average for manufacturing companies is around 70 days.

[6] The cost of sales figure may not be given in published accounts unless Format 1 or 3 (Companies Act 1985) is used. For the stock turnover figure, ratio (h), the 'sales' figure, must then be substituted for 'cost of sales'.

[7] Bank overdrafts are usually shown under current liabilities. When roughly the same overdraft has been in operation for many years it might be more appropriate to include it under long-term debt. Whatever method is used does not matter too much provided the *same method* is used for the comparative ratios for previous years in the company, and for the ratios for similar companies. *This principle applies generally to all ratios.*

[8] The average current ratio (d) is now around 1.5, and the liquidity ratio (e) around 0.8. But these figures should be taken as giving only a rough indication of the ratios which should be achieved by any particular firm or business, since individual and industry variations from these norms are, in practice, considerable. For any particular business *the important thing is the* TREND *in the ratio*, and whether it is in the right direction or not.

[9] The traditional gearing ratio

$$\frac{(200{,}000 + 50{,}000) = 250{,}000}{1{,}250{,}000} \times 100 = 20 \text{ per cent}$$

has been the ratio most used in the United Kingdom for comparing long-term debt with invested capital. Often all or part of bank overdraft is included in long-term debt and therefore included also in capital employed. Preference share capital is always included with long-term debt in this ratio on the pragmatic grounds that in practice preference share dividends are almost always paid.

Sometimes the ratio has been expressed in the form of 'long-term debt to net worth'. In our example this would be:

$$\frac{250,000}{1,050,000} \times 100 = 25 \text{ per cent (approx.)}$$

Traditionally, too, the maximum safe gearing has been regarded as 33 per cent. If we express the ratio in the other form, i.e. as long-term debt to net worth, this maximum will then be 50 per cent. This is another way of saying the same thing.

However, two points need to be made here. First, the use of gearing both in the United Kingdom and the USA (the American term for gearing is *leverage*) has tended to increase over the years, and nowadays gearing rates well above these figures are usually regarded as 'safe'. Second, this ratio, like most others, varies considerably from industry to industry. Some industries (e.g. property, public utilities and hotels) typically have ratios well above the average figure.

Because of the difficulty in separating short- and long-term debt, a 'debt to net worth' ratio which compares total debt (i.e. short-term loans and current liabilities, as well as long-term debt and preference shares) is now much more widely used. The practice started in the USA and is now common in the United Kingdom.

The basic difference between the 'traditional gearing' and the 'debt to net worth' ratios is therefore the inclusion of short-term loans and current liabilities in the latter. The proportion of these short-term loans and current liabilities in the total debt figure is referred to as *secondary gearing*.

[10] Ordinary shareholders' funds include reserves but exclude preference shares. Net worth can mean *net worth to ordinary shareholders* (in which case it is synonymous with the above), or it can mean *net worth to all shareholders*. In the latter case preference shares are included. In all ratios in which profit is compared with funds/net worth, the principle should be that if preference shares are excluded from the denominator (funds/net worth) the preference dividends must be excluded from the numerator (profit). *In practice, since preference shares now usually form only a very small (if any) part of capital, the difference is not all that important.*

---

shop makes few sales. But if a customer wants a particular antique, money is probably not too much a problem, so selling price will bear a little extra margin. On the other hand, a supermarket operates under conditions of great market price competition. Margins are very tight. It is not practical for businesses operating in such circumstances to increase or reduce prices substantially. Where the market fixes the price the only way to increase profits is to increase turnover.

The conclusions that we have arrived at for these ratios are that ROI should be as high as possible, but that, even if it is desirable, it will often not be practical to have too high a margin on sales.

But how high or how low is satisfactory? A clue to the right answer has already been provided. In discussing the margin on sales we noted that the value for this ratio is likely to vary very much from one industry to another. If we compare the ratios of our business with those of similar companies operating in similar trade or industries, we shall have a good guide as to what they should be. For the ROI ratio – which we want to be as high as possible – we shall be satisfied if it is as high or higher than the industry norm. For the margin on sales ratio we shall expect it to match up with the industry norm. If there is a substantial deviation, either above or below, we shall regard this as grounds for further investigation.

Contrasting the figure for our business with the industry's norm is therefore the first basis for comparison. With what other figures should we compare this year's results of our business? Is it entirely fair to assess the way our business has been managed this year with the industry average? It may be that in previous years the business was managed badly. Can we expect management today to put it all right immediately? Presumably we shall be satisfied if it improves the performance of the business, and this will be reflected in the *trend*. It may be, too, that this year there are some external factors over which management has no control. These can be taken into account by incorporating them in a forecast, plan or estimate for this year's figures. Presumably, too, we shall be satisfied if management's performance this year compares favourably with the estimate.

Putting all these together the answer to the question as to how high or low a ratio should be is that we need to compare this year's figure with:

- the INDUSTRY NORM, i.e. with other businesses (preferably of a similar size) operating in similar trades or industries
- the TREND, as shown up by past ratios of the same business
- the ESTIMATES, or forecasted figures for this year for the business

These are the comparisons to be made in ratio analysis, though the significance of the last one will depend on the amount of planning that the business does. Any organisation which takes planning at all seriously wil have cash budgets and profit forecasts prepared in detail at least for a year into the future. However, these estimates will not normally be available to anyone outside the business.

Although we have arrived at these comparison indications for ratio analysis from a consideration of one group of ratios only, it is obvious that they apply to *all* ratios, though their relative importance may vary from one ratio to another. So far as ROI and margin on sales is concerned they are very important. In theory the ROI should be the same for any industry. In a world where a perfect economic market exists the return that any industry makes on the capital invested will never fall below the national average. If it were to fall, the investors who supply the funds, and who get a reward based on the profit from these funds, would move their capital elsewhere, seeking a higher return. Businesses, if uneconomic in this sense, would close down. In practice there is an imperfect market, business assets cannot be immediately converted into other assets, nor can skills learnt be transferred quickly into other idustrial processes. Neither capital nor labour is, in reality, free to move according to market forces.

In reality the ROI earned in one industry will vary from that earned in another. The correct comparison for a particular return of a business is therefore the industry norm, and not the national average. Similar remarks apply to the margin on sales, though it will be remembered that it is not necessarily always desirable for this ratio to be as high as possible, or for it to be even above the industry norm.

Table 16.1 goes on to give some additional information (the total wages expense, depreciation expense and the number of employees are all required to be given by the Companies Acts, as indeed is a lot of other information not relevant to the needs of our analysis here). A number of ratios are then worked out for these accounts. Finally the notes give some aid to understanding the significance of the ratios. The notes also attempt to bridge the gap between the standard terminology first introduced by the Companies Act 1981, and the present accepted UK accounting practice. The latter can, of course, still be used for accounts which do not have to be presented in accordance with the formats as now laid down by the 1985 Act. Traditional accounting practice has deep roots and is likely to linger with us for a while!

Not all ratios will be used for every analysis. Earlier in this section we indicated the main uses of the various groups of ratios. Even within these groupings a great deal of selectivity needs to be exercised. Bankers concerned with cash repayments will place considerable emphasis on the cash ratios and, in particular, the liquidity ratios (sometimes called the bankers' ratios!). Not all the ratios, too, that *might* be used have been worked out. Most of the ratios that are likely to be necessary can, however, be worked out from the ratios given. Thus, analogous to the 'days sales outstanding', ratio (g), which indicates how long an average debtor takes to pay the company, we can construct a similar ratio for the number of days the company takes to pay its creditors. This will be

$$\frac{\text{Creditors}}{\text{Cost of sales per day}}, \text{ i.e. } \frac{147{,}500}{1{,}375{,}000} \times 365 \simeq 39 \text{ days}$$

This ratio will clearly be of particular interest to creditors.

The rules relating to the practical application of ratio analysis to published accounts can now be summarised as follows:

1. Decide which ratios are relevant.
2. Calculate these ratios for this year and preceding years (and those for any projected balance-sheet and profit-and-loss accounts which may be available).
3. Compare with industry or other *norms*.
4. Work out the *trends*.
5. Investigate the causes for any unsatisfactory indications thrown up by (3) and (4) above.

Analysing the complete accounts of a small business

In this section we concentrate on analysing the complete accounts of a small business. Whether the business is a company, partnership or sole trader is immaterial for this analysis. In all these cases we are dealing with the complete accounts which will be drawn up at the request of, and will be available to, the proprietor, manager or owner.

Many small businesses are unique. Comparison with industry or other norms, as suggested in the analysis of published accounts (rule (3) above), may, for this reason, be impractical. It may, in any case, be inappropriate to compare the performance of some small business with that of the industry average. If the difference in size is very great, if the economies or diseconomies of scale are substantial, making comparisons of this nature will not be comparing Cox's Pippins with Cox's Pippins!

In our last chapter the performance of large and small businesses is compared from various points of view. Here we are concerned to say that for many reasons it may not be appropriate to compare a particular small business with an industry's yardsticks. Sometimes small businesses are members of a trade association which runs an inter-firm comparison (usually set up by the Centre for Interfirm Comparison – an offshoot of the British Institute of Management). In that case useful managerial ratios can be obtained against which to compare the firm's own figures.

In all other cases we are thrown back on trying to find alternative ways of analysing the accounts of a small business. Fortunately rule

(4) above shows how this problem can be solved. Those small businesses for which, for any reason, industry norms are inappropriate or inapplicable must rely on *trend* analysis.

Before analysing trends in either balance-sheet or profit-and-loss account figures (i.e. the £ values, not ratios) it is essential to put these accounts into common-size format. This means, for each year, presenting all the balance-sheet figures relative to a balance-sheet total (fixed assets + current assets) of 100. The profit-and-loss accounts are similarly prepared, with all expenses shown relative to a sales turnover figure of 100. In effect the figures for the balance-sheet items and the charges in the profit-and-loss account are then expressed as percentages. The analysis of changes in these common form figures is referred to as *decomposition analysis*.

Table 16.2 shows the recommended approach in tabulated question form. Investigation of unsatisfactory trends will pinpoint areas of possible managerial inefficiency.

Funds-flow analysis

All UK companies which have had sales or gross income of over £25,000 per annum are required (by *Statement of Standard Accounting Practice No. 10*) to produce yearly, as part of their 'accounts', a statement of sources and applications of funds (more shortly a funds-flows statement or funds statement).

The aim of a funds statement is to show the sources and uses of funds employed in the business during the year. The term 'funds-'means 'cash and near cash', or more precisely 'cash and credit'. It is therefore nearly but not quite synonymous with cash.

There is no single format which must be followed in presenting a funds flow. It is usual to show separately the change in working capital, and it is usual to segregate on the 'sources' side those funds which are internally generated (e.g. profits, and cash flow from depreciation) and those that are externally generated (e.g. issue of new shares).

Funds-flow statements can be prepared from 'the accounts'. Probably the best way is to set the balance-sheets at the start and at the end of the year side by side, work out the differences and then separate these differences into 'sources' and 'uses'.

Table 16.1 gave two such balance-sheets, together with a profit-and-loss account for the year and, under 'additional information', the depreciation expense for the year. This depreciation charge, as we said, must be shown in published accounts to comply with the

Table 16.2 Financial analysis checklist

Profit and expenses analysis

1. What are the trends in net sales, net profits and return on investment?
2. What are the trends in costs and margins?
3. From inspection of profit-and-loss accounts are there any unfavourable trends in expenses?
4. Are there any unfavourable trends in the ratios of any individual variable expense to net sales or to cost of goods sold?
5. Are there any other useful efficiency ratios from the management point of view, e.g. expenses of a particular product or group in relation to cost of sales? These ratios do not necessarily have to be expressed in money terms.

In general 'input-related' expenses should be compared with cost of goods sold, and 'output related' to net sales. Input-related expenses are all those expenses concerned with obtaining raw materials and other resources and converting them into finished goods. Carriage inwards, for instance, is an input-related expense. For expenses such as telephone, stationery, manager's salary, etc., the best approach is to work out the increase of the current year's expense over the previous year's as a percentage, and compare this with the appropriate rate of inflation.

Current assets analysis

6. What are the trends in current assets, current liabilities, and their effect on the current ratio?
7. Has the liquidity of the current assets increased or decreased, and what is the effect on the liquidity ratio?
8. What are the trends in:
   (a) cash
   (b) debtors
   (c) stock?

Capital and assets analysis

9. What is the trend in total assets? Are they becoming more or less liquid?
10. What is the trend in net working capital?
11. What is the trend in long-term debt and its effect on the gearing ratio?
12. What is the trend in fixed assets and in the ratio of fixed assets to net worth?

In general

13. Check if the firm is a stronger or less strong credit risk.
14. Consider the effectiveness of management in the past.
15. Consider the operating characteristics of the business.
16. What are the patterns of cash flows (e.g. seasonal factors) and what are the causes of any fluctuations?
17. What degree of security is available in the assets?
18. What is the likely pattern of financial claims and requirements?

Ensure the figures used in your trend analysis have all been prepared on a similar basis (particularly take care with unaudited accounts).

Table 16.3 Sources and application of funds statement

			£
Cash and short-term funds at start of year			17,500
SOURCES OF FUNDS		£	
Arising from trading:			
Profit on ordinary activities before tax		175,000	
Depreciation		50,000	225,000
			242,500
APPLICATION OF FUNDS	£		
Payment of taxation		80,000	
Payment of dividends		50,000	
Increase in working capital:			
Stock	25,000		
Debtors	45,000		
Trade creditors	(17,500)	52,500	
			182,500
Cash and short-term funds at end of year			60,000

Companies Acts. It is usual to show it by way of a note to the accounts. (Depreciation is added back to profit because it is an expense included in profit that is not represented by a cash flow. Depreciation is an *allocation* of cost.)

Table 16.3 shows a simple sources and applications of funds statement prepared from these accounts. There are no externally generated funds in this example. No tangible fixed assets have been purchased or sold during the year. Had there been, these sums would have been included under 'uses' and 'sources'.

In much the same way as with ratio analysis, the *trend* over a number of years usually provides the most interesting information. It will be useful to see how much of the funds has come from trading, from borrowing, from issue of new shares or from sale of fixed assets. On the other side, it will be helpful to see whether the funds have been used for long-term investments in fixed assets, to pay interest and dividends, or to build up working capital. Funds-flow statements will show whether, broadly, long-term funds have been used to finance long-term assets, and short-term funds working capital.

The pattern of past funds-flow statements will also usually provide a good basis for calculating future flows of funds. This will give some indication of whether current financing methods will provide adequate sources to cover dividend and interest payments over the next few years.

Value-added statements

In a value-added statement we aim to show how much value a business entity has added to the cost of 'bought-in' goods and services. Looked at the other way round, after cost of goods and services have been deducted from sales turnover we are left with the value added to these by the labour and capital employed in the business. The difference is therefore wages expenses and depreciation, and the residue is the trading profit. See Figure 16.1.

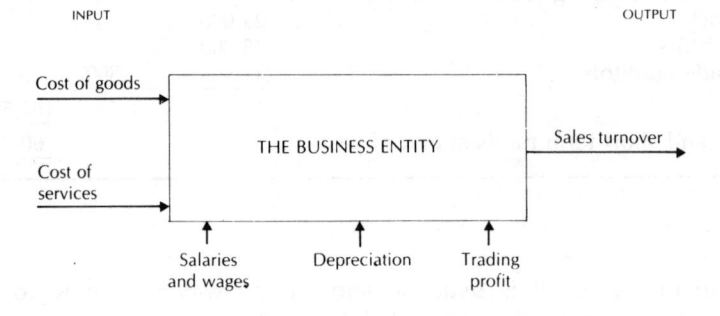

Figure 16.1

On the continent value added has received much attention. There are indeed good reasons why value added should be used either in addition to, and perhaps even as a substitute for, profit. Economists are particularly fond of this measure since the sum of all firms' added values equals national output. It is therefore possible to tie up the work of the firm at microeconomic level with macroeconomic figures. However, just because value added has this quasi-statistical benefit does not mean that it is, *per se*, the right measure for a firm. There are several reasons for not using it. Conceptually, comparing the efficiency of two similar firms on this basis is likely to be unsatisfactory. One firm may use its own labour to do most of the work (giving a high value added), another may subcontract some of the work outside. Depreciation, too, is a problem. Depreciation policy is largely an individual management decision. Different ways and rates of allocating depreciation will give different added values. But the main disadvantage of value added as a method for assessing business performance in the United Kingdom is a practical one. UK businesses are required to declare their profit and capital employed figures, but not their value-added figures. Many listed companies do produce such statements for their shareholders, but it is still the exception rather than the rule. It is not always possible to draw up a value-added statement from a published profit-and-loss account (it depends on the chosen format) unless certain information is given in addition to that at present required by law. For international companies this would be particularly difficult since only the amount of employees' wages in the United Kingdom has to be shown.

Even if value added can be used, there are problems in the definition of this term. *Gross value added* or *net output* is sometimes used. The UK Census of Production defines net output as the gross output *less* cost of purchases (adjusted for increases or decreases in the value of stocks), together with the cost of industrial services, and, where applicable, duties. Gross value at factor cost is found by deducting from net output the cost of non-industrial services (e.g. rent). This definiton therefore approximates to the definition of net output or value added as used in national accounts statistics. In the Census of Production these figures are divided by the number of employees to give net output per head and gross value at factor cost per head. The definition of employees is itself rather involved. Proprietors, and directors in receipt of a definite wage, are included. These fine distinctions are not of much concern when dealing with many organisations, but for small companies they are obviously of crucial importance.

Productivity is a term widely used in referring to output per employee. It is usually taken to mean net output per head or gross value per head. On this basis value added is an integral part of 'productivity'.

Many value-added statements go on to show how the value added has been disposed of as between the government, the suppliers of capital and the amount that has been retained in the business. In Table 16.4 we show how a value-added statement for the 'ratio analysis' accounts shown at the start of Table 16.1 would appear, using a slightly more comprehensive format to illustrate the main headings likely to be met in practice.

The use of value-added figures for comparing the performance of small and large businesses is discussed in Chapter 21.

Inflation accounting

'At the beginning of a year you start off with a bag of sugar which costs £100. During the year the general price level goes up from 100 to 200. At the end of the year you sell the bag of sugar for £400 at a time when the replacement cost is £350.' QUESTION: What profit did you make?

Table 16.4 Value added statement

Sources of income	
Sales	1,825,000
Royalties and other trading income	—
	1,825,000
Less Cost of goods and services	1,132,000
Value added by trading	693,000
Income from Investments, etc	—
Total value added	693,000
Total value added represents: Employees' remuneration	450,000
Depreciation	50,000
Trading profit	193,000
	693,000

There are no complications and no other transactions; all you have to be concerned with is exactly what is given above. *Before* proceeding any further (or looking down the page!) would you, the reader, *please* write down your answer to this problem. On your answer depends a lot. We shall know what type of accountancy you believe in – and you will know too!

Profit, of course, is *sales* less cost of sales and expenses. There are no expenses and the sales figure is not in dispute. The problem is what cost of sales figure to set against the sales figure. There are three likely candidates and the three profit-and-loss accounts showing these figures are set out below:

	I		*II*	*III*
Sales	400		400	400
Less Cost of sales	100	$(100 \times \frac{200}{100} =)$	200	350
Profit	300		200	50
	Historical cost (HC)	General price level (GPL (CPP))	Replacement cost (RC (CCA))	

If you are an historical cost (HC) advocate, you believe that the correct cost is the £100 historic (input) cost of purchase. This is the figure that will have been entered in your purchases, or stock books of account. It is the one thing you are certain about; it is, in your view, the only true cost. About a third of the accounting world sees it your way!

Perhaps you believe that money is the measure of all things. Since the general price level (GPL) has gone up from 100 to 200, so that the current purchasing power (CPP) of the £100 you laid out originally is now £200, you will believe that the correct cost of sales is £200. Almost a third of the accounting world believes that GPL (the UK version was called CPP) accounting is correct (or more accurately should be shown *as well as* the historic accounting figures).

If you argue that selling a bag of £400 at a time when the replacement cost is £350 must give you a profit of £50, then you belong to the replacement costing school (as do the authors!). Your argument is that to get back to square 1 (i.e. the initial position when you had one bag of sugar), you must spend £350. Your net gain is (400 – 350) = 50. This must be your profit.

Replacement cost (RC) accounting started in the 1920s when a Dutch economist, Professor Limperg, first developed its theoretical basis. About a third of the accounting world believes in RC, or at any rate believes that it should be shown as an adjunct to the historic accounting balance-sheet and profit-and-loss account. The UK version of RC was called current-cost accounting (CCA).

Earlier we said that your answer to our question would show what 'type' of accountancy you believed in. Each 'type' gives a different profit figure. It may seem surprising that accountants and others concerned with financial figures are not agreed on such a basic thing as this. The reason is best shown by giving some historical (in the true sense!) background. For many years accountants always took the input figure as being sancrosanct. So long as there was no (appreciable) inflation there was no problem. In our example the 200 and the 350 cost of sales figures would all have remained at 100. For all those years accountants had their own implicit, but slightly different, ideas of what profit really was. These differences never came to the surface until substantial currency debasement occurred. This forced accountants and others to declare openly what they understood by profit. 'Understood' is the relevant word. It is rather like defining a colour such as pink. Until scientists try and define pink (in terms presumably of a range of lightwave lengths) we all have our own idea of what pink is. When forced to say openly what we understand by 'pink', it is likely that we shall have different ideas of what we mean by that vague word – particularly if we have strong political views!

To comply with *Statement of Standard Accounting Practice (SSAP) No. 16* all UK companies had to provide CCA accounts (i.e. a CCA balance-sheet and profit-and-loss account) as a supplement to their normal (historic) annual accounts. There were exemptions. The principal one was for small companies.

The arguments about inflation accounting methods for reporting profit will continue. It all depends, as we have seen, upon what one understands by profit. Omar Khayyam summed up all the hassle when he wrote:

> Myself when young did eagerly frequent Doctor and Saint and heard great Argument . . . but ever more came out by the same Door as in I went.

Omar Khayyam was a realist. When it came to *reported accounts* figures he would probably have held, as we do, that some of the academic arguments are rather a waste of time.

One thing, however, is certain, and that is that, in *practical* terms, replacement accounting is important. Many companies these days keep all their asset accounts at replacement costs (this was the case even for companies who did not have to, or did not wish to, prepare CCA published accounts). For stock accounts this means keeping all inputs and all cost of goods sold outputs at replacement costs. For fixed asset accounts (and their associated accumulated depreciation accounts) this means updating the values of the assets to present-day replacement costs. This may be done by reference to up-to-date suppliers' prices, if these are available; more likely they will be recorded, as we said, at historical costs increased by a suitable specific inflation index itself based on information published by the government's Central Statistical Office.

Keeping asset accounts in replacement costs is not difficult and can be done within the framework of normal (historical) double-entry book-keeping. All that is required is that the values of the assets (stock or fixed assets) are systematically updated. The corresponding double entry for the increase in value of the asset will be an entry in a stock or fixed asset revaluation account. What is important is that all inputs and outputs in these acccounts are *all kept at replacement costs*. The greater availability these days of simple computerised record-keeping systems makes this comparatively easy.

The benefits from keeping asset accounts in replacement costs are *enormous*. All costing, all estimating, all capital investment appraisal decisions can then be based on relevant practical, present-day, figures. These benefits are likely to far outweigh the slight additional expense (getting a copy of the Central Statistical Office's set of tables for specific inflation indices for the various types of industries assets), and slight additional work (increasing all assets by their appropriate inflation indices).

CHAPTER 17

Alternative Choice Decisions

INTRODUCTION	315
PAST AND FUTURE COSTS	316
SEVERAL SINGLE-FIGURE ESTIMATES	320
BASIC PROBABILITY RULES	322
EXPECTED VALUE AND BAYES'S DECISION RULE	323
PROBABILITY FORECASTS	325
STATES OF NATURE AND PAY-OFF TABLES	328
UNCERTAINTY	332
SENSITIVITY ANALYSIS AND THE ASSESSMENT OF PROBABILITY FIGURES	333

Introduction

In the first part of this chapter we discuss the factors to take into account when evaluating possible alternative courses of action. This will involve a consideration, *inter alia*, of the various costs and benefits associated with decision-making; in particular we shall be concerned to discriminate between those costs which are relevant in making any decision and those which are not. Opportunity cost, differential cost, variable cost, book value, etc., will be the 'costs' considered.

Implied in these choices between different projects, investments or other courses of action is that we have good estimates of the costs and benefits associated with each of these possible decisions. But the future is inherently uncertain. As Omar Khayyam says:

The worldly Hope men set their Hearts upon
Turns Ashes – or it prospers.

In our next chapter, on capital investment appraisal, we note that with his emphasis on cash in hand and present value, Omar Khayyam was not so much a dreamer as perhaps the first chartered accountant with his feet very firmly on the ground!

It follows that a single-figure estimate of the future must be only the first stage in considering courses of action which relate to the future. There a number of ways of dealing with this uncertainty. In broad terms they include:

- SEVERAL SINGLE ESTIMATES – typically a high (HI), low (LO) as well as the single best figure estimate.
- ATTACHING PROBABILITIES to the likelihood of reaching certain figures.
- Considering how outside factors such as economic conditions (generally referred to as STATES OF NATURE) could affect the single-figure estimates for each of the alternatives.
- Taking account of emotional attitudes when the UNCERTAINTY is total, and it is almost impossible to put any sensible probability figures on events.

These approaches do require some mathematical expertise. Most students and some small business managers these days have a reasonable quantitative background. Nevertheless the analysis will be restricted to those methods of proven practical help in making decisions.

Past and future costs

As our mentor said, 'the moving finger writes and having writ moves on; nor all your piety nor wit shall lure it back to cancel half a line'.

What Omar Khayyam really meant (but he tended to use rather high-flown language) was quite simply, 'No man can alter what has happened', or more precisely still, 'Sunk costs (or benefits) are irrelevant when making a business decision'. And since costs not in any way associated with a decision clearly will not alter, it follows that the only relevant costs in a business decision are those differential or incremental costs which will be incurred and which will alter with the decision. The same applies to benefits.

Frequently this obvious precept is not observed in practice. It is common to hear given as a good reason for retaining a share investment the fact that the current price is lower than the price at which it was purchased. 'I mean to keep it till it shows a profit', or some such phrase, is given in justification. But of course what has happened in the past, whether this share has made a loss, and others perhaps a profit, is irrelevant from the point of view of deciding if it should be kept now. For that decision the only consideration is how the respective share prices are expected to behave in the future. The past (except as a guide to how it might behave in the future) is irrelevant.

The term 'marginal cost' is sometimes used as a substitute for differential cost. Strictly, marginal cost should be confined to the additional costs from output changes only. Opportunity cost is a synonym for differential cost, with the proviso that the two alternatives are restricted to the one under consideration and the next-best available choice. The rationale for this is that if the decision is taken to go ahead with the alternative under consideration, then the advantages (and disadvantages) of taking the next-best choice must necessarily be given up. The measure of this loss is the opportunity cost.

One particular type of cost requires special consideration. It occurs in decisions as to whether to sell a particular piece of plant or machinery or not. Is its book value, i.e., the value of the asset as recorded in the books of account, relevant or not? Consider the sale of a piece of machinery purchased, say, three years ago for £5,000 and depreciated at £1,000 per annum. Its net book value, or written-down value, will now be £5,000 - £3,000 = £2,000. Suppose we are proposing to sell it for £2,500 cash. The incremental cash benefit is clearly the £2,500.

However, it may be argued that the effect on the profit-and-loss account is different and should be taken into account. This is not the case. If the machine is not sold, the profit-and-loss accounts for the next 2 years will be charged with a total of £2,000 (£1,000 each year). If the machine is sold, there will be a credit to the profit-and-loss account for profit on sale of the machine of £500. The difference between these two is the same £2,500. Of course, it might be that the slight difference in the timing of the debts and credits to the profit-and-loss account will be important. This would be the case if, for example, it was important to present the bank manager with a good profit figure for the current year. On this extreme supposition the sale of the asset to give a temporary 'lift' to the books of the accounts might be justified. However, over the remaining two years in total the net effect is nil. If there is an estimated scrap value at the end of the two years, this will affect both the net cash and the net effect on the profit-and-loss account equally. Tax considerations (since they may result in an incremental payment) could result in differences which should be taken into account. However, they are arrived at by a calculation which is entirely separate from the book-keeping entries and the statement of accounts. We conclude that the book value of an asset is irrelevant for decisions as to whether to dispose of it or not.

Any cost or benefit which is not affected by the alternative under consideration can be disregarded. The proprietor's salary, for example, will not be altered whichever choice is made. It can therefore be ignored. Suppose the alternatives under consideration are buying a part from outside, or continuing to manufacture it on the premises. All benefits, all selling and distribution expenses, and most administrative and production costs, other than those directly associated with the manufacture of the part, will not be affected by the decision. Consequently they need not be considered.

Although we are only concerned with differential costs, it is often wise in practice to put down all the costs under each of the alternatives to arrive at the net differences. This means that a lot of the expenses will be entered more than once. The advantage of this 'zero-base' procedure routine is that no items of costs are likely to be overlooked. When attention is focused solely on differential items it is easy to omit one or two items.

There are two types of cost which might seem at first sight to be differential costs, but in practice rarely are. These are:

- Variable costs
- Allocated costs

The term 'variable costs' is short for 'costs directly variable with volume'. It is a classification of costs which is useful when considering changes in volume of production or sales in the future. This is not the same as considering two alternative choices of action now. In certain circumstances, for example when one of the alternatives involves a change in output, then the variable costs may be differential costs. In general they are not.

In general, too, when estimating the relevant differential costs, allocated costs can be ignored. Allocated costs are those overheads which are charged to a particular product, batch, department or process on some *pro rata* basis. Whatever method is used the amount of cost *pro rated* to the part manufactured on the premises (to continue with the previous example) will not be saved if the part is purchased from outside sources. For example, the total costs to the firm for rent, heat and light are certain to remain unaltered by the decision.

It is comparatively easy to see that this is true in the case of a simple expense such as rent. Unless the freed floor space will actually be used for additional revenue-producing items (such as the manufacture of new products) or it can be rented out, there will no change in total costs and benefits for the business. It is not so easy to decide whether this same principle applies for the labour saving. Most alternative choice calculations include figures for differential salaries or wages. Typically the main benefit from the introduction of more automated machinery will be the direct labour saved. There is a tendency in such circumstances to work out the theoretical reduction in wages that should arise, and to use this figure in the calculation. The problem in real life is that getting rid of staff is not likely to foster good labour relations. What may happen is that employees will be given other work until 'natural wastage', sufficient to absorb the surplus, has occurred. The true saving in wages is often much less than the calculated figure. Worse still, if jobs are 'found' to keep the extra staff employed, it is very difficult afterwards to revert back to the prior position. Put another way, a little bit more fat has been added, and cutting away fat is never easy. Wage and salary differentials in these calculations need to be gross wages inclusive of tax, National Insurance, pension fund payments, and all fringe payments in so far as they are a cost saved to the company.

To summarise, in any particular alternative choice decision, the costs and benefits that are relevant are only those which will be affected by taking one course of action rather than another at that point in time. The cost elements that are relevant may, however, vary with the nature of the choice. The classic example of this is in the decision as to whether it is cheaper to use a car or not. Background information was given in Chapter 11 that is:

VARIABLE COSTS	Per mile (pence)
Petrol, oil	6.0
Maintenance, repairs	2.0
Total variable cost per mile	8.0

FIXED COSTS	per annum (£)
Road fund licence	80
Insurance	120
Depreciation	900
Garage	100
Total fixed costs per year	1,200

Many simplifying assumptions are made in presenting the costs in this form. Some of them are common to those met in all marginal costing problems: for instance, the assumption that all costs can be split into those that are variable with the unit (mileage) and those that are fixed. It is evident that this will not be entirely true here. Maintenance (a service every 5,000 miles) may be so; repairs probably will not be. Garage costs may be fixed, but the figure will be difficult to determine unless we assume that the garage rented. Some of the depreciation will increase with mileage, though it will not be reflected in any cash flow until the car is sold.

The alternative choices under consideration are those of travelling by car, or by train. The convenience of having a car available is assumed to be balanced roughly by the extra benefit from relaxing and being able to work in a train. In other words, in this alternative choice example, we are solely concerned with money costs and benefits. It is evident that this is a vastly oversimplified exercise and we are merely using it for presentation purposes.

What costs are relevant for the following decisions?

1. Whether to take the car on a business trip to visit a supplier's factory in Somerset. The supplier will meet you at the station. The car is in your possession and is taxed.
2. Whether to tax the car for the next six months. At the end of the last period (when the new registration letter comes in) you are proposing, in any case, to buy a new car. Ignoring any effect that your decision might have on its resale value, should you leave it in your garage and make your remaining business trips by train, or should you tax and use it?
3. You do not own a car but are considering buying one rather than continuing to use the taxis and trains which are available where you live.

The costs which have to be taken into account vary for each of the above. For the first decision the only relevant costs are the variable costs. For the second, the 6-months road fund licence and any rebate on your yearly insurance premium forgone will be additional costs. For the final decision all costs will be relevant. Of course, if the garage is in your possession and could be hired out, any decision to have your own car will imply an opportunity cost for the rent forgone.

Several single-figure estimates

Up to this chapter we have assumed single-figure estimates, i.e. that the figures (cost and benefits) relating to any decision have all been determined. This is in accordance with the best tradition strictly kept to in the past in all examination papers! It is not, however, in accordance with the real-life situation. The decision-maker can never assess absolutely accurately what will happen in the future; sometimes, indeed, he is totally unsure. When we are totally unsure we use the term 'uncertainty' rather than 'risk'. Strictly uncertainty should be restricted to those situations where various discrete possibilities may arise (and one has no idea at all which will occur) rather than the situation where any figure at all may prevail; however, the distinction is somewhat blurred in practice.

Generally there is some idea of what the future costs and benefits are likely to be. This means, in mathematical terms, that the probability that some figures will be achieved are higher than that of others. In our typical 'exam question' the figure that was always given with such unrealistic certainty was presumably the single (or 'most likely') figure. The first step towards a more sensible approach is to add to this 'most likely' estimate one or two other possible estimates. The most useful of these will be the likely lowest (usually referred to as Low or LO) and the likely highest (High or HI). These LO and HI figures will not be the most extreme figures, but the lowest and the highest 'likely to be reached under reasonable conditions and with a reasonable probability'. The advantages of this approach are twofold. Within the LO-HI figures we have the 'range' of likely figures, and also by looking at the consequences following from using each of them we can see how sensitive the final result will be to the figures at each end of the likely range as well as to the 'most likely' estimate.

This 'three-level' approach is extremely useful, and will often be the one best suited to the needs of the small business. In practical terms it will mean constructing three profit-and-loss accounts and three budgets for all the periods effected by the decision. If the effect on the balance-sheet may be of importance, three balance-sheets will have to be prepared, too. Since most projected profit-and-loss account and budget work depends principally on estimates for sales, the 'three levels' are likely to be three different sales levels. Typically in work of this nature costs will be split up into those that vary with sales and those that will remain fixed. Of course some managed costs – i.e. costs at the discretion of management – may be modified to reflect changing volume levels.

An example of a profit-and-loss account forecast constructed on these lines is given in Table 17.1. The centre column is the only one which would have been available under the traditional single-figure forecast approach. It is evident that the three-level approach is much more informative.

A careful look at all three estimates is always essential. Frequently

Table 17.1 Profit forecast for year ending December 198X

	£ LO	£ Most likely	£ HI
Sales (£10 per unit)	800,000	1,000,000	1,100,000
Variable manufacturing costs (£5.50 per unit)	440,000	550,000	605,000
Contribution	360,000	450,000	495,000
Managed fixed costs	45,000	70,000	80,000
Short-run margin	315,000	380,000	415,000
Committed fixed costs	280,000	280,000	280,000
Profit before tax	35,000	100,000	135,000
Tax at (say) 50%	17,500	50,000	67,500
Profit after tax	17,500	50,000	67,500

the results are not the same as might be expected on *a priori* grounds. Profits, for instance, will not vary linearly with sales. Sometimes a drop in sales will not be reflected by much of a drop in profits. Cash flow may indeed go up. Always it is essential to see how sensitive key factors such as profit and cash are to differing levels of sales at different times.

Although the 'three-level' approach is simple and may be adequate for the needs of the small business manager, it will be advisable in major decisions to consider the use of more sophisticated approaches. One way is to attach probability figures to the various estimated figures. With the amount of statistical information available today and the easy accessibility of microcomputers and programmable electronic calculators, probability analysis is now a technique which is available to small business managers. Some mathematical knowledge is a prerequisite; this is covered briefly in the next section.

Basic probability rules

Common sense tells us that if we toss an evenly balanced coin there is half a chance that it will come down tails and half a chance it will come down heads. The sum of the two probabilities is ½ + ½ = 1, demonstrating the basic rule that 'the probability of all the various, mutually exclusive states (ignoring the very faint possibility that it comes to rest on its side!) must add up to 1'. Clearly, too, the range of possible probabilities goes from 0 to 1 (the measure of cast-iron certainty).

Alternative choice decisions 323

When two independent events take place the probability that both will occur is called the *joint probability*. The adjective 'independent' may need some clarification. In statistical terminology independent events are those in which the occurrence of one event will not affect the probability of the occurrence of the other event. Thus if we toss a coin and also toss a dice what happens to one will not alter the probabilities associated with the other. Tossing a coin and a dice can be used to demonstrate the rule of calculating joint probability, namely:

Joint probability of two events = Probability of one event × Probability of other event

In symbols:

$P(A \& B) = P(A) \times P(B)$

where $P(A)$ is the probability of event A occurring, etc. Clearly, too, $P(A \& B) = P(B \& A)$, since $P(A) \times P(B) = P(B) \times P(A)$.

If we toss a dice 120 times, a given side should occur on average around $(\frac{1}{6} \times 120) = 20$ times. Suppose that each of the times the dice was thrown we also tossed a normal double-sided penny in the air. How often would the combination of the given side of the dice and a head (say) of the coin occur? Since the side will occur twenty times on average, the combination of the given side and the head of the penny will be 10 times on average, i.e. as a fraction $^{10}/_{120} = \frac{1}{12}$. Since the probability of the side turning up is 1:6, and of the head of the penny turning up is 1:2, the joint probability (which we have seen to be $\frac{1}{12}$) is the product of the side probability ($\frac{1}{6}$) and the head ($\frac{1}{2}$). We have demonstrated the joint probability rule for independent events:

Joint probability of side and head		Probability of side		Probability of head
$\frac{1}{12}$	=	$\frac{1}{6}$	×	$\frac{1}{2}$

Expected value and Bayes's decision rule

Reverting to the original situation, suppose we are told the following: if the coin comes down 'heads' we receive 60p, but if it comes down 'tails', nothing. What are we prepared to pay for this? What is its value to us?

Presumably the simple answer is (on average) just 30p. We could express this expected value by an equation such as:

    Probability × Sum   =   Expected value (EV)
    ½ × 60p   =   30p

Had the terms included, as well, a payment of 40 p in the event that the coin come down 'tails', the total value to us would be arrived at in similar way. Thus:

    Probability × Sum   = EV
    ½ × 60p   = 30p
    ½ × 40p   = 20p
    TOTAL EXPECTED VALUE 50p

Hence, to calculate the total expected value of any particular decision choice, we multiply the money value of each choice by the probability of its occurrence, and add up these products.

Bayes's decision rule says that when there are several possible courses of action available, the decision-maker should make that choice which has the highest total expected value. For example, the two possible choices might be either to throw a dice or toss a coin. Suppose that if a 1 or a 2 is thrown on the dice, then 90p is paid; if a 3, 4, or 5, then 150p is paid; and if a 6, then 600p is paid. Is this preferable to a straight choice with a coin of 500p if it is 'heads', and nothing if it is 'tails'? The calculations of the two possible decision choices are:

           Probability × Sum   = EV
    DICE   2/6 × 90p   = 30p
           3/6 × 150p   = 75p
           1/6 × 600p   = 100p
           TOTAL EXPECTED VALUE 205p

    COIN   ½ × 500p   = 250p
           ½ ×   0p   =   0p
           TOTAL EXPECTED VALUE 250p

Bayes's decision rule therefore gives the coin as the best choice.

A helpful and widely used way of presenting choices of this nature to business managers is by way of a decision tree. Diagrammatically this dice/coin alternative choice can be shown as in Figure 17.1.

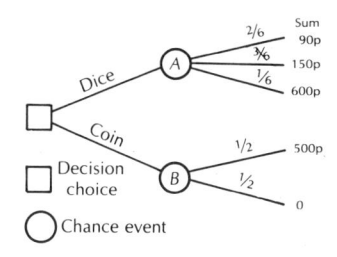

Figure 17.1

To arrive at the total expected value at A, we multiply all the possible sums by their respective probabilities. This gives a total expected value of 205p (as against 250p, for B). Proceeding leftwards, the correct decision choice as between the two is to take B, as this has a higher expected value. Decision-tree analysis proceeds by this method of moving from right to left. The method can be summed up as follows:

1. Proceed from right to left.
2. At every chance event find the total expected value.
3. At every decision point choose that course of action with the highest total expected value.

Probability forecasts

In probability forecasts, figures for estimated probabilities have to be made for all the factors which may vary. If we revert to the example used earlier in this chapter we shall have to assess probabilities for each of the three sales levels. Since it is extremely unlikely that sales will be 'exactly' any of the three figures given, in practice we shall be assigning probabilities to reaching ranges of sales whose mid-points are those three (LO, Most likely, HI) figures. It is not easy to see how these probabilities can be arrived at. Later we shall be discussing how to assess probability figures, and how much reliance to place on our assessment. For the moment, however, we take it that we are able to arrive at meaningful probability estimates for any variables we wish to consider. Let us assume that the probabilities of sales being around £800,000, £1,000,000 and £1,100,000 are 0.3, 0.5 and 0.2 respectively. These probabilities add up to 1, in accordance with the basic rule noted earlier.

It would now be easy to recast the profit forecast calculations in Table 17.1 to arrive at a new (and presumably 'better' – if the probability figures are accurate) expected value for profit after tax. However, probability analysis gives us the ability to be more sophisticated in our approach. So far we have assumed that only the sales figure is uncertain. But we are dealing with the future, and all future costs will have some degree of uncertainty associated with them. Take the variable cost figure. As it stands the variable manufacturing cost per unit is a constant £5.50. Can we be sure that this will be maintained in the future? It might go up a little to, say, £5.60, or down to, say £5.30. Again assume for the moment that we can assess the probabilities associated with these three figures and let us take them to be 0.6 (for the basic figure of £5.50) and 0.2 for each of the two variations, in each case provided the sales are £800,000 or £1,000,000. For sales of £1,100,000 it may be that we would assess slightly different probabilities (say 0.8, 0.1 and 0.1).

We are now able to produce a profit forecast incorporating probability figures for both sales forecasts and variable manufacturing costs. We shall need to use our formula for calculating joint probability. A tree diagram is a suitable format for presenting the calculation. Figure 17.2 shows the results.

The joint probability along the top branch of 0.06 is calculated by multiplying the probability of the sales being £800,000 (i.e. 0.3), by the probability of the variable cost being £5.60 (i.e. 0.2). The other joint probabilities are calculated in the same way.

It will be evident that this probability analysis approach is a fairly powerful tool. It need not be restricted to the case when only two factors are regarded as variable. Costs other than manufacturing costs may be variable. All that is required is that probability estimates be made for the various levels of these costs.

When there are many variables this method may become unwieldy. The simplest approach then is to assume that each of the variables is normally distributed about its mean and that some measure of how widely it is distributed about this mean can be determined. In practical terms this means arriving at some measure of distribution such as the standard deviation (s.d.) or coefficient of variation. This is discussed in the next section.

If such figures can be meaningfully arrived at, all that is necessary is to use one of the many computer programs employing the Monte

SALES	VARIABLE MANUFACTURING COST		OTHER COSTS £	TOTAL COSTS (TC) £	PROFIT AFTER TAX (PAT) (SALES − TOTAL COSTS) × 50% £	JOINT PROBABILITY (JP)	JP × PAT £
(£10 per unit)	COST PER UNIT £	COST £					
£800,000 (0.3)	5.60 (0.2)	448,000	325,000	773,000	13,500	(0.06)	810
	5.50 (0.6)	440,000	325,000	765,000	17,500	(0.18)	3,150
	5.30 (0.2)	424,000	325,000	749,000	25,500	(0.06)	1,530
£1,000,000 (0.5)	5.60 (0.2)	560,000	350,000	910,000	45,000	(0.10)	4,500
	5.50 (0.6)	550,000	350,000	900,000	50,000	(0.30)	15,000
	5.30 (0.2)	530,000	350,000	880,000	60,000	(0.10)	6,000
£1,100,000 (0.2)	5.60 (0.1)	616,000	360,000	976,000	62,000	(0.02)	1,240
	5.50 (0.8)	605,000	360,000	965,000	67,500	(0.16)	10,800
	5.30 (0.1)	583,000	360,000	943,000	78,500	(0.02)	1,570
					Expected Value of Profit After Tax		44,600

Notes: 1. Probability figures are in brackets
2. 'Other costs' are managed fixed costs and committed fixed costs.
3. The variable manufacturing cost (3rd col.) is the cost per unit (2nd col.) × number of units (1st col. divided by 10). For example, for the first row, £448,000 = £5.60 × 80,000.

Figure 17.2 Tree diagram for calculating expected profit after tax

Carlo simulation method. These programs are readily available for most microcomputers. In effect the computer program runs through some 1,000 calculations or iterations, sampling at random values for each of the variable factors. The answer is usually printed out in the form of the net profit after tax and the 95 per cent probability intervals each side for the profit, and all the variables going to make up the profit. The technique appears to be complex but is relatively easy to operate.

States of nature and pay-off tables

Up to now we have assumed that the small businessman can assign some figures or probabilities to all the various costs involved in any major decision in a fairly straightforward manner. Where there are several possible courses of action it may be that the expected gains or benefits will depend upon outside factors over which he will have little or no control. For example, whether he should build an extension to his existing factory which makes car components might depend upon whether a Japanese car manufacturer goes ahead with his plan to set up a new car production plant in his area. If he is a satellite business to a nationalised industry, his future planning must take into account his view of what political party will shortly be in power. Most business development plans depend upon estimates as to whether we are in for a period of economic expansion (*boom*), whether things are likely to go on much as they are (*normal*), or whether we are in for a troubled economic period (*recession*). Such outside or exogenous factors are usually referred to as 'States of nature'. In this section we try to show how a small business manager can best decide which course of action to take when the expected benefits from each will vary depending on which state of nature occurs. These benefits are usually referred to as 'pay- offs', and it is common to present the alternatives in the form of a 'pay-off table'. Table 17.2 is an example.

It does not matter particularly for our analysis what these various choices are. They might well be, for instance, differing amounts of investment in additional factory space. Thus choice C might represent the largest commitment. The net benefit or pay-off will be high (+15) if there is a boom, since the extra investment will bring in high additional profits from sales; conversely if there is a serious recession, the net cash loss (−30) will represent the investment costs with no offsetting additional profits. It is important to realise that the pay-offs are always net figures. In practise we shall almost always be con-

Alternative choice decisions 329

Table 17.2

Choices	States of nature		
	Boom (0.6)	Normal (0.3)	Recession (0.1)
A	+9	0	−9
B	−1	+5	+10
C	+15	+0	−30

Note: All figures are £000 throughout.

cerned with returns that continue for several years into the future. The pay-off figure in the table will then be the net present value of the cash flows, as defined in Chapter 18. However, for ease of exposition, we shall assume for the moment that the pay-off figures are firm. The problem is simply one of deciding which course of action is appropriate given these figures. There are a number of possible approaches.

EXPECTED VALUE

Probably the simplest method of all is to assign probabilities to the occurrence of the various states of nature and work out the expected value of the three alternative choices and then use Bayes's decision rule to decide on the best course of action. It may not be easy to arrive at sensible probability figures for the likelihood of recession or other states of the economy, though, in fact, independent authorities such as the Paris-based Organisation for Economic Co-operation and Development (OECD) do give remarkably accurate forecasts for member countries. If there is doubt – and there may well be – then sensitivity analysis must be used, i.e. the effect on the final decision of various other probability figures must be explored. For the moment let us take it that firm probabilities can be assigned and let us take a fairly optimistic view of things and assume that the probability of a boom is 0.6, of a normal period 0.3, of a depression 0.1. These probabilities have already been included in Table 17.2. Table 17.3 shows the expected value calculations.

Table 17.3

			Ranking
EV (A)	= 0.6 × 9 + 0.3 × 0 + 0.1 = (−9)	= 4.5	2
EV (B)	= 0.6 × (−1) + 0.3 × 5 + 0.1 × 10	= 1.9	3
EV (C)	= 0.6 × 15 + 0.3 × 0 + 0.1 = (−30)	= 6.0	1

Risk

Choice C, however, has a very definite disadvantage. The range of possible values (+15 to −30) is far greater than for either of the other two choices. The greater the range, or variation around the mean point, presumably, the more unsatisfactory is that choice. In an ideal world we would like to be absolutely certain that the value we had calculated would be achieved. However, C has a great deal of variation. In everyday terminology we might say that it was a 'risky' project. How, then, can we quantify this risk, or measure the deviation of the possible pay-offs from the expected value?

The deviations from the EV of C of 6.0 will be $15 - 6 = 9$, $0 - 6 = -6$ and $-30 - 6 = -36$. If we add these deviations to arrive at some summary measure then, unfortunately, the minus deviations will cancel out to an extent the positive ones. Statisticians invariably use the squares of the deviations (this neatly gets round the plus and minus problem!). They also weight the square of the deviation by the probability of it occurring. In fact, their measure for risk or deviation about the mean, called the standard deviation (s.d.), is defined as the square root of the sum (Σ) of the probability (p) multiplied by the square of the deviation (d) from the mean. That is:

$$\text{s.d.} \times \sqrt{\Sigma p d^2}$$

For project C we have:

$$\text{s.d. of } C = \sqrt{0.6 \times (9)^2 + 0.3 (-6)^2 + 0.1 (-36)^2}$$
$$= \sqrt{189} = 13.75$$

Similarly the s.d. of A is 6.04 and of B is 3.81.

From an absolute standpoint these figures for the standard deviation give a good measure of the dispersion about the mean. But are these figures comparable? After all, the deviation of C is taken from a mean of 6, and the deviation of B from a mean of just under one-third of this (1.9). If the pattern of the two spreads are the same, we would expect that the absolute dispersion around a figure three times the size of another would be three times as great. So to arrive at a meaningful measure for relative dispersion we must relate the s.d. to the size of the mean, i.e. in our case to the EV. The ratio of the s.d. to EV is the coefficient of variation (V), see Table 17.4.

In statistical work relative dispersion is regarded as a good surrogate for risk, and the coefficient of variation as the best measure of relative dispersion and hence of risk. We may wonder whether this is right. When we talk generally about riskiness of a project, do we have in mind the square root of the sums of the squares of the deviations divided by the mean? It seems rather doubtful! The majority of people probably do not even understand the definition. Perhaps it is used because it is mathematically convenient and easy to manipulate. Whatever our reservations may be, we have to accept that it is used as the measure of riskiness. Indeed, statisticians reverse the process and say that when they (like Alice!) talk about risk, they *mean* the coefficient of variation. This neatly gets around the problem! Even if we accept this in general terms the definition suffers from one obvious practical disadvantage – which is that equal deviations from the mean either up or down are regarded (in the formula) as being equal. Does this too, make sense? A gain of 20 or 30 up is highly desirable, but a drop of 20 or 30 may be disastrous. It might well mean that the business would go into liquidation and hence have no future at all! Later in this section we show ways of taking these downside risk considerations into account.

On the right of Table 17.4 we have shown the rankings in terms of 'riskiness'. It is now a question of comparing a project such as C which has a high EV but also a high degree of riskiness with another, more stable, but less rewarding one. Later (page 355) a method of combining such factors is shown. Usually, however, the small business manager will be able to assess intuitively which combination of reward and risk he wishes to have, once he has facts presented to him in a simpler manner, as in Tables 17.3 and 17.4.

Table 17.4

					Ranking
	V (A)	$= \dfrac{s.d.}{EV}$	$= \dfrac{6.04}{4.5}$	= 1.3 approx.	1
Similarly	V (B)	=	$\dfrac{3.81}{1.9}$	= 2.0 approx.	2
and	V(C)	=	$\dfrac{13.75}{6}$	= 2.3 approx.	3

PERFECT INFORMATION

Sometimes in real life we can obtain perfect information about the likely states of nature – though presumably for a price. For one of the examples we gave at the start of this section perfect information (PI) could perhaps be obtained. One way or another (and perhaps it is best not to discuss how!) it might be possible, for instance, to find out if the Japanese car manufacturer will go ahead and build his production plant in our area. The question is, what is this information worth to us and therefore how much should we be prepared to pay for it? It is in fact unlikely that we can obtain perfect information about the states of nature in our present example; no economist or economic organisation is likely to guarantee its forecast absolutely. Nevertheless this example has served us well so far, so let us assume (rather wildly!), just for the sake of exposition, that such information could be obtained. What is the expected value of such perfect information (PI) to us?

There are three possibilities. Perfect information may tell us that boom, normality or recession will occur. If it is boom, then we should take the C choice, and this is worth 15 to us; if normality, we would choose B; and if recession, then B again. However, the likelihood of getting each of these information forecasts is not the same. From where we stand, boom has a 0.6 likelihood of being the *ex cathedra* advice, so the EV of this PI is 0.6 × 15. And the same applies for normal and recession states. In total the expected value of perfect information is:

$$\text{EV (PI)} = 0.6 \times 15 + 0.3 \times 5 + 0.1 \times 10 = 11.5$$

There is some variation, in these values of 15, 5 and 10, from the EV (PI) of 11.5. In precisely the same way as before we can work out the coefficient of variation to be

$$\text{V (PI)} = \sqrt{0.6 \, (3.5)^2 + 0.3 \, (6.5)^2 + 0.1 \, (1.5)^2} = 4.5$$

We are now in a position to put the choice of seeking perfect information (the net figure for PI will be the EV (PI) of 11.5, *less* any cost of getting it) against the other three choices, and make sensible comparisons on the basis of EV and risk.

Uncertainty

Earlier we drew a distinction between risk and uncertainty. A risky solution was one in which some probability figures, however vague, could be assigned to the various factors. Throughout we have emphasised that the way to take account of the vagueness of the probability figures is to use sensitivity analysis. Suppose, however, the truth is that we have no idea at all of what the likely probabilities are? How can we cope with this situation? At first sight the problem might seem to be easily solved. If all choices are completely uncertain, then they are equally uncertain. So we assign equal probabilities to them. Using our basic pay-off table, this would give us the expected values:

$$EV\ (A) = 1/3\ (9 + 0 - 9) = 0$$

and similarly EV (B) = 4.66 and EV (C) = −5. These answers, even if mathematically correct, are somehow emotionally unsatisfactory. In conditions of total uncertainty is this really how people think and decide? It seems unlikely. Perhaps we need to look further and deeper. One possible approach, rather pessimistic in attitude, is concerned to ensure that if things go badly we shall at least be as well off as possible. On this basis B is the best choice, since the maximum loss is only −1. With A, it could be −9 and with C a terrible −30. Earlier in this chapter we argued that some technique to protect us against the most serious adverse outcomes was necessary. *Maximin* – as this is called – or choosing the best of the worst, does this.

The alternative optimistic approach, *maximax*, is to choose that alternative which gives the possibility of the highest gain. Clearly this signals C, since the maximum gain possible is 15, whereas if A or B had been chosen the best that could have occurred would be 9 and 10 respectively. Maximax – or choosing the best of the best – gives the risk-seeker his best chance.

There is one even more emotional approach which has some appeal and may be nearer to the true motivation in most of us than either of the above. No one likes to look like a fool. We all seek to protect ourselves against the inevitable regret if we make a wrong choice. Suppose we choose B: what is the greatest possible regret we could suffer? This will be 15 − (−1) = 16 when boom occurs (if normal or recession is the state of nature, the figures will both be Nil). The corresponding figures for A and C are 19 and 40. Minimax regret – minimising the regret for making the wrong choice – therefore indicates B.

Sensitivity analysis and the assessment of probability figures

Apart from the last section, we have throughout this chapter assumed that some probabilities can be assigned to the various figures that enter into our decision-making process. Throughout, too, we have emphasised that the way to take account of the difficulties associated with arriving at good estimates for these figures or probabilities is by using sensitivity analysis. In our basic example using the pay-off tables this would mean using other sets of probabilities as well as the 0.6, 0.3 and 0.1 which we employed. Typically each probability estimate would be increased or decreased by 0.1 or 0.2 or more, depending on the perceived likelihood of variation from the initial set. A considerable number of calculations will then be necessary, but they would all be along exactly the same lines as with the basic probabilities.

For the small business manager, involved in making a major decision, however, his time and effort will be nothing by comparison with the possible benefits. The essential point in this approach is that the results of the various sensitivity analyses will be looked at from the point of view of their effect on any critical factor. This factor may be expected profit; more likely it would be cash. If some of the combinations of probability figures give a cash flow at any time in the future which may endanger the survival of the business, then it may be best to give up the proposition, even though the possible benefits are great. To sum up: 'What's to come is still unsure.' Single-figure estimates or probability estimates must always be the subject of sensitivity analysis. Even though in our example we fail to do so, there can be no exemptions for the small business manager in practice from this simple rule.

The extent to which sensitivity analysis will be necessary with the probability figures will depend on the reliability of these figures. In broad terms probability figures which are firmly based on past statistical data are likely to be more accurate than mainly subjective estimates of the future.

These days an impressive amount of quantitative information is available even to the small business manager. Sometimes this will be provided by government, local authorities, trade associations or other institutions exogenous to the small firm; some will be provided by the small firm itself – for instance, past profit- and-loss accounts, budget estimates, costings, stock lists, debtor's records, etc. A good example of the latter arises in considering the probability of 'stock-outs', i.e. the situation when goods cannot be supplied from stock and the customer either waits or places his order elsewhere. In Chapter 19 the costs associated with a stock-out are considered; here we are concerned with the probability of a stock-out occurring. Can one give probability estimates? The answer must surely be that if good stock records are available showing the pattern of sales from stock, and if we have reason to believe that the same pattern will continue into the future (and this is likely to be the case if there are a number of customers and there are no reasons for them changing their demand), then these stock records will provide extremely reliable probability figures for the likelihood of a stock-out. From the stock records a note will be made of the number of times the stock falls below the chosen level in the period. The ratio of this number of times to the total number of stock level checks is the required probability figure.

At the other end of the spectrum let us consider how one might attach probability figures to future sales estimates when, for various reasons, past figures are not likely to provide a good guide.

Putting probability figures on likely sales estimates in a subjective way is best done by (i) thinking of the probabilities in terms of betting odds and then translating to mathematical figures, and (ii) thinking in terms of equal chances, either side of a given figure. To demonstrate the latter technique, the best way to arrive at the most likely figure for sales is to think of a series of possible figures and choose that one which, on reflection, is felt to be equally likely to be exceeded or not reached; this is easier and better, we are saying, than trying to choose the single most likely figure directly.

It is most important, in practice, to get contributions from all people who could give sensible estimates. Again, staying with the business sales figures example, there might be, for instance, three sales representatives who could give estimates of the sales of the business. The best approach here is to use some variation of the *Delphi technique*. In this technique each member is asked to give his assessment individually, *without reference* to other members of the group. There are two possible ways of dealing with the inevitable differences. One is to weight them by some perceived ability of each individual as an assessor. The other is to get the group to meet and try and reconcile the differences in assessments. The disadvantages of the latter approach in a small business group is that seniority and ranking are likely to mean that a junior will subordinate his views to that of his superior, even though in fact they may be equally (or more!) valuable. A solution to this problem is to use a variation of the courtmartial approach! The junior ranking officer on the Board is always asked his decision first, so that there can be little question of his views being affected by his colleagues.

The ability and reliability of individuals to assess estimates properly (and hence the weight that should be given to these views) should be based mainly on their track record as forecasters: that is, on the evidence from the past that they have assessed the future sensibly and not perhaps through rose- coloured spectacles. Where an individual has consistently overestimated future sales by, say, 10 per cent in the past, then obviously his estimates must be discounted by that factor.

Large businesses have a particular problem in that groups (e.g.

boards of directors) typically make the important decisions and the emotional attitudes of groups, and of individuals that compose these groups do differ. It used to be thought that groups were more conservative or risk-averse than their individual members. This would seem to tie up with the traditional view of the size as being a stabilising, moderating, influence. Research, however, would seem to indicate that groups are in fact more bold and less risk-averse than their component members. The spin-off to small businesses is obvious . One man may tend to be too cautious. Perhaps the advice to the small business manager is 'Boldness [within reason!] be my friend.'

CHAPTER 18

Capital Investment Appraisal

INTRODUCTION	337
THE DISCOUNT FACTOR	338
PRESENT-VALUE CALCULATIONS	340
IRR, PV, PROFITABILITY INDEX AND OTHER DCF TECHNIQUES	343
TRADITIONAL TECHNIQUES	345
BUILDING UP THE CASH FLOWS	346
INFLATION	351
PRESENT-VALUE TABLES	353
THE INTEREST RATE AND RISK	354
REPAIR OR REPLACE: UNEVEN LIVES	356
LEASE OR BUY	358
CAPITAL RATIONING AND LINEAR PROGRAMMING	360
SUMMARY AND CONCLUSIONS	361
Appendix 1 *Present value tables*	363
Appendix 2 *Annuity tables*	364

Ah, take the cash . . .
    Omar Khayyam

Introduction

This chapter is concerned with capital expenditure in small businesses. Capital expenditure, which is expenditure typically on fixed assets such as plant and machinery, differs from other expenditure in two important respects. First, the benefits from the investment, whether in terms of labour savings or cash flow from additional profits, are likely to continue over a considerable number of years. Some technique is therefore needed to take account of the fact that cash flows in earlier years are more important than in later years. The principal reason for this difference is that cash received early on can earn interest and hence cannot be equated directly with an equivalent cash flow received later. Capital budgeting using proper discounted cash flow (DCF) techniques can take this *time value* of money into account. Much of this chapter will be concerned with an explanation of these techniques so far as they relate to small businesses. Secondly, the sums of money involved in the decisions are usually substantial and consequently more care needs to be exercised before committing the business to the purchase of the asset.

It is sometimes held that discounted cash flow techniques are too sophisticated for small businesses and are more appropriate to large firms with large cash flows. Nothing could be more wrong. Capital budgeting is not difficult, and it is even more important for small firms than large. A piece of new or replacement plant and machinery will set any firm back, but its cost will be only a fraction of the yearly cash flow for many businesses; for a small business it is likely to be a substantial part.

Two other factors are of importance in capital investment appraisal. These are inflation – the effects of which are frequently ignored in practice in DCF calculations – and the risk inherent in estimated future cash flows. Small businesses are particularly vulnerable to risk. Risk analysis is comparatively simple, yet few small businesses take account of it in their planning. Both factors will be considered later in this chapter. We start off, however, with a brief discussion of the mathematics involved in capital investment appraisal.

The discount factor

Suppose you are owed £1,000. Instead of being paid in one year's time, when the debt is due, you are offered the alternative of £800 now. Suppose, too, that money spare can earn 25 per cent gross (tax is ignored for the moment). Should you accept the offer?

If you go for the alternative, the interest on £800 for one year at 25 per cent is $800 \times 25/100 = £200$, so at the end of the year you will have $800 + 200 = £1,000$. But that is precisely what you would have had if you had not exercised your option. In the form of an equation:

£1,000 in one year's time = Present value of £800

Capital investment appraisal 339

Now to convert 1,000 into 800 we have to multiply by the factor of 0.8, so we can write:

$$1{,}000 \times 0.8 = 800$$

Sum   Discount factor = Present value

Using the standard abbreviations of DF for the discount factor, and PV for the present value, we have:

Sum × DF = PV (18.1)

This is the basic equation for all DCF or capital budgeting work. It does not matter whether the money is paid or received. The same interest would be earned in either case. To arrive at the value now (present value) of a sum of money to be paid or received in the future, all that is necessary is to multiply it by the right discount factor.

What is the appropriate discount factor will depend upon the interest rate and the number of years into the future when the sum is due – Appendix 1 to this chapter shows the discount factors (or, as they may be called, present value factors) for varying interest rates and periods until payment.

It will be obvious to those with a mathematical background that equation 18.1 is similar to that used in the compound interest formula for calculating the sum (S_n) to which a principal (P) will accrue at an interest rate (r) over a number (n) of periods of time. That formula is:

$$S_n = (1 + r)^n P \qquad (18.2)$$

where $(1 + r)^n$ is the compound interest factor. We can rewrite the formula as:

$$S_n \times \frac{1}{(1 + r)^n} = P \qquad (18.3)$$

This new formula is now identical to equation 18.1, with $1/(1 + r)^n$ as the discount factor (DF).

Formula 18.2 converts a principal into a sum in the future by multiplying by a compound interest factor. Our basic formula (18.1 or 18.3) does the reverse. It converts a sum in the future to a present value now by multiplying by a discount factor. The discount factor is the reciprocal of the compound interest factor. In our example the discount factor for one year at 25 per cent was easy to arrive at. It was

0.8, and application of the formula does give $1/(1 + 0.25) = 0.8$. For two years the discount factor is not so easy to arrive at by common sense, but the basic formula gives it quickly as $1/(1 + 0.25)^2 = 0.64$. In practice, of course, the discount factors are not calculated; they are obtained by looking them up in a table.

Present-value calculations

We start off with two examples of present-value calculations, given in the form of questions, and then consider the implications of our answers.

EXAMPLE 1

What is the present value of equal sums of £1,000 received at the end of each of three consecutive years? Money spare can command 10 per cent. Using the basic equation (Sum × DF = PV) for each of the years we have:

Year	Sum £	×	Discount factor (10%)	=	Present Value £
1	1,000		0.909		909
2	1,000		0.826		826
3	1,000		0.751		751
			TOTAL PRESENT VALUE		£2,486

The present value is therefore £2,486.

It is easy to check that these two, i.e. £1,000 at the end of each year for three years, and £2,486 now, at 10 per cent, are the same, by finding what they are each worth after three years (columns A and B in Table 18.1).

Alternatively, we can imagine that the £2,486 is lent for three years at 10 per cent, and the capital is returned, intact, at the end of the third year (column C). These are two ways of looking at DCF. Remembering that money spare is worth 10 per cent the comparisons are shown in Table 18.1.

In this example the sums of money are the same each year. When this is the case, it is possible to shorten the calculation dramatically. If we multiply the sum of £1,000 by the factor of 2.486 we arrive at the present value. This factor is the sum of the three individual year's

Capital investment appraisal

Table 18.1

	A £1,000 for 3 years	B £2,486 now	C £2,486 lent
Sum at start	—	2,486	
Interest for first year		249	249
Sum received after one year	1,000	—	—
Total at end of one year	1,000	2,735	249
Interest for second year	100	274	25
Sum received after two years	1,000	—	249
Total at end of two years	2,100	3,009	523
Interest for third year	210	301	52
			249
Sum received after three years	1,000	—	2,486
Total at end of three years	£3,310	£3,310	£3,310

factors and can be read off directly from the cumulative or annuity tables. Appendix 2 to this chapter gives the figure as 2.487. This difference is due to the 'rounding off' of the factors in both sets of tables to 3 decimal places, and is totally unimportant in practice.

EXAMPLE 2

At what interest rates will it be worth while to invest £41,500 in a business project which is likely to bring in the following estimated sums of cash:

Year	Sum (£)
1	15,000
2	20,000
3	30,000

Since the interest rate is not known, we have to proceed by the method of trial and error. If we try 22 and 24 per cent we have (using the factors given in Appendix 1).

Year	Sum (£)	DF (22%)	Present value (£)	DF (24%)	Present value (£)
1	15,000	0.820	12,300	0.806	12,090
2	20,000	0.672	13,440	0.650	13,000
3	30,000	0.551	16,530	0.524	15,720
	TOTAL PRESENT VALUES		£42,270		£40,810

It is important to ask what these figures mean. The effect of multiplying a cash sum by a discount factor is to bring it back to its present-day value. A direct comparison can then be made with the sum paid out on the project 'now'. The advantage of choosing now as the time when the comparisons are to be made is fairly obvious – we are making the decision now!

		At 22%	At 24%
	Cash in: PV of cash flows	42,270	40,810
Less	Cash out on investment	41,500	41,500
	NET PRESENT VALUE (NPV)*	£770	£ (690)

*That is, PV of cash flows *less* investment cost.

Since discount factors always get less as interest rates rise, it is evident that for rates lower than 22 per cent the NPV will always be positive, and that for rates higher than 24 per cent it will always be negative, and the higher the rate, the greater will be this gap.

Again it will be evident that at around 23 per cent the NPV will be nil, i.e. the present value of the cash flows will be equal to the project investment sum. On the face of it the exact rate could be determined by interpolation (and the calculation gives the rate to be 23.05 per cent). However, interpolation implies a relationship between the present value and the interest rate which is linear, and this is not the case. In practice determining the exact rate to several decimal points is usually quite unnecessary. For most work, determining the rate to the nearest whole number is all that is necessary and most sets of tables enable this to be done easily.

In Example 1 we showed that when the present value is precisely equal to the investment amount, this meant that the discount rate is that rate of return that the estimated cash flows are actually earning on the project. This rate of return is usually called the *internal rate of return* (IRR), or sometimes the DCF rate, though the term DCF is generally used to describe any type of capital investment appraisal analysis that properly takes into account the time value of money. To make matters worse, the term used in the USA for internal rate of return is *yield*!

Example 1 also brings out an important point concerning the IRR calculations. It will be noted that, in the comparisons, money spare was always reinvested at the 10 per cent rate. i.e. at the internal rate. This is called the 'reinvestment assumption' and will be of importance to us when we are discussing the validity of IRR against the present-value approach for making capital investment appraisals.

IRR, PV, Profitability Index and other DCF techniques

If, in Example 1 of the previous section, we had said that the sums of £1,000 generated at the end of each of the three years had required an investment of, say £2,100 at year 0 (now), then the net present value of the cash flows at 10 per cent would have been £2,486 − £2,100 = £386. Since this is positive the simple answer to the question as to whether to invest or not at this 10 per cent rate must be in the affirmative. Had the initial investment required been greater than £2,486, the net present value would have been negative and investment would have been unwise. Of course, these easy figures, given purely as an example, totally oversimplify the problem. In real life, estimates of future cash flows cannot be determined with any accuracy and we need techniques to deal with risk and uncertainty. Cash flows, too, will typically go on for a much greater number of years than are shown in these examples. However, the principle is still the same. Tax and inflation, too, will both affect the values of the net cash flows. All these factors will be discussed later in this chapter. For the moment we ignore them and make the assumption that the net cash flows have been determined and that 'single-figure' estimates for the cash flows each year are acceptable.

When the discount rate is given (here it is 10 per cent: a very low rate in today's conditions) the term *present-value (PV)* analysis is used. When, as in Example 2, the precise interest rate of return is calculated, we noted that the term *internal rate of return (IRR)* is used. There is not, in reality, much difference between these two approaches. In Example 2, if we had used any discount or cut-off rate below 23 per cent, the net present value would have been positive, i.e. for all rates below the IRR rate the NPV would have been positive. If we are just looking for, say, a 20 per cent return, then PV analysis will give a positive NPV indicating that we should go ahead. IRR analysis gives the 'exact' rate of return as 23 per cent. This figure is greater than 20 per cent, so IRR analysis signals the same decision.

An advantage of PV analysis is that only one calculation is required. In IRR analysis several calculations, trying various discount rates, are usually required. It is sometimes argued that IRR analysis is superior to PV on the grounds that PV analysis is not possible until a cut-off or criterion rate has been agreed. IRR analysis, on the other hand, can proceed purely on the basis of the agreed investment costs and yearly benefits. In practice, there is no difference. Once IRR analysis has thrown up the precise internal rate of return, judgement is still required as to whether this is an acceptable rate or not. The managerial decision as to the appropriate rate required has been postponed, not avoided.

Internal rate of return analysis has one other apparent advantage over present-value analysis. Once the rate of return on a project has been established, a quick and accurate method for comparing projects is available, for clearly the higher the rate, the better the project. Present-value analysis takes no account of the *size* of the investment in the project. A large project will tie up much more money than a smaller project and therefore may not be preferable even though it shows a slightly higher absolute NPV figure. The solution to this problem of how to rank projects under PV analysis is to use the *profitability index (PI)*. This index is defined as:

$$PI = \frac{\text{PV of cash benefits}}{\text{Investment cost}}$$

The PI really gives the benefit per £ (or other unit of money) invested. It is conceptually a more satisfactory method for ranking projects then the internal rate of return approach. This is because IRR analysis assumes that spare funds (if any) during the life of the project are reinvested at the project's own internal rate of return. The reinvestment assumption is not likely to be very realistic. The project's own rate of return should be fairly high for investment to be seriously considered (rates of around 20 to 25 per cent or higher are typical these days), and it is not likely that spare funds will be able to earn this amount. Present-value (and PI) analysis requires only that spare funds earn the 'criterion' (i.e. agreed discount) rate. This is almost certain to be a lower and much more realistic rate. In general, the profitability index is the best technique for appraising projects and ranking them.

In Example 1 the yearly cash inflows each year were equal. When this is the case it is sometimes more convenient to 'annualise' the initial investment cost and compare this annual cash cost with the yearly cash benefits, rather than the other way round (as in conventional IRR or PV analysis). If we assume, again, that the investment amount is £2,100 and that a 10 per cent criterion rate is appropriate, then the annualised cost of £2,100 over a 3-year period is simply

$$\frac{2{,}100}{2.487} = £844.39 \text{ per annum}$$

(again using the same factor given in Appendix 2).

Each year is now strictly comparable. Each year the benefit is £1,000 and the equivalent cost is just over £844. *Annualised cost or annualised equivalent*, as this approach is called, gives the same go-ahead signal as conventional analysis.

A number of corporations, including British Telecom, use annualised cost, mainly on the grounds that the concept is simpler to understand and apply than the usual techniques.

Traditional techniques

Most small businesses, and many large businesses too, still use methods of investment appraisal that do not properly take into account the time value of money. The two most common methods are:

- Payback
- Accounting return on investment (or return on funds employed)

Both these have serious conceptual disadvantages, and in view of the simplicity of 'DCF' techniques it is surprising that they are still so prevalent.

In the *payback* method the number of years before the original capital investment is 'paid back' (i.e. before the cumulative yearly cash returns equal the inital investment) is determined.

Payback has two serious disadvantages. First, it totally ignores all cash beyond the payback period. This can be a very serious drawback as many substantial projects, vital to a firm's long-term survival, do not start to bring in cash for quite a number of years. Indeed, the whole point of capital investment is to make a profit, not just to break even. Second, even within the payback period, cash flows are not properly evaluated.

Thus, consider these two projects, each requiring an initial investment of £3,000:

		X	Y
CASH FLOWS	Year 1	£2,000	£1,000
	Year 2	£1,000	£2,000
	Year 3	£1,000	£1,000

Both have a 2-year payback, so would appear to be equally desirable. However £1 this year is worth more than £1 next year, because of the interest it can earn, so X, with its faster cash flow, is really more desirable.

The *accounting return on investment* method determines the average return on investment for a project. In the above example the average return over the 3 years for both projects is £4,000/3 = £1,333: the average rate of return is the same for both, i.e. £1,333/3,000 × 100 = 44.4 per cent. However, we know that X is preferable to Y.

In using the accounting rate of return, there are other problems, too. How do we define 'return'? Is it profit before or after tax? Should we use initial or average investment? Should we add back depreciation to our return to try to arrive at cash? One thing is certain: in DCF analysis we are setting actual cash flows against cash flows, i.e. we are comparing like with like.

For all these reasons the accounting rate of return is not to be recommended. Payback, on the other hand, does have advantages. A short payback period does mean that the firm's initial investment is soon recovered. When used as a simple indicator of risk, in *conjunction with* a proper analysis, payback does have an important 'part' to play. However, this part is only that of a supporting role to the main character! Once again we revert to the main DCF techniques – IRR and PV – and now concern ourselves with the mechanics of arriving at those net cash flow figures which so far we have taken for granted in our calculations.

Building up the cash flows

What happens when any investment project is first evaluated? How are the cash flows, which, it is hoped, will occur over the years, arrived at in practice? Sometimes these cash inflows will be the benefits from labour savings, as, for instance, if the investment is in a piece of more highly automated machinery. The savings in wages in this case can be estimated comparatively easily from technical data supplied by the makers and from an inspection of the effectiveness of the machinery when put into operation by other users.

When the investment is in new buildings or plant (or both) which should increase production and generate new sales the estimate of future cash flows is more difficult.

The broad approach is to start off with the estimated sales, then calculate those additional costs which will be incurred to service the sales. As the project gets under way, yearly sales should increase. The corresponding costs will be split up into those that vary with sales (e.g. raw materials) and those that are fixed (e.g. the rent of the factory space). The ratio of direct costs to sales may be determined from past figures, and this ratio will be applied to further yearly sales. Once the fixed costs are arrived at, they will be the same each year.

Provided yearly sales can be estimated, it will be fairly easy to produce projected profit-and-loss accounts. One word of caution is necessary here. These estimates are *incremental* sales, costs and cash flows from the additional investment. A cost whose amount is unaltered is not an incremental cost. By 'fixed' costs we mean costs which are additional for the project but which do not vary (appreciably) from year to year with the estimated increases in the new sales generated over the years.

It is evident that costs, profit and cash flows all depend on sales. The real problem is how to estimate sales. In Chapters 2 and 13 this problem was attacked, and little more can be added at this stage. Let us assume, therefore, that additional sales for a particular year in the future have been estimated. A projected profit-and-loss account constructed on this basis might be (in abbreviated form) as follows:

	PROFIT-AND-LOSS ACCOUNT (ESTIMATED)		£
	Turnover		100,000
Less	Raw materials	40,000	
	Variable costs	15,000	
	Fixed costs	15,000	
	Depreciation	10,000	80,000
	PROFIT BEFORE TAXATION		£20,000

What is the cash flow from this? Making the assumption, usual in long-term planning, that the change in debtors, creditors, accrued liabilities and stock over the year will not be great – and will in any case even out from one year to the next – the net cash flow will be

$$100,000 - 70,000 = 30,000$$

The expenses will be set out in considerable detail under the main headings of distribution costs, administration costs, etc. From the calculation point of view it is easier to regard cash as net profit plus depreciation, i.e. 20,000 + 10,000, giving the same yearly net cash flow of 30,000.

We now need to introduce, for the first time in this chapter, the important effect of tax on the net cash flow. These additional profits, will generate additional tax payments. As we have seen in Chapter 9 the Inland Revenue does not allow the company's assessment of the charge for depreciation to stand in arriving at taxable profits. The Revenue insists that its own charge for depreciation, i.e. the capital allowance, is deducted instead. If we suppose that these *additional* tax allowances are estimated to be £12,000 in the year in question, the tax calculation (assuming all other expenses are allowable) will be:

		£
	Profit before taxation	20,000
Add	book depreciation	10,000
		30,000
Less	tax allowances	12,000
	TAXABLE PROFIT	£18,000

Additional corporation tax is due on this figure (assuming, too, that the business has enough taxable profits to cover tax allowances at the current marginal tax rate.

The exact time when this tax will have to be paid depends on a number of factors. Chapter 9 showed that for a partnership the first payment can be between 9 and 21 months after the year end, depending on the choice of the accounting year end. For a company, mainstream corporation tax will be paid 9 months after the accounting year end for all companies incorporated after 1965. The cash flow from profits is likely to have occurred fairly evenly throughout the accounting year, and any capital purchase may of course have been at any time during that year. In each case the exact date when tax must be paid needs to be established and the appropriate discount factor used. In the next section this point will be taken up further. For the moment we make the simplifying assumption – often closely approximated to in practice – that all incremental tax payments are paid a year later.

It does not matter particularly what form is used for arriving at the net cash flows. In large corporations, capital expenditure requisition forms usually include a worksheet to be filled in with columns for the investment in the new equipment, receipts from sale of old machinery (if any), tax savings from the purchase of new machinery, annual benefits, incremental tax on the benefits, salvage value (if any) at end of life, and so on. One form for the cash-flow layout suitable for calculations in small businesses is given in the following example of a capital investment appraisal.

INVESTMENT APPRAISAL EXAMPLE

An engineering workshop is proposing to invest in a new special purpose lathe costing £38,000. Purchase of this lathe will enable the engineering company to dispose of its existing machine for an estimated sum of £12,000. The life of the new lathe is expected to be some 6 years. At the end of this time the salvage value – because the lathe is custom-built for the purpose – is likely to be only some £4,000. Savings will be mainly labour savings from using one man less on the lathe and will amount, in all, to approximately £14,150 per year. There will be no redundancy payments since this man can be moved to fill another (genuine) job vacancy in the workshop at the same salary level. Taxable profits are likely to be available to cover any incremental capital allowances and the tax rate can be taken to be the small business marginal rate of 27 per cent. At a 30 per cent cut-off rate, is investment in the new lathe worth while? Assume the old lathe, if not sold, also had an expected life of 6 years and nil salvage value then, and that no regional development grants are available for the new lathe.

Incremental capital allowances can be taken to be a writing down allowance of 25 per cent on the net investment in the new lathe. The net investment in the new machine is:

New lathe	38,000
Less Sale of old machine	12,000
	26,000
Less Scrap value of new lathe 4,000 × 0.207	828
Net investment	25,172

Capital allowances are therefore:

Year	25% of	=	Capital allowance	Written down balance
1	26,000		6,500	19,500
2	19,500		4,875	14,625
3	14,625		3,656	10,969
4	10,969		2,742	8,227
5	8,227		2,057	6,170
6	6,170		1,543	4,627

At the end of Year 6 we have assumed that the new lathe will be sold for an estimated net salvage value of £4,000 so that a balancing allowance of (4,627 − 4,000) = 627 will be given in Year 7.

The suggested form for the cash layout for savings is shown in Table 18.2. Since the NPV is positive, investment in the new lathe is worth while if the required rate of return on investment is 30 per cent. The payback period can be seen (by comparing the cumulative total of the net cash flows in column (e) with the net investment amount) to be a fraction under 2 years.

It should be noted that column (c) does not enter directly into the calculation of the net cash flow. This figure, i.e. column (e), is made

Table 18.2

Year	Cash flow from savings (a)	Tax on savings (b)	Capital allowances (c)	Tax saved by capital allowances (d)	Net cash flow (e)	PV factor (30%)	PV of cash flows
1	£14,150		£6,500		£14,150	0.769	£10,881
2	14,150	£3,820	4,875	£1,755	12,085	0.592	7,154
3	14,150	3,820	3,656	1,316	11,646	0.455	5,299
4	14,150	3,820	2,742	987	11,317	0.350	3,961
5	14,150	3,820	2,057	740	11,070	0.269	2,978
6	14,150	3,820	1,543	555	10,885	0.207	2,253
7		3,820	627	417	(3,403)	0.159	(541)
8				169	169	0.123	21

Total PV of CASH FLOWS   32,006

The net present value is therefore 32,006 − 25,172 = £6,834

up of column (a) less column (b), plus column (d). This layout also has the advantage that it can be used for any type of capital investment. The headings to column (a) and column (b) can be renamed more generally as 'cash flow from benefits' and 'tax on cash flow benefits' respectively. The term 'benefits' will cover cash flow from profits if the investment will increase production and sales, and for a 'lease or buy' appraisal it will cover the lease payments saved. In the unlikely event that the expected scrap value at the end of the useful life of the old lathe had been material, this disposal value could be entered in the appropriate year in column (a). An alternative could be to deduct the scrap value, suitably discounted and any incremental associated tax adjustment from the net investment figure. Regional incremental development grants are best treated this way, too. This approach has the conceptual advantage that it keeps separate the capital investment adjustments and the yearly benefits accruing from the use of this capital. Whichever approach is used does not matter much. The net present value figure will not be altered.

Quite frequently the investment amount will not all be paid out in the base year. When the project involves purchase of land and a factory and then putting machinery into the building, a more likely pattern of cash flow might be (say):

| Land and buildings | £26,000 |
| Plant and machinery | £12,000 (one year later) |

Taking the purchase of the land and buildings as being in year 0 (the base year) and the present-value rate as still being 30 per cent, the net investment, discounted back to now, would be:

	£
Land and buildings	26,000
Plant and machinery 12,000 × 0.769	9,228
NET INVESTMENT	35,228

and the sale of the old machine would be deducted from this figure and the scrap value of the new machine (suitably discounted) deducted as well.

Inflation

Strictly there are two ways of dealing with inflation:
(1) Using present-day (year 0) purchasing power amounts throughout. This is a rather theoretical approach and is rarely, if ever, used in practice.

(2) Using actual money amounts, with a criterion rate which implicitly includes an allowance for expected general inflation. This is the approach which is commonly employed when inflation is taken into account. To use it properly it is necessary to forecast specific price changes for each category of cash flow. Forecasting general inflation rates, let alone specific rates, is of course very difficult and depends largely upon one's individual assessment of the state of the economy in the future. Chapter 17 attempted to deal generally with such problems of uncertainty about the future. Since we are concerned with specific categories of cash flow, it may be best to rely on trends determined from past figures. The Central Statistical Office publishes figures of inflation rates for specific categories of goods and materials. In the example we are using the benefits are labour savings, so we need to assess future wage rises. For a particular small business it may be quite satisfactory to rely on one's personal judgement. Whether a statistical or a subjective approach (or a combination of the two) is used, some way of assessing future savings from the wages no longer needed to be paid out must be determined. Let us suppose that our best estimate is that there will be a 5 per cent yearly increase in benefits. We could now put these new cash flows into the savings, and tax on savings, columns. The new NPV figure will be considerably higher than the corresponding figure before inflation was taken into account. In general the incidence of inflation is an argument in favour of investment since the investment amount is likely to remain practically unaltered, and the benefits are likely to increase substantially.

From the small business point of view, what is the upshot of all this? Should inflation be taken into account or not? The answer is that in theory it must be; in practice, it very often is not. The reason for this dichotomy is simple. Most estimates of cash savings in the future have been found to be overoptimistic. Studies of figures for the estimated and the actual benefits realised show a shortfall of around 30 per cent, or even more. If inflation is not taken into account, the resultant decrease in savings and net present value go some way to compensate for this common failing in almost all savings estimates.

Many businesses – large and small – do not take account of inflation in their cash flows and, by implication, accept that this is a hedge against overoptimistic estimation. The practical consequences are not serious, provided the reasons for this omission are understood.

Present-value tables

We have already noted that there are basically two types of present-value tables (or discount factor tables – the terms are interchangeable), that is:

- those which show the present value of a single unit sum of money given or received n years from now
- those which show the *cumulative* present value of the same unit sum of money in each of the years 1 to n (inclusive) – these tables are referred to as annuity tables

Although the time periods in these tables are usually expressed in years, they can be used for *any* period if the corresponding interest rate is applied. Thus if the interest for a 6-month period is 10 per cent (which is not quite the same as a 20 per cent annual rate, because we are throughout using *compound* interest) and we wish to find the present value now, we merely use the 10 per cent PV factor from the tables.

All these tables imply an end of period receipt (or payment) of the sum of money. It follows that in many ways the 6 months interest factor would be the most appropriate to use in DCF calculations. In the basic example earlier in the chapter the cash flows from savings were mainly wages savings, and wages were paid throughout the year. These savings were not therefore as we assumed so far, all made at the end of the year. Evidently for the first a 6-month discount factor is better, for the second year an 18-month factor, and so on.

Why is it that in capital investment appraisals, year-end factors are still used when many of the savings do occur, on average, around the middle of the year? Partly the answer must be that this is because it is a matter of customary practice. In fact, this practice is not as bad as it might seem. Many DCF appraisals are between alternative methods of achieving the same object. For example, should we buy one machine or another? Purchase of either machine will result in labour savings. If we apply year-end factors to both calculations we shall be making errors, but these errors will be similar in both calculations. The difference between the calculations whether we (wrongly) use year-end factors or (rightly) middle-year factors will be much the same. Moreover, the use of year-end factors will reduce the benefits more than mid-year factors, and this too will help to compensate for inherent overoptimism in the estimation of yearly cash benefits!

Using the appropriate discount factor for tax payments is important. With a 100 per cent capital allowance these sums are likely to be fairly substantial and their estimated payment date fairly close to year 0. If the sum will be received in, say, 15 months from now and the annual rate used in the present-value calculations is, say, 20 per cent then the discount factor is a quarter down from the year 1 factor to year 2 – i.e. $0.833 - \frac{1}{4}(0.833 - 0.694) = 0.798$. Strictly this is incorrect, since, as we noted earlier, we are dealing throughout with compound interest factors. However, for practical purposes, straight-line interpolation between yearly periods for calculating discount factors is quite adequate.

The interest rate and risk

We have throughout kept the cost of financing an investment decision, and the return that the investment is expected to make, separate. When we calculate that a project's internal rate of return is, say, 25 per cent, by implication we are then proposing to compare that 25 per cent with a cost of financing. The difference will be the net benefit. This difference needs to take some account of the riskiness of the project.

So far in all our examples the interest rate has been given. How, in real life, does a business decide on the rate it will use? For large businesses with the possibility of a number of projects and various ways of raising capital it could be argued that some mix of capital should be employed. For small businesses the typical situation is that projects are 'one-off', and money is raised, or made available, to finance that one project. For small businesses, therefore, the cost of financing is usually the marginal cost of the finance for that particular investment project.

Even when we arrive at the cost of capital we are still faced with this problem of risk. The cost of capital must be paid; the hoped-for return on the proposed project is not certain. Some projects are inherently more 'risky' than others. Clearly for these projects we shall add more to the 'risk-free' rate of return than for others (see Figure 18.1).

Some capital investment appraisal departments of large corporations formalise this concept by using different 'hurdle' rates for passing or failing projects with differing degrees of inherent riskiness.

A small business is more likely to be faced with the problem of deciding between alternative projects. Some will have a high return but a high risk, and others which appear to be safer will offer a lower expected rate of return.

Capital investment appraisal 355

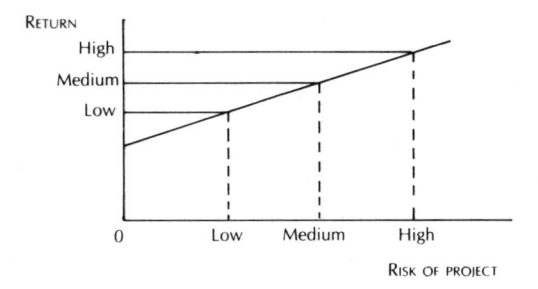

Figure 18.1

In Chapter 17 we showed how standard deviation can be used as a surrogate for risk. Plotting on a graph past individual investment projects and using the horizontal axis this time for the rate of return, and the vertical axis for standard deviation (s.d.), expressed as a percentage, we might obtain a series of points as in Figure 18.2.

Clearly project A is better than C because it has the same risk but a higher expected DCF rate. Project B, too, is better than C because it has the same rate but is assessed to be less risky. What is required is a combination of a small s.d. (risk) and a high rate of return, so the results should be, as far as possible, in the general directions indicated by the arrows. The points A, B, F lie on the 'efficiency frontier'. Once the efficiency frontier for a business has been roughly determined, the aim must be to improve on this position. That is, to take a

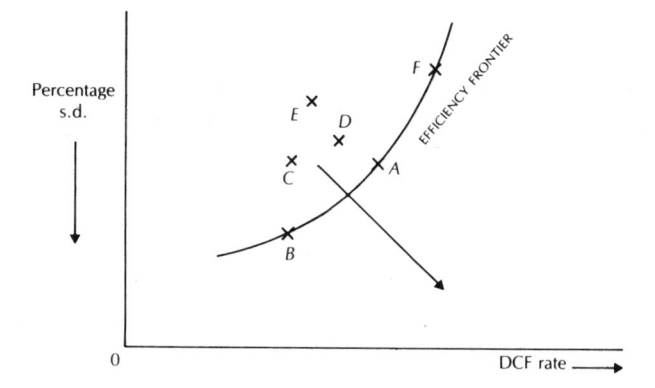

Figure 18.2

project beyond this frontier – if that is not possible, at least in the right direction.

We have seen that there are problems in arriving at the cost of capital and the appropriate discount rate to use in assessing a particular project. Many large businesses fix a criterion rate. They also, frequently, stipulate a payback period usually for a period of between 2 and 3 years. This criterion rate is not normally determined by using any theoretical approach. It will have been determined by what has been found to work at a practical level. It will be changed every year or so when market conditions such as availability of funds and interest rates have altered substantially.

For the small business much the same applies, except that since most of the borrowing for investment in fixed assets will come from one of the clearing banks, the medium term (3 to 7 years) loan rate may be used for the assessment. (This rate may well be the 6-months inter-bank rate, plus perhaps 1 to 4 per cent, or it may be a fixed rate determined by the bank after negotiation with the borrower.) To sum up, this rate, together with some additional rate, subjectively assessed by the small business manager to reflect the risk of the project and the profit required, will be the appropriate criterion rate to use in the project appraisal.

Repair or replace: uneven lives

In this section and the next, we deal with certain practical problems in capital investment appraisal. In this particular section we restrict the capital investment appraisals to clearly defined alternatives: namely, granted that we already have a certain asset (typically a piece of machinery), shall we replace it now or at some other point in time, e.g. in one or two years' time? This problem is of common occurrence in industry. Strictly the alternatives are to replace now or replace later. This later alternative probably means repairing now, and hence the term 'repair or replace'. In practice replacement, too, implies, most likely, a choice between the purchase of two or more possible machines. In the broadest sense, therefore, repair or replacement problems include the choices of both repairing or replacing, and choosing between different machines. Since machines have different economic lives this type of appraisal also covers the problem of 'uneven' lives.

It is important to realise that if the decision is made now to repair, another set of calculations may be required at the end of the next year to decide whether to replace then, or repair for another year or two, since the estimates of the various costs, lengths of life, etc., are likely to have changed by then. Indeed, although analysis at this time may indicate perhaps that the best alternative is to replace in, say, two years' time, the correct decision, when looked at in one years' time, might have been to replace immediately.

Since 'repair or replace' problems provide outstandingly the most frequent project appraisal decisions which the small business manager will have to make, it will be convenient to summarise here the costs which need to be taken into account. As in all capital investment appraisals the costs (or benefits) which need to be considered are only the *differential* costs. Sunk costs, i.e. costs that have already been incurred, or costs which do not change as a result of the decision, are irrelevant. Costs which should be taken into account include:

- the capital cost of the replacement
- the resale value of the existing equipment
- the costs of the changeover
- the repair and maintenance costs
- the costs of lost production or of lower quality output
- other running costs

Broadly there are three methods of comparing the alternatives. They are:

(1) *Comparing the net present value* of the various options for perpetuity. Conceptually this is the most satisfactory. In practice, however, assumptions have to be made as to reinvestment many years from now, and even though the discount factor drastically reduces the effect that these later figures have on the final calculation, the air of unreality is enormous.

(2) *Determining the least common multiple* of the different possible lives of the alternatives and making the calculations over that number of years. This method is particularly useful when considering the problem of investment in two alternative types of machine each with differing lives. Thus if there are two machines being considered with lives of 2 and 3 years respectively, then a fair comparison can be made if we make it over a period of 6 years (the lowest common multiple of 2 and 3).

(3) *Artificially terminating the life* of one or more of the alternatives at a convenient point in time. This is a technique which can be used for a large number of widely different types of capital investment appraisal. When applied to repair or replacement problems it is particularly useful for comparing machinery with lives of a similar, but not identical, nature. Thus if the alternatives are restricted to replacing now with one machine which has an estimated life of 9 years or

another with an estimated life of some 7 years, the lowest common multiple approach would require the comparison to be made over a period of 63 years. This is not practical, and the much simpler solution is to assign a 'notional' scrap value to the 9-year machine as at the end of 7 years. A straight comparison over the period of 7 years on a comparable basis can then be made.

Lease or buy

The other popular and practical use of capital investment appraisal for a small business manager is in the 'lease or buy' decision. This term needs some clarification. The decision as to whether to have one machine or another, or indeed any machine, may be the subject of a capital investment appraisal in which the costs are set against the likely future cash benefits. In a 'pure' lease or buy appraisal we are solely concerned with the ways of financing the acquisition of that piece of plant or machinery once the decision to have it has been made. Of course, in practice, they may be combined with the appraisals setting off future cash benefits against one or the other methods of financing.

In most project appraisals the future cash benefits are uncertain. In leasing, the terms of the lease agreement will lay down the exact payments, so both the costs (the purchase of the plant) and the benefits (the lease rentals saved) are known pretty accurately. Lease or buy appraisals are therefore particularly suitable for fairly sophisticated capital investment work.

The principal differences in the cash-flow effects of leasing as opposed to buying and borrowing will arise from the different treatment of tax. Tax writing-down allowances which could have been obtained if the plant had been bought will not be obtained if the plant is leased. Leasing rentals normally will be fully allowable for taxation. Of course, if the lessee is not in a taxpaying situation, these cash-flow differences will not apply.

Apart from these tax points (and the receipt of grants where appropriate) ownership does not normally give rise to any significant differential cash flows.

Situations may exist where there are advantages to ownership or leasing which cannot readily be reduced to specific cash flows; these advantages may, none the less, be very real. For instance, a small business may wish to build-up assets in the balance-sheet for presentation to bankers or even with a view to eventually obtaining a stock exchange quotation. In such a case buying will have advantages over

Capital investment appraisal

leasing. Another company may know that borrowing must be contained within existing arrangements, in which case leasing may have advantages over borrowing in purchasing plant.

In 'lease or buy' capital investment appraisals it is best to assume that the business has decided to lease, and then determine, from this basis, the additional costs and benefits in the event that the alternative of buying is decided upon. The advantage of this approach is that the purchase of the new machine is the investment cost, as in any other conventional DCF appraisal.

The changes in cash flow (if the alternative of purchase is taken up) will be:

- CASH OUT   Purchase of plant
- CASH IN   Tax savings from writing-down allowances
- CASH IN   Rentals saved (i.e. rentals not now having to be paid)
- CASH OUT   Tax payments on the additional taxable profit caused by the rental savings

The cash-flow layout in our basic example can be used, without any adjustments, for lease or buy capital investment appraisals. It is evident that lease or buy decisions are a very straightforward application of normal DCF procedures.

In many small business situations the need for new machines (perhaps to replace an existing one which is no longer operational) is so overriding that no appraisal is really necessary. The very existence of the business depends on the machine. If this is truly the case, then the best use of a DCF calculation is in the 'pure' lease or buy appraisal, i.e. solely in deciding how to finance the asset. We noted that in these circumstances the cash flows contained in the terms of lease will be much more precisely determined than in other capital investment appraisals. It follows that the appropriate cut-off rate to use in the 'lease or buy' appraisal will not need to include anything like as substantial a figure for risk. For 'lease or buy' appraisals a rate only slightly in excess of the basic fixed cost of borrowing (assuming this is the alternative method of financing) is therefore the appropriate rate to use.

We have concerned ourselves with the capital investment appraisal considerations of lease or buy in this section. It is fair to add that in the practical situation it is frequently liquidity considerations that will be the overriding factor, and they will indicate the lease decision.

Capital rationing and linear programming

When there is a budget ceiling or restriction on the amount of funds that can be made available, we have a 'capital-rationing' situation. Although bank funds are fairly readily available today, small businesses which have yet to establish themselves and are not able to present a proven track record will have problems in borrowing funds.

In general, even in the capital-rationing situation, the profitability index will still be a good indicator. However, if the cash constraint is strictly enforced, it may be that a number of smaller, less profitable proposals will give a higher net present value in total than one larger project which has a higher profitability index. An example will make this clear. Let us suppose there is rigid budget constraint of £90,000 and there are only these possible projects available:

Proposal	A	B	C	D
Profitability index	1.15	1.13	1.11	1.07
Investment amount	£60,000	£37,000	£52,000	£45,000

In this capital-rationing situation a combination of B and C is preferable to A despite the fact that A has a higher PI, for the net present values are:

$$
\begin{aligned}
A \quad 60,000\,(1.15 - 1.0) &= 9,000 \\
B \quad 37,000\,(1.13 - 1.0) &= 4,810 \\
C \quad 52,000\,(1.11 - 1.0) &= 5,720 \\
&\ 10,530
\end{aligned}
$$

Because B and C are able to make more use of the available cash funds the combined net present value that they generate is higher than that of the apparently more profitable single project A. We conclude that in the capital-rationing situation net present value is the appropriate technique to use.

Even this firm conclusion needs to be interpreted with care. An analysis such as this may need to be extended to take account of intermediate cash flows generated by the project or the effect of these cash flows on yearly balance-sheets and profit-and-loss accounts. If there is any likelihood of these causing any problems during the anticipated lives of the projects, it is essential to produce projected balance-sheets, profit-and-loss accounts, and budgets and inspect them carefully for any possible adverse implications.

We have already noted that bank managers are rather traditional in their approach to the analysis of customers' accounts. They tend to use trusted and well-tried figures such as 0.75 for the quick asset ratio, and a loan to proprietor's funds top limit of about 1.0 in analysing the balance-sheet; they like to have adequate security; and they want to see how their proposed loan can be repaid over the years from projected funds-flow statements or budgets presented to them. All these are constraints which exist in forms which are eminently suitable for a linear programming (LP) approach. LP packages are already available for microcomputers. No special knowledge is required to use them. Slightly more sophisticated programs will also print out the values for dual variables. These variables test the sensitivity of the solution to changes in the various constraints. We give one quite extreme example, just for demonstration purposes. If, in the example given earlier in this section, four proposals had been evaluated by an LP program and a budget constraint of £88,999 had been included, the LP print-out would show project A as the optimum solution since the alternative of B and C together would have been rejected. Yet common sense says that by relaxing the budget constraint by just £1, some £1,500 extra benefit in terms of NPV could be obtained. A suitable analysis would show the benefit from relaxing the budget constraint by the £1. Such an analysis will frequently show, in practice, that the budget constraint is not crucial, though other constraints, such as earnings in a given year or return on investment, probably are. In other words, relaxing one of these constraints in one of the years by only a little may allow a much more satisfying project or a mix of projects to be chosen.

Summary and conclusions

Earlier in this chapter we argued that both the accounting rate of return and payback do not properly take account of the interest-earning capacity of cash flows and that they should be replaced by DCF methods such as *internal rate of return, net present value, profitability index, annual cost* or *annual equivalent*. We added the caveat that payback has got a place in capital investment projects as an adjunct to a proper DCF approach. A short payback period is a good practical indicator of risk. In some cases, too, the accounting rate of return method should also be included as it shows the effect that the capital investment appraisal will have on the profit-and-loss account of the business. This may be important to the small business manager who needs to present his bank manager with yearly accounts which are acceptable.

Nevertheless, only DCF methods deal properly with *time*. The internal rate of return is the most widely used of these. Because of its inherent 'reinvestment' assumption, it is not conceptually the best method, though the differences are mostly slight.

The net present value approach is *prima facie* better. Its only disadvantage is that the present value of the cash flows of one single project cannot be compared directly with the cash benefits from another unless the investment amounts are approximately the same. In that case, the best appraisal technique to use is the profitability index. The PI gives, in effect, the present value per unit of money invested. It is the best single technique for alternative project appraisal work. The only occasion when it might not be used is in the capital-rationing situation, when, as we said in the preceding section, net present value is the better indicator.

We have argued throughout this chapter for the use of a proper analysis for evaluating a proposed capital investment project. In this summary we have tried to compare the various techniques giving the situations where one may be preferred to another. The differences between these various techniques are, however, very slight indeed. In practice, any DCF approach is likely to give much the same answer. What is important is that some DCF analysis, i.e. one properly taking account of the true value of money, is used.

Such an analysis is in fact extremely simple. It is barely an oversimplification to say that all that is required is to multiply the estimated cash flows in any period by the appropriate discount factor. For a small business manager, success, even survival, may well depend on the correct evaluation of even one project proposal. So to argue that the analysis is difficult, not necessary, or not worth the effort, is stupid. In any case many simple calculators these days include NPV buttons, so the effort is negligible.

But how accurate are capital investment decisions made with the use of DCF analysis? A year or two after a project has really got under way some sort of comparison between the actual results and the estimate can be made. In essence all that is necessary is a comparison of the actual investment cost with the estimated cost, and a similar comparison of actual yearly benefits with their estimates. The difference in each case will be the variance. Just as in standard costing, variances will be looked into, and their causes identified.

The advantages of a follow-up procedure of this kind for capital investment decisions are considerable. The very fact that the project proposal estimates will later be 'audited' will tend to make for greater care in their preparation at the time. The main benefit, however, will come later, from an analysis of the variances. Lessons will be learnt from these as to the reasons for departures of actual benefits from estimates. These can be of crucial help in making the next capital investment project appraisal a proper evaluation.

Years Hence	1%	2%	4%	6%	8%	10%	12%	14%	15%	16%	18%	20%	22%	24%	25%	26%	28%	30%	35%	40%	45%	50%
1	0.990	0.980	0.962	0.943	0.926	0.909	0.893	0.877	0.870	0.862	0.847	0.833	0.820	0.806	0.800	0.794	0.781	0.769	0.741	0.714	0.690	0.667
2	0.980	0.961	0.925	0.890	0.857	0.826	0.797	0.769	0.756	0.743	0.718	0.694	0.672	0.650	0.640	0.630	0.610	0.592	0.549	0.510	0.476	0.444
3	0.971	0.942	0.889	0.840	0.794	0.751	0.712	0.675	0.658	0.641	0.609	0.579	0.551	0.524	0.512	0.500	0.477	0.455	0.406	0.364	0.328	0.296
4	0.961	0.924	0.855	0.792	0.735	0.683	0.636	0.592	0.572	0.552	0.516	0.482	0.451	0.423	0.410	0.397	0.373	0.350	0.301	0.260	0.226	0.198
5	0.951	0.906	0.822	0.747	0.681	0.621	0.567	0.519	0.497	0.476	0.437	0.402	0.370	0.341	0.328	0.315	0.291	0.269	0.223	0.186	0.156	0.132
6	0.942	0.888	0.790	0.705	0.630	0.564	0.507	0.456	0.432	0.410	0.370	0.335	0.303	0.275	0.262	0.250	0.227	0.207	0.165	0.133	0.108	0.088
7	0.933	0.871	0.760	0.665	0.583	0.513	0.452	0.400	0.376	0.354	0.314	0.279	0.249	0.222	0.210	0.198	0.178	0.159	0.122	0.095	0.074	0.059
8	0.923	0.853	0.731	0.627	0.540	0.467	0.404	0.351	0.327	0.305	0.266	0.233	0.204	0.179	0.168	0.157	0.139	0.123	0.091	0.068	0.051	0.039
9	0.914	0.837	0.703	0.592	0.500	0.424	0.361	0.308	0.284	0.263	0.225	0.194	0.167	0.144	0.134	0.125	0.108	0.094	0.067	0.048	0.035	0.026
10	0.905	0.820	0.676	0.558	0.463	0.386	0.322	0.270	0.247	0.227	0.191	0.162	0.137	0.116	0.107	0.099	0.085	0.073	0.050	0.035	0.024	0.017
11	0.896	0.804	0.650	0.527	0.429	0.350	0.287	0.237	0.215	0.195	0.162	0.135	0.112	0.094	0.086	0.079	0.066	0.056	0.037	0.025	0.017	0.012
12	0.887	0.788	0.625	0.497	0.397	0.319	0.257	0.208	0.187	0.168	0.137	0.112	0.092	0.076	0.069	0.062	0.052	0.043	0.027	0.018	0.012	0.008
13	0.879	0.773	0.601	0.469	0.368	0.290	0.229	0.182	0.163	0.145	0.116	0.093	0.075	0.061	0.055	0.050	0.040	0.033	0.020	0.013	0.008	0.005
14	0.870	0.758	0.577	0.442	0.340	0.263	0.205	0.160	0.141	0.125	0.099	0.078	0.062	0.049	0.044	0.039	0.032	0.025	0.015	0.009	0.006	0.003
15	0.861	0.743	0.555	0.417	0.315	0.239	0.183	0.140	0.123	0.108	0.084	0.065	0.051	0.040	0.035	0.031	0.025	0.020	0.011	0.006	0.004	0.002
16	0.853	0.728	0.534	0.394	0.292	0.218	0.163	0.123	0.107	0.093	0.071	0.054	0.042	0.032	0.028	0.025	0.019	0.015	0.008	0.005	0.003	0.002
17	0.844	0.714	0.513	0.371	0.270	0.198	0.146	0.108	0.093	0.080	0.060	0.045	0.034	0.026	0.023	0.020	0.015	0.012	0.006	0.003	0.002	0.001
18	0.836	0.700	0.494	0.350	0.250	0.180	0.130	0.095	0.081	0.069	0.051	0.038	0.028	0.021	0.018	0.016	0.012	0.009	0.005	0.002	0.001	0.001
19	0.828	0.686	0.475	0.331	0.232	0.164	0.116	0.083	0.070	0.060	0.043	0.031	0.023	0.017	0.014	0.012	0.009	0.007	0.003	0.002	0.001	
20	0.820	0.673	0.456	0.312	0.215	0.149	0.104	0.073	0.061	0.051	0.037	0.026	0.019	0.014	0.012	0.010	0.007	0.005	0.002	0.001		
21	0.811	0.660	0.439	0.294	0.199	0.135	0.093	0.064	0.053	0.044	0.031	0.022	0.015	0.011	0.009	0.008	0.006	0.004	0.002	0.001		
22	0.803	0.647	0.422	0.278	0.184	0.123	0.083	0.056	0.046	0.038	0.026	0.018	0.013	0.009	0.007	0.006	0.004	0.003	0.001	0.001		
23	0.795	0.634	0.406	0.262	0.170	0.112	0.074	0.049	0.040	0.033	0.022	0.015	0.010	0.007	0.006	0.005	0.003	0.002	0.001			
24	0.788	0.622	0.390	0.247	0.158	0.102	0.066	0.043	0.035	0.028	0.019	0.013	0.008	0.006	0.005	0.004	0.003	0.002	0.001			
25	0.780	0.610	0.375	0.233	0.146	0.092	0.059	0.038	0.030	0.024	0.016	0.010	0.007	0.005	0.004	0.003	0.002	0.001	0.001			
26	0.772	0.598	0.361	0.220	0.135	0.084	0.053	0.033	0.026	0.021	0.014	0.009	0.006	0.004	0.003	0.002	0.002	0.001				
27	0.764	0.586	0.347	0.207	0.125	0.076	0.047	0.029	0.023	0.018	0.011	0.007	0.005	0.003	0.002	0.002	0.001	0.001				
28	0.757	0.574	0.333	0.196	0.116	0.069	0.042	0.026	0.020	0.016	0.010	0.006	0.004	0.002	0.002	0.002	0.001	0.001				
29	0.749	0.563	0.321	0.185	0.107	0.063	0.037	0.022	0.017	0.014	0.008	0.005	0.003	0.002	0.002	0.001	0.001	0.001				
30	0.742	0.552	0.308	0.174	0.099	0.057	0.033	0.020	0.015	0.012	0.007	0.004	0.003	0.002	0.001	0.001	0.001	0.001				
40	0.672	0.453	0.208	0.097	0.046	0.022	0.011	0.005	0.004	0.003	0.001	0.001										
50	0.608	0.372	0.141	0.054	0.021	0.009	0.003	0.001	0.001	0.001												

Appendix 2 Annuity tables
Cumulative present value of £1 received annually for n years

Years (N)	1%	2%	4%	6%	8%	10%	12%	14%	15%	16%	18%	20%	22%	24%	25%	26%	28%	30%	35%	40%	45%	50%
1	0.990	0.980	0.962	0.943	0.926	0.909	0.893	0.877	0.870	0.862	0.847	0.833	0.820	0.806	0.800	0.794	0.781	0.769	0.741	0.714	0.690	0.667
2	1.970	1.942	1.886	1.833	1.783	1.736	1.690	1.647	1.626	1.605	1.566	1.528	1.492	1.457	1.440	1.424	1.392	1.361	1.289	1.224	1.165	1.111
3	2.941	2.884	2.775	2.673	2.577	2.487	2.402	2.322	2.283	2.246	2.174	2.106	2.042	1.981	1.952	1.923	1.868	1.816	1.696	1.589	1.493	1.407
4	3.902	3.808	3.630	3.465	3.312	3.170	3.037	2.914	2.855	2.798	2.690	2.589	2.494	2.404	2.362	2.320	2.241	2.166	1.997	1.849	1.720	1.605
5	4.853	4.713	4.452	4.212	3.993	3.791	3.605	3.433	3.352	3.274	3.127	2.991	2.864	2.745	2.689	2.635	2.532	2.436	2.220	2.035	1.876	1.737
6	5.795	5.061	5.242	4.917	4.623	4.355	4.111	3.889	3.784	3.685	3.498	3.326	3.167	3.020	2.951	2.885	2.759	2.643	2.385	2.168	1.983	1.824
7	6.728	6.472	6.002	5.582	5.206	4.868	4.564	4.288	4.160	4.039	3.812	3.605	3.416	3.242	3.161	3.083	2.937	2.802	2.508	2.263	2.057	1.883
8	7.652	7.325	6.733	6.210	5.747	5.335	4.968	4.639	4.487	4.344	4.078	3.837	3.619	3.421	3.329	3.241	3.076	2.925	2.598	2.331	2.108	1.922
9	8.566	8.162	7.435	6.802	6.247	5.759	5.328	4.946	4.772	4.607	4.303	4.031	3.786	3.566	3.463	3.366	3.184	3.019	2.665	2.379	2.144	1.948
10	9.471	8.983	8.111	7.360	6.710	6.145	5.650	5.216	5.019	4.833	4.494	4.192	3.923	3.682	3.571	3.465	3.269	3.092	2.715	2.414	2.168	1.965
11	10.368	9.787	8.760	7.887	7.139	6.495	5.937	5.453	5.234	5.029	4.656	4.327	4.035	3.776	3.656	3.544	3.335	3.147	2.752	2.438	2.185	1.977
12	11.255	10.575	9.385	8.384	7.536	6.814	6.194	5.660	5.421	5.197	4.793	4.439	4.127	3.851	3.725	3.606	3.387	3.190	2.779	2.456	2.196	1.985
13	12.134	11.343	9.986	8.853	7.904	7.103	6.424	5.842	5.583	5.342	4.910	4.533	4.203	3.912	3.780	3.656	3.427	3.223	2.799	2.468	2.204	1.990
14	13.004	12.106	10.563	9.295	8.244	7.367	6.628	6.002	5.724	5.468	5.008	4.611	4.265	3.962	3.824	3.695	3.459	3.249	2.814	2.477	2.210	1.993
15	13.865	12.849	11.118	9.712	8.559	7.606	6.811	6.142	5.847	5.575	5.092	4.675	4.315	4.001	3.859	3.726	3.483	3.268	2.825	2.484	2.214	1.995
16	14.718	13.578	11.652	10.106	8.851	7.824	6.974	6.265	5.954	5.669	5.162	4.730	4.357	4.033	3.887	3.751	3.503	3.283	2.834	2.489	2.216	1.997
17	15.562	14.292	12.166	10.477	9.122	8.022	7.120	6.373	6.047	5.749	5.222	4.775	4.391	4.059	3.910	3.771	3.518	3.295	2.840	2.492	2.218	1.998
18	16.398	14.992	12.659	10.828	9.372	8.201	7.250	6.467	6.128	5.818	5.273	4.812	4.419	4.080	3.928	3.786	3.529	3.304	2.844	2.494	2.219	1.999
19	17.226	15.678	13.134	11.158	9.604	8.365	7.366	6.550	6.198	5.877	5.316	4.844	4.442	4.097	3.942	3.799	3.539	3.311	2.848	2.496	2.220	1.999
20	18.046	16.351	13.590	11.470	9.818	8.514	7.469	6.623	6.259	5.929	5.353	4.870	4.460	4.110	3.954	3.808	3.546	3.316	2.850	2.497	2.221	1.999
21	18.857	17.011	14.029	11.764	10.017	8.649	7.562	6.687	6.312	5.973	5.384	4.891	4.476	4.121	3.963	3.816	3.551	3.320	2.852	2.498	2.221	2.000
22	19.660	17.658	14.451	12.042	10.201	8.772	7.645	6.743	6.359	6.011	5.410	4.909	4.488	4.130	3.970	3.822	3.556	3.323	2.853	2.498	2.222	2.000
23	20.456	18.292	14.857	12.303	10.371	8.883	7.718	6.792	6.399	6.044	5.432	4.925	4.499	4.137	3.976	3.827	3.559	3.325	2.854	2.499	2.222	2.000
24	21.243	18.914	15.247	12.550	10.529	8.985	7.784	6.835	6.434	6.073	5.451	4.937	4.507	4.143	3.981	3.831	3.562	3.327	2.855	2.499	2.222	2.000
25	22.023	19.523	15.622	12.783	10.675	9.077	7.843	6.873	6.464	6.097	5.467	4.948	4.514	4.147	3.985	3.834	3.564	3.329	2.856	2.499	2.222	2.000
26	22.795	20.121	15.983	13.003	10.810	9.161	7.896	6.906	6.491	6.118	5.480	4.956	4.520	4.151	3.988	3.837	3.566	3.330	2.856	2.500	2.222	2.000
27	23.560	20.707	16.330	13.211	10.935	9.237	7.943	6.935	6.514	6.136	5.492	4.964	4.524	4.154	3.990	3.839	3.567	3.331	2.856	2.500	2.222	2.000
28	24.316	21.281	16.663	13.406	11.051	9.307	7.984	6.961	6.534	6.152	5.502	4.970	4.528	4.157	3.992	3.840	3.568	3.331	2.857	2.500	2.222	2.000
29	25.066	21.844	16.984	13.591	11.158	9.370	8.022	6.983	6.551	6.166	5.510	4.975	4.531	4.159	3.994	3.841	3.569	3.332	2.857	2.500	2.222	2.000
30	25.808	22.396	17.292	13.765	11.258	9.427	8.055	7.003	6.566	6.177	5.517	4.979	4.534	4.160	3.995	3.842	3.569	3.332	2.857	2.500	2.222	2.000
40	32.835	27.355	19.793	15.046	11.925	9.779	8.244	7.105	6.642	6.234	5.548	4.997	4.544	4.166	3.999	3.846	3.571	3.333	2.857	2.500	2.222	2.000
50	39.196	31.424	21.482	15.762	12.234	9.915	8.304	7.133	6.661	6.246	5.554	4.999	4.545	4.167	4.000	3.846	3.571	3.333	2.857	2.500	2.222	2.000

CHAPTER 19

The Management of Working Capital: Inventory and Cash

INTRODUCTION	365
THE MANAGEMENT OF INVENTORY	367
'Dependent' and 'independent' stocks	368
Materials requirement planning	369
Annual requirement values	369
Economic order quantity model	370
THE MANAGEMENT OF CASH	374

Introduction

Studies indicate that between 80 and 90 per cent of the time of a business manager is spent on working capital. The importance of working capital management can therefore hardly be overemphasised. However, before we discuss efficient working capital management, we need to define what we mean by 'working capital' and discuss how it is separated traditionally from the other assets and liabilities of the firm.

The accounting definition of working capital is: CURRENT ASSETS *less* CURRENT LIABILITIES. Current assets are those assets which are normally converted into cash within one year and current liabilities are liabilities which normally must be met within one year. The Companies Act 1985 emphasises this time distinction when it lays down in its mandatory formats for accounts that those debtors and creditors which must be met within a year are separated from those which are not. Working capital management is therefore the administration and control of those current assets and current liabilities.

Tables 8.4 and 8.5 showed the balance-sheets of small and large companies. Ignoring the not very large differences between manufacturing and non-manufacturing small companies, we can see that, typically, a small company has a higher investment in current assets than a large company. Trade and other debtors and trade and other creditors are both substantially higher, too, for small companies. Stocks and work-in-progress are a substantial item for all companies.

Bank overdraft and loans and other short-term loans form the next largest item. In Chapter 6 we noted the heavy reliance, these days, of small businesses on bank money. It is because of the importance of bank finance to the small business manager that we segregated all dealings with banks to separate chapters.

We noted that this segregation of all bank money highlights a serious conceptual difficulty arising from the analysis of the operations of a business on the basis of the conventional split in balance-sheet items. Is a bank overdraft or short-term loan always to be regarded as a current liability? Frequently overdrafts *do* continue for many years, often fluctuating round some hard-core base figure. For how many years must they continue before it is accepted that in effect they are long-term capital? Banks may institutionalise this when they convert existing overdrafts into medium- or long-term loans. This involves no real change so far as the small business manager is concerned, yet in conventional terms it will affect the presentation of the liability side of his balance-sheet.

There is indeed no hard-and-fast dividing-line between *capital* and *current* liabilities. Much the same applies to the split between *fixed* and *current* assets, at least so far as their management is concerned. It is sometimes said that fixed assets are 'lumpy' in that they involve the one-off commitment of large funds for a long time. Current assets, by contrast, are viewed as a continuing investment in a variety of alternative forms (stock, debtors, creditors) each at different levels. Again this separation is caused more by accounting treatments (for example, fixed assets are depreciated according to formal and rather unrealistic rules) than by any real difference. For the small business manager preparing his plan, cash paid out, whether on fixed assets or for raw material stock, is still cash. And against this he will set the supply of money. Whether this is from debtors, from the bank, or elsewhere, makes no difference to him. In the long run he is only concerned with the figures for cash and profit emerging from the operations of all parts of his business. They are all part of the business plan.

However, it must be accepted that most business managers do follow the conventional split and separate working capital management from other forms of asset and liability management. Having made our caveat, we therefore now follow the traditional approach. We discuss separately the management of stock (or inventory – the terms are synonymous) and cash, and, in the next chapter, debtors, trade creditors and accrued changes.

The management of inventory

The importance of proper inventory management hardly needs underlining. Too much inventory means too much money tied up in stock: money earning nothing for the business. This excess can be due to the retention of obsolete stocks; more likely it will be due to too high a level of the normal items currently being produced and sold. Too low a level of inventory brings its own problems. If stock is not available when ordered by a customer the trading relationship is in jeopardy and further sales may be lost. It follows that finding and maintaining the right level is a matter that demands attention.

In Chapter 16 we argued that the correct stock turnover figure to use in ratio analysis was the one in which cost of sales was divided by stock, since then both figures were valued in the same terms, i.e. at cost value. In practice, the sales figure is sometimes used as a surrogate for cost of sales if that figure is not readily available (this will apply if one of Formats 1 or 3, Schedule 4, of the Companies Act 1985 is not used). This is satisfactory for trend analysis since the average mark-up is likely to remain much the same. This stock to cost of sales, or to sales figure, should remain fairly constant. Any reduction over a period of time may indicate that stock levels are too high; at the least it will signal the need for further investigation. The best approach, then, is to split the overall stock figure into main categories and determine which of the individual turnover ratios has declined. For a manufacturing small business the obvious categories will be raw materials and consumables work-in-progress, finished goods and goods for resale. The end result of this analysis should be a much clearer indication of where the excessive stock build-up has occurred.

The underlying assumption behind this turnover approach is that inventory should rise pro rata with sales. It is easy to test if this assumption is correct, by working out the proportion of sales or of cost of sales to stock for periods in the past and checking if this ratio is constant. If these figures are plotted on graph paper, the points should be on a straight line passing through the origin. 'Should' is the operative word; in practice, the points are not likely to be exactly on a straight line, and usually the line of best fit does not pass through the origin. To avoid merely recording a rise due to inflation it is preferable to record both stock and sales figures in real terms, i.e. to reduce them by the amount of inflation. In many cases the points do lie fairly close to a line, and this line can fairly be used for forecasting inventory levels. In that case the equation for determining inventory (y) in relation to sales (x) will be of the form

$$y = a + bx$$

where a is the 'basic' stock, and b is the proportional increase in stock for each unit of sales. Sometimes the rise in inventory is less than proportional to sales. In that case the relationship between the two may be that inventories increase as the square root of sales. The same approach can still be applied. The only difference is that the units along the 'y' axis will now be the square root of inventory. What relationship, if any, actually applies will vary from one business to another. For each business the method will be to test which scale for the y axis (either inventory, square root of inventory, or some other similar function) gives a good line when these past figures are plotted against past sales.

For assessing what present and future stock levels should be, this approach might appear to be adequate. However, it is doubtful if this is entirely true. In the percentage of sales method we just relate past stock figures to past sales. The crucial point is that no attempt is made to find the level of inventory which is correct in its own right. If all past figures were 50 per cent too high, then this analysis would predict future levels which themselves were too high. How can one go about finding the 'right' level?

'Dependent' and 'independent' stocks

The first step must be to accept there are two different types of inventory and that the two types need to be treated differently. Broadly, inventories can be split into *dependent* and *independent* items.

When the rate of use of an item is not linked to that of another item it is an 'independent' item. Most finished goods, factored supplies, etc., are independent items. Those items whose use is dependent on another item are 'dependent' items. Sub-assemblies which go into a higher-level finished product, for example, are dependent items. Many raw materials and most work-in-progress are likely to be dependent items.

Later we shall be concerned with forecasting the demand and the appropriate stock level, for independent items. First, however, we need to deal briefly with the control system for dependent items.

Materials requirement planning

The basic principle here is to work out backwards from the forecasted demand for the higher-level independent items the requirements for components going into the making of these items. This process is called *materials requirement planning* (MRP). In general MRP requires fairly frequent updating, as previous master plans for finished goods are altered with alterations in sales demands. There are two ways of dealing with these changes. In the regeneration process, previous plans are discarded and a new master schedule is prepared. The approach is analogous to zero base budgeting. In the net change approach, only changes from the last MRP schedule are worked through and their effects on altered bills of materials, requirements, etc., taken into account. Except for planning in very small workshops, MRP will always need to be implemented on some form of data-processing equipment. MRP is part of the overall budgeting process.

We now revert to the main problem, i.e. the management and control of inventory of independent items. The first step is to recognise that the type of control may vary. It is only those items with a high cost and a high usage which may justify sophisticated methods of inventory control (with a computerised stock package the additional cost of including the low-cost items may be so small that it may be sensible to include them as well).

Annual requirement values

Initially a business needs to work out the *annual requirement values* (ARVs) for all independent items of stock. The ARV for each item is obtained by multiplying its unit value by its estimated annual usage. The next step is to list all the items in order of their annual requirement values. Frequently it will be evident from inspection of this list that items fall naturally into two or three groups. If we call those items with a high ARV the *A* group, those with a lower value the *B* group, and those with the least value of all, the *C* group, then it is obviously only the *A* group items that require a high level of control: this will mean precise record-keeping and (in view of the money tied up) a fairly low level of buffer inventory – say less than 2 weeks. At the other end of the spectrum the C items will need few records and control: their levels of inventory can be allowed to be comparatively high – say in excess of 3 months. Most B and C items will be controlled by some fixed re-order quantity system. In the widely used 'two-bin' system, for example, the second bin acts as the safety stock, and 're-ordering' (i.e. ordering again) is automatically signalled when the first bin is empty.

Many small businesses will need only two categories of stock. Pareto's law suggests that in practice around 80 per cent of the total stock-holding value is made up by only 20 per cent of the stock items. This is a generalisation, and the percentages will vary from one business to another. Nevertheless, it has been found that these percentages are remarkably constant and they provide a good yardstick for splitting up items of stock into two basic groups.

Economic order quantity model

The final problem remaining is that of determining the correct stock level for holding A-level items, i.e. for those items whose value may justify the use of some fairly sophisticated mathematical approach. Let us start by taking a very naive example, just to establish the basic problem. Suppose we are only concerned with one product, that there is no manufacturing process, and suppose that for the coming year S units will have to be carried in inventory to meet sales of that amount. No safety stocks are held and sales are constant throughout the year. One way to deal with the situation is to order all S units *ab initio* and run them steadily down throughout the year. The average quantity in stock would then be $S/2$. However, it is more likely that we will order several times during the year. If Q is the quantity ordered, and N the number of times this quantity is ordered, then $N \times Q = S$ (since in total we must have S units passing through inventory). Average inventory will be $Q/2$.

There will be two types of cost:

1. ORDERING AND PURCHASING COSTS. If we assume that the cost for an order is fixed (and is O, say), then the amount of these costs will be $O \times N$.
2. CARRYING COSTS. The main element of these is likely to be the interest cost of the money tied up in stock. Presumably carrying costs will vary with the amount of stock. If the cost per unit per annum is C, say, then, since the average stock is $Q/2$, the amount of these costs will be $CQ/2$.

Total costs are therefore $ON + CQ/2$.
But $NQ = S$, or $N = S/Q$. Hence

$$\text{Total costs } (TC) = OS/Q + CQ/2 \qquad (19.1)$$

We wish to minimise total cost. Differentiating with respect to Q (and using partial derivatives to emphasise that S, C and O are to be regarded as constant for the present):

$$\frac{\partial(TC)}{\partial Q} = \frac{-OS}{Q^2} + \frac{C}{2}$$

Putting $\partial(TC)/\partial Q = 0$ we have as the value for Q which gives the least cost:

$$Q = \sqrt{\frac{2OS}{C}} \qquad (19.2)$$

Formulae (19.1) and (19.2) show the total cost and the best quantity to order; the latter is usually referred to as the *economic order quantity* (*EOQ*). Strictly the *EOQ* formula should come first, since the first step is to determine what is the most economic way of ordering and this will then give the required minimum total costs.

In the form that we have arrived at, this *EOQ* model is of very limited use. It does, however, have a number of associated applications, and provided certain changes and refinements are introduced it can be of considerable help in giving the right stock level.

Probably the most important application of the *EOQ* model is for dealing with the parallel situation when batches of goods are to be made in the workshop rather than when materials are to be ordered. When the product is to be made internally there will be substantial set-up costs connected with each decision to 'make'. These set-up costs replace the ordering costs. The formulae are now of practical use in determining the size of batches of standard products which should be produced from stock.

For the *EOQ* model to be used effectively for *A* items of independent stock, we need to introduce a number of refinements. These are:

- variable 'ordering' costs
- quantity discounts
- lead times
- safety stocks and stock-out costs

We conclude this section by considering each of these, in turn.

ORDERING COSTS may not be constant. In the application of the EOQ model to the size and frequency of batch production, the set-up costs are likely to be in the form of $O + VQ$, where V is a constant. Replacing ordering costs in the EOQ model by this new formula in fact does not affect the model (basically this is because the constant V disappears on differentiating). The practical upshot is that the EOQ model can still be used provided 'ordering' costs can be split into a fixed and a directly variable (with quantity) component.

QUANTITY DISCOUNTS may not always be available to the small firm, but if they are they must be taken into account since discounts affect the price per unit and hence the economic order quantity. To find out whether it is worth while we need to compare the benefits from taking the discount with the net costs. The savings from having a lower purchase price will be the discount per unit multiplied by the usage. There will also be additional carrying costs and savings in ordering costs since fewer orders will be put through if we are bulk-buying. If Q_1 is the economic order quantity without taking any discount as determined by formula (19.2) and Q_2 is the new EOQ, after taking the discount, the additional carrying cost will be, *vide* formula (19.1).

$$\frac{C(Q_2 - Q_1)}{2}$$

and the saving in ordering costs will be

$$\frac{OS}{Q_1} - \frac{OS}{Q_2}$$

Comparing the two savings (from the use of the discount and from the fewer ordering costs) against the additional carrying costs will indicate whether a quantity discount should be taken or not.

LEAD TIMES will present few problems. All that is required is that the reordering is worked out well in advance so that the extra time between placing the order and receiving the materials can be taken into account.

SAFETY STOCKS AND STOCK-OUT COSTS are a very different matter. However good the system for predicting the correct stock levels, there will be times when demand for finished goods will exceed expectations. Unless large buffer or safety stocks are kept, a 'stock-out' will occur. What level of safety stock is sensible will mean weighing the cost of carrying additional inventory against the cost of a stock-out. For dependent items the cost of a stock-out will be reflected in the additional costs due to the interruption of production.

For independent items the cost will vary with the effect on the customer. If the customer waits, the only cost is the intangible loss of goodwill due to the irritation he must feel. If he takes that order elsewhere, but maintains the relationship unharmed, the cost is the contribution (sales value *less* variable costs) forgone. If he takes his business elsewhere from then onwards, the cost is the present value of the discounted stream of expected future contributions on orders lost. It may not be too difficult to determine the tangible components of these. Contributions can be easily found; past records will show that proportion of customers who permanently go elsewhere when one order cannot be met immediately, and these same records may provide a good guide to their likely sales requirements. Past records indeed should provide some measure of the expected probability distribution of inventory usage. By implication we are assuming again that the past is a good guide when planning for the future. An example will show how to determine expected costs associated with levels of safety stocks.

Suppose that past records indicate that the usage of a particular finished good item in inventory is likely to follow this pattern over the coming month:

Usage (in units)	150	200	250	300	350
Probability	0.20	0.35	0.30	0.10	0.05

Suppose that a typical batch to be produced is around 200 units, and that the stock-out cost has been estimated at £6 per unit and the carrying cost for the month is £1 per unit. What level of safety stock is it economic to keep?

In Table 19.1 we show the calculation of the expected stock-out cost, and the carrying cost, which together make up the total cost, for various levels of safety stock. If 150 units of buffer stock are kept, there is no chance of a stock-out and the only cost is the carrying cost, which is (150 × £1) £150. If 100 units of safety stock are kept, a stock-out of 50 units may occur. The stock-out cost of this is (50 × £6) £300. Since the probability of this occurring is 0.05, the expected value of the stock-out cost is (0.05 × £300) £15. Together with the carrying cost of £100, this gives a total cost of £115. The other calculations follow along the same lines. We are concerned with the total cost, and the last column shows the minimum value for this is £110. This will occur when the safety stock is 50 units. Accordingly, we should carry 50 units only to minimise total cost.

Table 19.1

Safety stock (units)	Stock-out (units)	Stock-out cost (£6 per unit)	Probability	Expected stock-out cost	Carrying cost	Total cost
150	0	0	0	0	150	150
100	50	300	0.05	15	100	115
50	100	600	0.05	30		
	50	300	0.10	30		
				60	50	110
0	150	900	0.05	45		
	100	600	0.10	60		
	50	300	0.30	90		
				195	0	195

The management of cash

The term 'cash' includes petty cash, i.e. coins and bank-notes, held at the business for day-to-day transactions, as well as balances in bank accounts. Those short-term deposits and marketable securities which can be converted to cash in a day or two are normally also regarded as 'cash'.

The simplest way to deal with petty cash is by the 'imprest' system. In this system, traditionally used in the armed forces, a fixed sum is drawn out initially and then replenished at regular intervals to cover disbursements. In the imprest system proper, the replenishment sum is not a round figure but exactly covers the sums paid out. It follows that the person in charge of the petty cash will be responsible for the initial sum, either in cash or in appropriate disbursement vouchers.

Petty cash, as its name implies, is likely only to be used for trivial payments and for small cash receipts from customers. The total sum involved will not be great. Cash management, in the generally accepted sense of the term, will therefore be concerned with larger sums, most of which will be paid or received through the firm's current account at its bank. In Chapters 13 and 14 the mechanism of the financial plan and the operating of a cash budget were discussed at some length. Here we need to discuss two points of practical relevance. First, there may well be a substantial difference between the balance as shown in the cash book and the balance on the firm's account with the bank. Secondly, in some circumstances, there may be a cash surplus. The effective management of this surplus is important.

The difference between the balance as shown in the cash book and the balance at the bank is referred to as the 'float'. A float arises because of the delay in charging the bank account of the business writing out the cheque. Any cheque will take time to travel by post to the recipient, but here we are principally concerned with the time required for clearing through the banking system.

Typically a cheque takes 3 working days to be cleared. This applies to all 'out-of-town' (or country) cheques. A 'same-day' clearance does operate for cheques of at least £5,000 presented through the 'town' clearing system. Town cheques must be drawn and paid through one of the branches operating within the City of London area. It is evident that town cheques are unlikely to be issued by most small businesses.

When a cheque is received and paid into the business's bank, the account is credited immediately (through always in theory, and often in practice, the bank manager will not allow this amount to be paid out until it has been cleared 3 days later). It follows that when cheques are paid in and out fairly frequently and regularly, the balance of the firm's account with the bank may be well above the balance as shown in the cash book. To encourage this beneficial position payments into the bank should be expedited as much as possible. This is particularly helpful for the small business operating on an overdraft and incurring substantial interest charges. Managing the float, i.e. making arrangements like this, and taking account of the float in planning the cash position of the business, is an important part of cash management.

In the USA, with its wider geographical context, many schemes and devices (e.g. the 'lock box') have been used to expedite cash collection. These are of limited value to the small business here. Nevertheless, this is an area of management which has not received enough attention by the small businessman in the UK.

Small businesses sometimes have substantial sums of money available, even if only for short periods. Seasonal businesses are one good example. Cash balances, even if not likely to remain for long, should already be in a high interest current account or building society easy access account.

For sums which remain for a period of a month or more, many opportunities are open. In particular:

1. A BUILDING SOCIETY ACCOUNT. Building societies have entered into a tax arrangement with the Inland Revenue, the effect of which is that interest is paid net of basic-rate income tax to lenders. Notice of withdrawal is likely to be required.

2. THE MONEY MARKET. Amounts involved for the practical operation of this market must be in the region of tens of thousands of pounds. Deposits typically will be for 3 or 6 months, but shorter or longer periods are possible. Banks will make the necessary arrangements, though dealing direct with suitable local authorities may well be cheaper.
3. STOCKS AND SHARES. Particularly suitable are government securities. These do not have to be sold through the stock exchange account system (which takes a considerable time) but can be realised in a matter of a few days. An alternative to this is a portfolio of diversified Alpha stocks.

For those small businesses which have considerable sums available over substantial periods, a more sophisticated planning approach to surplus-cash management may be appropriate. The EOQ model, as outlined earlier in this chapter, can be adapted for use here.

The problem that this model helps to solve is that of how often, and in what quantity, amounts of cash should be transferred out of current accounts into deposits on the money market, or more typically into securities. In each case there is some cost involved in the movement. Now that the dust of 'Big Bang' has settled down, it is easy to be precise about the costs of buying and selling securities. They are, typically:

	Purchase	Sale
Transfer stamp (½%)	0.50	
Commission (around 1.65%)	1.65	1.65
VAT on commission (at 15% – approx.)	0.25	0.25
	2.40	1.90
	1.90	
Total cost of buying and selling (as a percentage of securities value)	4.30	

This 'transfer' cost corresponds to the 'ordering' cost in the EOQ formula. It is directly variable with the market value of the securities. The dividends, interest, capital growth foregone, correspond to the carrying cost. They are much more difficult to assess (If the authors could advise on how to estimate these they would not be writing this book!). They are, obviously, very much a matter of subjective assessment. However, in any choice, such as this, it helps if the uncertainty entities in the decision are reduced by the application of the accountant's equivalent of an Occam's razor!

CHAPTER 20

Credit Control

THE MANAGEMENT OF TRADE DEBTORS	377
Credit Policy	378
Evaluating the credit applicant	379
Credit ratings	381
Collection policy	384
TRADE CREDITORS AND ACCRUED CHARGES	386

The management of trade debtors

The term 'accounts receivable' (and its shortened version 'receivables') is gradually replacing the older term 'trade debtors' in the United Kingdom. Its main advantage is its clarity; no one can doubt that a receivable will (it is hoped!) be received. Debtors and creditors are less indicative terms. Both terms have been used interchangeably throughout this book. Accounts payable is the corresponding phrase for creditors. Both accounts receivable and payable are terms which, like many in the finance area, come from the extension of US practice into the United Kingdom.

Debtors arise when sales are made, not for cash, but on 'account terms'. Account terms are typically net 30 days, which means that the net figure as shown on the sales invoice is due and payable in 30 days' time. Sales made on these conditions are referred to as 'credit sales' since the customer is given credit for this period. This is confusing, particularly as 'credit policy', i.e. what level and amount of credit to give to a customer, is a widely used term in debtor management. Debtor policy would be a better term.

We shall here discuss overall credit policy, evaluating the credit applicant and collection policy. Credit policy will involve an analysis of the trade-off between the profits on the sales that give rise to receivables, and, on the other hand, the cost of carrying these receivables, together with the cost of any bad debts. Evaluating the credit applicant means determining the financial worth and intentions of the customer; this helps in arriving at a sensible credit policy. Collection policy, by contrast, is historical. Once a sale has been made, a proper collection policy will see that the appropriate procedures are installed that will ensure the collection of the debt as expeditiously as possible.

Credit policy

For small businesses eager to get sales in a competitive market, having the right credit policy can be crucial importance. In today's cash-conscious market, sales can easily be lost too often to other suppliers who are prepared to give more liberal credit terms. On the other hand, a small business may well feel in a very weak position when selling to large corporations. In such circumstances it will not be easy to apply pressure for payment of outstanding accounts. To the large corporation the loss of one small supplier may not be a major factor. Some large businesses 'stretch creditors' unmercifully; it will be the small supplier, short of cash, who will be in difficulties in that situation.

The granting of trade credit in terms of assessing the financial worth of a potential customer will be dealt with in the next section. Here, we are only concerned to note that it is a part of a firm's general credit policy. In theory a business should go on relaxing the standards of its credit as long as the gains from the increased sales generated exceed the costs from additional receivables. Since money is tied up in the additional receivables, we need to find the return on this incremental investment. An example will make this clear. Suppose a business sells one product for £10 per unit. Variable costs are £8, so the contribution per unit is £2. Suppose that annual sales on account terms are currently running at a steady £24,000 per annum. We are considering a more relaxed credit policy and expect that as a result the average collection period will increase from the present 2 months to about 3 months (so that sales turnover will go down from 6 times per annum to 4 times). It is hoped that the result will be to increase sales to £30,000 per annum. A return on the additional investment of around 20 per cent (before tax) is required. Is this more liberal approach likely to be worth while? The steps in the calculations are:

		£
Additional profit on incremental sales	£2 × 600 units	= 1,200
Present level of accounts receivable (annual sales/sales turnover)	24,000/6	= 4,000

Expected level of accounts receivable after change in policy	30,000/4	= 7,500
Additional receivables	(£7,500 −£4,000)	= 3,500
Additional investment in receivables	8/10 × 3,500	= 2,800
Required return on additional investment	20/100 × 2,800	= 560

Since the additional profit (£1,200) exceeds the required return on the additional investment, the proposed relaxation would appear to be financially viable.

There are, however, a number of warnings that need to be made relating to this deceptively simple and straightforward analysis. First, it will always be difficult to assess the likely additional sales and the increase in level of receivables from any change in credit policy. If a customer has been kept to a fairly tight payment schedule, any relaxation of this control may make him believe that he can pay more or less when he likes. In the calculation above we are concerned with the actual time taken to pay and not any notional relaxation of terms. There is a parallel situation here when offering cash discounts. If a customer's terms of payment are net 30 days, and he is actually taking 50 days to pay, offering terms of 2½ per cent 10 (i.e. a 2½ per cent discount off invoice price if payment is made within 10 days) is not as costly as it might seem. The difference in payment is (50 − 10) = 40 days, so that the actual equivalent annual rate is 2.5 × 365/40, or just under 23 per cent and not, as it would appear, if we took the notional saving of 20 days, a ridiculously costly figure of nearly 46 per cent.

The other major assumption made is that the additional units can be produced at a variable cost of £8 per unit. For small increases over short periods of time this is almost certainly a reasonable supposition. However, when the increase is substantial, some non-variable costs will become variable. For example, the existing plant and the fixed-cost facilities associated with it may vary. The longer the period, the more likely that fixed costs such as rent, proprietor's salary, etc., will vary. Keynes said that 'in the long run we are all dead'. In the very long run all costs are variable.

Evaluating the credit applicant

There are a number of ways in which the creditworthiness of a potential new customer can be evaluated. Broadly they can be categorised into:

- Bank references

- Trade references from other suppliers
- An analysis of the financial accounts of the business
- Personal opinions (or those of one's own salesmen) based on interviews, meetings with the customer, or visits to premises, etc.
- Credit ratings and reports from credit bureaux and agencies such as Dun & Bradstreet

A bank manager will give a reference based on the record of the dealings of the customer with his bank. The customer may have accounts with several banks. Bank references are cautious and give little away.

Trade references can be the most useful of all. In some trades, credit organisations are active. The information they give is likely to be well informed and comparatively uninhibited.

Chapter 16 dealt with ways of analysing the accounts of a business. Here we are merely concerned to note that in the credit-evaluation situation the short-term cash or liquidity ratios are the ones that require especial attention.

In addition to all these sources the opinion that the small business manager forms of the customer is of crucial importance. It is usual to place great emphasis on the three Cs: Character, Capacity and Collateral. *Character* refers to the integrity of the potential customer. Does he intend to operate honourably? *Capacity* means the ability of the business to trade successfully. Partly, this can be assessed by personal observation of the customer, his premises and his way of operating; partly it must be based on his track record. *Collateral* means the specific assets that the customer has available to pledge if security is required. In normal open account trading security is not usually offered or required. However, since it may be, if the trading relationship starts to deteriorate, it is helpful to know *ab initio* what strength is available in this matter.

Any credit-control system must include a periodic review of customers' accounts to see that they are not exceeding their credit limits. In today's economic conditions clients frequently ask for special terms. For a small business manager, anxious to increase his sales, this pressure will be difficult to resist. However, granting special terms to one customer can create a great deal of 'negative goodwill' with other customers if they discover that they have arbitrarily discriminated against!

Credit ratings from agencies and bureaux are probably the most important method for evaluating the credit worthiness of a new customer. We deal with them separately in the next section.

In the section following that, we deal with collection policy. One of the main aims of a good collection procedure is to ensure that bad debts are properly dealt with. However, a liberal policy in granting credit can result in the creation of bad debt problems. In the previous example any additional bad debt losses (if any, and if they can be determined) arising from the proposed relaxation in credit terms should be deducted from the additional profit on the incremental sales to give a revised calculation of the net benefit.

Credit Ratings

Although credit reference agencies have been around since the end of the nineteenth century it is only in recent years that they have been widely used and seen as commercially acceptable. This change has been due to a number of factors, the most important of which have been the increasing demand for credit by businesses and the increased technical capacity provided by electronic data equipment – particularly through the use of on-line computer terminals.

Until some 10 years or so ago the market was dominated by Dun & Bradstreet (D & B). However, there are now three major agencies:

- Dun & Bradstreet itself
- UAPT/INFOLINK
- CCN

These cover most of the market needs of both small and large businesses. There are, as well, a number of other commercial organisations who do not specialise in credit ratings as such, but who nevertheless cover this area and will provide credit services if required.

Credit agencies operate according to fairly strict rules. They will require the applicant to apply for one of the services they supply and to give a good reason for wishing to do so. The genuine small businessman, anxious to obtain bona fide information about potential customers, will have no problems in being accepted. Nevertheless, credit agencies insist that the information they supply is only to be used for the purpose stated, and is not to be passed to third parties.

The information that credit agencies use comes from a number of sources. Broadly, these are:

- accounts and other details filed with the Registrar of Companies
- public record information (e.g. county court judgements)

- information from national and local papers
- past bank references sought by the agency.
- the electoral register

In addition, most credit agencies (Dun & Bradstreet in particular) generally approach the credit subject directly – without, of course, giving away the name of their client(s) (they operate throughout on the strictest client/customer confidentiality terms). Most companies are only too keen to co-operate, and sometimes supply copies of accounts which are more recent than those filed with the Registrar. Credit agencies also have a substantial number of business analysts on their staff. They monitor information, make comparisons and look for trends. All the evidence is that early detection of trends (whether in profits or in the period of settlement of debts) is one of the best indicators of business failure and liquidation.

All the agencies, will, if required, extend their search of a company to include that of the directors themselves, and that of the other companies on whose Boards they sit. Some individuals have a clean record themselves, but hide their activities under the disguise of one or more companies which are nothing more than corporate extensions of their own selves.

All the agencies, too, are emphatic that their services only extend to the provision of information for an agreed fee. The decision as to whether to extend credit to a potential customer or not is entirely up to their small business manager client.

The services and the reports available from each of the agencies are many and varied. The small business manager may ask for a basic search, a basic search together with annual returns and/or legal judgements, or a full search. The small business manager, who is in the precarious position of having one large industrial organisation as his major customer, may feel justified in asking for a further comprehensive report giving, *inter alia*, details of the companies industrial relations record and problems, its risk, whether in exports to politically unstable third world countries, or in products of a potentially hazardous nature, or in its dependence on one customer or category of customers, or its dependence on one or more major plants (with the risk of fire), or on one or more suppliers, or sources of materials.

The three agencies do provide slightly different services and indeed are organised in rather different ways. INFOLINK is a non-profit-making business which is controlled by its members. It concentrates particularly on making available to those of its clients with an appropriate terminal, a very wide range of services. It is heavily computer based and indeed is reputed to have at its Croydon premises one of the largest computers in the UK.

The youngest of the three agencies is *CCN*. It has a large viewdata network in the *UK*. Many of its files were acquired some years ago, some by acquisition. It has a number of exclusive 'club' services, some of which will not be suitable for the average small business manager.

From all this it may well seem to the man in the street, that there is likely to be a lot of information about himself (which he might feel is private!) available on file to anyone who is prepared to pay for it. The Consumer Credit Act 1974 does give certain rights to an individual who thinks that he has been unfavourably discriminated against in a credit decision. He can force the disclosure of the name of the credit agency used. He can obtain, on payment, a copy of the appropriate file, and he can insist on any incorrect information on himself being deleted, or put right.

Although the credit market is dominated by these three main agencies there are, as we noted, a number of commercial organisations such as ICC, ICS, Company Formations etc., who include credit rating in the package of services they provide. The most important of these is ICC, a city based company. ICC provides:

- Company Formation Services (ready made companies, special formations, unlimited companies, guarantee companies, foreign, public and non-resident companies).
- Registered Office and Company Secretarial Services (provision of registered office address, maintenance of statutory registers, filing of returns with Registrar of Companies etc.).
- Search and Agency Services.

The work that ICC will undertake under the last heading is comprehensive. They will provide, free, while the caller waits, the registered office of any UK company and immediate information on the date of the last filed Report and Accounts, and Annual Return, and Date of Incorporation.

They provide for a fee:

- a Status Report giving notes on the companies' performance and prospects and including a ratio analysis, figures for comparable industries, and a credit assessment.
- a Credit Rating giving more details than the Status Report and highlighting any strengths and weaknesses.
- a Datacard fast-fact sheet giving ratios and financial results for the previous four years.
- a Name Check, that is, a computer check to prevent conflict with an existing company name or trade mark.
- a Name Watch to keep a constant check on new names which

might conflict or provide a competitive problem to the client's own business.
- Company Information, that is, a same-day search service from Companies House offices at London, Cardiff or Edinburgh. The results can be sent by telex, typed, or on microfiche.
- Ancillary Services connected with Legal Notices, Document Registration, Legalisation of Documents at Embassies, Consulates etc.
- a Nationwide Search from Local Authorities or from most registries including those of:
    - The Trade Marks Registry
    - The Registry of Births, Deaths and Marriages
    - The Probate Registry
    - The Bankruptcy Registry
    - The Registry of Friendly Societies
    - The London Chambers of Commerce (Business Registry)
    - The Registry of County Court Judgements
    - The Registry of Bills of Sale
    - Lloyds Register of Shipping
    - The Public Records Office
    - District Land Registries
    - The Charities Commission
- Updating Service, that is, a computer check on the filing of statutory returns, including either advice of the filing of the return, a copy of the return, or notification when a return is overdue.

It is evident that a wide range of credit rating services are available to the small business manager. We have already noted the importance to the small business of having good information on existing or potential customers. Shopping around to find the most suitable service is essential. Money spent on good credit checking is never money wasted in the long term.

Collection policy

These days many companies take as much credit as they can, regardless of the agreed terms of trade, and do not pay their account until they are chased. Any effective collection policy must therefore enable the small business proprietor to be aware of the length of a debt and then to apply the appropriate procedure for collecting it.

The best debtor information control system is based on an 'aged

Table 20.1 'Aged debtor' list

Customer's name	Credit terms and limit	Total outstanding	Current	Over 30 days	Over 60 days	Over 90 days	Notes/proposed action
TOTAL							Average days sales outstanding...
Previous month							Average days sales outstanding...
Same month last year							Average days sales outstanding...

debtor' list. This list should be prepared once a month (or even more frequently. Table 20.1 shows a suitable format.

If the periods of debt outstanding are increasing, the small business proprietor must find out why, and act accordingly. Is it due to one or two large debtors? Is the right amount of attention being paid to large and small debts? Clearly it would be stupid to spend as much time on a debt of £10 as on one of £500. Are office administrative methods adequate? Collection is so important in practice that before discussing how to chase bad payers a few points on the initial procedure are worth noting. Briefly:

- SEND THE INVOICE AS SOON AS POSSIBLE: do not wait till goods are dispatched. Most customers relate their own paying procedure to the invoice date.
- SEND STATEMENTS AS SOON AS POSSIBLE AFTER THE MONTH END, i.e. at the very latest by the third or fourth of the following month. Many statements are not sent out till the middle of the month or even later.
- GIVE FULL DETAILS ON THE INVOICE, and state clearly terms of sale and settlement on all statements and invoices. This avoids 'delaying tactics' by customers.

The advantages of a standard policy for chasing bad debtors are obvious. A sensible policy will be based on the following:

- CHASING LETTERS SHOULD PLAY ON THE EMOTIONS, e.g. 'After a long and good relationship it saddens me to see that your account is now etc., etc.' This is usually more effective than a simple 'bloody-minded' approach!
- DO NOT HESITATE TO CHASE THE DEBT. Many small businessmen believe that to chase debts from important customers will result in a loss of business. This fear is more imagined than real. Many corporate managers respect someone who stands up for himself.
- PERSONAL CONTACT IS BETTER THAN WRITING. A visit is the best of all – the customer may well be embarrassed into writing a cheque! Failing a personal visit, a telephone conversation is usually better than a letter.
- WITHHOLDING SUPPLIES (*de facto*, even if not openly stated to be by intent) will be very effective if the customer needs your product or services and cannot get them easily elsewhere.

These are good, general, pragmatic, rules. Nevertheless, it must be recognised that debtors have individual idiosyncrasies and these need to be taken into account. Some respond best to a series of gentle reminders, others only to harsh treatment!

For very bad payers policy must be based on an appraisal of the reasons for non-payment. If the money is believed to be there (e.g. some other suppliers are being paid), then a very tough collection policy is in order. Some customers are frightened by a solicitor's letter and the threat of a court action. In general, however, bad-debt collection agencies are more cost-effective than solicitors in pursuing debtors. Both are likely to be expensive. For small debts they may not be worth the expense. If the reason that the customer is not paying is simply that he does not have the money with which to do so, an entirely different approach is necessary. Some agreement on payment, or part-payment over a period, will be better than nothing. A voluntary creditor's arrangement may be better than enforced liquidation.

Trade creditors and accrued charges

In this section we deal with certain non-bank sources of short-term financing. Bank sources have already been covered in Chapters 6 and 7. In this particular section we are concerned with trade creditors and accrued charges; the latter term is frequently shortened to 'accruals'.

Trade credit is a common form of short-term financing. It arises when goods and services are sold on 'open-account' terms. Open account, as we noted, means that the customer is not required to pay cash at the time of delivery but is extended credit for a period of (typically) 30 days. To record the supply of goods, and later the payment for them, an *account* in the accounting books is opened — hence the term. There are other forms of trade credit financing, such as *bills of exchange, promissory notes* and *notes payable*. Bills are used in export financing, but they are rather specialised and are not dealt with here.

Many suppliers are prepared to give discounts. These discounts are either trade discounts or cash discounts. Trade discounts represent a reduction in the invoice price; they are frequently made for large orders and therefore may not be available to the small business. Earlier in this chapter we noted that cash discounts can be expensive when offered to customers. It may also be expensive not to take cash discounts offered by suppliers. Once again the calculation must be based on the actual days saved and not the notional days.

Postponing payment beyond the agreed period is called 'stretching'. An American version of this term, 'leaning on the trade', is (as usual) rather more colourful and interesting! Stretching accounts payable is a useful, substantial, and apparently simple form of finance. There are, however, two costs associated with stretching. These are the cost of any cash discount forgone, and more importantly, the intangible cost of lack of goodwill and possible drop in credit rating. Suppliers do view with apprehension a firm which continues to pay its accounts late. They may refuse to make any further deliveries, or they may insist on rather strict payment terms in the future. No general rules can be laid down as to when it is or is not sensible to stretch creditors; it all depends on the importance of maintaining the trade relationship to the payer on the one hand and the need for cash on the other. When a firm is intending to stretch creditors the best approach may well be to inform the supplier in advance, advising him the reasons for the action, and the extent to which it is intended to delay payment. This is usually preferable to presenting him with a *fait accompli*!

Accrued charges are for expenses which have been incurred but which have not been paid. Broadly, they can be split into three groups: operating expenses of the business such as electricity, etc.; wages; and taxation. All, to an extent, represent costless financing. Dealing with the payment of operating expenses follows along much the same lines as for trade creditors; wages and taxation require special consideration.

Wages represent a very high proportion of the total expenses of a business. Frequently the proportion is around 50 per cent, though the figure varies widely from business to business. Since an employee's co-operation and enthusiasm are vital to the business's ongoing operation, great care must be taken with wage payments. Nevertheless, accrued wages are, to some degree, discretionary. Changing from weekly wage payments to monthly payments may be something which workers are prepared to accept today. Some temporary 'subbing' will be necessary but the benefits to the typical small firm with a large bank overdraft in terms of reduction in bank interest (and possibly some savings in administration charges) can be substantial.

Taxes do have to be paid. The Inland Revenue, pressed for money itself, does press for payment rather more urgently than it used to do. In Chapter 9 ways of reducing the total tax bill and deferring the liability were discussed. In dealing with the Inland Revenue's legitimate demands for payment, the best approach is along exactly the same lines as with trade creditors, i.e. to make (physical!) contact with the tax collector (visit – failing that, phone) and arrange with him in advance some agreed schedule!

CHAPTER 21

Vale

FINANCIAL WAYS OF ASSESSING A BUSINESS'S CONTRIBUTION	389
Return on investment (ROI)	389
Profit per person employed	394
COMBINING THE FINANCIAL WAYS OF ASSESSING A BUSINESS	395
ROI and profit per person	395
Capital, labour and value added	395
CONTRIBUTIONS THAT A BUSINESS CAN MAKE BEYOND THOSE MEASURED BY FINANCE	397
DIFFICULTIES IN THE OVERALL COMPARISONS OF CONTRIBUTIONS FROM SMALL AND LARGE BUSINESSES	400
Profit figures	400
Industry concentrations	401
SUMMARY AND CONCLUSIONS	403
A summary comparison of small and large businesses	403

Financial ways of assessing a business's contribution

Return on investment (ROI)

Throughout we have said that profit per pound (money) of capital, or per pound of net assets, is the traditional way of measuring the efficiency of the financial performance of a business. Comparing small and large businesses' contributions – even using this simple approach – is not easy.

Bolton gave the following figures:

390 Small business: planning, finance and control

PROFIT AS A RATIO OF NET ASSETS, TOTAL ASSETS AND EQUITY,
SMALL FIRMS AND QUOTED FIRMS (1968)

	Profit before interest as a ratio of net assets	Profit before interest as a ratio of total assets	Per cent profit before interest as a ratio of equity
Small firms	17.8	11.2	18.7
Quoted firms	13.5	9.5	16.5

and Wilson provided these:

PROFITABILITY (NET INCOME AS PER CENT OF NET ASSETS)

	1973	1974	1975
Smaller	18.4	16.4	14.9
Medium-small	22.7	19.5	16.9
All small companies	21.0	18.2	16.1
Large companies	18.3	16.3	14.9

Table 21.1 gives the immediate post-Wilson years.

Figures for the most recent years are given in Table 21.2. These show the make-up of the Return on Net Assets ratios and also the differences between major sectors (that is, manufacturing and non-manufacturing).

Although *Business Monitor* continues to give figures for large businesses, it has not published comparable data for small businesses beyond 1982. *Ex cathedra* information is to the effect that this situation will probably be rectified fairly shortly. Nevertheless, these are the only figures available in late 1987. Comparisons between small and large businesses beyond 1982 cannot be made. Some further additions and comments on these figures however can be made here.

First, the variability of the ROI ratio is probably greater for small businesses than for larger ones. Wilson says: 'The average ratios again conceal a very wide dispersion of profits rates. Just over half of small companies had their profit ratio within the range of 0.29.9 per cent in 1975, compared with over three-quarters of large companies.'

Such comment does appear to support the frequently held view that large firms are more stable, less flexible, more set in their ways, less easily adjustable to changes in volume of activity, or even to changes in that type of activity, than are small firms. And that small firms, by contrast, are less stable, probably have a less rigid workforce establishment (i.e. they hire and fire more easily) and are more

Table 21.1 Profitability of SBs, 1977–81 (%)

	1977 ROTA	1977 RONA	1977 ROE	1978 ROTA	1978 RONA	1978 ROE	1979 ROTA	1979 RONA	1979 ROE	1980 ROTA	1980 RONA	1980 ROE
All companies												
Small	6.9	17.0	13.4	7.7	20.1	16.9	6.0	15.9	11.4	3.6	9.4	2.1
Medium	11.1	17.7	14.3	10.5	16.7	14.2	10.0	16.3	14.6	7.8	12.2	13.9
Small & Medium	10.1	17.6	14.1	9.8	17.2	14.6	9.2	16.3	14.2	7.0	11.9	12.7
Large	12.3	17.0	12.2	11.2	15.6	11.1	13.0	18.4	14.8	10.6	14.8	9.0
Manufacturing companies												
Small	8.4	21.1	21.3	8.8	21.2	18.9	2.9	7.5	neg	2.1	5.4	neg
Medium	13.0	20.5	16.4	11.3	17.7	13.8	10.5	16.7	14.4	12.0	14.2	15.5
Small & Medium	12.3	20.6	16.9	10.9	18.1	14.3	9.5	15.9	13.4	11.9	13.4	14.3
Large	11.9	16.6	12.6	11.1	15.7	11.9	10.8	15.4	12.3	10.4	11.3	5.5

Source: *Business Monitor MA3*, HMSO.

ROTA: Return on Total Assets = $\dfrac{\text{earnings before interest and tax}}{\text{current and fixed assets}}$

RONA: Return on Net Assets = $\dfrac{\text{earnings before interest and tax}}{\text{total assets current liabilities, excl. bank overdrafts (= capital employed)}}$

ROE: Return on Equity = $\dfrac{\text{earnings after interest, tax and minorities}}{\text{shareholders' interests}}$

Table 21.2

SMALL & MEDIUM	All industries (excl. oil)		Mftg Industries		Non-mftg (excl. oil)	
	1982	1981	1982	1981	1982	1981
Gross trading profit	4,653	4,382	1,629	1,525	3,024	2,857
Less depn	2,122	1,984	757	710	1,365	1,274
Trading profit (after depn)	2,531	2,398	872	815	1,649	1,583
Total net assets	22,959	21,452	8,756	8,261	14,203	13,191
RONA	11.02	11.18	9.96	9.87	11.61	12.00

LARGE (Mftg & Non-mftg)	Manufacturing				Non-mftg (excl. oil)	
	1984P	1983P	1982	1984P	1983P	1982
Gross trading profit	22,354	18,531	16,439	11,550	9,886	8,716
Less depn	6,571	5,918	5,570	3,112	2,737	2,699
Trading profit (after depn)	15,783	12,613	10,869	8,438	7,149	6,017
Total net assets	90,772	82,941	77,808	53,338	45,819	41,781
RONA	7.39	15.21	13.97	15.82	15.60	14.40

LARGE (UK only – Mftg & Non-mftg)	All industries (excl. oil)		Mftg		Non-mftg (excl. oil)	
	1984P	1983P	1984P	1983P	1984P	1983P
Gross trading profit	26,913	22,881	16,570	13,997	10,343	8,884
Less depn	7,850	7,147	5,006	4,657	2,844	2,490
Trading profit (after depn)	19,063	15,734	11,564	9,340	7,499	6,394
Total net assets	116,956	104,064	69,473	63,301	47,483	40,763
RONA	16.30	15.12	16.65	14.75	15.79	15.69

Source: *Business Monitor*, 17th edn, HMSO.

Notes to Table 12.2

P = Provisional figures
1. All figures are in £'s million.
2. Only limited companies are included.
3. Sample proportion varies widely from 1 in 1 to 1 in 360 for very small companies
4. Size is here defined by capital as follows:

   Large : Capital greater than £4.16m
   Medium: Capital between £100,000 and £4.16m
   Small : Capital less than £100,000

   (where capital is shares, reserves, minority interests, deferred tax, and all loans and overdrafts)
5. Gross trading profit is:
   after directors fees etc., exceptional expenditure, and
   before gains or losses on fixed assets, depreciation provisions, interest on all debt.
6. RONA is the ratio of trading profit (after depreciation) to total net assets, expressed as percentage.

open to changes in product type and production. But to some extent we anticipate conclusions which, even now, depend on work later in this book.

Second, the denominator of the ROI ratio is capital, which means that the supply of capital is important, and that any comparison between the ratios for small and large businesses must take into account any imbalance in the supply (and cost, by way of interest rates) of money to them. In fact there is some imbalance. Banks charge small businesses more for loans.

Third, all the figures given so far relate to small or large businesses across the board. The pattern from industry to industry will vary considerably. Most studies by economists of the advantages/disadvantages of scale are on an industry-wide basis, and typically are concerned with the concentration of the three or four largest firms in a given industry.

Comparisons, such as already have been made, as to business structure and performance between countries will not be valid if industrial patterns are substantially different. This is likely to vitiate conclusions drawn between, say, a country such as the United Kingdom and an emergent country. It does not necessarily mean that comparisons between the United Kingdom and France or West Germany are invalid.

Profit per person employed

At the level of the firm this particular ratio has not been widely used. Maximising profit per unit of labour makes little sense to a businessman, though increasing output per unit, if labour is a crucial factor, is accepted as giving a good measure of efficiency so far as that one dimension is concerned. The Bolton Report showed that 'net output per person employed rises with size of firm even among small firms'. The Report went on to add that small firms generally paid lower rates than larger firms and there was evidence that the skill mix was lower in small firms. However, it concluded that, even after these adjustments, 'the residual difference in output per unit of labour input [as between small and large firms] lies . . . nearer 18 than 3 per cent'.

More recent figures taken from the UK Census of Production 1981[1] show how net output per head broadly rises with size of firm (number of employees), as does wages per person (Table 21.3).

Table 21.3 Output and wages in SBs

Establishment size (No. of employees)	Net output per head	Gross value added at factor cost per head	Wages per person Operatives	Others
1–99	£10,382	£8,389	£4,755	£6,617
100–99	£10,625		£4,612	£6,678
200–499	£11,554	£9,356	£5,135	£6,726
500–999	£12,387	£9,984	£4,836	£6,931
1000–1499	£13,940	£10,799	£5,333	£7,159
Average (all)	£12,290	£10,040	£5,182	£7,191

Comparing the output figures with those given in the return on investment section above, we conclude that small firms, in general, may earn a slightly higher return on capital but a lower return on labour. This may be due, in part, to the greater use of capital in plant and machinery in large businesses in any industry. It may also be, to some extent, because those industries in which large firms operate are capital-intensive industries.

This tentative conclusion leaves the question of what sort of financial measure of a business's efficiency is the right one to use still open.

---

[1] Prepared by the Business Statistics Office of the Department of Trade and Industry.

Other financial measures have been proposed. Return on sales is one. This has considerable use in comparisons for similar firms within an industry, but since the profit margin varies so much between industries it has no application on any wider basis.

If profit is the basic figure, then ROI and profit per person are presumably both of importance in assessing efficiency. In other countries value added has found, as we have noted, an equal or greater emphasis. In that case capital per unit of net output and labour per unit of net output will be the candidates.

Combining the financial ways of assessing a business

ROI and profit per person

The real problem is to decide which of these two ratios to use. How, for instance, do we decide between two firms, such as the typical small business, which may give a high ROI and a low profit per person, and the typical large business? The traditional answer has been to rely only on return on capital. This can be justified if capital is the sole scarce resource, but in practice capital-rationing is not a problem for some large firms. The simplest approach to this problem is to construct an efficiency frontier.

Since we are throughout concentrating on comparisons between small and large businesses, Figure 21.1 shows efficiency frontiers for groups of each of these firms. In general, firms to the left and below the efficiency frontier will be 'inefficient'. For small businesses, with typically a restraint on capital, the aim must be to move as far as possible in the direction *OA*; for large firms *OB* is the relevant direction for greater efficiency. Efficiency, however, has yet to be defined. It is taken up in the next section.

Capital, labour and value added

For value added, capital per unit of net output and labour per unit of net output are customarily used. These ratios are therefore similar to those in Figure 21.1; but are *inverted*. Inefficient firms will now lie to the right and above the efficiency frontier (see Figure 21.2). The effect is the same: the difference is merely one of customary presentation.

In Figure 21.2 the efficiency frontier of a large group of firms of mixed size is represented by the 'curve' *CD*. This is the technical

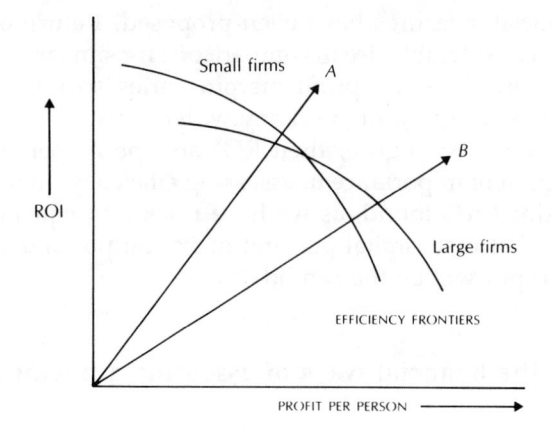

Figure 21.1

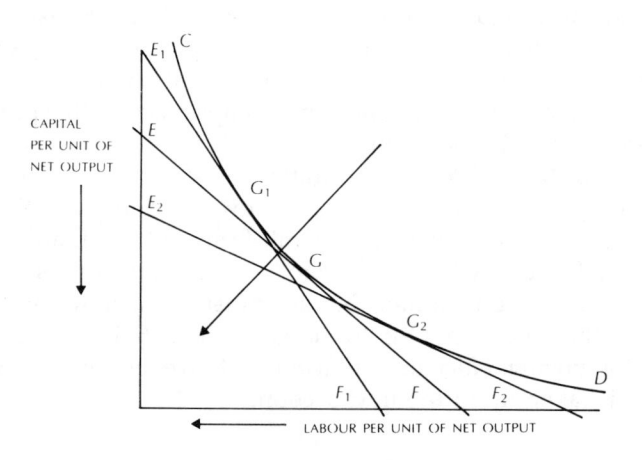

Figure 21.2

efficiency frontier, where a technically more efficient firm is one which is able to produce (for a given level of net outputs) with less of one input and no more of the other input. Price (or cost) efficiency is indicated by the line EF, where the intercepts on the axes are relative costs of capital and labour. On this basis the firm represented by the point G is the best bet in terms of both technical and cost efficiency.

However, the slope of EF will vary depending on the size of the business. For a small firm, as we noted, capital is not only in shorter supply but also dearer. The reverse is true for a large firm. E_1F_1 and E_2F_2 represent the cost-efficiency lines for small and large firms in the group. G_1 and G_2 are more realistic representatives of those firms that are both technical and cost efficient than G, since it is a fact of life that different-sized firms have different costs of capital and indeed availability to the labour market. More accurately we should draw (as in Figure 21.1) the technical efficiency curves for small and large business, or indeed any comparable group, and find the most efficient firm in terms of 'total' efficiency, by drawing the appropriate cost-efficient line for that group. However, the basic point that is being made here is that the efficiency frontier curves and the relevant cost-efficient firms will vary, as between small and large companies, because of the difference in the supply and cost of capital to these groups and the availability of labour to them.

Contributions that a business can make beyond those measured by finance

So far we have only considered financial ways of assessing a company's overall performance. Many large companies also employ subsidiary measures. Some of the ratios for assessing these were discussed in Chapter 16. Some large companies employ a large number of internal indicators. As long ago as 1952 General Electric (GE) established the following eight key result areas:

1. Profitability
2. Market position
3. Productivity
4. Product leadership
5. Personnel development
6. Employee attitudes
7. Public responsibility
8. Balance between short-range and long-range goals

and performance in each of these was, GE argued, important.

It is evident that some of these internal ways (e.g. public responsibility) do have a spin-off benefit to the community at large, though the reason for including them as key result areas was simply that they were a help to business efficiency. But is business efficiency the only way one should judge a company? Does not a good approach to public responsibility give some benefit in its own right? Should we be concerned with a business's overall contribution to society and the economy? Should we give some credit for its contribution to research, good treatment of its employees, and so on? And on this enlarged view of total contribution, how do small companies fare by comparison with large ones?

In *innovation, research and development,* the traditional wisdom has always been that small firms have the edge over large firms in inventiveness. Dr Roy Rothwell of the Science Policy Research Unit at Sussex University, and Dr Walter Zegveld of the Dutch TNO Organisation have cast some doubts on this widely held view. They say that 'universities, independent inventors had made the major contribution to radical inventions only up to 1930. Since then corporate R & D (mainly by large firms) played the dominant role.' Also, 'at least half the inventions . . . by small firms and independent inventors owed their successful commercial exploitation to the development work . . . of large firms'.[1] Dr Rothwell cites a 5-year study by the US National Science Foundation which recorded that:

> Averaged over all countries, small firms contributed about one-third of all innovations, the majority share being taken by large firms. Medium sized firms played only a minor role (less than 20 per cent) except in France (the other countries were the US, UK, West Germany and Japan).
>
> Small firms' contribution was highest in the US (35 per cent) and France (31 per cent), followed by West Germany (26 per cent) and the UK (23 per cent).
>
> In the US small firms produced a reasonably even distribution of 'radical breakthrough', 'major technological shift', and 'improvement'-type innovations (27 per cent, and 30 per cent and 37 per cent respectively). A similar pattern was found for large firms.
>
> In the UK, however, the innovative output of small firms was composed entirely of radical breakthroughs. Large firms showed a similar, though less pronounced tendency.

In *contribution to exports* small firms have appeared to do moderately.[2] In some social matter, e.g. the employment of women,[3] small firms probably do better than large. In other social matters, e.g. pollution,[4] they may do less well. But these are difficult to assess accurately.

---

[1] W. Zegveld and R. Rothwell, 'Small and Medium Sized Manufacturing Firms: Their Role and Problems in Innovation. Europe, the USA, Japan and Israel'.
[2] See the Bolton Report, paras 3.30, 3.33.
[3] For example, Françoise Rey, Essec, France.
[4] Ibid.

In matters relative to the *labour force* and *labour relations*, the balance of the evidence is that small firms do better than large. In job generation the most persuasive document was a report[1] from the Massachusetts Institute of Technology which showed that two-thirds of new jobs created in the USA between the years 1960 and 1976 were in companies employing 20 or fewer people. However, the lack of comprehensiveness and the partiality in the choosing of the data sample, the wide variances in the regions and the fact that the report dealt with another country (one in which small businesses are a major as opposed to a very minor component of the economy), means that the relevance of the report is arguable, to say the least. It achieved its popularity and esteem in this country partly because we wished to see evidence of how some sectors of the economy (small business) could be used to solve our worrying problem of high unemployment.

In job satisfaction the evidence is probaby not quite so clearly in favour of small firms as was at one time thought to be the case. A number of writers[2] have reported on field studies which appear to indicate that employees in small firms are much happier, much better motivated, and above all have a much-enhanced feeling of 'belonging' to a caring organisation than those in large firms. But most of these studies have been on the continent.

In the area of *industrial relations* the difference between small and large companies is very strong. In strike-free working days the close relationship between the stoppages and plant size has long been known. In an article in the *Oxford Bulletin of Economics and Statistics* Paul Edwards confirmed that 'there is a pronounced tendency for the frequency of strikes to increase with plant size', but goes on to say that 'the extent of this increase is exaggerated when official strike figures are employed'.[3] Even so the tendency is clear.

Trade-union presence is one factor which may help to explain these figures. The greater the presence, the more the likelihood of industrial action, and of course the correlation between trade-union activity and plant size has long been realised. In his international analysis of trade unionism under collective bargaining, Clegg noted, in 1976, the importance of bargaining structure: plant bargaining leads to a larger number of strikes than industry or regional bargaining.[4]

---

[1] David L. Birch, *The Job Generation Process*, MIT Program on Neighborhood and Regional Change, 1979.
[2] For example, the writings of Dr Pleitner, Small Business Institute, St Gallen, Switzerland (summarised in a contibution to his 'Job satisfaction of entrepreneurs and employees in small business firms', International Symposium on Small Business, Washington, D.C., November 1976).
[3] *Oxford Bulletin of Economics and Statistics*, vol. 42, no. 2, May 1980.
[4] H.A. Clegg, *Trade Unionism under Collective Bargaining*, Blackwell,1976.

A great deal of work has been done on strikes and other industrial action. Many factors which were thought to influence strikes have been found not to have any effect. William Brown, in *The Changing Contours of British Industrial Relations*, says: 'Popular notions that [strikes] are affected by the presence of women and by the production technology have received no support.'[1] He concludes by emphasising the importance of size of the establishment and of the bargaining structure by which it is characterised.

Difficulties in the overall comparisons of contributions from small and large businesses

Profit figures

We have already discussed many of the problems in arriving at a 'true' profit figure. Return on investment uses a capital or asset base. Since some of the assets are quite likely not to have been revalued, it is probable that any (historical accounting) ROI ratio has errors both in its numerator and denominator.

However, there are certain additional reasons why the declared profit of a small business may be arbitrary and incorrect. The principal reason is probably that the profit figure can be affected by the decision of the proprietor as to the way he will take his reward out of the business. He may do this either by way of dividends, as a wage or as a salary, or as directors' fees or emoluments, or by way of a loan or withdrawal. For large businesses the treatment is fairly standard and directors' interests are in many case not usually the dominant expense factor. For small businesses the proprietor's discretion is likely to be absolute, and because the amount is likely to be very material in relation to the profit figure his treatment of the sum of money he pays himself will arbitrarily affect his reported profit figure substantially.

The method which the proprietor adopts will be governed by tax considerations, i.e. he will be concerned to find which of the many ways will minimise his current tax liability, or defer tax till a year later. Whether certain items can be treated as capital or an expenses item is also likely to some extent to be within the discretion of management. For a small company this amount, too, is likely to be material in relation to the profit figures.

---

[1] William Brown (ed), *The Changing Contours of British Industrial Relations*, Basil Blackwell, 1981.

In almost all countries, but to very different extents, tax avoidance by small businesses does occur and does affect published data on profitability. Studies by Tamari in Israel[1] and Stekler in the USA[2] revealed substantial differences between declared profits and 'corrected' profits. Tamari found declared profits were increased by 50 per cent after adding back excessive salaries, household expenses, the cost of foreign travel, car allowances, entertainment charges, and so on, which tax officers ascribed to the personal accounts of major shareholders. Stekler shows that profits also increased by 50 per cent, after increasing for excess management charges defined by him as the difference between that paid to managers of loss-making companies and that paid to profit-earning companies, on the assumption that the loss-making companies were unable to pay salaries in excess of the market rate.

National statistics for small firms will reflect the typical practices in each country, and the extent of the downward bias in the profitability figures is virtually impossible to quantify. All these factors make any international comparisons of profitability statistics virtually impossible to make.

However, the overriding difficulty in making such comparisons is the simple fact that in most countries any national figures for profit, or the equivalent, for small companies are extremely difficult to find. In the United Kingdom the Wilson Committee commented that the level of information about small businesses here was very poor, particularly by comparison with the situation in the USA.

Industry concentrations

Financial comparisons between small and large companies on a country-wide basis may be invalid if the industrial patterns differ substantially. In some industries scale economies are so great that no small business can survive (except as a satellite). Air frame, space, shipbuilding and vehicles are obvious examples of these. However, the main European countries are now all highly industrialised with not dissimilar economic structures. Even where there are material variations, and some countries have more or less of one type of industry, this will not necessarily vitiate inter-country comparisons.

---

[1] M. Tamari, 'Industrial Corporate Profits in Israel 1956–70', *Economic Review*, No. 40, 1973.
[2] H.O. Steckler, 'Profitability and Size of Firms', Institute of Economic Research, Berkeley, University of California, 1963.

Table 21.4 Gross Domestic Product per person

	1986 (at current prices and exchange rates)	1981 (at 1980 prices and rates)	Percentage gain 1986/1981
France	1.274	1.216	4.77
West Germany	1.458	1.321	10.40
United Kingdom	0.959	0.936	2.40
OECD total	1.301	0.994	30.80
OECD Europe	0.961	0.890	8.00
EEC	1.035	0.955	8.40
UK/West Germany	66%	71%	
UK/France	78%	77%	

Trend in UK Gross Domestic Product (1980 = 100)

Years	1975	1976	1977	1978	1979	1980	1981	1982	1983	1984	1985
GDP	92	93.9	96.5	99.9	103	100	98.3	100.1	103.1	106.4	110

Source: OECD (Organisation for Economic Cooperation and Development), tables for Gross Domestic Product and Population

Notes:
1. Population figures for 1986 for the UK, OECD total, OECD Europe and EEC are estimates.
2. Gross Domestic Product is expressed in billions of dollars.

A survey in the UK, reported in *The Changing Contours of British Relations*, showed a remarkable similarity in average work-force size as between establishments in differing industries. Vehicles, as we suggested, are an obvious exception. They have an average workforce establishment size of 729. All the other 10 industries varied very little from the manufacturing average figure of 294 (the smallest was 163, the largest 430). Intra-industry patterns are not as different as commonly supposed, at any rate in the United Kingdom. In so far as this is also applicable to other European countries it would tend to imply that even differing industry patterns will not vitiate inter-country comparisons on an across-the-board basis. For the United Kingdom the obvious countries for comparison purposes are its neighbours, France and West Germany. Table 21.4 gives some comparative figures for economic performance based on gross domestic product (and, as a footnote, the trend enter UK GDP).

In the late 1950s and the 1960s growing big was seen in our country as the way to industrial efficiency, to obtaining the substantial economies of scale in purchasing and production, and to fighting off the competition in the newly-enlarged world market of the American giants. We have already seen that return on investment not only does not rise but may actually fall with increase in size. The direct relationship between concentration and profit has not been well explored. A 1976 study by Dalton and Penn[1] concluded that 'changes in concentration do not have a significant impact on profit rates within concentration groups', but their work was done in the USA and was even there somewhat limited in scope.

So if the rewards of size are not reflected in the financial and economic indicators, why is being big so important? Certainly there has been some swing away from this view. 'Small is beautiful' has had a good press. But still size is seen as being strong. Still governments permit mergers and take-overs even when the monopolistic and political dangers are evident. Why is this? Partly the explanation may be that it is just the institutionalisation of the innate desires in us to grow, to be big, to be powerful. But there is more to this than the projection of business empire-builders' egos. Anyone who has worked in a Monopolies Commission office or in that of any of the equivalent bodies which in continential countries are set up to advise governments as to whether mergers should be allowed to go through will understand. The economists in these offices may apply sensible criteria to evaluate proposals put to them, but they know that their recommendations will only be acted on by their government if the political considerations are favourable. Power and politics are key criteria for concentration as well as finance and economics.

Summary and conclusions

A summary comparison of small and large businesses

We have dealt at some length with the problems relating to the assessment of the contributions of small and large businesses. Most of the figures we have quoted relate only to the United Kingdom; some had a wider application.

Condensing the facts, as in the summary which follows, inevitably leads to oversimplification. However, making comparisons is helped by a short simple presentation.

---

[1] J.A. Dalton and D.W. Penn, 'The Concentration-Profitability Relationship: Is there a Critical Concentration Ratio?', *Journal of Industrial Economics*, December 1976.

Bearing these caveats in mind we have:

	Small businesses	Large businesses
FINANCIAL MEASURES OF APPRAISAL		
Return on investment, or return on assets		
Profit, productivity or value added per person (employee)		√
NON-FINANCIAL MEASURES OF APPRAISAL		
Job security		√
Industrial relations	√	
Job satisfaction	√	
Job generation	√	
Research and development		
Innovation	√	
Development		√

where a √ represents an ('in general') better performance.

We have shown no tick against return on invested capital. The traditional slight superiority of small businesses over large in ROI seems to have been eroded or temporarily reversed around 1980 and 1981. It is interesting to set the gross domestic product indicators, given in Table 21.4 against these figures. In pollution, contribution to exports (Bolton's figures) and a number of other areas there are no clear indications of superiority by either small or large businesses.

Some of the non-financial measures can be regarded as 'internal' ones, i.e. they are aimed at controlling performance; others relate to ways of assessing contribution to society beyond those covered by the profit figure. The margin between these two, as we noted, is a little blurred. Are good industrial relations and job satisfaction solely internal matters, their benefit adequately reflected in the profit figure through greater industrial efficiency, or do they rank, as well, as being desirable in their own right? Do people matter as such? If we answer 'yes', then most of the non-financial measures might be counted twice! Even if we do not allow this double-weighting, small businesses seem to come out fairly well in the non-financial measures of appraisal section and particularly well in what can be described as the human-aspects areas.

If we are principally concerned with these areas, then perhaps the aim should be to increase the relative number of small companies in the United Kingdom. There are of course very practical limits to what can be done. We have already noted that plant size is remarkably constant across industries, but some heavy industries clearly must have large plant size to get economies of scale, etc.

There is some evidence that employees in small firms work longer hours and yet appear on the whole to be happier. It may be that highly motivated people will naturally go into small firms, since they will feel that their initiative is more likely to be rewarded there. The fact is that there are some people who are entrepreneurs and some who are not, some who like challenges, some who are free independent spirits, some who like a quiet life, and some who like to work within prescribed limits. In any well-ordered society jobs should not only be available to all but in the right proportion. On this argument the balance as between small and large firms in any economy should take account of the number of persons who like to work in companies, in small businesses, in co-operatives, and so on. But this is a very 'grey' area!

Select Bibliography

Chapter 1

Bolton Report, *Report of the Committee of Enquiry on Small Firms*, Cmnd 4811, 1971.
Wilson Report, *Interim Report on the Financing of Small Firms*, Cmnd 7503,1979.
The European Climate for Small Businesses: A 10 country Study, Economist Intelligence Unit, 1983.

Chapters 2, 3, 4, 5

Department of Industry, *Helping Small Firms Start Up and Grow: Common Services and Technical Support*, HMSO, 1982.
C. Barrow, *The Small Business Guide*, BBC Publications, 1983.
Department of Industry (Small Firms Division), *Starting up a New Business*, 2nd edn, HMSO, 1982 (free).
Croner's Reference Book for the Self Employed and Small Business (annual), Croner Publications.
The Small Business Kit, 2nd edn, National Extension College, 1982.
The Daily Telegraph Guide – Working for Yourself (annual), Kogan Page.
M. Mogano, *How to Start and Run Your Own Business*, Graham & Trotman, 1982.
All the major banks and most of the major accounting firms produce pamphlets for managers of small businesses. These pamphlets are intended primarily for clients, but can usually be obtained free on application.
Sara Williams, *The Lloyds Bank Small Business Guide*, Penguin, 1987.
Derek Waterworth, *Small Business: Marketing for the Small Business*, Macmillan, 1987.
Peter Gorb, Philip Dowell and Peter Wilson, *Small Business Perspectives*, Armstrong Publishing, 1981.
Burns and Dewhurst (eds), *Small Business and Entrepreneurship*, Macmillan, 1988.

Chapters 6, 7, 8

M. Tamari, 'The Financial Structure of the Small Firm – An International Comparison of Corporate Accounting in the USA, France, the UK, Israel

and Japan', *American Journal of Small Business*, vol. IV, no. 4, Spring 1980.
Money for Business, Bank of England and City Communications Centre, 1981.
Money for Exports (annual), Overseas Department of Bank of England.
Burns and Dewhurst (eds), *Small Business in Europe*, Macmillan, 1986.
Tony Lorenz, *Venture Capital To Day*, Woodhead Faulkner, 1986.
A.L. Minkes, *The Entrepreneurial Manager*, Penguin, 1987.
Making a Small Business Bigger, Lloyds Bank Finance Series 2, Lloyds Bank, 1979.
Peter F. Drucker, *Innovation and Entrepreneurship*, Heinemann, 1985.
W.A.J. Pollock and G. Golzen, *Franchising for Profit*, Chartac, 1985.
A. Gemmel, *The Unlisted Securities Market Chartac*, 1985.

Chapter 9

Williams and Wilman, *The Lloyds Bank Tax Guide 1987/88*, Penguin, 1987.
Croner's Reference Book for the Self Employed and Small Business (annual), Croner Publications.
Coopers & Lybrand, *Tax Saving for the Family Business*, Harrap, 1987 (and similar publications from all major accounting firms).
Employer's Guide to PAYE (annual), Board of Inland Revenue.
Homer, R. Burrows and Gravestock, *Taxwise Workbooks Nos 1 and 2*, Tolley, 1986/1987.

Chapters 10, 11, 12, 13, 14, 15

F. Wood, *Business Accounting*, vols 1 and 2 4th edn Pitman, 1987.
Colin Drury, *Management and Cost Accounting*, Van Nostrand Reinhold (UK), 1986.
J.F. Weston and E.F. Brigham, *Managerial Finance* (British edn by J. Boyle and R.J. Limmack), Holt, Rinehart & Winston, 1986.
K.N. Bhaskar and R.J.W. Housden, *Accounting Information Systems and Data Processing*, Heinemann/CIMA, 1985.
Choosing a Small Business Computer (2616), Chartac, n.d.

Chapter 16

C.A. Westwick and W.J. Westwick, *Source of British Business Comparative Performance*, Chartac, 1986.
R.H. Parker, *Understanding Company Financial Statements*, Penguin, 1987.
W. Reid and D. Myddelton, *The Meaning of Company Accounts*, Gower, 1982.
G. Foster, *Financial Statement Analysis*, Prentice-Hall, 1978.
M. Tamari, *Financial Ratios: Analysis and Prediction*, Paul Eleck, 1978.
B.V. Carsberg, M.J. Page, A.J. Sindall and I.D. Waring, *Small Company Financial Reporting*, Prentice Hall 1985.
G. Holmes and A. Sugden, *Interpreting Company Reports and Accounts*, Woodhead Faulkner, 2nd Edition, 1982.

408 Select Bibliography

Chapter 17

Dallenbach, George and McNickle, *Introduction to Operations Research Techniques*, 2nd edn, Prentice Hall, 1983.
Jim Dewhurst, *Business Mathematics*, Macmillan, 1988.

Chapters 18, 19 and 20

J. Sizer, *An Insight into Management Accounting*, 2nd edn, Penguin, 1983.
R. Brealey and S. Myers, *Principles of Corporate Finance*, McGraw-Hill, 1983.
Terry Hill, *Small Business: Production/Operations Management*, Macmillan, 1987.
T.J. Hill, *Production/Operations Management*, Prentice-Hall, 1983.
T.J. Hill, *Manufacturing Strategy: The Strategic Management of the Manufacturing Function*, Macmillan, 1985.
James van Horne, *Financial Management and Policy*, 7th edn, Prentice-Hall, 1985.
Small Business Administration, 'Business Plan for Small Manufacturers', and other articles on small business (available, free, from SBA, PO Box 15434 Fort Worth, Texas 761219, USA).

Chapter 21, and Generally

R. Rothwell, 'Small and Medium Sized Manufacturing firms and Technical Innovations', *Management Decision*, 1978, pp. 349–59.
Charles Handy, *The Future of Work*, Basil Blackwell, 1987.
R.F.J. Dewhurst, 'Ways of Assessing a Company's Performance', paper given at the 11th European Small Business Seminar, September, 1981.
E.F. Schumacher, *Small is Beautiful*, Blond & Briggs, 1973.
G. McRobie, *Small is Possible*, Abacus, 1982.
Sue Birley, *The Small Business Casebook* (reprint), Macmillan, 1982.
G. Bannock, *The Economics of Small Firms*, Basil Blackwell, 1981.
Issues of *Small Business Digest*, published by National Westminster Bank plc.
Business Monitor, HMSO.
G. Haskins, A. Gibb and A. Hubert, *A Guide to Small Firms Assistance in Europe*, Gower, 1987.
Publications for small businesses by Investors In Industry.
Background to the Government Small Firms Policy, Small Firms Division, Department of Trade and Industry, November, 1983.
Robson Rhodes Report, Department of Trade and Industry, HMSO, 1983.
US Government Printing Office, *The State of Small Business: a Report to the President*, March 1984.
Journal of Small Business Administration (sundry articles).
Publications of the Small Business Research Trust, Dean Trench Street, Westminster, London SW1P 3HB.

Index

acceptance credit bill finance 90, 120
accountants 205
accounting principles 196–9
accounting return on investment 344, 345, 361
accounting year (and relationship to tax year) 163, 164
accounts: analysis of 294–311
accruals 386
Advance Corporation Tax (ACT) 170–2
advice, sources of market information 26–7
Agricultural Mortgage Corporation 127
annualised cost 344, 345
annual requirement values 369, 370
annuity tables 364
Argenti, John 49
arrangement fee 108
articles of association 31
associate company 200
Association of Certified Accountants 205
audited accounts 154, 201, 204, 205
Aziz, K. 287

balance-sheet 190–3; Companies Acts formats 199–205
Bank of England 109–10
bankruptcy 43, 49
banks: borrowing from 102, 103; structure 116, 117
Bannock, G. 51
base rate 108, 109

Bayes's decision rule 323–5
benefits in kind 174
Birch, David L. 399
block discounting 121
Bolton Committee 3–7, 132, 389, 390
borrowing 23–5
breakeven point 211–20
British Technology Group 149
Brown, William 400
Buchele, R. B. 52
building societies 375
Building Societies Act 1986 114
business entity 196, 197
Business expansion scheme 146, 174
Business Monitor MA3 133, 138–1, 390–3
business plan 77–99
buy-outs 35

capital gains tax 173
capital rationing 360, 361
capital, working 20, 21, 365–88
cash: breakeven point 218; management of 374–376
cash book 270
Census of Production 311, 394
Central Statistical Office 314
Centre for Interfirm Comparison 306
certificates of deposit 129
cessation of trade 165, 168
chain ratio method 14
cheques 375
Clegg, H. A. 399
close companies 174
committed costs 207

Index

Companies Acts 4, 30, 199–205, 269, 274
Companies, Registrar of 31, 199, 201, 294
conservatism 198
consistency 199
Contracts of Employment Act 33
contributions in costings 215–27
convertible preferred ordinary shares 143
Co-operative Development Agency 33
co-operatives 33, 34
corporation tax 168–173
cost: differential 316, 317
   marginal 317
   opportunity 206, 317
   prediction 207
cost–volume–profit 210–25
Council for Small Industries in Rural Areas (COSIRA) 36
credit factoring 119
credit rating 380–4
current-cost accounting 313
Customs and Excise 32

Dalton, J. A. 403
debentures 112
decision tree 325–7
decomposition analysis 307
Delphi technique 335
deposits 108
differential prices 225
disclosure required in accounts 201
discretionary costs 207
diversification 57–9
donations 201
drawings 30
Dun & Bradstreet 381
Dupont 297

economic order quantity 370–4
economies of scale 44, 45
Economist Intelligence Unit 6, 7
Edwards, P. 399
efficiency frontier 395, 396
Employee Protection Act 33
Equity Capital for Industry 150
Estate Duties Investment Trust 148
expected value 323–5

Export Credits Guarantee Department (ECGD) 122–4
export finance 122–4

Fair Trading, Office of 33
Finance for Industry 148
Financial Services Act 1986 146
Financing of Small Firms, The 111
FINCO 279–86
franchising 34, 124–37
Friendly Societies, Registrar of 33
funds-flow analysis 307–9

Ganguly, P. 51
gearing 23, 300, 302
General Electric 397
going concern 197
goodwill 200
Government Statistical Service 14

Health and Safety at Work Act 33
hire purchase 120–1
historic cost 197, 206, 207

imputation system 170
industrial relations 399, 400
Industrial and Commercial Finance Corporation 148
Industrial and Provident Societies Act 33
industry concentration 401–3
industry norm 304
inflation accounting 311–14
information, perfect 331, 332
Institute of Chartered Accountants 205
inventory see stock
investment income, tax on 159
Investors in Industry (3Is) 148

job costing 228–30
job satisfaction 399

labour costs 231–3
lease or buy 358, 359
leasing 121–2
ledgers 272, 276, 277
life-cycle concept 47–57
limited companies 30–2
Limited Partnership Act 30
limiting factors 222, 223
Limperg, Professor 313

linear programming   360, 361
Lloyds Bank   117, 118
loan guarantee scheme   127, 128
loan limits   105
London Enterprise Agency   36

Mainstream Corporation Tax (MCT)   171, 172
management   54, 55
management buy-outs   35
market build-up method   14
market research   15, 237
marketing plan   237
materials   208
materials requirement planning   369
maximax and maximin   333
memorandum of association   31
mergers   402, 403
microcomputer   279–92
Monopolies Commission   403
Monte Carlo simulation method   326–8

National Economic Development Office   14
negative pledge   114

opportunity cost   206, 317
Organisation for Economic Co-operation and Development (OECD)   329, 402
overdraft   109–11
overheads   231–3
Over the Counter (OTC) market   146, 147, 155

Paciolo, Luca   196
Partnership Act   30
partnerships   29
Pay-As-You-Earn (PAYE)   181–3
payback   345
perfect information   331, 332
Pletiner, Dr   399
position audit   154
preference shares   143
present value   340–2
prime costs   234
Private pension plans   165
probability   322–8
process costing   228–30
production budget   241–4

production plan   237
productivity   395
professional negligence   29
profit per person   394–7
profitability index   343–5
published accounts, analysis   295

ratio analysis   295–306
realisation   196
registration of company   31
repair or replacement   356–8
replacement cost   312–14
research and development   50, 398
Retail Price Index   226
retirement pension   175
return on investment   296, 297
Rey, Françoise   398
risk: and interest rate   354–6; in decisions   330–3
Rothwell, R.   398

sale and leaseback   122
sales, budget   241
   estimates   11–15
   margins   297
schedules, tax   159–61, 166–8, 176, 181
security   23, 24, 110- 112, 113
self-employed   159, 166, 183, 189
sensitivity analysis   333–6
share capital   142–6
share premium   200
sickness benefit   183
small business, definition   3–5
spreadsheet packages   289–92
sole traders   28, 29, 158–66
standard deviation   330–2
Statements of Standard Accounting Practice   205, 313
stock   230, 231
   working capital   367–70
   dependent and independent   368, 369
Stock Exchange   145–7
stock-outs   334, 335, 372–4
strikes   399, 400
Supply of Goods and Services Act   33

target income   219, 220
Technical Development Capital   148

third market 146, 147
Trade Union and Labour Relations Act 33
trade unions 399
trend analysis 304–08
trial balance 272

uncertainty 332, 333
underwriters 145
Unlisted Securities Market 145–7, 153

value added 310, 311, 395
valued-added tax (VAT) 179, 244–9, 269
variable budgets 255–7
variances 260–4
variation, coefficient of 330, 331
venture capital 147–50
voting rights 143

Wilson, Sir Harold 111
Wilson Committee 3, 132, 133, 390, 401
word-processing 292

Zegveld, W. 398